Changing Minds

Changing Minds

Contributions to the Study of Buddhism and Tibet in Honor of Jeffrey Hopkins

edited by

Guy Newland

Snow Lion
Boulder
2017

Snow Lion
An imprint of Shambhala Publications, Inc.
4720 Walnut Street
Boulder, Colorado 80301
www.shambhala.com

9 8 7 6 5 4 3 2 1

Printed in the United States of America

♾This edition is printed on acid-free paper that meets the American National Standards Institute Z39.48 Standard.
♻Shambhala Publications makes every effort to print on recycled paper. For more information please visit www.shambhala.com.
Distributed in the United States by Penguin Random House LLC and in Canada by Random House of Canada Ltd

The Library of Congress catalogues the previous edition of this book as follows:
Changing minds: contributions to the study of Buddhism and Tibet in honor of Jeffrey Hopkins / edited by Guy Newland.
p. cm.
Includes bibliographical references.
ISBN 978-1-55939-160-3 (alk. paper)
ISBN 978-1-61180-528-4 (second edition)
1. Buddhism—China—Tibet. I. Hopkins, Jeffrey. II. Newland, Guy.
BQ7612.C44 2001
294.3'923—dc21 2001001417

Table of Contents

Editor's Introduction

Twenty-five years ago I first met Jeffrey Hopkins as my instructor in a popular undergraduate course on Buddhist meditation at the University of Virginia. I liked the course—and studied with him for almost thirteen years—because of the way Hopkins presented Buddhist ideas. He did not posture as the authoritative curator of a mummified body of knowledge. He did not mystify the tradition and he certainly did *not* act as a missionary for it. On the other hand, he did not attempt to "account" for Buddhism in terms of any extrinsic academic ideology. Instead, Hopkins was interested in encountering Buddhist worldviews as living systems of human meaning; his classes were invitations to participate in that encounter. They were based on his own meticulous translations of primary-source Tibetan or Sanskrit texts, sometimes produced in collaboration with Tibetan colleagues. The message that I got, from his teaching and his books, was: There are and long have been real people, whole communities and civilizations, for whom the ideas and texts we are now studying are profoundly important. We should show them the respect of taking their ideas seriously. That means finding out how far we can go in understanding how others make sense of the world—and seeing how our minds change in the process.

Hopkins presented Tibetan Buddhism as a living system of meaning in part by bringing to campus distinguished Tibetan scholars from the refugee communities of India. At that time, in the middle of the 1970s, this was something quite rare; most of my fellow undergraduates had heard the term "Dalai Lama" only as a Johnny Carson punch-line. Sometimes a monk would accompany Hopkins to class and speak to us in Tibetan, with Hopkins translating. Hopkins taught many undergraduate and graduate courses in this way while I was at the University of Virginia.[1] There is no doubt that the presence of visiting Tibetan scholars on campus greatly enriched my education in the graduate Buddhist Studies program. Instead of having only Hopkins representing and mediating Tibetan Buddhism to us, we had continuing opportunities to work with scholars whose credentials to speak from within and on behalf of the tradition were unimpeachable. Some graduate students in the program likely developed, outside of class, spiritual connections with these lamas that were deeper and more important to them than their academic relationship with Hopkins.

That was not my experience; I was not drawn into the program mainly by the Tibetan scholars. After all, they could not speak English and only Hopkins and the more advanced graduate students could really question them directly. For me, the heart of the program was Hopkins. He had no superficial flash as a public speaker, but he had intellectual substance and passion. He conveyed his prodigious learning with an intensity that John Buescher conjures from the past in the opening article of this volume. Buescher gives us Hopkins at work—guiding students through the complexities of Sanskrit syntax, teaching them how to pull from the tangle something that would change their minds:

> "It's the self of persons and of things that we're looking for," Jeffrey said, as he pointed to Nāgārjuna's text in front of him. "The thing that seems to cover over them and make them a whole, single entity, assembling things out of their parts. We've got to take them apart to see it." Parsing the words of the text, then translating them, the operation became unexpectedly exacting. Sweat rolled down in tight little streams under my shirt. We were unprepared for this drill, this scalpel. Jeffrey, however, proceeded on, laying bare our ignorance, peremptorily rejecting any uncertain or wrong answer. As he thundered his demand for the right answer, we searched for it. We desperately wished we could find it, some seat of the soul, some little treasure amid the remains of the words that now lay in pieces all about us.

Did these teaching methods leave room for students to challenge the tradition itself, to form their own critical evaluation of it? In my undergraduate courses with Hopkins, he seemed to regard it as satisfactory if a student could think through some of the complexities of Tibetan Buddhist doctrine. He certainly did not forbid "etic" analysis or independent critique, but he did little to encourage it. This might not seem ideal, but it did not strike me as so different from many other courses that I had taken, in Russian literature, Greek tragedy, or experimental psychology, for example. In each case, the premise was that there is a very complicated, very unfamiliar story to be told. The novice must expect to spend time on the ground of the storyteller, learning the story well and getting the details straight, before launching an idiosyncratic metanarrative on what the story (in this case someone else's religion) is "really" about.

As a graduate student, my experience was that Hopkins wanted—even demanded—work that was not only intimately grounded in the details of the tradition, but also had something to say, something useful or insightful. As I gained mastery of a research topic (and not before), he clearly expected more of me than a re-transmission of what learned lamas had said. For example, he told me that my seminar paper on the *Abhisamayālaṅkāra* was "boring" because it simply reorganized information from the tradition. On another occasion, Hopkins asked me to present a paper in an interdepartmental colloquium series, assigning me a topic from the work of the Sa skya scholar sTag tshang. I decided on my own that I would instead give a psychoanalytic treatment of Tsong kha pa on the three principal aspects of the path. When he heard my talk, rather than being upset that I had presumed to offer an independent analysis, he was clearly pleased. The same was true when I submitted my dissertation; when I used various Western theories to give an independent account of the religiosity of dGe lugs scholasticism, Hopkins's criticisms were aimed only at strengthening my argument.

Hopkins's scholarship likewise evidences concern to avoid arrogant pseudo-objectivity on the one hand and naive adulation on the other. Hopkins has taken special pains to avoid the first of these extremes and has been more careful in that regard than some. By being open in his appreciation for some aspects of the traditions he studies, Hopkins has at times chosen to risk appearing to some as an academic front-man for religious dogma. In books such as *Meditation on Emptiness* and *The Tantric Distinction*, Buddhist thought-systems are not specimens to be dissected at arm's length.

Instead, Hopkins recreates his encounter with another world of meaning, a very particular and intricate Asian Buddhist world which can never again be imagined as completely separate from "our" world. Describing his version of a methodological middle way, Hopkins (1999: 4) writes that his aim is "to evince a respect for the directions, goals, and horizons of the culture itself" without "swallowing an Asian tradition as if it had all the answers or… pretending to have a privileged position."

Should it scandalize us that a professor of "our" Western academy presents another culture not as a stack of data, but as a voice speaking to us, saying something that we can hear—of course imperfectly—and *perhaps* benefit from? It would give us but little pause if the topic were, say, ethnobotany. Because the cultural realm under consideration is religious, certain secular academic taboos come into play and, especially at a public institution, some concerns reasonably apply. Personally I have little patience for dogmatism or triumphalism under any guise, but I have never seen it in any work by Hopkins. Unfortunately, in some circles even the insinuation that a scholar might have a religious commitment or a spiritually motivated interest seems enough to discredit otherwise impeccable work.

Just this year, someone from the University of Chicago trusted me enough to ask privately, and quite seriously, "Is it true that studying with Jeffrey Hopkins is just like being in a monastery? Is it true that his students see him as just like a guru from whom they are receiving religious instruction?" I am tempted to trace the genesis of such egregiously mistaken notions, but more appropriate here is to state flatly that my experience contradicts them. Many who are or have been involved in the University of Virginia Buddhist Studies program are Buddhists. This is irrelevant to the *quality* of the program *one way or the other* and it is clearly fallacious and offensive to suggest otherwise.[2] During my years in Virginia I did not consider myself a Buddhist and I never felt that this created any kind of problem for me. No one in the program asked me about my personal beliefs or made any implication about what they ought to be.

For a fair approximation of Hopkins's approach, we can look to these comments by D. Seyfort Ruegg (1995: 156-157):

> [U]nderstanding and analysis of our sources must initially be what has been termed "emic" rather than "etic." That is, in the

> first instance, an effort has to be made, as far as is possible, to determine how the categories and terms of a culture relate to each other structurally and systematically, and so to place ourselves within the cultural contexts and intellectual horizons of the traditions we are studying, making use of their own intellectual and cultural categories and seeking as it were to "think along" with these traditions. This is much more than a matter of simply developing sympathy or empathy, for it is an intellectual, and scientific, undertaking. And very clearly it is not one of merely converting from one religion to another . . . . Rather it is one of learning how to work with, and within, a tradition of thinking by steeping oneself in it while rejecting the sterile "us" *vs.* "them" dichotomy.

In his own comments on method, Hopkins (1984: 7 and 1999: 5) cites Wilfred Cantwell Smith's view that we should go beyond "us" talking about "them" to a conversation in which, finally, it is "we all" talking with each other about "us," inevitably "heirs of many cultures." Taking Buddhism seriously in this way may require us to set aside creaky presumptions that secular and materialistic ideologies constitute a more evolved viewpoint that can objectify, encompass, and explain the more primitive religious mind. As Hopkins (1984: 7) writes, "It is important to consider any religious system as a challenge to one's own thought... ." And since religions make contradictory truth-claims, it is quite obvious that this *precludes* accepting religious views uncritically, regardless of one's starting perspective.

Jeffrey Hopkins's scholarship has focused without apology on texts, primarily the literature of Tibetan Buddhist scholastic elites. These traditions claim to be transmitting an unbroken lineage of profound meaning derived from Indian treatises, and ultimately from the Buddha. Of course, this claim is duly represented in Hopkins's writing. Hopkins does not expect, or imply an expectation, that his readers will simply accept such claims uncritically. Neither does Hopkins assume that Tibetan Buddhist texts are clear reflections of an earlier Indian Buddhist reality. He has been primarily interested in the religious reality of the *Tibetan* Buddhist religious systems themselves, which have their own intrinsic interest and worth. These systems include Tibetan translations, commentaries, critiques, and synthetic reformulations of Indian Buddhist texts, some of which are extant in Indian languages. In such cases, accurate representation of how Tibetan scholars read these texts is the first aim of Hopkins's scholarship. In the background, there is the hope that what might be gleaned from these commentaries could open up new perspectives on the older Indian texts.

These priorities were reflected in the Buddhist Studies program while I was a student at Virginia. For those of us choosing to concentrate on Tibetan Buddhism, the program required at least four full years (including intensive summer work) of Tibetan, two years of Sanskrit, and a year of Pali. Clearly, *Tibetan* rather than Sanskrit (a language known to few traditional Tibetan scholars) was the primary foundation for the study of Tibetan Buddhism. Still, I passed a written comprehensive examination on Pali and a separate written comprehensive exam on Sanskrit. Almost everyone in the program while I was there took a bit more Sanskrit and considerably more Tibetan than the minimum, and everyone did additional work on languages, including Buddhist Hybrid Sanskrit, French, Hindi, and Japanese.

To take another case, the priority of Tibet is also reflected in Hopkins's translation of the term *dgra bcom pa* as "Foe Destroyer." Rather than "correcting" a Tibetan reality by second-guessing the translators who—perhaps consciously and for religious reasons—chose a philologically debatable translation of the Sanskrit, Hopkins is faithful to the Tibetan construction. Yet another example is Hopkins's career-long interest in Tibetan doxography (*grub mtha'*) or "tenets" literature, a genre in which various Indian Buddhist philosophers are categorized into four ascending schools, each with a number of sub-schools. Well aware that such literature cannot be relied upon as a source of historical information about Indian Buddhism, Hopkins refers to Tibetan doxography as "an artificial creation" and "a pretended amalgamation" (1996: 175). That such systems are not historical depictions of Indian Buddhism strengthens their value as indicators of the *Tibetan* religious imagination. If we believe that earlier formulations of a religious view are somehow more pure or authentic—and therefore more worthy of academic concern—then we can readily dismiss doxography along with much of the rest of Tibetan scholastic literature.[3] But Hopkins sees the constructions of the continuing tradition as well worth our attention and he chooses to concentrate on their internal structure and dynamics.

Scholarly respect for a tradition requires deep mastery of its language. Hopkins's spoken Tibetan is fluent. He gives his graduate students a systematic education in Tibetan grammar and the translation of classical Tibetan. In class after class, year after year, he never allowed us to get off the hook by "going for the meaning" in a way that bypassed painstaking lexical and grammatical analysis. In this way, all of his graduate students gained an invaluable skill, the ability to read and to translate even very complex Tibetan religious texts with a high degree of accuracy and a minimum of "reading in." I am always grateful to him for this especially.

Hopkins's own translations hew to the literal and have sometimes been faulted on this account.[4] Yet Hopkins's "emic" approach to Buddhist idea-systems is a perfect match for his philological method. Every effort is made to find and bring forward the internal structure of the object studied. He has never transmogrified Tibetan Buddhism into something seductively attuned to Western interest in existentialism, spiritualism, or transpersonal psychology. Certainly he does not want his books to be of use *only* to other academics; he has frequently published with so-called "dharma" presses (such as Snow Lion) that serve both scholars and non-scholars. Also, he consistently renders Tibetan words in an accessible but precise phonetic system of his own devising, rather than in the standard method which is intelligible only to those who know both Tibetan and Roman letters. But this kind of accessibility does not entail any adulteration or compromise for the sake of mass appeal. A Hopkins translation conveys with uncompromising—even discomfiting—precision the unfamiliar ideas and syntactical complexity of the Tibetan texts it renders.

To be honest about oneself as a person, an author and a scholar; to be rigorous in one's methods; to be passionate in the search for understanding; to be conscientious and indefatigable in one's work; to be generous with one's readers and inspiring to one's students: these are high ideals for which we may all strive. Hopkins has embodied them. His life-work will endure as an important part of the history of Buddhist Studies.

* * *

Don Lopez and Joe Wilson conceived that this book should come into being to honor Jeffrey Hopkins in his sixtieth year. At their suggestion and with the encouragement of Anne Klein, I undertook the project, soliciting contributions only from a close circle of Hopkins's friends, admirers, and former students. Then, with some assistance from Snow Lion and outside readers, I selected the articles in this volume for publication. As Paul Hackett shows in the closing article of this volume, Hopkins's research has covered a wide range of concerns, centering on dGe lugs scholarship but ranging far beyond it in several directions. A thin cross-section of that diversity is reflected in the scholarship here.

John Buescher opens our volume with an atmospheric and evocative real-life detective story. Caught in the act of teaching Mādhyamika Buddhism, Hopkins appears as a philosophical sleuth on the trail of truth. Buescher then weaves into this portrait its unexpected resonances, years later, in a baffling international news-event—the sudden appearance of a previously unknown dental relic of the Buddha.

The Mādhyamika theme continues through the next two articles, by Guy Newland and Donald Lopez. My article is inspired in part by the efforts of Hopkins to describe the Mādhyamika view for a general readership. I summarize some of the philosophical claims Tsong kha makes in *Lam rim chen mo*, reflecting in particular on the notion of conventional reality. Lopez's piece distills a careful synopsis of Tsong kha pa's treatment of the object of negation (*dgag bya*) in Mādhyamika analysis. Then, based on his own new translations, he treats us to a riveting critique of this position by the brilliant twentieth-century iconoclast dGe 'dun Chos 'phel.

Contributions by Dan Cozort and Elizabeth Napper keep the focus on Tsong kha pa and his *Lam rim chen mo*, but move away from Mādhyamika. Cozort provides a useful, clear, and detailed analysis of Tsong kha pa on the special dangers of anger, which is said to "cut the roots of virtue." What, exactly, does this mean? How deep is the damage of anger? Cozort finds Tsong kha pa working with mixed success to explicate this doctrine and integrate it into his system. Like Cozort, Napper scrutinizes *Lam rim chen mo* in her contribution, "Ethics as the Basis of a Tantric Tradition: Tsong kha pa and the Founding of the dGe lugs Order in Tibet." She lays out exactly how Tsong kha pa *used* his sources, subtly and skillfully reshaping grammar, nuance, and context in order to build a new and unique system of religious meaning. She concludes with some frank observations about the impact that the distinctive features of this system (such as its emphasis on monastic ethics) have had on the later tradition. Napper's impeccable work, synthesizing insights from many years of work with *Lam rim chen mo* and its sources, merits the appreciation of everyone who studies the dGe lugs order.

The next two articles shift our attention to the contemplative traditions of rDzogs chen and Mahāmudrā. Anne Klein takes us into the realm of Bon rDzogs chen poetry. Her original translations gracefully depict a natural, open awareness—unrecognized by ordinary persons—in which reality is experienced as spontaneous and unbounded wholeness. She carefully explains who reads such poetry, to what end, and she compares the handling of contradiction and nonduality in Buddhist Mādhyamika with that in Bon rDzogs chen. Roger Jackson then gives us an outstanding treatment of a little-known topic, the tradition of dGe lugs Mahāmudrā (*phyag rgya chen po*). As he notes, Mahāmudrā is more usually associated with meditative practices central to the bKa' brgyud tradition of Tibetan Buddhism. Questions about the role of and basis for a dGe lugs form of Mahāmudrā lead Jackson to broader insights about inter-sectarian connections.

As Hopkins (1999: 47) suggests, our understanding of early dGe lugs has been much aided by recent advances in our grasp on the teachings of Shes rab rgyal mtshan and the Jo nang "other emptiness" doctrine. Here we offer two articles which touch on this issue, demonstrating how the self-empty *vs.* other-empty controversy set the stage for otherwise disparate debates. Displaying his formidable knowledge of Tibetan Perfection of Wisdom literature, Gareth Sparham shows how debates about the authorship and authority of key commentaries evolved within the context of controversy between dGe lugs and Jo nang views. Then, Joe Wilson gives us a generous and cogent explication of how and why the concept of a basis-of-all (*ālayavijñāna, kun gzhi rnam par shes pa*) is subject to radically different constructions in the Jo nang and dGe lugs traditions.

While cross-cultural and comparative themes are touched upon in other contributions, José Cabezón and Harvey Aronson bring them into focus. Cabezón analyzes the structure and content of Tibetan colophons, looking for evidence of an implicit theory of authorship and literary production. Simplistic notions of authorship are quickly problematized by the multiple layers of productivity through which a book is generated. Cabezón has given us a unique and nuanced study, full of allusions to and connections with the conversations of Western literary theory. Such cross-cultural comparison arises from historical contact; in the case of Tibetan Buddhism, that contact includes the unprecedented phenomenon of large numbers of Westerners taking up Buddhist practices and striving to embody Buddhist virtues. Using object-relations theory and his own experience as a clinician, Harvey Aronson warns of the pathological pitfalls that may afflict the self-sacrificing American bodhisattva, but argues for a model of healthy altruism.

Our volume concludes with Paul Hackett's comprehensive survey of the published works of Jeffrey Hopkins. We are grateful to Hackett for an ambitious essay charting the range and depth of Hopkins's *oeuvre*. Inasmuch as Hopkins's recently published *Emptiness in the Mind-Only School* has been hailed by many as his best work ever,[5] and inasmuch as it is the first of a three-volume series, Hackett's work will perhaps but serve as a starting point for future bibliographic analysis.

In sum, this volume is presented as a tribute to the work of Jeffrey Hopkins as a teacher and as a scholar. Paul Hackett has written eloquently of Hopkins's impact:

> Most people who have pursued knowledge and learning would be hard pressed not to remember at least one teacher sometime, somewhere, who first inspired them and instilled in them a sense of value in learning. This ability, the capacity not only to convey meaning, but also to motivate remains an art which stands apart from mere erudition. For some, it comes naturally; for others it requires effort; though in each person who manages to master it, there is always evident an idiosyncratic artistry by which their knowledge and experience is conveyed. So it is with Jeffrey Hopkins, who has repeatedly demonstrated not only his depth of knowledge, but also his skill as a teacher and writer.[6]

As we see in this volume, he has inspired and enlivened us in many different ways. So now we say: Thank you!

Notes

1. He did *not* always teach this way and when he did have Tibetan scholars in his courses they did not come to every class session.

2. As Ruegg (1995: 157, n. 19) writes, "[T]he claim that a Buddhist is, as such, disqualified from lecturing on Buddhism in a university department of religion (where few seem, however, to be concerned about whether a Christian is disqualified from teaching courses on Christianity) [and] … the opposite claim that only a Buddhist can be so qualified … are egregious examples of intellectually sterile arguments carried on with scant regard to the scientific (not to mention spiritual) issues involved."

3. Here I am repeating a point that I (1996: 202) have previously made in almost the same words.

4. E.g., by de Jong, who argued that Hopkins should abandon his translation of *gnod* as "harm."

5. On the book-jacket of *Emptiness in the Mind-Only School of Buddhism*, Kapstein blurbs it as "Hopkins's most important work to date"; Cabezón as "a scholarly tour de force" and Lopez as "his magnum opus … a magisterial study."

6. These words appear in an earlier—unpublished—version of Paul Hackett's contribution to this volume and are cited here with his permission.

References

Cabezón, José

1995 "Buddhist Studies as a Discipline and the Role of Theory." In *Journal of the International Association of Buddhist Studies*, 18(2).

de Jong, J. W.

1989 "Review of Jeffrey Hopkins' *Meditation on Emptiness:* An Exchange." *Journal of the International Association of Buddhist Studies*, 12(2): 126-128.

Gómez, Luis

1995 "Unspoken Paradigms: Meanderings through Metaphors of a Field." In the *Journal of the International Association of Buddhist Studies*, 18(2).

Hopkins, Jeffrey

1983 *Meditation on Emptiness*. London: Wisdom Publications.

1984 *The Tantric Distinction*. London: Wisdom Publications.

1996 "The Tibetan Genre of Doxography: Structuring a Worldview." In *Tibetan Literature: Studies in Genre*. Edited by José Ignacio Cabezón and Roger R. Jackson. Ithaca, NY: Snow Lion Publications.

1999 *Emptiness in the Mind-Only School of Buddhism*. Berkeley: University of California Press.

Lopez, Donald S. Jr.

1995 "Foreigner at the Lama's Feet." In *Curators of the Buddha*. Edited by Donald S. Lopez, Jr. Chicago: University of Chicago Press.

1998 *Prisoners of Shangri-La*. Chicago: University of Chicago Press.

Newland, Guy

1996 "Debate Manuals (*yig cha*) in dGe lugs Monastic Colleges." In *Tibetan Literature: Studies in Genre*. Edited by José Ignacio Cabezón and Roger R. Jackson. Ithaca, NY: Snow Lion Publications.

Ruegg, D. Seyfort
1995 "Some Reflections on the Place of Philosophy in the Study of Buddhism." In *Journal of the International Association of Buddhist Studies*, 18(2).

Chapter 1

The Buddha's Conventional and Ultimate Tooth[1]

John Buescher

The first year Jeffrey came to the University of Virginia, he inhabited an office in a colonnaded, almost-empty building, across a dark patch of grass from the room of Edgar Allan Poe. Poe's room had been refurbished with props and memorabilia as a replica of how it might have looked in his student days—a bed, a trunk, a chair, a writing desk, a raven's quill pen. Initiates from the Raven Society, we imagined, came in the night to attend to the room. They sought to create the impression that Poe had been revived, that he had just stepped out for a moment and left his cloak slung over the back of the chair. Perhaps he was rambling out in the mountains in an opium fog in the autumn cold.

In "A Tale of the Ragged Mountains," Poe made the India of a prior age materialize in the hills around Charlottesville. Sitting outside Jeffrey's office, in his small Sanskrit class, we did that, too. We dreamed, so that we might awaken, not from the dream of India, but from the dream of Self. To do that, as Poe wrote, we first had to recognize the dream: "Now, when one dreams and, in the dream suspects that he dreams, the suspicion *never fails to confirm itself*, and the sleeper is almost immediately aroused. Thus Novalis errs not in saying that 'we are near waking when we dream that we dream'" (Poe: 790).

A magnolia blocked the sunlight that tried to enter Jeffrey's office through its tall window. But adjoining his office was a cavernous room with high, soaring walls, oak chairs and, in the center, a massive table, upon which pale light streamed through an ancient skylight. We held our hours-long Sanskrit classes in that late-afternoon light.

I remember one class in particular. On that day the querulous sounds of tourists outside, disoriented, looking for Poe's room, echoed with our own unsteady parsing of the Sanskrit, and Jeffrey's unwavering, relentless questions. As we tried to analyze the grammar of the text in front of us, moving across the lines one slow syllable at a time, Jeffrey dissected our ignorance. The text turned into a riddle-book. And our little class turned into the text whose corpus we probed. The passive, objectified text we parsed yielded uncomfortably active, first person knowledge. We were after the Self, but to pin it down and look at it, we made it appear as an "It."

We struggled to escape from the peculiar syntax in the second chapter of Candrakīrti's *Prasannapadā*, his commentary on Nāgārjuna's *Mūlamadhyamakakārikā*. But even more difficult than the syntax—and more peculiar—was the reasoning in the text. Jeffrey had chosen to begin *in medias res*, to pin us down with Nāgārjuna's "ultimate analysis," demonstrating that, contrary to the way things appear, they do not (inherently) exist, they are "empty of (inherent) existence."

Nāgārjuna's tome runs through chapter after chapter, dissecting item after item of the "conventional" world with excruciating and near-unbearable thoroughness (like pulling one tooth after another). The second chapter—an analysis of going and coming—dissolves motion. And our own progress through it seemed to slow down until we were barely dragging ourselves along. We merged with the "goer" in the text, and, like Zeno's arrow, found it harder and harder at each moment to go anywhere.

Jeffrey paused, poured some tea from his Thermos, took a sip, and listened to the silence that now overwhelmed the faint echoes that traveled across the lawn from Poe's room. Riddles hung in the air, alive with our tense, quiet breathing. Why is a raven like a writing-desk? Why is a word like a thing? Is there any "motion"? Any "goer"? Any "going"? Any "place being gone over"?

Gatam na gamyate tāvadagatam naiva gamyate / Gatāgata vinirmuktam gamyamānaṃ na gamyate, wrote Nāgārjuna (92). We ground to a halt in the Sanskrit, and Jeffrey picked us up and carried us to the other side of it:

> Respectively, the gone-over is not being gone over,
> The not-yet-gone-over is also not being gone over,
> A being-gone-over separate from the gone-over
> And the not-yet-gone-over is not known. (Hopkins, 1974: 6)

But where had we arrived? It seemed to be a place where people spoke an outlandish dialect of English, in which, for example, you could begin a sentence with the word "respectively." The translation amounted to only a relic of the Sanskrit, no more than a similitude of English. In Sanskrit, the sounds helped us imagine Nāgārjuna ringing the changes on word-elements by varying declension and conjugation, exploding them out of their boundaries—sort of an ancient Jazz Novena. In this English, all that disappeared. But still we were now left to inspect the strange mystery that presented itself in the bare meaning.

Jeffrey talked now about poor young Socrates, with his notion of forms, and wholes and parts, about his having been wound back and forth by Zeno's teacher, old man Parmenides:

> I like the way you make out that one and the same thing is in many places at once, Socrates. You might as well spread a sail over a number of people and then say that the one sail as a whole was over them all. Don't you think that is a fair analogy?
>
> Perhaps it is.
>
> Then would the sail as a whole be over each man, or only a part over one, another part over another?
>
> Only a part.
>
> In that case, Socrates, the forms themselves must be divisible into parts, and the things which have a share in them will have a part for their share. Only a part of any given form, and no longer the whole of it, will be in each thing. (Plato, *Parmenides* 131b-c: 925)

Jeffrey stopped then and smiled. Fine elegant teeth. His smile, certainly, but even his teeth, at that moment, seemed urgent indications of some truth just beyond us, a truth both painful and comical at once. At that moment, backstage in the theater of my imagination, twenty-five centuries of Western Philosophy began rehearsing the Comedy of Dentition. And yes, the sets may be a little worn, ladies and gentlemen, and the actors a little long in the tooth, but we present to you now a series of moving images in illustration of our point—

One: A couple of Sophists debate with Socrates. They get him to agree, for the sake of argument, that since he knows something, and, since he cannot know something and not know something, therefore he—like they—must know all things. An onlooker, wanting proof, asks each of the Sophists to say how many teeth the other has in his mouth. They say he's making fun of them, and refuse.

Two: Aristotle declares as false the sophistical argument of the form that someone who has teeth (always) has teeth. He also concludes that women are less intelligent than men because they have fewer teeth.

Three: Augustine disputes the notion—obviously both absurd and contrary to Scripture—that humans may have been around before Adam, by testifying that he himself has found the huge, marvelous teeth of creatures—but of giants, not of humans—along the seashore.

Four: Francis Bacon has the revolutionary idea that if you want to know how many teeth some person or animal's got, don't pray, or consult an oracle, scriptures, or ancient authorities, but open their mouth and count them.

Five: Thomas Jefferson founds a modern University on the basis of Enlightenment ideals and mastodon bones and tusks. *Applause*.

In that building, the ghost of Jefferson, the University's *pater familias*, still lived. Jefferson never lost a tooth, unlike our *pater civitatis*, George Washington, who lost every tooth but one. Washington, "as every schoolboy knows," had a set of wooden teeth that irritated him. Like many things that "every schoolboy knows," however, this was false—the belief, not just his teeth. He did have dentures, two sets of them, but they were not wooden ones. The first was made from cows' teeth, the second was carved from hippopotamus tusks. His uncomfortable and ill-fitting teeth had first belonged to other creatures.

Even in a dismembered body, there still lingers a vital power in what remains. On a high cliff overlooking dGa' ldan Monastery south of Lhasa, ravens, crows and vultures consume dismembered human corpses, the teeth and the bones of which are pounded with stones, ground down, mixed in dough balls, and offered to the birds to eat. Down in the monastery, a monk manufactures relics for pilgrims and tourists, pressing tiny balls of red-tinted dough onto the sacred tooth of Tsong kha pa, which is affixed on a lap-sized platform. These little flattened beads, touching the actual tooth, gain power from the impression.

You don't really *have* teeth, do you? Your relationship with them, as Jeffrey would say, feels much closer than that. It's more like you are your teeth, or like your teeth *are you*. And where are you located anyway? Maybe there is some oral Self, located around the mouth, the tongue, the teeth. Maybe the Self, after it has been investigated, parsed, analyzed, dissected, and chopped up, remains in the teeth. You are what you eat, but maybe you are what you eat *with*, too. (Or—ask Washington—maybe not.)

The odd thing about teeth: Most of they time they definitely are you, but when they start to loosen, they enter some twilight, borderland existence. You can worry a tooth loose with your tongue. I saw my daughter doing this several times last summer, concentrating inside her closed mouth, first pushing the tooth out of place, then moving it back, in and out, over and over. Each time she did, it oscillated back and forth, first feeling as if it was a part of her—ineluctably, primordially *her*—and then not a part of her—utterly hard and alien, frustratingly, annoyingly *not her*. When finally it released itself, she held it in her hand and examined it with relief, triumph, and fascination.

Even after it came out, an aura of Self still lingered about the tooth, or an aura of precious power, some uncanny duplicate remains of a Self that might travel on its own. The Tooth Fairy gives my daughter a dollar for each tooth she finds in the dark hidden under a pillow. She carries away every tooth to the Underworld, playing with dismemberment and death. I have a secret: In the Underworld, the Tooth Fairy offers my daughter's red-blood-flecked, milk-white baby teeth to the goddess Persephone, who uses them to bite into her red and white pomegranate seeds.

"It's the self of persons and of things that we're looking for," Jeffrey said, as he pointed to Nāgārjuna's text in front of him. "The thing that seems to cover over them and make them a whole, single entity, assembling things out of their parts. We've got to take them apart to see it."

Parsing the words of the text, then translating them, the operation became unexpectedly exacting. Sweat rolled down in tight little streams under my shirt. We were unprepared for this drill, this scalpel. Jeffrey, however, proceeded on, laying bare our ignorance, peremptorily rejecting any uncertain or wrong answer. As he thundered his demand for the right answer, we searched for it. We desperately wished we could find it, some seat of the soul, some little treasure amid the remains of the words that now lay in pieces all about us.

The Translation of Relics

When the Buddha passed away in Kūśinagarī, the local clan, the Mallas, cremated his body. They intended to keep the remains as a treasure, the ashes and whatever else there was—pieces of bones, and teeth, perhaps. Representatives of other clans came to Kūśinagarī, however, claimed kinship with the Buddha, and demanded that the Mallas hand over the relics to them. They refused, and everyone began brandishing their weapons, but a Brahmin resolved the dispute by dividing up the relics into eight parts, and distributing them. Each recipient of a share carried it back home and installed it in a stūpa.[2]

From that point, however, the Buddha's relics moved forward through time in more uncertain ways, in mythical ways. They continued to be divided and reassembled, carried one place and then another, back and forth, disappearing and reappearing over and over in time and place. One story, for example, says that soon after the relics had been divided following the cremation, the Buddha's chief disciple, Mahākāśyapa, became concerned for their safety, so he secretly went from stūpa to stūpa, taking out the relics, and then put them all back into one urn and buried them in a single vault (Jayawickrama: 44-46).

Two hundred years later, Aśoka, who established an empire over the area, decided to propagate the Faith, it was said, by dividing up the Buddha's holy relics into as many portions as he could. He opened the original stūpas or (depending on the version of the story) located the relics that Mahākāśyapa had collected. He built a vast number of stūpas throughout his empire, and these became pilgrimage centers to increase the people's piety, and radiate the relics' spiritual blessings and power over the entire land. He laid out the Buddha's body, as it were, onto the body politic[3] (Strong: 116-119; Geiger: 5.19ff).

The fifth-century Chinese monk and pilgrim Fa-xian reported on his travels to India that a stūpa in Nagarahāra held one of the Buddha's teeth, and a shrine there held the gilt frontal bone from his skull (Giles: 15, 17). Two and a half centuries later, Chinese monk Xuan-zang traveled through the Northern Indian kingdoms.

In a nunnery in Balkh he found a tooth of the Buddha, and in Kāpiśa an inch-long milk-tooth of the boy Gautama, as well as a piece of the Buddha's skull and even his top-knot of hair. The stūpa in Nagarahāra was by then in ruins, and the tooth that Fa-xian had reported was no longer there. Xuan-zang also found the place in Kūśinagarī where the Buddha had been cremated, and described the earth there as a mixture of clay and charcoal. "Whoever with true faith seeks here, and prays," he wrote, "is sure to find some relics of [the] Tathāgata" (Beal, 1911 [1]: 67, 92; [2]: 39).

The early Pāli version of the *Mahāparinibbāna Sutta* doesn't mention any of the Buddha's teeth surviving the funeral pyre, but only "bone" (Walshe: 274-276). Other later accounts—including some that made it into Tibetan texts—say as many as four of his teeth remained (Bigandet, 2: 89; Obermiller: 66; Rockhill: 147). However, the remains were said to include the Buddha's four eye-teeth, or canines, which survived "in a state of perfect preservation" along with his two collarbones, and the frontal bone—which collection, taken together, would seem far too miraculously symmetrical to be plausible to a forensics investigator. According to the scriptures, the Buddha would certainly not have lacked teeth in the first place. The descriptions of the marks of a Buddha say that he has forty brilliantly white, dense, and even teeth[4] (Conze: 584, 586).

Mahāyāna texts, in their accounts of the events just before the Buddha's death, relate that the Blessed One answered his disciples' anxieties about his imminent passing away by reassuring them that his "true" body was adamantine and indestructible (Yamamoto: 75-83). This might have inspired them not to worry about the disposition of his human remains but to look instead to his teachings—or the diamond-like truth in them—for something that would last. Or it could have convinced them that the remains had transmuted into some otherworldly crystal, an interpretation that actually did become elaborated into a description of the Buddha's relics sinking down through the vast eons into the foundations of the Earth and rising back into the Heavens, transmuting into various jewels, and even performing miracles—raining flowers down on the land, pacifying strife, and teaching the doctrine (Obermiller: 178-179). Either of these interpretations would make the questions of a later forensics investigation looking for and at the sacred remains hopelessly quotidian and meaningless.

Be that as it may, we can imagine Aśoka taking the teeth—if there were teeth—along with the other relics, on an imperial tour of his empire, distributing small bits and portions to eighty-four thousand corners of the land, placing them inside that same number of stūpas. The teeth, inside an urn in Aśoka's chariot, would have appeared to "go" on "the place-being-gone-over." But did they? Did the Buddha's teeth go anywhere?

Jeffrey seemed to have an answer—he demanded one, of course—but we realized that he was looking, too. He stood up. Until now, he'd found no goer, no going, no place being gone over. But he'd been sitting down. Now he began walking around the room, slowly circling the table, circumambulating it. He analyzed each moment as he set his foot down, each part of the foot as he placed it, and each portion of the area under it, dividing it up in smaller and smaller parts: "Where's the goer who's going, who exists in the independent, substantial way we feel the goer *must* exist?" Then: "Philosophers these days say these problems—like these about going and coming, whole and parts—just result from verbal confusions. They don't amount to anything *real*. Nothing to worry about, just 'category mistakes.' Right?" He smiled. And his smile, and his teeth, moved in a great slow circle around the room.

One of the Buddha's teeth moved to Sri Lanka in the fourth century, when Buddhists could no longer protect their relics and holy objects in India. A Sinhalese princess smuggled the tooth across the straits by hiding it in her hair, and the Sri Lankan king enshrined it in a temple he built for it in his capital, Anurādhapura. A seventeenth-century king finally installed it in Kandy, in the Dalada Maligawa, the "Temple of the Tooth," next to the royal palace.

A pious devotee carried another of the Buddha's teeth from India to the kingdom of Uḍḍiyāna. Another carried it further north to Khotan. Then in the fifth century, Fa-xian brought it to Nanjing. Over the following centuries, during political upheavals in China, the tooth disappeared and reappeared, moving first to Chang-an and then to Beijing, where, in the eleventh century, monks enshrined it in the Zhao-xian Pagoda inside the Ling-guang Monastery. During the Boxer Rebellion in 1900, artillery from the embattled Western imperialist forces in Beijing reduced the monastery and its pagoda to rubble. In the ruins, however, monks found a stone casket that contained the little tooth reliquary. In 1964, Buddhists completed a new pagoda in Beijing on the site of the destroyed monastery and installed the tooth reliquary in it.

In 1996, Beijing lent Burma its Buddha tooth for a few months. Officials in Rangoon put it on display at the Kaba Aye Pagoda. On the evening of December 25th, someone hid a bomb in a vase near where crowds of pilgrims walked by the tooth to offer it water and flowers. The bomb exploded and killed four people and wounded eighteen. It didn't damage the tooth.

Burma's military leaders blamed opposition activists. As the Chinese news agency Xinhua reported it, "destructive elements planted time bombs on the site to harm the friendship between China and Myanmar, disrupt stability in the country and disturb the Buddhist laity's faith in and reverence for the religion" (Xinhua, 12.26.96). Opposition leaders denied responsibility and pointed to the military government itself as having done it so that they could pin the blame on the opposition.

Another Burmese government in modern times had already borrowed the Buddha tooth enshrined in Sri Lanka. During the Karen uprising in 1950, Prime Minister U Nu arranged to have the Sri Lankan tooth tour Burma, like Aśoka's grand tour of his kingdom by chariot. But the Burmese substituted a small, twin-engine De Havilland Dove for the chariot, and had a young Australian pilot it. He has recently reminisced about the experience for a reporter from the *Sunday Times* of London: "I shook for days afterwards, for much of the flight was across the restless Gulf of Martaban, and the loss of the aircraft would have entailed the loss, not only of the sacred relics which were beyond price, but also the co-operation and goodwill of millions of followers of Buddha."

He was right to be worried and to consider the safety of the tooth as supremely important. In the early morning of January 25, 1998—one year and one month after the Rangoon bombing—three Tamil Tigers crashed a truck loaded with explosives into the gate of the Dalada Maligawa. The explosives detonated when they hit the gate. The Tamil Tigers died in the suicide bombing; twelve other people died as well, and twenty-one were wounded. Most of the victims were pilgrims on their way to see the tooth.

The explosion did not harm the inner Temple of the Tooth—or the tooth itself—but blew apart and flattened sections of the outer temple. The Associated Press reported that "Some Buddhist monks sitting in front of the temple sobbed and others chanted prayers in unison, while the army collected remains" (AP, 1.26.98).

Rescue workers made piles of the shattered debris and body parts that the explosion had blasted apart, fragmented, and scattered about in the mud around the monks, around the elephant-sized bomb crater in front of the temple. "There is no need to get upset since the tooth has not been harmed," the Minister of Cultural

Affairs said on television, attempting to prevent a backlash against the Hindu minority. Sinhalese armies in the first century B.C.E. fought a bloody war with an invasion force of Tamils (at the time, also Buddhists), and Sinhalese monks holding up sacred relics on spears accompanied their armies (for their protection) into the field. After the Sinhalese acquired the Buddha-tooth, an invading army from India, it was said, once briefly got hold of it and carried it back to India, but Sinhalese forces re-captured it and returned it again to Sri Lanka.

A thought about all these soldiers and monks and pilgrims carrying the Buddha's teeth from one place to another, making them disappear and reappear: The Burmese, for one, have displayed, from time to time, replicas of the Buddha's tooth—but they have explicitly acknowledged them as replicas. (In fact, the Burmese military government is currently building two pagodas just to display Buddha-tooth replicas.) But especially when political power depended on possessing relics, political and religious leaders who had none would surely have been tempted to display replicas or duplicates of relics as actual relics. Among Buddhists (as among Christians) the possession of sacred relics, with competing claims of authenticity, has fueled political competition between pilgrimage centers and between religious or political factions.

Dispute over the Buddha's tooth relics has even extended to dueling claims between Buddhists and non-Buddhists. The *Catholic Encyclopedia*, for example, says, of the Sri Lankan tooth, that in 1560 (before the Temple of the Tooth was built), the Portuguese (who had captured and occupied Kandy) took it to Goa, where they "publicly burned [it] there in presence of the viceroy. The Buddhists claim otherwise, and show in proof of their claim a piece of ivory about two inches long by one inch in diameter, which is said to resemble the tooth of a crocodile rather than of a man" (*s.v.* Kandy, Diocese of).

The Catholic Church, of course, has not been entirely innocent of encouraging "pious frauds" in the relic trade. Thomas Aquinas sanctioned honoring saints' relics because they have been "temples, and organs of the Holy Ghost dwelling and operating in them, and . . . destined to be likened to the body of Christ by the glory of the Resurrection." But he still thought it necessary, as a cautionary note, to quote Jerome quoting an earlier writer about deluded pagan ritual: "They worship with kisses I know not what tiny heap of dust in a mean vase surrounded with precious linen,"[5] (Aquinas: 2158 [*Summa* 3.25.6]). Nor has the Church always been above waging war to protect and defend (or just take possession of) its holy places and relics. Few of these relics would bear too close a scrutiny, but as John Calvin observed, most people don't look at a sacred relic with a critical eye: "Some people, in that way, in seeing, see not at all, that is to say, they do not dare to cast their eye on it judiciously in order to ascertain what it is"[6] (Calvin: 54).

Jeffrey sifted through the Sanskrit grammar, looking for the Self who was a "goer," as determined as if he were some treasure-seeker looking for a golden relic, or some midnight grave-robber out of Poe. The Aśoka of the legend understood that relics become precious treasures. He collected all the Buddha's relics he could find and then divided them up again, into the smallest imaginable grains and distributed them, like investing shares of spiritual capital, multiplying reliquaries, stūpas, all over his empire to mark the limits of his power.

But could he increase the real basis of his political power by the distribution, multiplication, and display of the Buddha's holy teeth? Indian magicians, Jeffrey told us, could create illusions for entire crowds, making them see a banquet laid out before them, for example. But they didn't create illusions out of thin air. They had to use a "base" for the illusion, some kind of small object, like a stone or a piece of wood. They would focus the crowd's attention on it and then convince them that they actually saw something else—a horse, an elephant, a banquet.

Such a thing could undoubtedly be done with a tooth, too: Hold a tooth in your hand and conjure up an entire golden body of a Buddha. Or hold a dog's tooth in your hand and conjure up a Buddha's tooth, as a well-known Tibetan proverb acknowledges: "Through having faith, even a dog's tooth will begin to shine."[7]

But we must not reduce the world to *just* a magic show: The conventional truth of my daughter's tooth—its mere existence—does not contradict its *seemingly* contradictory ultimate truth—its emptiness of *inherent* existence. That is, at least, according to Tsong kha pa, whose tooth (if it is his tooth) the monk back at dGa' ldan uses to make copies that serve, in some way, as his tooth-but-not-tooth. Tsong kha pa's tooth is not Śākyamuni Buddha's tooth is not a dog's tooth is not my daughter's canine tooth is not a pomegranate seed. Or is it?

Aśoka, the pious grave robber, in his royal chariot, "translated" (to use the old Catholic term) the Buddha's remains around his empire. Jeffrey continued to circle his "aggregates" (*skandha*: that is, his body and mind) around the table, "translating" Nāgārjuna's remains—which is to say, his argument: "The self does not inherently exist because of (1) not being the aggregates, (2) not being other than the aggregates, (3) not being the base of the aggregates, (4) not depending on the aggregates, and (5) not possessing the aggregates. An example is a chariot" (Hopkins, 1983: 178).

After all, through its various translations and commentaries, the text remains a portable reliquary; it exhumes and displays and protects and wheels about the ancient body of the teaching. The text reanimates that body—one reason why an intelligent person should prefer, according to the Perfection of Wisdom literature, a single copy of a text that clearly describes the truth over an entire universe filled with relics of the Buddha: The text forms the base on which the relics can come back to life (Conze: 249-258). But Nāgārjuna's commentators draw from the sūtras the example of a chariot, like Aśoka's chariot. The Emperor has no (inherently existent) chariot—or aircraft, for that matter, either a De Havilland Dove or something larger—that could entirely escape from the risk of disintegrating into its constituent parts at any moment. Would an airline captain better prepare his passengers with an announcement like, "You may wish to fortify your deluded sense of the inherent existence of our aircraft, as it hurtles through the near-void six miles above the Earth, protecting you from the dark vacuum only by a mere thin skin of aluminum"? Or would he do better (if we could really imagine it) to announce that "You passengers aren't going over any place being gone over, nor—even if you look carefully in or out of the plane—is anyone going anywhere at all." *Gatis ca gantā ca gantavyaṃ ca na vidyate*, literally, "Going, goer, and place of going do not exist" (Nāgārjuna: 107; Hopkins, 1974: 30). Would the passengers find that comforting?

On April 26, 1994, two hundred sixty-four people out of the two hundred seventy-one on board a China Airlines Airbus landing in Nagoya died when it crashed and exploded before it got to the gate. *Gate gate pāragate pārasaṃgate bodhi svāhā*. "Gone, gone, completely gone . . . ," as we chant at funerals from the *Heart Sūtra*. And on February 16, 1998, at the end of a second approach in heavy fog at night, a China Airlines Airbus returning vacationers from

Bali crashed and disintegrated at Taipei's Chiang Kai-shek International Airport outside the city. All one hundred ninety-six people on board and at least seven on the ground died. "The fiery impact scattered charred bodies and body parts along the road and throughout the sparsely populated area," the Associated Press reported (AP, 2.17.98).

Jeffrey still looked for the goer, the Self that was going. He had searched where one would have expected it to be—somewhere in his own mind and his own body, which he'd set in motion around the table—and hadn't found it there. Now he looked everywhere else he could think of, in the corners of the room, under the table, under the chairs, in his briefcase. Each time he looked someplace, he bellowed, "Where is it?" Then he turned to look somewhere else. "Is it here? Is this the self? NO! Is this it? NO! Come to some strong conviction about it! Eliminate every possibility! Don't just let the mind escape the way we usually do and slide around the problem. Is this the self? NO!"

Trapped. The hair on the back of my neck stood up. The light in the room had now faded, and so had the sounds, except for Jeffrey's voice and his methodical search through all the places in the room where the Self might be hiding. In Jeffrey's search we all searched for the Self. And now we feared that we wouldn't find it. A wild moment opened up, in which we very much wanted to find some Self, as if we hoped for the "invention of a relic" to wrap in preciousness and "translate" out into the world, but in which we glimpsed sidelong something dreadful—that we would find the Self and that it would dissolve when we exhumed it, like some rotten tooth, perhaps, that would shatter under pressure.

A Dental Phantom

Now, let me tell you a story, and see what you make of it: One of the Tibetan reporters on our staff at the Voice of America came into work one April morning and said he had been watching Taiwan TV on cable the night before and had seen a strange news feature story about "some Chinese dressed up like Tibetan monks," who were getting on a plane to fly to Bangkok, where they would display a tooth of the Buddha and bring it back to Taiwan. Sorting through the newswire copy, we turned up other pieces of a story. We discovered, most importantly, that Chan Master Hsing Yun, the head of two huge Buddhist Temples and Centers—the Fokuangshan Temple in Taiwan, in Kaohsiung, and the Hsi Lai Temple in Hacienda Heights not far from Los Angeles—is organizing the expedition.

In 1989—seven years before Vice President Al Gore had lunch with Master Hsing Yun at the Hsi Lai Temple and ran into a number of monks and nuns there who each wanted to donate five thousand dollars to the Democratic National Committee—the Dalai Lama had visited the place and had eaten lunch there.

Public relations copy from the Temple says that when the Dalai Lama visited Hsing Yun in Los Angeles, "The two great masters had a very wonderful meeting." At the welcoming ceremony, however, with perhaps a thousand people watching, a nun from the Temple offered to write down His Holiness' comments on the magnificent surroundings in a guest book she held in which other celebrities had described the grand beauties of the Temple. His Holiness thought for a moment and then said that although he recognized the Temple's beauty, as a Buddhist monk he felt that impressive surroundings had much less value than having a good and simple heart.[8]

Beginning in 1991, Hsing Yun repeatedly invited the Dalai Lama to come to Taiwan, but until Lee Teng-hui won his election, His Holiness had no opportunity to go. Hsing Yun, however, found himself at a disadvantage after Lee's election because he had publicly supported Lee's opponents. When Lee's government allowed and invited His Holiness to visit in the Spring of 1997, it chose not to put Hsing Yun in charge of the arrangements. When His Holiness did visit, Hsing Yun arranged an elaborate welcoming ceremony for him at his Fokuangshan Temple in Kaohsiung, but Hsing Yun himself had found a reason to be out of the country at the time. The government also did not involve Hsing Yun with the arrangements for the Dalai Lama to set up an office in Taipei, which opened around the time of the visit.

Now here we see Hsing Yun, as pictured in the Taiwan Press, about to fly to Bangkok, to receive a precious Buddha's tooth from an aging Tibetan monk, a Sa skya monk referred to as "Kunga Dorje Rinpoche." On a visit to India in February, Hsing Yun had reportedly convinced this Tibetan to give him the tooth so he could take it to Taiwan. This "Kunga Dorje Rinpoche" claims that in the 1960s he witnessed the Red Guards destroying his monastery, threatening the tooth that monks had kept there ever since they had brought it to Tibet from India in the thirteenth century. He took the tooth, therefore, and kept it for the next thirty years in his *gau*, the portable silver reliquary box that Tibetans sometimes wear when they travel. In 1985, he says, he escaped to India with the tooth (TTNN, 4.8.98).

This all sounds odd to us, from one end of the story to the other. But one problem stands out: *What* tooth? Has anyone ever heard of a tooth of the Buddha in Tibet? We're hearing about a Buddha tooth enshrined in Tibet for centuries or in exile in India for a decade or more, but no one on our staff of well-educated, well-connected and inquisitive Tibetan news reporters can find any Tibetan who knows anything about it. (One of Hsing Yun's disciples' Chinese web sites—of the "Nan Tien Monthly"—says that "Every Tibetan knows the story about the tooth as it has been passed down.")

We consult Shakabpa's *Political History of Tibet*. He cites ancient texts that describe Tibetan King Khri srong lDe btsan, in the eighth century, sending Tibetan expeditionary forces to India on forays to collect precious objects, including "relics" (*ring bsrel*) of the Buddha (Shakabpa: 189-190). When these forces returned, they sent the relics they had collected to bSam yas Monastery for safekeeping. But no tooth of the Buddha appears in the account. And this was supposed to have happened in the eighth century, not in the thirteenth.

We call the Dalai Lama's Chief Minister in Dharamsala, Sonam Topgyal, about the story: "I heard a rumor about a tooth brought from Tibet," he says, "and I wanted to investigate it. However, when I did, and I looked in our history books, they made no mention of a tooth of the Buddha in Tibet. Certainly, if there were such a tooth, we in His Holiness' Exile Government would have known about it." He had also heard a rumor a couple months before about a monk—in retrospect, this was Hsing Yun—who had traveled to India looking for such a tooth: "I heard a while ago there was a Taiwanese monk in Bodhgaya," he says, "who came to collect a tooth, so I wanted to know who that monk was, but when I asked, none of the Tibetan monks there knew."

How about the Sa skya monk, "Kunga Dorje Rinpoche," and the ten or so other Tibetan monks who had been reported in the Taiwan press to have signed a document attesting to the authenticity of the tooth? We call up every Sa skya lama we can think of in the United States. They have never heard of such a person as Kunga Dorje Rinpoche. (Nor have they ever heard of any such tooth.) No official in the Dalai Lama's organization in India that we talk to has ever heard of such a person, either. And Jamphel Choesang, Secretary of the Bureau of the Dalai Lama in New Delhi, tells us that if the monks had been Tibetans living in India, they would have had to apply to his office for travel papers in order to go abroad, but none had done so.[9]

Kunga Tsering, the Secretary of the new Tibet Religious Foundation of the Dalai Lama in Taiwan (His Holiness' liaison office there), tells us his office knows nothing at all about any of this, except what's appeared in the Taiwan press. When he read about the document of authenticity signed by the Tibetan monks accompanying the tooth, he did everything he could to get a copy of it, but with no success. Nor can he find out the names of the monks (if they were monks) who have signed it. And, he says, although Hsing Yun's organization has invited representatives of almost every other political and religious organization in Taiwan to the welcoming ceremony for the tooth, they have not invited his office or even informed them about it. The Dalai Lama's representative in Taiwan is watching the whole episode play out on television.

In fact, the Dalai Lama himself, at the time, is visiting Japan, attending a meeting in Kyoto of Buddhist leaders who are pledging to preserve the shrines and holy places of Buddhism in India and Nepal. A reporter asks him about the tooth that's going to Taiwan. He says he doesn't know anything about it.[10]

An aged Tibetan Sa skya monk in exile in India is giving a tooth of the Buddha to Hsing Yun rather than to the Dalai Lama, or to the head of the Sa skya sect, the Sa skya Khri 'dzin. How could that be? The China News Agency in Taiwan reports that the Tibetans traveling with Hsing Yun said that "Hsing Yun was chosen to take over the most precious object in the Buddhist world because of his wisdom and compassion, as well as his great contribution to Buddhist activities worldwide and his promotion of exchanges between different sects of Buddhism" (CNA, Hsu, 4.8.98). Another report quotes the monks as saying that, since they're getting old, they fear they might not be able to "keep it from vandalism" in India (CNA, "Delegation," 4.8.98). Hsing Yun's own organization says the Tibetan monks decided that "Master Hsing Yun is the most honorable one who possesses enough merits to be able to hold and preserve Buddha's tooth" (Nan Tien Monthly, "Buddha's

Tooth"). During the handover ceremony in Bangkok, "Kunga Dorje Rinpoche" reportedly says that he is giving it to Hsing Yun because the Master has a good reputation, because he's made an effort to preserve Buddhism, and because he's agreed to build a temple for it (TTNN, 4.8.98). This resonates somehow with another report in the Taiwan press, that Hsing Yun "denied claims Fokuangshan had paid a lot for the tooth, saying it had nothing to do with money"[11] (HKS, 4.7.98).

They hand over the tooth in Bangkok, at a ceremony in which monks read prayers in Mandarin, Thai and Tibetan (CNA, "Delegation," 4.7.98). Hsing Yun's "Buddha's Dental Relic Escort Organizing Committee," which had flown in from Taiwan, has handled the logistics. But Thai newspapers report that, despite the fact that the Bangkok Mayor and thousands of other Thais pay their respects to the tooth during its one-day display (practically invisible, ensconced inside a small golden stūpa) in the city, the visitors include neither the Thai royal family nor Thai government officials (AFP, 4.9.98).

The Tibetan monks took the tooth to Bangkok from India, it is said, because no direct air flights connect India to Taiwan—puzzling, given that Hsing Yun has arranged a charter flight to Taipei on China Airlines from Bangkok: Why couldn't the monks charter a flight from India to Taipei? Also, it is said, Thailand has close relations with Taiwan: Hsing Yun tells reporters that Thai authorities have resisted "pressure" from Beijing to send the tooth "back to China" (AP, "Can a Tooth," 4.7.98). Much of the press dutifully repeats this claim as true, but we don't; we can find no evidence at all, besides Hsing Yun's claim, that China has pressured Thailand or even that China wants the tooth. The Associated Press reporter in Beijing perceptively protects his rear by writing that "It wasn't immediately clear why China would want the tooth, if, as it claims, the tooth is not legitimate" (AP, "In Apparent Dig," 4.8.98).

And China (or, at least, a spokesman for the government-sponsored Chinese Buddhist Association) does claim exactly that. "The two teeth remaining in the mortal world," the spokesman says, "are currently enshrined and worshipped in Sri Lanka and Beijing" (Xinhua, 4.8.98). He points out that no one ever heard of this other tooth, until it suddenly appeared almost overnight: "Generations of Dalai and Paṇ chen Lamas have never mentioned the existence of such a tooth in the region. We have no idea where the third Buddha's tooth originates."[12] Hsing Yun's press people, however, were referring to religious texts that said that four teeth were recovered after the Buddha had been cremated, and that the "emperor of the sky" took one, while the other three went to India, China, and Sri Lanka[13] (AFP, 4.9.98).

Jeffrey, now finished looking under the table and chairs, saw a trash can and walked over to it. "You have to come to the conviction that you've figured out all the possibilities that it might be, so that you can carefully examine every one. The person, if it inherently existed, would have to be the same as or different from the body and the mind. We looked for it. The goer—among other things—the one that seems proud of going, is made happy by going, is threatened by going, inconvenienced by going, tired out by going, excited by going, and so on. It's not the same as the mind or the body, or the mind and the body together. So now we're looking at the possibility that it's different from them. But it couldn't be too different, could it? Otherwise it would lose all contact with the mind and body. It would be too far away. So maybe it's hovering close by, right around here somewhere." And he peered into the trash can.

The first reports about the tooth, especially in the Western press, tend to repeat uncritically everything the tooth's promoters have claimed, perhaps because many in the West—especially since the Reformation—would automatically regard all "Buddha's teeth" (or any other religious relics) as equally papistic and mythical; all beliefs about relics as equally preposterous. One Buddhist tooth equals any other Buddhist tooth (real or imaginary), just as one Marian apparition or one Elvis sighting equals any other. BBC reporters describe the episode as it begins to unfold, but apparently never ask themselves whether something likely to be a real tooth of the Buddha has been recovered. But this predisposes them, it seems, to repeating the story they've heard without questioning it: "The relic, which is more than two thousand years old, has been in India since it was smuggled out of Tibet during the turbulent years of China's cultural revolution" (BBC, 4.8.98). Eventually, however, before the story drops completely out of the BBC's view, its World Service has qualified one part of the tooth-promoters' claim: "The relic, believed to be more than two thousand years old, was smuggled out of Tibet to India during the Chinese cultural revolution" (BBC, 4.9.98).

But by this time, some people, even in Taiwan, have begun to have real doubts. The Taiwan press even has a minister of a fringe,

Christian, saucer-cult weigh in on the subject by offering his services to help compromise between those who say it's real and those who say it's not (Hsin Hsin Wen, 4.10.98, "Fei-tieh"). Let's agree it's most probably the Buddha's tooth, he says, but that it's his *false* tooth. *Ha ha*. He gives other helpful advice, too: No reason to fight about it, he says. With all those offerings of milk that people gave the Buddha, he must have had dental problems, anyway, and probably lost most of his teeth. With all that fasting, too, why would he have needed teeth? And with all that meditation, he probably even forgot he had any.[14]

As the criticism of the tooth grows, its defenders shift their arguments. One line of criticism attacks the motives of the tooth's promoters. This criticism describes the arrival of the tooth as the religious and government leaders' cynical ploy to mask their own failure. Lee Teng-hui isn't even Buddhist, but Christian, the papers point out, yet many high officials in his secular government are set to participate in the tooth-welcoming ceremonies.

To make up for a string of foreign relations losses to Mainland China, it's said, the government is trying to set Taiwan up as a new pan-Asian spiritual power, a protector of the Dharma. The tooth is "the most important treasure which guards both the order and the Nation," in the words of a Hsing Yun follower, who apparently sees the Master's procurement of the tooth as similar to the government's acquisition of an F-16.[15] One commentator writes that the current upsurge in religion in Taiwan actually points to a failure, to the fact that people have lost confidence in politicians and are looking for another place to put their trust (Hsin Hsin Wen, 4.3.98, "Chia-chih").

The promoters of the tooth, responding to such criticism, say that the arrival of the tooth won't solve any problems—foreign relations losses, China Airlines mishaps, official corruption scandals, rising crime, or any other. It will not automatically bring good luck, as it has been so widely reported and commonly anticipated. It will simply give the Faithful an opportunity to purify their minds and gain merit. Before leaving for Bangkok, Hsing Yun tells reporters "that the true meaning of venerating the holy tooth is to learn the wisdom, mercy and morality of the Buddha," and says, "The tooth won't relieve Taiwan of misfortunes unless people make their own efforts" (CNA, 4.7.98).

The other line of criticism directly attacks the authenticity of the tooth. One scientist explains to reporters how he could easily date the tooth by measuring carbon-14 levels in it (TTNN, 4.10.98, "T'an shih-su"). The press informally polls Buddhist scholars in Taiwan and find them to be mostly skeptical. One scholar points to the Buddha's dismissal of image and artifice in preference for the truth, and to the early Buddhists' refusal to make any representation of the Buddha, except insofar as his teachings embodied him. Some, however, are willing to allow that even if the tooth is not real, the growth of piety resulting from its enshrinement might be a good thing (TTNN, 4.10.98, "Fo-chiao").

In response, the tooth's promoters emphasize the uncertain nature of verification in this world as well as the benefits of Faith. Hsing Yun gives an interview in which he tells the reporter about his own toothaches, and how much he has to pay to treat them. The huge dental bills for the thousand students studying at his Temple, he says, he has reconciled himself to paying. "I prefer to have good teeth in my mouth," he says, "even if I can't make good words come from my mouth." How many good words, he says, came through this Buddha tooth? And these still remain true and real today. Maybe this, he says, makes the tooth this most precious thing in the world: "If you have faith in it, it is true. If you don't have faith in it, then even true things are also false" (TTNN, 4.8.98, "16 k'e"). Senior Presidential Advisor Wu Poh-hsiung takes this line, too: "Whether the Buddha's tooth is genuine or phoney completely depends on how it is thought of and seen in people's hearts" (HKS, 4.7.98). One Buddhist scholar, however, puts his opposition to this sort of reasoning rather succinctly: "Hsing Yun said it doesn't matter if it's real or fake," he says, "but if this is a dog's tooth and everyone's worshipping it, that's stupid, isn't it?" (TTNN, 4.10.98, "Fo-chiao").

By the time Hsing Yun arrives back in Taiwan with the tooth, reporters ask him to respond to the widely reported denial by the mainland Chinese Buddhist Association that the tooth is genuine. He says that it is "not worth arguing over the issue." And, he says, "For a wonderful thing like this, it is meaningless to argue over what exactly is real and what is false .... Some say the Lord Buddha had left four teeth, some say three. How can you tell which is real and which is false?" (Reuters, 4.9.98).

A good question. How indeed? Especially as far away from Taiwan as Washington? One might try to work over the body of the problem, at a distance once-removed, like Poe's detective Monsieur

Dupin in "The Murders in the Rue Morgue" reasoning his way to the truth from evidence collected only in the newspapers, analyzing it in almost complete isolation from all the actual objects and events. A conceptual simulacrum or a model—even constructed from what the newspapers present—may serve as the real thing. The collected press reports embody the case. One may dismember and analyze it, and expect to identify the truth. To corner it.

Of all the possible relics of the Buddha that one might imagine, a tooth satisfies a certain kind of expectation more than, say, ashes or some grey nondescript lump of charred bone. A tooth is hard, complete, shiny, and recognizable in and of itself. One can more easily imagine it as a close replica of the Buddha's "actual presence" than any other part of the cremated remains could be, short of the entire skull. And a tooth has the advantage over a skull of not being so obviously a *memento mori*: Children even put teeth under their pillows. The tooth is a little duplicate of the Self we were looking for—hard, solid, substantial, seemingly complete in and of itself, like a fabulous jewel, a Moonstone, a Koh-i-noor, immediately recognizable as something personal, a perfect "point of attachment." The Buddha might even dwell inside it, somehow (Schopen: 158).

Jeffrey picked up the trash can and began rummaging around in it. "I don't see it here," he said. Then he suddenly turned the trash can over and emptied it out in the center of the table, sending broken pencils, apple cores, typing paper, and newspaper skittering across the surface of the oak table. Jeffrey began a methodical examination, picking up one bit of debris, one bit of trash, after another, and examining each piece. "Is this the Self? No."

One feeling predominates in Poe's stories—the feeling of being trapped. People are sealed up in underground storage rooms, buried in coffins before they're really dead, tied up by Inquisitorial torturers, engulfed in a maelstrom, and trapped on Earth while a comet hurtles toward them. Even messages get trapped in bottles. We felt some of that uncomfortable closeness now, around the table in that room.

Hsing Yun and his delegation and the tooth depart Thailand for Taiwan on a chartered China Airlines Airbus A300-600R, the same kind of aircraft that had crashed in February (*Nation*, 4.8.98, 4.10.98; Reuters, 4.9.98). The plane lands at Chiang Kai-shek airport, where a crowd of twenty thousand is waiting. TV and newswire photos show the Tibetan monks deplaning first, followed by Hsing Yun carrying the small golden stūpa that holds the tooth, followed by others in the hundred-and-sixty-some-member delegation.

Officials greeting the plane include Vice President Lien Chan, Premier Vincent Siew and Taiwan Governor James Soong. TV and movie stars line the red carpet, as well. At the last minute, Lee Teng-hui decides he has other work to do and, much to the relief of the secularists, doesn't attend the reception ceremony (Hsin Hsin Wen, 4.17.98, "Amen"). Two hundred "Buddhist virgins" in robes, however, lie prostrate on the tarmac with their long straight hair spread out carefully in circles, like fans upon the ground, paying homage to the tooth as it comes down the ramp and across the runway.

During an hour-long welcoming ceremony, Premier Siew offers prayers and gives a brief speech "praising Buddha's renunciation of fortune and position to seek ultimate truth and salvation" (CNA, 4.8.98, "Traffic Controls"). Hsing Yun then places the tooth reliquary in a sedan chair. An escort carries it over to several other China Airlines planes on the runway, which the assembled monks bless "in an attempt to confer safety on the flagship carrier" (AP, 4.10.98).

Police have set up strict protocols for traffic control around the airport and on the route from there to Hsing Yun's branch temple in Taipei. The tooth proceeds into the city at the head of a fifteen-car procession, stopping along the way at the site of the February crash, where Hsing Yun offers prayers for the dead. At the temple, he installs the tooth in a temporary shrine where, over the next few days, thousands of people, amid clouds of incense, offer prayers in its presence. Much of this is televised.

So, what do you think? What would you report on this, under deadline, to a Buddhist radio audience in Tibet?

Case Closed

"You have to force yourself," Jeffrey said, "to mark out all the possibilities beforehand, and commit yourself to those possibilities as being completely comprehensive and inclusive, so that when you eliminate all of them, you're left with an utterly inescapable conviction about what you've found." Poe's detective, M. Dupin, solved the mystery by examining and comparing the press accounts of the incident, and eliminating one hypothesis after another. Finally inviting the unsuspecting culprit to his room, Dupin allowed him in, then locked the door from the inside, put the key into his pocket, pulled out a brace of pistols, and aimed them at the man. Trapped. No way to escape, nowhere to hide. Jeffrey wanted us to do this with our minds.

At the beginning of December, Master Hsing Yun chartered a train. He and six hundred other people traveled with the tooth, over the "place being gone over," to Kaohsiung. Twenty to thirty thousand people were on hand for its arrival. Hsing Yun plans to seal away the tooth in a stūpa that will be the world's largest (TTNN, 12.14.98).

A few months after the tooth came to Taiwan, we made another call to Kunga Tsering at the Dalai Lama's Office in Taipei: He said that the excitement had died down. During the initial furor, the Taiwan press called his office day and night, asking about the tooth. He didn't have any evidence that the tooth was genuine, but Hsing Yun has enormous political influence in Taiwan, so he didn't really know what to say.

However, he now had some more information about the monk who gave the tooth to Hsing Yun. He is a monk, a Sa skya monk, named Kunga. But he's not a lama, not a *rin po che*. And he's not from India, but from Nepal, where he has lived for decades. On the day of the handover of the tooth, this monk Kunga flew to Bangkok, not from New Delhi, but from Kathmandu, and he flew out of Taiwan almost immediately after the ceremony at Chiang Kai-shek Airport. All this would explain why no one—especially no one in India—had ever heard of him before.[16]

And Gunga Tsering learned one more thing: Some time ago, this monk Kunga went back to Tibet on a visit to his remote birthplace, and the local people, treating him as a visiting celebrity, gave him various holy objects they had collected among themselves. Not to put too fine a point on it, but one might expect such objects to be of dubious provenance.

In the twilight of the seminar room, we were coming to the end of Jeffrey's search for the remains of the Self among the trash. He had worried at, picked at, and pointed to almost every bit of trash on the table, considering each—the Self as apple core, the Self as used tea bag, as term paper draft, as paper clip, as newspaper—and eliminating each, one by one, he'd put each one back in the trash can. As he neared the end, and only a last few scraps of newspaper remained on the table, we felt some palpable sense of unease, even a note of momentary panic. We looked, then, into the very newsprint of these last scraps, searching for the truth.

And then there it was. Jeffrey had examined and eliminated everything. Nothing was up his sleeves. The top of the table was absolutely clean and empty. The room was silent. Class was over. And we all smiled.

Notes

1. Thanks to Tseten Wangchuk and Nadine Leavitt, who helped me with the Chinese-language sources. Concerning the rendering of Tibetan personal names in this article, since many of the contemporary Tibetan persons referred to in this article have previously established romanized forms for their names either legally or in print, I have utilized established romanized forms for the names of such Tibetan scholars and authors as they appear in Library of Congress bibliographic citations. Other Tibetan names and terms appear in standard Wylie transliterations.

2. This much seems reasonably clear from the most ancient accounts of the Buddha's passing, and archaeological evidence appears to substantiate it: What seems to have been one of the original stūpas, containing ashes of the Buddha (labeled in a covered stone pot), was discovered intact more than a hundred years ago.

3. Surely apocryphal. The texts describing Aśoka as a kind of good-intentioned grave-robber, such as the *Aśokāvadāna*, the *Mahāvaṃsa*, and the *Thūpavaṃsa*, are relatively late and have many features that are obviously fantastical.

4. Are the extras wisdom teeth?

5. During the time I was writing this paper, my boss—a lapsed Catholic like me, but also an avid collector of Asian antique art who cruises Internet auctions—told me that someone was offering for sale a "class one relic" (an actual part of the body, in the terminology of the Council of Trent) of Saint Thomas Aquinas. Did I want to make a bid? (Technically, the seller was asking for bids on the reliquary; the relic itself was a "gift.") We stared at the image on the screen, but all we could see was the reliquary, which was sealed. Papers of authenticity from the Holy See came with it, however. We queried the seller by e-mail, and he replied, explaining that the relic was a coin-shaped, cross-section slice of the Angelic Doctor's tibia. We bid two hundred dollars. After the bidding closed, we discovered we'd lost it to a higher bidder, by ten dollars. The seller, then, who identified himself as an ex-Jesuit, e-mailed us that actually he had two Aquinas relics, both very much alike. He'd been planning to save one, but now he'd decided to let them both go. Would we like to have the second one for our original bid? Alleluia and Saints Preserve Us, we two Parochial School refugees thought, we are witnessing the multiplication of the holy relics in cyberspace. We wrote back, declining the offer.

6. "Car plusieurs, afin, en voyant, de ne veoir goutte: c'est a dire qu'ilz n'osent pas jecter l'oeil a bon escient, pour considerer ce que c'est."

7. *Mos pa byas na khyi'i so la yang 'od zer 'khrungs.* A variation: *Mos pa byas na khyi'i so la yang ring bsrel 'khrungs,* "If you have faith, even in a dog's tooth, a holy relic is born."

8. According to Tseten Wangchuk, His Holiness' translator for the Temple visit.

9. Almost entirely true. Some of the few exceptions include those Tibetans who wish to avoid the Tibetan Government-in-Exile's organization.

10. Kunga Tsering later told us that the Taiwan press reported that the Dalai Lama then said that once he'd been invited to see a Buddha tooth, and that when he went, it turned out to be an elephant tusk. The Head of the Dalai Lama's Liaison Office in Japan, Karma Gelek Yuthok, however, who was with His Holiness in Japan, told us he doesn't remember the Dalai Lama making any such statement.

11. The Taiwan press was reporting that Hsing Yun was making money from the tooth, but the truth of this seems something that only Hsing Yun or his accountant would be in a position to know.

12. The Chinese Buddhist Association has placed Chan Master Miao Dzong in charge of the Buddha Tooth Pagoda in Beijing. Master Miao Dzong has spent a considerable amount of his career repairing old Buddhist temples and rebuilding them, many of which (but not the Buddha Tooth Pagoda) were damaged or destroyed during the Cultural Revolution. Miao Dzong is a Patriarch of the Cao-dong (Jap. *Sōtō*) lineage of Chan Buddhism, while Master Hsing Yun, originally from Nanjing, is a Chan Patriarch of the other major lineage, the Lin-ji (Jap. *Rinzai*).

13. Referring, in part, to the Mahāyāna *Mahāparinirvāṇa Sūtra,* according to the tooth's proponents: "The Buddha's whole body turned into single grains of relics, except for the teeth which remained intact." A confusion—or difference of opinion—about what remained after the cremation is present in the ancient texts. Xuan-zang, for example, said that, besides bone, only nails and hair remained. Bu ston said there were fourteen portions of the relics made after the Buddha was cremated, and that four of these consisted of just the four eye-teeth, although he places two of them in India: one of them in the Trāyatriṃśa Heaven (Śakra, foremost of the *devas* who live there, is the "emperor of the sky" referred to by the tooth's promoters); and one (protected by *nāgas*) in the stūpa at Rāmagrāma. (However, according to other texts, the stūpa at Rāmagrāma was the resting-place of one of the "regular" portions of relics.) Any text that said that teeth had gone to China and Sri Lanka, of course, would have to have been written after they supposedly went there, in the fifth century C.E.

14. Christian-Buddhist dialogue in Taiwan doesn't appear to be progressing, judging by this minister's wacky misjudgment of his audience, although he can hardly be said to be representative of mainline Christians. But the Taiwan Baptist Mission's website reports, almost despairingly, in an article entitled, "Holy Molar Prompts a Frenzy of Buddhist Activity Across Asia," that

"Taiwan largely lives in spiritual darkness" because only two percent of the people have "accepted the Lord Jesus Christ," and that "international Buddhists are moving the tooth to Taiwan, likely hoping to fan the flames of revival and establish Taiwan as an outpost aimed at revitalization of the religion in Mainland China as well as Taiwan."

15. Or an ABM System, perhaps? Not an Anti-Ballistic Missile System, but an Adamantine Buddhistic Masticating System. A cartoon by CoCo, reproduced in the June, 1998, issue of Sinorama (69): In the office of "Hsing Yun, Dentist," the Master stands smiling by a dentist's chair, implement in hand. Patient "Taiwan," with a goofy smile, bounds sideways out of the chair and across the floor, off-balance by a new "false tooth" the size and shape of an airplane propeller. He thinks, "Having this false tooth implanted makes me too heavy. . . . "

16. A Voice of America listener in Darjeeling heard our radio interview with Sonam Topgyal in which he said that he knew of no Buddha's tooth in Tibet. The listener, a Sa skya monk, wrote a letter to the Tibetan Cabinet in which he wondered if there was a political motive behind this statement. He referred them to a rare Tibetan history text, *The History of sTag lung* (sTag lung: 192-195). It mentions four tooth relics, one of which was in Kalinka (modern Orissa). It says that sTag lung thang pa chen po (twelfth century C.E.) carried it to sTag lung in central Tibet, where his successor placed it in a stūpa.

In another late development (January of 1999) in the Tale of the Tooth, some Sa skya teachers now remember the monk Kunga. Staff at the Sa skya Khri 'dzin's office say he asked for a letter of support for "a temple project," which they gave him. They also remember him, at an unrelated moment, showing the Sa skya Khri 'dzin a reliquary and telling him that it contained a tooth of the Buddha, to which the Sa skya Khri 'dzin said, "*A le*," an expression meaning something like, "I see," or "Is that so?"

References

Agence France Presse (AFP)

1998.4.7 "Taiwan Buddhists Headed for Bangkok to Welcome Buddha's Tooth."

"Thailand Braces for the Arrival of Buddha's Tooth."

"Taiwan Set to Welcome Arrival of Buddha's Tooth."

1998.4.8 "China Says Taiwan-Bound Tooth of Buddha Is Phony."

"Thousands of Devotees Flock to See Buddha's Tooth in Bangkok."

"Thai Crowds Flock to Pray before One of Buddha's Teeth."

1998.4.9 "Thousands of Taiwanese Buddhists Greet Buddha's Tooth."

1998.4.11 "Thousands Pray before Buddha's Tooth to Escape Disaster."

Aquinas, Thomas

1947 *Summa Theologica*. Trans. by Fathers of the English Dominican Province. Vol. 2. New York: Benziger Brothers.

Associated Press (AP)

1998.1.26 "Sri Lanka Temple Attack Kills 11; Suicide Blast at Site Laid to Tamil Rebels." Gemunu Amarasinghe.

1998.2.17 "Plane Plows into Neighborhood outside Taipei, 205 Reported Dead."

1998.4.7 "Can a Tooth Bring Peace?"

"Taiwan Hopes Tooth Will Bring Peace."

"Taiwan to Get Holy Tooth Despite China's Claim of Owner ship."

1998.4.8 "In Apparent Dig at Taiwan, China Questions Authenticity of Holy Tooth."

1998.4.9 "Taiwanese Welcome 'Holy Tooth.'" Annie Huang.

1998.4.10 "Taiwanese Welcome Tooth Linked to Buddha." Annie Huang.

Beal, Samuel, trans.

1998 *Si-Yu-Ki: Buddhist Records of the Western World, Translated from the Chinese of Hiuen Tsiang (A. D. 629)*. Reprint. New York: Paragon Books.

Bigandet, Paul Ambrose, trans.

1911 *The Life or Legend of Gaudama the Buddha of the Burmese; with Annotations. The Ways to Neibban, and Notice on the Phongyies, or Burmese Monks*. 2 vols. 4th ed. London: Kegan Paul, Trench, Trubner & Company.

British Broadcasting Corporation (BBC)

1998.4.8 "Seekers after the Tooth." Enver Solomon.

1998.4.9 "Buddha's Tooth in Taiwan."

Calvin, Jean

1970 *Le Traité des Reliques*. In Jean Calvin, *Three French Treatises*, pp. 47-97. Ed. by Francis M. Higman. London: Athlone Press.

The Catholic Encyclopedia (online). <http://www.knight.org/advent> *s.v.* "Kandy, Diocese of."

China Daily [Beijing]

1998.4.15 "Buddha's 'Other Tooth' Sparks Controversy."

China News Agency [Taiwan] (CNA)

1996.10.26 "Buddhist Temple Founder Denies Clinton Campaign Donation."

1998.4.7 "Delegation Leaves for Bangkok to Escort Back Tooth of Buddha." Lin Wen-fen.

1998.4.8 "Delegation Off to Thailand for Holy Tooth."

"Traffic Controls to be Imposed for Arrival of Buddha's Tooth." Elizabeth Hsu.

Conze, Edward, trans.
1975 *The Large Sutra on Perfect Wisdom, with the Divisions of the Abhisamayālaṅkāra*. Berkeley: University of California Press.

Geiger, William, trans.
1912 *The Mahāvaṃsa, or the Great Chronicle of Ceylon* [by Mahānāma]. London: Pali Text Society.

Giles, H[erbert] A[llen], trans.
1981 *The Travels of Fa-hsien (399-414 A. D.), or Records of the Buddhistic Kingdoms*. Reprint. Westport, CT: Greenwood Press.

Hong Kong Standard
1998.4.7 "Big Welcome Prepared as Tooth Truth Unresolved." Jason Blatt.

Hopkins, P[aul] Jeffrey, trans.
1974 *Chapter Two of Ocean of Reasoning by Tsong kha pa: A Commentary on Nāgārjuna's* Fundamental Treatise on the Middle Way, *Proving the Emptiness of Going and Coming*. Dharamsala: Library of Tibetan Works and Archives.
1983 *Meditation on Emptiness*. London: Wisdom Publications.

Hsin Hsin Wen/The Journalist [Taiwan]
1998.4.3 "Fo-ya she-li lai-t'ai li-hsing chu-yi chiao-hsieh t'ou-hsiang." ("Buddha's Tooth Comes to Taiwan; Rationalists Give Up and Surrender.")
"Chia-chih mi-luan pu-tzu-ch'iu tsai-to te Fo-ya yeh mei-yung." ("If Your Value System Is Confused, However Many Buddha's Teeth You Have Doesn't Matter.")
1998.4.10 "Fei-tieh k'ao-shih Fo-ya chen-wei." ("Saucer Cultist Examines Authenticity of the Buddha Tooth.")"Fo-chiao shih-yie ching-ying yu-shu chieh he cheng-shang shih-li chang hou-teng." ("Skillfully Managing a Buddhist Enterprise with the Backing of Politics and Business.")
"Ying-ya tui-wu ch'ung-su hsuan-chu erh-yu." ("Receiving Line for the Tooth Filled with Whispers about the Election.")
1998.4.17 "Amen! Li Teng-Hui he Chu Shu-Hsien mei-yu ch'u ying Fo-ya." ("Amen! Lee Teng-Hui and Chu Shu-Hsien Don't Go to the Buddha Tooth Reception.")

Independent [London]
1998.4.9 "Buddha Relic Upsets Chinese."

Jayawickrama, N. A., ed. and trans.
1971 *The Chronicle of the Thūpa and the Thūpavaṃsa; Being a Translation of and Edition of Vācissarathera's Thūpavaṃsa*. London: Pali Text Society.

Nāgārjuna

1903 *Mūlamadhyamakakārikās (Mādhyamikasūtras) de Nāgārjuna avec la Prasannapadā commentaire de Candrakirti.* Ed. by Louis de la Vallée Poussin. St. Petersburg: Imprimerie de l'Academie Imperiale des Sciences.

Nan Tien Monthly [Taiwan]

1998 "Buddha's Tooth Reappears in the World/Buddha's Tooth to Taiwan." <http://www.ozemail.com.au/~nantien/htmls/special5.html>

"Mo-chih Fo-ya she-li chuan-ch'ou chin-tsun san-ko chi-yi chiang tso-wei Fokuangshan sun-mo Kuochenshan chi-pao." <http://www.ozemail.com.au/~nantien/htmls/tooth.html>

Nation [Bangkok]

1998.4.8 "Buddha's Tooth on Display Wednesday."

1998.4.10 "Devotees Gather to Pay Respects."

Obermiller, E[ugene], trans.

1986 *The History of Buddhism in India and Tibet by Bu-ston.* 2nd ed. Delhi: Sri Satguru Publications.

Plato

1961 *Parmenides.* Francis Cornford, trans. In Edith Hamilton and Huntington Cairns, eds. *The Collected Works of Plato*, pp. 920-956. Princeton: Princeton University Press.

Poe, Edgar Allan

1992 "A Tale of the Ragged Mountains." In *Edgar Allan Poe: The Complete Stories*, pp. 785-794. New York: Alfred A. Knopf.

Reuters

1998.4.9 "Taiwan Spurns China's Tooth Relic Controversy."

Rockhill, W[illiam] Woodville, trans.

1976 *The Life of the Buddha and the Early History of His Order, Derived from Tibetan Works in the Bkah-Hgyur and Bstan-Hgyur.* Reprint. San Francisco: Chinese Materials Center.

Schopen, Gregory

1997 "On the Buddha and His Bones: The Conception of a Relic in the Inscriptions of Nāgārjunikoṇḍa." In Gregory Schopen, *Bones, Stones, and Buddhist Monks: Collected Papers on the Archaeology, Epigraphy, and Texts of Monastic Buddhism in India*, pp. 148-164. Honolulu: University of Hawai'i Press.

Shakabpa, W[angchuk] D[eden]

1986 *Bod kyi srid don rgyal rab* ("Political History of Tibet"). Dharamsala: Library of Tibetan Works and Archives. 3rd ed.

South China Morning Post [Hong Kong]

1998.3.29 "Taiwanese Bank on Buddha Tooth."

1998.4.11 "Thousands Turn Out to See Buddha's Tooth on Show," Jason Blatt.

sTag lung Ngag dbang Chos rje

1992 *sTag lung chos 'byung*. Reprint. Lhasa: Ancient Tibet Text Publishers.

Strong, John S.

1983 *The Legend of King Aśoka: A Study and Translation of the Aśokāvadāna*. Princeton: Princeton University Press.

Sunday Times [London]

1998.8.16 "The Pilot and the Tooth Relic." Roger Thiedeman.

Taiwan Today News Network (TTNN).

1998.4.7 "Hsi-tsang kao-seng ch'ien-li hu-ch'ih Fo-ya ti-t'ai Hsing-Yun tai-kuo ying-ya." ("Tibetan High Lama Comes a Thousand Miles; Buddha's Tooth Arrives in Thailand; Hsing Yun Leads His Delegation to Receive It.")

"Ying Fo-ya 170 ren ch'i-ch'eng fu Manku." ("To Receive Buddha's Tooth, 170 People Leave for Bangkok.")

1998.4.8 "Fo-ya lai-le Manku t'ien-k'ung hsia Tsang-seng hsien 'chen-pao.'" ("Under the Skies of Bangkok, Tibetan Monk Presents the Precious Jewel.")

"16 k'e huai-ya jan ta-shih ts'an-wu." ("Sixteen Bad Teeth Awaken the Master.")

1998.4.10 "Fo-ya ti-t'ai wan-jen cheng-tu chan fa-hsi." ("Buddha's Tooth Arrives in Taiwan; Tens of Thousands Vie for a View.")

"T'an shih-su chien-ting k'e p'an-tuan Fo-ya nien-ling." ("Carbon-14 Dating Can Decide the Age of the Buddha Tooth.")

"Fo-chiao hsueh-che lun chen-ch'ueh k'an-tai hsin-yang." ("Buddhist Scholars Urge Correct Approach to Religious Faith.")

1998.12.14 "Fo-ya she-li an-feng Kaohsiung Fokuangshan." ("Buddha's Tooth Relic Placed in Kaohsiung's Fokuangshan Temple.")

Walshe, Maurice, trans.

1995 *The Long Discourses of the Buddha: A Translation of the Dīgha Nikāya*. Boston: Wisdom Publications.

Xinhua News Agency [Beijing]

1996.12.26 "Bombs Explode in Cave Housing Buddha Tooth from PRC."

1998.4.8 "Chinese Buddhists Doubt Authenticity of Third Buddha's Tooth."

Yamamoto, Kosho, trans.

1973 *The Mahayana Mahaparinirvana Sutra*. 3 vols. Tokyo: Karinbunko.

Chapter 2

Ask a Farmer

Ultimate Analysis and Conventional Existence in Tsong kha pa's Lam rim chen mo[1]

Guy Newland

In February of 1997, Geshe Lobsang Gyatso, Director of the Buddhist School of Dialectics in Dharamsala, India, was brutally assassinated. He was from the rugged and beautiful country of Khams, in eastern Tibet, and he was prone to enlivening his Dharma expositions with old stories about fording wild rivers, breaking horses and shooting guns (cf. Lobsang Gyatso: *passim*). Many times he said, to me and to many others, that if you need to know whether a certain potato will be a good one to plant, you had better not ask a philosopher. Ask a farmer. This earthy advice implies that it is a matter of common sense, and shared experience, to distinguish between two types of knowledge, one which interrogates the ultimate conditions of being but unfortunately does not seem to be of any practical use in getting things done, and another which ignores ontological inquiry in order to allow very practical distinctions. Lobsang Gyatso's comment is thus an implicit argument for the reasonableness, in terms of the practical conventions already familiar to all, of the Buddhist distinction between the two truths: conventional truth and ultimate truth.

This distinction has roots in the earliest teachings of Buddhism. The Buddha pushed his followers to investigate their own conceptions of person and self. He taught that when one analyzes the psychophysical elements of the person, the personal self that we believe in is nowhere to be found. Yet he used words like "I" and "mine" to refer to himself, his own motivations, and his own experiences. Moreover, from the outset, the notion of personal identity was critical to Buddhist ethics, in which karma is created and bears fruit as moral consequences in this life and future lives. Thus, the distinction between two types of knowledge about persons, as well as potatoes and other things, is a persistent theme within Buddhist philosophy. By extension, the problem of knowing which potato to plant is also the problem of how to choose between possible courses of action, the question of how empty persons can make distinctions between right and wrong.

Here I will summarize some of the changes Tsong kha pa Blo bzang grags pa (founder of the dGe lugs order of Tibetan Buddhism) rings on this theme in his massive *Byang chub lam rim chen mo* (*The Great Exposition of the Stages of the Bodhisattva Path,* hereafter cited as *LRCM*). Published in 1402, the *LRCM* was the first of five major works in which Tsong kha pa expounded his approach to Buddhist philosophy, an approach in which the validity of logic and ethical norms is maintained within a radical view of "emptiness," the theory that all phenomena are devoid of any essential or intrinsic nature. Like other Mahāyāna Buddhists, Tsong kha pa believes that all living beings have the potential to attain perfect happiness in buddhahood. The spiritual path to buddhahood involves balanced attention to two factors: wisdom—which knows the emptiness of all that exists—and altruistically motivated active engagement with other living beings. Wisdom destroys all reification and shows us ultimate truth, while leaving unscathed the conventional truths which allow us to exist, to make distinctions, and compassionately interact with others.

The root of our current unsatisfactory condition in a cycle of death and rebirth is our innate tendency to view the personal self in a reified manner (*LRCM*: 574). We also have innate tendencies to view all other phenomena in a reified manner. To achieve wisdom, or to know emptiness, means to overcome this reifying view, to realize that the self or essential being as thus conceived does not exist at all. In order reach this realization, according to Tsong kha pa, one must use reason to refute the existence, and to prove the nonexistence, of this reified self or essence. Having intellectually arrived at the correct philosophical view—that the self lacks a shred of intrinsic nature—one proceeds along the path to spiritual liberation through intense, deep, and extensive meditative familiarization with this view. At the same time, however, the practitioner also cultivates compassionate engagement with other living beings, making a commitment to help all of them reach perfect happiness.

A critical step in the refutation of "self," or "essence," is to carefully take the measure of and accurately identify the self, or intrinsic nature, that is to be refuted (*LRCM:* 579-580). Ethical commitments to compassionately engage with the lives of other beings break down if logic is misapplied so as to seem to refute the very existence of these beings. A precise identification of what analysis refutes will allow the practitioner to find the middle way, a view that slips free from the innate tendency to reify, without swerving into nihilism.

In *LRCM* (580ff.) and other works, Tsong kha pa argues that many of the previously prevailing Tibetan interpretations of Nāgārjuna's Madhyamaka philosophy misidentified the object of negation. In his view, many of these earlier Tibetan versions of Madhyamaka subvert ethical commitments by treating them and all other conventions only as provisional—provisional in the sense that their validity or legitimacy is obviated by the profound truth of emptiness. Tsong kha pa holds that profound emptiness must be understood as complementing and fulfilling, rather than canceling, the principles of moral action (e.g., *LRCM:* 582-584). His writings aim to inspire, and as a matter of historical fact, did inspire, vigorous striving in active virtue, and he insists that rational analysis is an indispensable tool in the spiritual life. In order to make cogent the compatibility of emptiness and ethics, Tsong kha pa had to show that the two truths do not contradict, undermine, or supersede one another. Emptiness of essence is the ultimate truth found under scrupulous analysis of how things exist, but it is fully compatible with valid conventional distinctions.

Ultimate Analysis

In order to further explore this view, let us first consider what Tsong kha pa's *LRCM* says about ultimate analysis. All Mādhyamika philosophers agree that there is nothing that exists ultimately. This means that when one uses reason to analyze exactly how it is that a person, or a potato, exists, just what its final ontological status is, one will not come upon, or find, any definitive basis or ground upon which to establish it. The reality of the potato seems to recede under analytic scrutiny. The mind seeking to know "what the potato REALLY is" does not arrive at the ultimate potato essence. If it did, then we would say that a potato can withstand ultimate analysis and that a potato ultimately exists. Instead, the mind analyzing the potato arrives at last at the emptiness of the potato, that is, the potato's lack of any essential nature. All Mādhyamika philosophers agree that there is nothing that can withstand ultimate analysis, by which they mean that there is nothing anywhere that ultimately exists, including of course the Buddha and the teachings of Buddhism. Even emptiness is itself empty; that is, when one searches for the ultimate essence of emptiness, it is unfindable, and one finds instead the emptiness of emptiness.

Following Candrakīrti's interpretations of Nāgārjuna, Tsong kha pa (*LRCM:* 606-607) argues that if things had any sort of essence or intrinsic nature of their own, this essential nature would have be located under ultimate analysis. Therefore, the fact that things are not found under ultimate analysis means that they lack intrinsic nature. The lack of intrinsic nature is logically equivalent and universally conterminous with the lack of ultimate existence. For Candrakīrti and Tsong kha pa, not existing under ultimate analysis, not existing ultimately, and not existing intrinsically or essentially are three ways of saying the same thing.

Mādhayamika treatises include many different arguments refuting any realistic thesis regarding the nature of phenomena. Tsong kha pa was well aware of these, and comments on them in other contexts, but in the *LRCM* he describes the process of meditative analysis mainly in terms of one particular argument known as *gcig du bral*, the lack of sameness and difference. Tsong kha pa's version of the argument begins by describing what has been known in the West as the Law of the Excluded Middle. Since it has sometimes been held that this principle is lacking in non-Western logics, let us read through one of Tsong kha pa's statements of it in the *LRCM* (730-731):[2]

> In the general case, we see in the world that when a phenomenon is mentally classified as accompanied, it is precluded from being unaccompanied, and when it is classified as unaccompanied, it is precluded from being accompanied. In general, therefore, same and different, as well as singular and plural, preclude any further alternative because the unaccompanied and the accompanied are [respectively] singular and plural.

Accompanied and unaccompanied are A and not-A. Since what is unaccompanied is singular and self-same, or non-diverse, and what is accompanied is plural and diverse, the basic principle that anything that exists must be either A or not-A is extended to imply that anything that exists must be either single or plural, must be either self-identical or diverse. Tsong kha pa (*LRCM*: 731) then applies this general principle to the realm of hypothetical intrinsic selves.

> When you determine in the general case [that an existent must be either] one or not one, then you will also determine that for the particular case [of something that exists essentially, it must be either] essentially one or essentially different.

So if a chariot, for example, had an essential or intrinsic nature, such would have to be demonstrated by rigorous analysis of whether it intrinsically exists as one with its parts or different from its parts (*LRCM*: 720-730). Is the chariot the same as its parts? No, for if it were, then just as the parts of a chariot are several and diverse, so too would be the chariot; or else, just as there is a single chariot, there would only be one part. If the chariot were identical to its parts, then, since we say that a chariot has parts, the possessing agent would be identical to the possessed object. If agent and object can be identical, then fire and fuel can be identical. Just putting a log in a cold fireplace should warm up the room. On the other hand, a chariot is not essentially separate from its parts, because if it were we would see cases of chariots appearing without any chariot parts, just as horses and cows can appear separately insofar as they are separate. Since a chariot cannot be found either among its parts nor essentially separate from them, it must lack an essential nature. This is because an essentially existent chariot would have to be findable under this sort of analysis.

Tsong kha pa (*LRCM*: 730-733) uses an analogous and somewhat more elaborate form of the same argument to demonstrate that the self, or person, does not essentially exist because it is neither essentially one with nor essentially different from the psychophysical aggregates.[3]

The knowledge that things lack essential reality is a liberating insight into emptiness, the absence of intrinsic existence. The unfindability of a chariot among its parts is not emptiness itself, but it is a sign from which emptiness can be deduced. Other signs which are indicative of emptiness, the lack of intrinsic or essential reality, are the instant-by-instant transience of all concrete things, and the interdependent nature of all existing things.

Another important point to note is that for Tsong kha pa the final basis for any proof or critique, including this refutation of essential reality, is information provided by ordinary conventional consciousness. We see that a log is different from a flame, that a horse is different from a cow, that being accompanied is different from being unaccompanied; and from this ordinary factual knowledge, we can develop arguments against essential nature. Our ordinary conventional consciousnesses are mistaken in that a log appears to them as though it were essentially real, but at the same time these conventional consciousnesses provide accurate and practical information. Not only can we use this information to light a fire—or select a potato for planting—but we need this information in order to form the argument against essential nature. As Tsong kha pa (*LRCM*: 739) says, "Even when you analyze reality, the final basis for any critique derives from unimpaired conventional consciousnesses."

Conventional Phenomena Are Not Destroyed by Ultimate Analysis

If potatoes and chariots and persons cannot withstand rational analysis, if their reality somehow recedes upon analysis, does this mean that reason refutes them? How can anyone talk about things having any kind of meaningful existence at all once they have been refuted by reasoning?

Tsong kha pa has an interlocutor pose this very question in *LRCM* (606). In response (*LRCM*: 606-610), he argues that this question comes about through conflating (1) the inability to withstand rational analysis with (2) invalidation or refutation by reason. It is reckless, he says, to claim that things are refuted by reason and yet exist nonetheless. But things may and do exist very well while being unable to withstand rational analysis.

In the foregoing analysis of a chariot, for example, the unfindability of the chariot under analysis is not taken as a sign of chariot's nonexistence. Rather, it is a sign of chariot's *not existing in such a manner as to make it findable under just this sort of analysis*. That is, it is a sign of the nonexistence of an essentially real chariot.

To ask whether something can withstand rational analysis is to ask whether it is "found" or demonstrated by a line of reasoning that analyzes what is finally real. This kind of analysis is intent upon seeking out the essential nature that is the core reality behind an appearance. When such a line of reasoning analyzes a potato, it does not find any such essential reality—and this is what it means to say that a potato is "unable to withstand rational analysis."

However, that this line of reasoning does not find a potato does not entail that it refutes the potato. Rather, it refutes an essentially existent potato, the kind of potato that it would have found had such been there to find. Potatoes, chariots, and persons exist, but this existence is established by ordinary conventional consciousnesses which give us practical and accurate information about the world around us. We should not expect them to be found under ultimate analysis, and we should not suppose that this undermines their mere existence in any way. Tsong kha pa (*LRCM*: 607) gives an example: We do not see sounds no matter how carefully we look, but this does not refute them. Likewise, when we are not satisfied with potato as we know it now, or as farmers and botanists explain it, but press on to search out its ultimate ontological basis, the unfindability of such an ultimate essence has no bearing on the ordinary sense of the question, "Is this a good potato?" Potatoes exist, and grow well, without any essence, without any findable ultimate potato reality.

Thus, ultimate analysis does not find the potato, but it also definitely does not find or indicate the potato to be nonexistent. If it did, the potato would have to *be* nonexistent. Ultimate analysis simply does not find the ultimate potato-reality it is looking for. This is an important distinction, and making this distinction clearly is one of Tsong kha pa's major contributions to the history of Tibetan philosophy. Conventional realities are not obviated by their profound emptiness of essence; instead, they have their own kind of validity.

Some interpreters of the Mādhyamika philosophers in Tibet suggest that speaking of the existence of potatoes and persons is, in effect, a concession to the moral situation and limited understanding of non-philosophers. On this reading, the Mādhyamika acceptance of conventional existence amounts to no more than an admission that *other* people, such as shepherds and farmers, talk about sheep and potatoes as if they actually existed; we the philosophers are beyond such conventions and for our own part know perfectly well that rational analysis refutes the existence of such things.

Tsong kha pa sharply rejects this interpretation of conventional existence. He stresses that ordinary conventional consciousnesses that provide accurate information about practical distinctions can be found among philosophers as well as farmers, and it is such consciousnesses that establish the standard of conventional validity. As it happens, most philosophers do not know which potato to plant, but some gardening philosophers might know, and the rest are equipped to learn about this if they choose. Philosophers know that the distinction between the one to plant and the one to eat cannot withstand ultimate analysis, but they can learn to make the distinction anyway.

Likewise, even the process of refuting essence, the process of pursuing ultimate analysis, is not something that can withstand ultimate analysis. Like everything else, ultimate analysis itself exists only in conventional terms, and must be carried out in reliance upon conventional terms. In this case, it is the philosopher rather than the farmer who is the specialist about a particular set of practical conventions.

In *LRCM*, ultimate analysis is spiritually liberating. On the other hand, complete spiritual fulfillment also requires the ability to act compassionately, and that involves making practical distinctions. Tsong kha pa believes in the clarifying power of analysis that is not ultimate, analysis that operates within the constraints and boundaries of conventional fact and language in order to clarify what does and what does not exist. He does not believe that all useful analysis need immediately reduce everything to emptiness. In other words, we can learn valuable practical things by analyzing which potato is good to plant, which action is good to do, which log good to burn, without at each step interrogating the final ontological status of the potato, action or log. On this point, Tsong kha pa (*LRCM*: 612-613) quotes a famous passage from Candrakīrti's *Prasannapadā* (54):

> Unskilled in ultimate and conventional truths, you sometimes apply analytical standards inappropriately and destroy the conventional. Because we are skilled in positing conventional truths, we stay with the world's position, and we use its standards to overturn the standards that you set so as to eliminate the category of conventionalities. Like the elders of the world, we drive out only you who deviate from the traditional standards of the world; we do not drive out conventionalities.

For example, some Buddhists claim that only groups of parts exist, and that since nothing apart from such grouping is evident, wholes and composites do not exist (*LRCM*: 722). Also, some Buddhists (and some others as well) speak as though only "verbs" (actions and processes) really exist, while "nouns" (objects, agents and persons) do not. Mādhyamika philosophers such as Tsong kha pa argue that these positions are wrong any way the problem is analyzed. In terms of the conventions of the world, there are no parts without wholes to which they belong and there are no actions without agents. Ultimately, just as wholes and agents do not exist, neither do parts and processes; conventionally, just as parts and processes exist, so too do wholes and agents.

Conventional Existence

Is it not the case, however, that worldly convention also enshrines, over against the Buddhist philosopher, some things that are completely wrong? What about the notion of a personal Creator God who oversees the affairs of the world and the dispensation of justice? In refuting such claims, Buddhist philosophers use rational analyses and arguments. From this, according to Tsong kha pa (*LRCM*: 627-631), some Tibetan writers concluded that potatoes and persons have the same status as the Creator God because both are refuted by analysis and yet sustained in the conventional beliefs of many ordinary people. Such Tibetan philosophers cannot accept even the conventional existence of a person or potato, for to do so would also entail accepting all the other conventions known in the world, including the convention of a Creator God. They believe that to deny the conventional existence of constructs such as a divine creator commits them also to denying the conventional existence of chariots, potatoes, and persons. As a result, they have no way to make any conventional distinctions on their own behalf; they hold that all distinctions are made by ignorance and are sometimes compassionately tolerated by the philosopher as a concession to the ignorant. For their own part, they claim neither to identify nor to assert any phenomenon. In the context of such an understanding, meditating on emptiness means to stabilize the mind without apprehending anything at all.

Tsong kha pa sharply and repeatedly disagrees with this sort of approach, which he regards as a grievous and nihilistic deviation from the Buddhist philosophical middle way. He argues that Māhdyamika philosophers have to be able to make conventional distinctions, and accurately explain how the world works at the conventional level, while using reason to refute even the conventional existence of constructs such as a Creator God.

A famous passage in Tsong kha pa's *LRCM* (627) lays out three criteria for saying that something exists conventionally:

(1) a conventional consciousness knows about it;

(2) no other conventional valid cognition contradicts its being as it is thus known; and

(3) reason that accurately analyzes its final reality—that is, analyzes whether something intrinsically exists—does not contradict it.

Since nothing exists ultimately, whatever fails to meet these criteria for existing conventionally does not exist at all.

The first criterion of conventional existence is that a conventional consciousness know about it. Tsong kha pa tells us that, in a sense, all conventional consciousnesses operate in a non-inquisitive manner; to some degree they function within the context of how something appears to them, without asking, "Is this how the object REALLY exists, or does it just appear this way to the mind?" At the same time, and vitally, he points out that conventional consciousnesses need not be utterly non-inquisitive. They operate within the context of how things appear, but within that context they can do analysis. In other words, they can analyze questions like, Is this potato a good one to plant? Is this action a good one to do?—as long as they do not analyze how it is that these things actually exist in the final analysis.

Everyone, philosopher or not, has this kind of ordinary conventional consciousness. Philosophers will ask questions like, "Is conventional knowledge REALLY accurate?" or, "Does this object exist this way in reality?" Nevertheless, they cannot think this way all the time. They have to make mundane distinctions about the time of day, what is and is not edible, the weather, and so forth. They also have to make other analytical distinctions which are highly specialized to their profession just as farmers make distinctions specialized to theirs. So, Tsong kha pa (*LRCM*: 630) reminds us that conventional knowledge is not only what is accepted by the non-philosophical village elders. Conventional knowledge is something we all have, on every side of every philosophical argument; it is the perceptual or experiential basis for the construction of conventional language; it shows up in the examples we use to prove our points.

However, as Tsong kha pa's latter two criteria for conventional existence make clear, some things that conventional consciousness seems to know about are in fact nonexistent. That is, careful analysis and accurate perception even at the conventional level can show that what some persons or consciousnesses take for fact is actually completely wrong. For example, an ordinary conventional consciousness might mistake a rope for a snake or a mirage for water. One does not have to analyze emptiness in order to refute these mistaken conceptions and perceptions. Tsong kha pa sees the belief in a Creator God as falling into a category like this. Belief in a flat earth, and other hypotheses refuted by science, all fall into this same category.

There are other things that seem to be a matter of ordinary, conventional experience, and which accurate conventional knowledge does *not* contradict, but which are nonetheless wrong. As Tsong kha pa (*LRCM*: 630) puts it, "There are things that have been apparently "known to the world" from beginningless time, and yet do not exist even conventionally inasmuch as reason contradicts them." As examples, one can cite the misconception (and misperception) that things have essential nature, or the conception that yesterday's mountain is today's mountain. Only ultimate analysis of how things really exist allows these ideas to be refuted. Yet they are refuted, and thus they do not exist even conventionally. Thus, it is not the case that Mādhyamikas accept *everything* that ordinarily seems to be common knowledge in the world.

On the other hand, Tsong kha pa accepts the conventional validity of things like potatoes and logs that appear as objects of consciousnesses that have not been fooled or distorted by factors such as disease or optical illusion. He further argues, as we have seen, that reasoned analysis can and must proceed from this basic set of accurate and reliable data. Even though the senses mistakenly present images of potatoes and logs that appear as though they were objectively, independently, and essentially real, they do allow us to accurately distinguish between a potato and a log. With further analysis at the conventional level, we can even learn which log will be good to burn and which potato good to plant.

Final Comment

When I first heard Lobsang Gyatso say that one should ask a farmer, rather than a philosopher, about which potato to plant, I found it more confusing than illuminating. It seems to propose a dichotomy between *two types of people*, one analytically trained and the other using non-analytical common sense. This kind of language, distinguishing between the perspectives of cowherds and philosophers, often does appear in Buddhist texts. In this context, though, it raised questions: Can't a scientist tell which potato will be more be more likely to grow? Doesn't a potato scientist have a rather analytical perspective that still enables, rather than inhibits, practical distinctions?

But now it is clear that Lobsang Gyatso's comment about the farmer and the philosopher cannot refer to two types of people; nor can it imply a simple dichotomy between analytical and non-analytical perspectives. The farmer, who could just as well be an agronomist, does not represent a non-analytical person but rather a certain type of *analytical* perspective which we *all* have, an accurate but conventional perspective which works with the given to make practical distinctions. The philosopher in the example is likewise not really a person, but represents a different sort of analytical perspective, the perspective of a mind pursuing ultimate analysis, the interrogation of final ontological status. The down-to-earth quality of Lobsang Gyatso's example is in fact its most subtle nuance; it shows how this particular set of philosophical distinctions is grounded in common experience, and arises as a natural derivative or explication of everyday practice.

For Tsong kha pa, the point is these two types of analytical perspective are both legitimate and necessary dimensions of the path to liberation; neither subverts or contradicts the other. Each shows us something valuable, something we need in order to find happiness, which the other alone cannot bestow. The final mind of buddhahood is culmination of mastery in both of these realms, the farmer philosopher who sees all potatoes just as they are, equally devoid of essence, and yet always knows which one to eat and which one to plant.

Notes

1. An earlier version of this work was presented at the World Congress of Philosophy in August of 1999 (Boston) and appears in the selected proceedings of that conference. The "seed" for this paper was my memory of a very brief conversation with Jeffrey Hopkins, about Gen Lobsang Gyatso, which took place in the late 1980s over the Cocke Hall photocopier at the University of Virginia.

2. Another interesting example, in which Tsong kha pa cites Nāgārjuna as his source, is found at *LRCM:* 599: "Limiting things to two possibilities—either they intrinsically exist or they do not—derives from the universal limitation that anything imaginable either exists or does not exist. Similarly, the limitation that what truly exists must either truly exist as single or truly exist as plural is based on the universal limitation that anything must be either single or plural. When there is such a limitation, any further alternative is necessarily precluded; hence, it is utter nonsense to assert a phenomenon that is neither of those two. As Nāgārjuna's *Vigrahavyāvartanī* [26cd in Lindtner: 79] says:

> If the absence of intrinsic existence were overturned,
> Intrinsic existence would be established."

3. Following Buddhapālita's reading of Nāgārjuna, Tsong kha pa (*LRCM:* 731-733) deploys various arguments against the position of sameness:

> (1) If the self and psychophysical aggregates were the same, it would be pointless and redundant to speak of a self because the self would be identical to the aggregates.
>
> (2) Since the components of a chariot are plural and diverse, then the chariot would also have to be plural and diverse. Likewise, just as one person has many aggregates, one person would also have many selves. Or, if there is no more than one self, there would, absurdly, also be just one aggregate.
>
> (3) The self that is identical to the aggregates would have to arise and disintegrate, changing as the mind and body change. In fact, Tsong kha pa accepts this kind of impermanent self, but he argues, following Nāgārjuna, that impermanence is impossible in a self that exists by way of an unchanging essence.
>
> (4) If the self were identical to the mind and body, then, since we say that a person has a body and has a mind, the possessing agent would be identical to the possessed object. If an agent and object could be identical in this way, then fire and fuel could be identical. Just putting a log in a cold fireplace should warm up the room.

On the other hand, if a person had an essential character which was *different* from the essential character of the aggregates, then selves should be in evidence apart from psychophysical aggregates—just as horses and cows are seen separately. Yet they are not. Thus, since it is impossible for the self to have an essence which is either one with or different from the aggregates, it is impossible for the self to have any essence. The self or person exists only nominally and conventionally, and yet is nonetheless able to function as an agent.

References

Candrakīrti

MVPP *Mūla-madhyamaka-vṛtti-prasanna-padā*. Tibetan translation: P5260, vol. 98 in *The Tibetan Tripiṭaka* (see Suzuki). Also, the edition cited here, Dharamsala: Tibetan Publishing House, 1968. The Sanskrit of the cited passage appears in *Mūlamadhyamakakārikās de Nāgārjuna avec la Prasannapadā Commentaire de Candrakīrti*, edited by Louis de la Vallée Poussin (Osnabrück: Biblio Verlag, 1970), p. 69.

Lindtner, Chr[istian]

1982 *Nagarjuniana*. Copenhagen: Akademisk Forlag.

Lobsang Gyatso

1998 *Memoirs of a Tibetan Lama*. Translated and edited by Gareth Sparham. Ithaca, NY: Snow Lion Publications.

Suzuki, D.T., ed.

1955-61 *The Tibetan Tripiṭaka, Peking Edition*. 168 vols. Tokyo and Kyoto: Reprinted under the supervision of the Otani University, Kyoto.

Tsong kha pa Blo bzang grags pa

LRCM *Lam rim chen mo/ sKyes bu gsum gyi rnyams su blang ba'i rim pa thams cad tshang bar ston pa'i byang chub lam gyi rim pa*. P6001, vol. 152 in *The Tibetan Tripiṭaka* (see Suzuki). Edition used for citations: mTsho sngon mi rigs dpe skrun khang, n.p., n.d.

Chapter 3

Painting the Target

On the Identification of the Object of Negation (dgag bya)

Donald S. Lopez, Jr.

Since the time of his 1973 doctoral dissertation, Jeffrey Hopkins has gone to great lengths to demonstrate that even for the "scholastic" dGe lugs sect of Tibetan Buddhism, emptiness is not only a topic for philosophical exegesis, but is also the object of sustained and systematic meditation. Both in *Meditation on Emptiness* (1983) and *Practice and Theory of Tibetan Buddhism* (coauthored with Geshe Lhundup Sopa in 1976, republished in a revised version as *Cutting Through Appearances* in 1989), Hopkins delineated a standard procedure for coming to a meditative understanding of emptiness, a procedure known as the "four essentials" (*gnad bzhi*). They are (1) identification of the object of negation (*dgag bya ngos 'dzin pa*), (2) ascertaining pervasion (*khyab pa nges pa*), (3) establishing the property of the position (*phyogs chos sgrub pa*), and (4) ascertaining the probandum (*bsgrub bya nges pa*).[1]

The procedure derives from the classic Buddhist doctrine that all suffering is ultimately the result of ignorance, the belief in self. According to the Madhyamaka school as interpreted by Tsong kha pa, the belief in self can only be destroyed through recourse to reasoning: the belief in self is an innate conception that besets all sentient beings, but it is incapable of withstanding reasoned analysis. Numerous reasonings, such as the lack of being one or many, are therefore set forth in Madhyamaka texts, each designed to prove that the self does not exist. Precisely what is meant by "self" is consequently of great importance. For Tsong kha pa, self refers to an intrinsic existence that is falsely ascribed to persons and to other phenomena. He is fond of citing Candrakīrti's gloss of "self" in his *Bodhisattvayogacaryācatuḥśatakaṭīkā* as "that which does not rely on another" (*gzhan la rag ma las pa*) (Candrakīrti: 103.4).

Both the self of persons and the self of phenomena must be negated, but the self of persons is usually attacked first because it is more intimate. The first step in the fourfold procedure is therefore the identification of this self, called "the object of negation." dGe lugs authors often quote Śāntideva (at *Bodhicaryāvatāra* IX.140ab) on this point, "Without contacting the imagined object, its nonexistence cannot be apprehended." The first step thus involves a watchful awareness of precisely what the self is like.

The next three steps involve making this self the subject of a logical statement. A Buddhist syllogism has three parts: a subject, a predicate, and a reason. In order for the syllogism to be valid, certain relations must obtain among these three parts. First, there must be pervasion (*khyab pa*), which means that whatever falls under the category of the reason must necessarily fall under the category of the predicate. Second, the reason must be a property of the subject. If both of these relations pertain, then the predicate is a property of the subject and the syllogism is correct. For example, the first correct syllogism learned by dGe lugs monks is, "The subject, the color of a white conch, is a color, because of being white." Here, the subject is the color of a white conch, the predicate is being a color, and reason is being white. In order for this statement to be correct, it is necessary first for it to be true that there be pervasion, that is, that whatever is white is necessarily a color. Second, the reason must be a property of the subject, that is, the color of a white conch must be white. Because both of these relations obtain, the predicate is a property of the subject (the color of a white conch is a color), the syllogism is correct, and the thesis (the subject plus the predicate) is proven.

In meditation on emptiness, the self is made the subject of a syllogism. Any number of reasons may used to prove that the self does not exist, such as the diamond slivers, the reasoning of the four extremes, the reasoning of the four alternatives, the reasoning of dependent arising, the sevenfold reasoning, or the reasoning of the lack of being one or many (Hopkins: 125-196). For example, the syllogism could be, "The subject, the self of persons, does not intrinsically exist, because of not being either intrinsically the same as or different from the aggregates." Here, the aggregates refer to the classic Buddhist division of the constituents of the person into five groups: form, feeling, discrimination, conditioning factors, and consciousnesses. Since everything in the universe is either the same as or different from one of these constituents, anything that is not does not exist. That is, there is pervasion between the reason and the predicate. The second step in the proof of the syllogism would be to establish that the reason is a property of the subject, in this case, that the self is not the same as or different from the five aggregates. Establishing that this is indeed the case requires a long and detailed investigation, examining each of the aggregates (and their subcategories) in turn in an effort to determine whether any of them is the self. Assuming that such effort fails to result in the identification of the self with one of the aggregates, the next step would be to determine whether the self is somehow different from the aggregates. For this to be the case, the self would have to exist entirely apart from the mind and the body. This is a claim that is rejected in Madhyamaka. With it now established that the reason is a property of the subject, one moves automatically to the conclusion that the predicate is a property of the subject, that the self does not exist.

Applying this to the four essentials, the first essential is to identify the object of negation, in this case the self. The second essential is, having made the object of negation the subject of a syllogism, establishing the presence of pervasion in that syllogism. The third essential is to establish that the reason is a property of the subject. The fourth essential should follow spontaneously, the conclusion that the predicate is a property of the subject. This is the goal, to understand that the self does not exist.

The locus classicus for this procedure in dGe lugs literature seems to be the "instructions on the view" (*lta khrid*), a genre that originates with Tsong kha pa himself. Three such works are to be found in his collected writings, and one of these, *dBu ma'i thal 'gyur ba'i zab lam dbu ma'i lta khrid*, contains the procedure that would be repeated in scores of similar works in subsequent centuries, such as *gSung rab kun gyi snying po lam gyi gtso bo rnam gsum gyi khrid yig gzhan phan snying po*, translated by Sopa and Hopkins in *Practice and Theory of Tibetan Buddhism*. The colophon of Tsong kha pa's text indicates that the work was actually composed by mKhas grub rje (identified as dGe legs dpal bzang po), based on instructions from the master himself. After a brief introduction, the text turns to an explanation of how to identify the object of negation.

> Second, regarding the actual practice, the divisions of selflessness are enumerated as two: persons and phenomena. Regarding the order of understanding, the self of persons is the object of negation on the basis of negation, the person. The complete elimination of that is the selflessness of persons. The self of phenomena is the object of negation on the basis of negation, the aggregates. The complete elimination of that is the selflessness of phenomena. It is not asserted that there is a difference of coarseness and subtlety between the two, but because of a difference in difficulty and ease of ascertainment, the order of understanding is determined [such that] you initially meditate on the selflessness of the person and then meditate on the selflessness of phenomena.
>
> Thus, the method of meditating on selflessness has two parts, meditation on the selflessness of persons and meditation on the selflessness of phenomena. The first has two parts, meditating on the lack of intrinsic nature of the I and meditating on the lack of intrinsic nature of the mine. The first has two parts, the yoga of space-like meditative equipoise and the yoga of illusion-like subsequent attainment. The first has four parts: [1] perceiving clearly the I that is the substratum for the innate awareness that thinks "I am," and understanding the essential point of making the I appear; [2] when the extent of the mode of appearance of the I has been established, ascertaining the pervasion, which is the determination that because there is no third possibility other than identity or difference, the I and the aggregates are either intrinsically identical to each other or they are intrinsically different from each other; [3] ascertaining the property of the position through ascertaining that the two, I and my aggregates, are neither intrinsically the same nor different; and [4] the sign of the lack of being one or many that ascertains the probandum of the sign: the elimination of the object of negation in the basis of negation.[2]
>
> First, it is said that the mere I that lacks attributes and is simultaneous with the innate awareness thinking "I am" is not just a sound-generality but is like something established

objectively, it appears to the awareness perceiving it to be intrinsically established, it appears to be established by its own entity, it appears to be established by its own defining characteristic, it appears to be truly established. If it were established in the way that it appears, it would be a self of persons, truly established, and so forth, and the awareness that conceives it to be established in the way that it appears would be the innate conception of self.

When a child perceives the reflection of a face in a mirror, everything about it looks like a face; there is no differentiation of those factors of the reflection that look like a face and those that do not. In the same way, everything [about the I] appears to be established objectively, without there being some factors of the I that appear to be established objectively and some factors that are not established objectively. For someone not trained in the terminology of "reflection" and "face," they appear to be mixed as one. Therefore, the awareness conceives of the reflection as a face. For the awareness thinking "I am," the appearance of being established objectively and the appearance of not being established objectively are mixed into one [such that] one conceives of its appearance as established objectively. When you analyze how [the I] appears to the awareness thinking I, if the way that the I appears to the awareness that is the innate conception of I is shaky, do not analyze it. When the awareness thinking "I am" emerges and is produced, you should ascertain how it appears at that very time. If you analyze how it appears later, it will have become mixed with other things and you will not ascertain it.

Therefore, the way to ascertain it is to arrange your body properly, straighten your spine, and make your mind alert and steady. First, post the sentry of introspection that thinks that it must ascertain what the mode of appearance is like for the awareness that is the innate conception of I when the thought "I am" is produced. Then, even if the production of the awareness thinking "I am" does not occur, fabricate it and concoct the awareness thinking "I am." Analyze its mode of appearance as soon as it emerges and is produced. You will thereby understand what its mode of appearance is like without it being mixed with other objects. Also, the awareness analyzing the mode of appearance is simultaneous with it [i.e., the mind thinking "I am"]; the awareness that ascertains the mode of appearance comes in its second moment.

In general, the aggregates do not appear to the awareness that is the innate conception of the I and, specifically, they do

> not appear at the same time as the awareness thinking "I am." If one wonders whether something like the aggregates appears to it, the appearance arises prior to it [i.e., the awareness thinking "I am"], the aggregates do not appear to it. If you watch gently from a corner without losing the awareness that thinks in that way, there is something like a separate mode of appearance that is none of the aggregates which appears to the awareness thinking I; that I does not appear as a mere name to the awareness thinking I, but like something that is capable of setting itself up. Through holding that the I is established in the way that it appears, one is bound in saṃsāra. Therefore, when you have analyzed well what the mode of appearance is like for innate awareness thinking "I am," you have ascertained the object of negation. (2a-3b [821-824])[3]

Here, Tsong kha pa begins by noting the division of selflessness into two exhaustive categories, the selflessness of persons and the selflessness of all phenomena other than persons. He defines each in technical terms, describing the selflessness of persons as the absence of the object of negation on the basis of negation. The object of negation is the self of persons, and it does not exist. The basis of negation is the locus for the discovery of the absence of the self; it is the person, and it does exist. In the case of the selflessness of phenomena, the object of negation is the self, or quality of independence, of the aggregates, and it does not exist. The basis of designation is the aggregates, which do exist. For the Prāsaṅgika, there is no difference in coarseness and subtlety between the two selflessnesses (according to Svātantrika and Cittamātra, the selflessness of phenomena is more subtle than that of persons). However, because the sense of the personal self is more familiar and intimate than that of phenomena, the self of persons is made the first target of meditation.

Tsong kha pa will consider meditation on the selflessness of the person under two categories, the emptiness of the I and the emptiness of the mine, the latter referring to any object, but particularly parts of the body, that are conceived to be intrinsically under the control of the person. He further divides meditation on the selflessness of the person into two parts, the yoga of space-like meditative equipoise and the yoga of illusion-like subsequent attainment. The first refers to the state of deep meditation in which only the vacuity that is emptiness appears to the mind. The latter refers to the post-meditation state in which ordinary objects again appear to the mind, but should be regarded as if they were illusions, knowing that although they appear to be real, in fact they are not.

Tsong kha pa turns next to an enumeration of the four essentials. He calls the first, the identification of the object of negation, "perceiving clearly the aspect of the I, the substratum for the innate awareness that thinks, 'I am,' and understanding the essential point of making the I appear." What he means by this phrase is that there is, or, more accurately, there appears to be, an I that is the referent of the mind that thinks, "I am." It is this I that must be identified at this point in the meditation. But this I is elusive, and special techniques must be employed to cause it to show itself. Once the object of negation has been identified, it must be subjected to logical analysis. From the many reasonings available to the Madhyamaka, Tsong kha pa here chooses the absence of identity and difference. The resulting syllogism would be, "The subject, the I, does not intrinsically exist, because of not being intrinsically identical to or different from the aggregates." The second essential is therefore the establishment of the pervasion, whatever intrinsically exists, including the I, must be either intrinsically the same as or different from the aggregates. The third essential is to show that the I is, in fact, neither intrinsically the same as nor different from the aggregates. This leads immediately to the fourth essential, the ascertainment of "the probandum of the sign, the elimination of the object of negation in the basis of negation." This is a technical way of saying that the thesis of the syllogism, that the I does not intrinsically exist, has been proven to the meditator, who now understands that the person has no self.

The remainder of the translated excerpt is devoted to the identification of the object of negation. Tsong kha pa begins by stating that the naked I, the referent of the thought "I am," is not simply a meaningless word, a sound generality (*sgra spyi*), but seems to have an independent existence; indeed, if it did in fact exist as it appears to, it would be the self. He describes this I as "the mere I that lacks attributes." Here he is referring not to the mere I (*nga tsam*) that exists conventionally, but to the I that is not qualified by being either correctly imputed to be nominally existent or falsely imputed to be intrinsically existent. Like all phenomena, this I appears to intrinsically exist, but sentient beings do not actively assent to that appearance in all cases. When they do, this I serves as the object of the innate conception of self, the fundamental ignorance present in all sentient beings. He also describes it as "without attributes" to differentiate it from the I that is the object of the artificial conception of self, acquired through exposure to erroneous philosophical schools, such as Sāṃkhya, where a variety of attributes of the self, such as permanence, are claimed.

It is Tsong kha pa's position, then, that the I is not utterly nonexistent; it is possible to use the term simply as a name for the mind and body, without indulging in the conceit that the I has some independent existence, that the I is the self. There are, in fact, two ways in which the I appears, one correct and one erroneous. The first is the appearance of the I to the mind that understands emptiness and thus knows that the I is a mere designation. The second is the appearance of the I to the innate conception of intrinsic existence. It is this latter appearance that Tsong kha pa is concerned with here. This is why he continually uses phrases like, "what the mode of appearance is like for the awareness that is the innate conception of I when the thought of 'I am' is produced."

However, it is difficult to make the subtle distinction between the I that does not exist and the I that does. For ignorant sentient beings, it is impossible to do so; any thought of an I that does exist is invariably and inseparably tied up with thoughts of an I that does not exist. Tsong kha pa compares their situation to that of a child who looks at the reflection of a face in a mirror and mistakes the reflection for the face. Tsong kha pa seems to suggest that, unlike the classic example of the rope and the snake, there is a veridical relation between the reflection and the face, that, perhaps, the color of the hair and eyes of the face are accurately reflected in the mirror. Yet the reflection is not the face, since it cannot perform the functions of the face, such as speaking or eating. The problem is that the child, who does not know what a reflection is, is incapable of differentiating those elements of the reflection that are true and those elements that are false and believes that the reflection is the face.

Tsong kha pa is describing, by analogy and in highly analytical language, the unanalyzed experience of the ignorant in a meditation manual in which that experience is to be analyzed. However, in order for that analysis to take place, the unanalyzed experience, the ordinary sense of the I, must first be identified. That is, in order eventually to differentiate the I that exists from the I that does not, they first must be undifferentiably mixed. To further complicate matters, he counsels, "When the awareness thinking 'I am' emerges and is produced, you should ascertain how it appears at that very time. If you analyze how it appears later, it will have become mixed with other things and you will not ascertain it." That is, the sense of self in which the I that exists is mixed with the I that does not exist must be identified precisely at the moment of its emergence into awareness; if one waits and it becomes "mixed with other things," it will be impossible to discern.

Tsong kha pa next instructs the meditator to assume the posture of meditation and lie in wait, poised for the thought "I am" to emerge, at which point it will be possible to study it and determine what it is like, that it does, indeed, seem to be independent. The innate conception of I is always present, but it only becomes manifest in explicit thoughts, such as "I am." It is therefore necessary to wait for such thoughts to occur before the way that the I appears to exist can be scrutinized. This is undoubtedly a difficult process, using one part of the mind to analyze another. It would seem rare that the thought "I am" would naturally occur under circumstances in which the mind is poised to examine it. Hence, it is perhaps not surprising that Tsong kha pa instructs the meditator to fabricate the thought, "I am." If this can be done successfully, the thought will be present at the same moment as the introspection assigned to analyze it, such that the way that the I appears can be immediately determined in the next moment.

There are many cases in Buddhist meditation in which the meditator imagines the presence of something that is not there. In *śamatha* practice, the meditator visualizes a golden buddha floating in space; in tantric practice, the meditator visualizes his or her body as the body of a buddha, adorned with the major and minor marks of a superman. But in such cases, what is being imagined is something salubrious: contemplating the body of a buddha is a form of *buddhānusmṛti* and a source of great merit; visualizing oneself as a buddha now is the special technique for becoming a buddha in the future. But here one is actively cultivating the source of all suffering, the belief in self. And if the sense of self will not emerge, it must be concocted. But what is the relation of this concoction to the innate conception of self?

Tsong kha pa goes on to state that the aggregates—the mind and body—do not appear to the mind when the thought "I am" occurs; the aggregates may appear prior to the emergence of the thought, "I am," but once it emerges, the I appears alone, as something independent of the aggregates and autonomous. When this appearance of something that is none of the aggregates, that exists objectively, has been scrutinized, then the meditator has identified the object of negation.

dGe lugs *lta khrid* and *lam rim* texts composed in subsequent centuries would present similar instructions in less technical language, providing, as Tsong kha pa did not, specific techniques for fabricating the false sense of self. A typical example was translated by Sopa and Hopkins in *Practice and Theory of Tibetan Buddhism*. The passage appears in *gSung rab kun gyi snying po lam gyi gtso bo rnam gsum gyi khrid yig gzhan phan snying po* by the Fourth Paṇ chen Lama (1781-1852/4):

> Even in sleep we hold tightly, tightly in the center of the heart, the thought "I, I." This is a consciousness innately misconceiving [an inherently existent] self. For example, without your having done a bad deed another accuses you, "You did such and such a bad deed," and thinking, "I, I," tightly, tightly in the center of the heart, you reflect, "Without my doing such a bad deed he/she accuses me like this." At that time, the way the I is apprehended by a consciousness innately misconceiving inherent existence is clearly manifest.
>
> Therefore, at that time, how and as what the mind apprehends the self should be analyzed with a subtle part of the mind. If the later analytical attention is too strong, the former consciousness that conceives "I, I" will be abandoned and will not appear at all [and thus cannot be watched]. Hence, allow the general mind to generate firmly and continuously the entity of the consciousness thinking "I," and analyze it with another subtle portion of consciousness.
>
> When you analyze in this way, the first essential is to understand how the I is conceived by a consciousness innately misconceiving an inherently existent self: "This I is not other than my own five aggregates, or body and mind. The I is not any of the five aggregates taken singly nor is it either of the two, body and mind, taken singly. Also, the I is not just conceptually imputed to only the glittering collection of the five aggregates or a collection of the two, body and mind. Hence, there is an I that from the beginning is self-sufficient." This deluded conception of an I that from the start is self-sufficient is the innate apprehension of an inherently existent I. The [inherently existent] I that is its object is what is negated [in the view of selflessness].
>
> This way of identifying what is negated should be realized nakedly in your mental continuum without its being just an

> idea explained by others or a general image evoked by words. This is the first essential, ascertaining the mode of appearance of what is negated.[4] (95-96)

Similar instructions appear in scores of *lta khrid* and *lam rim* texts, always stressing the importance of artificially cultivating the sense of self by imagining situations of false accusation or great pride.

dGe 'dun Chos 'phel's Critique

A number of interesting questions might be raised about the four essentials, focusing especially on the first of the four, the identification of the object of negation. First, there is the logical question of whether it is possible to state a valid syllogism about a subject that does not exist. Tom J. F. Tillemans and I have treated this question elsewhere (Tillemans and Lopez). Second, one might consider the question of taking the conception of self—regarded by the dGe lugs as both innate and primordial, existing in all sentient beings from time immemorial—and making it the subject of a syllogism. It is a hallmark of Tsong kha pa's thought that reason is more powerful than ignorance and that an ignorant consciousness can therefore be displaced by wisdom. Nevertheless, that our most intimate and reflexive sense of personal identity should be susceptible to the syllogism is a fascinating assumption worthy of further reflection. Third, one might consider the psychology of this particular form of meditation. One must assume that anyone familiar enough with Madhyamaka reasoning to employ it in meditation must know quite well, at least intellectually, that the self does not exist. What does it mean then, to sit down and attempt to prove to oneself what one already knows to be the case? What force does the syllogism carry in such a situation? And what does it mean to seek a clear and accurate sense of this self that does not exist, as the first of the four essentials requires? How does one actively cultivate an emotional assent to what one knows intellectually is utterly nonexistent? And finally, precisely how innate and natural can the conception of self be if, in order for it to appear clearly, it must be actively concocted through pretending to be falsely accused of being a thief?

Despite the persistence of the instructions among the dGe lugs, this procedure has not passed uncritically through the centuries; some of the questions raised above have been addressed within the tradition. A recent critique derives, not surprisingly, from the brilliant scholar dGe 'dun chos 'phel (1903-1951). For those unfamiliar with his life and work, dGe 'dun Chos 'phel was born in northeastern Tibet in 1903. During his monastic training, both in A mdo and later at 'Bras spung, he distinguished himself as a debater in the areas of logic and Madhyamaka philosophy. He left the monastery in 1934 to accompany the famed Indian scholar Rahul Sankrityayana, who had come to Tibet in search of Sanskrit manuscripts, returning with him to India, where dGe 'dun Chos 'phel would spend the next twelve years. During this time, he traveled extensively, translated Sanskrit classics into Tibetan, assisted European scholars in their studies, wrote a history of early Tibet, and composed a famous treatise on erotics (translated by Jeffrey Hopkins as *Tibetan Arts of Love*). In 1945 he helped found the Tibetan Progressive Party, which sought to liberate Tibet from its "theocratic" government so that it might become a democratic republic within China. Upon his return to Lhasa in 1946, he was arrested on the fabricated charge of counterfeiting currency and was imprisoned until 1949. He died in 1951.

Shortly before his imprisonment, dGe 'dun Chos 'phel gave teachings on Madhyamaka philosophy to a rNying ma disciple and instructed his student to compile these teachings, which were published under the title *Klu sgrub dgongs rgyan* in 1951. Upon its publication, *Klu sgrub dgongs rgyan* became a controversial work for its critique of dGe lugs scholastic philosophy; it was hailed by the rival sects and condemned by the dGe lugs orthodoxy. Since his death and especially since the fall of the Dalai Lama's government with the subsequent Tibetan diaspora in 1959, dGe 'dun Chos 'phel has emerged as a prescient culture hero for the current generation of Tibetans both in exile and in Tibet, and this, his last work, is recognized as testimony to his stature as the most important Tibetan thinker of the last century.

Klu sgrub dgongs rgyan is both stylistically and topically divided into two distinct parts. The first part of the work concludes with a series of four-line stanzas, many ending with the line, *tha snyad tshad grub 'jog la blo ma bde* ("I am not happy with the proof of conventional valid knowledge.") This section is in effect a self-contained work, composed in dGe 'dun Chos 'phel's distinctive prose style, a style that makes frequent use of colloquialisms. And it deals with one topic, the critique of valid knowledge (*tshad ma*). A close friend of dGe 'dun Chos 'phel, Bla chung A pho (Shes rab rgya mtsho), reports that after his return to Lhasa in 1946, dGe 'dun Chos 'phel presented him with this portion of what would become the *Klu sgrub dgongs rgyan*, written in his own hand on an Elephant Brand pad of Indian paper.

The remainder of the work is more disorganized, with the author returning to a topic that he has dealt with ten pages before, often merely paraphrasing what he has already said. Long discussions of a technical topic are interrupted by an aside of one or two sentences on an unrelated issue, before launching into a new discussion. And while the first part of the text deals consistently with the question of valid knowledge in a way that is accessible to those uninitiated in the fine points of *mtshan nyid*, the remaining two-thirds of the book wanders all over the Madhyamaka map, offering up opinions on a range of topics incomprehensible to those who have not spent time in the dGe lugs curriculum. For example, the author discusses *dbu ma pa la khas len yod dam med* (Does the Madhyamaka have a position?); *chos can mthun snang ba* (the commonly appearing subject); *don dam pa'i khyad par sbyar ba* (the use of the qualifier "ultimately"); *grub mthas blo bsgyur ba* (the mind being influenced by philosophy); *drang nges* (scriptural interpretation); *kun rdzob dpyod pa dang don dam dpyod pa'i skabs* (the contexts for conventional and ultimate analysis); *rigs pas dpyad bzod* (the ability to withstand analysis); *rigs shes pa'i ngor ma snyed pa* (not being discovered by reasoning); *ma snyed pa dang med pa nges pa* (not being discovered vs. being determined not to exist); and *snang rung ma dmigs pa* (the non-observation of the suitable to appear). It is here that the text deals directly with Madhyamaka and where the majority of the criticisms of dGe lugs occur.

But even in the first section, we find dGe 'dun chos 'phel turning his razor-sharp intellect and scathing wit against the dGe lugs geshes of his day, whom he sees as pedants obsessed with sectarian supremacy and doctrinal consistency, losing in the process all appreciation of the poetic power of the sūtras.

> When the scholars of today hear a scripture that refers to neither existence nor nonexistence they first seek out the identity of the speaker of the scripture. If the scripture is a statement of an earlier [i.e., non-dGe lugs] Tibetan scholar, they dismiss it [saying]: "The one who says something like that is a nihilistic fool." If the scripture is identified as a statement of the Buddha, Nāgārjuna, and so on, they patch it with words like "'does not truly exist' is the meaning of the statement that '[something] does not exist'" and "'is not conventionally nonexistent' is the meaning of 'is not nonexistent'" so that it fits with their own

> wishes. In fact, the only difference is that if they direct refutations at the Buddha, they fear being labeled evil persons with evil views, [whereas] if they are able to refute earlier Tibetans they are labeled heroic scholars. Apart from that, there is no difference in the frequency of occurrence of conventions like "does not exist," "does not not exist," "inexpressible," and "free from elaboration" in the sūtras and Nāgārjuna's Collections of Reasoning [on the one hand] and the scriptures of earlier Tibetan scholars [on the other]. Therefore, some refute the statements of the earlier Tibetan scholars that say that the mode of being is inexpressible and inconceivable, saying that they are fools and nihilists, and some show some slight respect, saying that there are not great errors in the thinking of those earlier Tibetan scholars and adepts—it is just that at the time that they spoke, the fine points of someone like the Foremost Lama [Tsong kha pa] had not yet appeared. There are no errors in the thinking of the Bhagavan himself. When the Buddha spoke he simply said such things as "The perfection of wisdom, unutterable, inconceivable, inexpressible" and "When you engage in what is, you engage in signs; when you engage in what is not, you engage in signs." Those beautiful patches of our dGa' ldan Mountain system, such as "When you engage in that which is truly established, you engage in signs" and "When you engage in what does not exist, you engage in signs" simply do not appear [in the sūtras]; the Buddha left them out. If it is true [that the earlier Tibetan scholars were imprecise,] then even the way that the Buddha taught the doctrine is something that lacks precision. (287-288)

Shortly after this passage, dGe 'dun chos 'phel briefly considers the standard dGe lugs procedure for identifying the object of negation. He writes:

> According to their system, this mind that ordinarily thinks "I am" is not the conception of self and therefore is not to be refuted. Therefore, this is how they identify the innate conception of "I": For example, when someone says, "You are a thief," you say, "Why am I a thief?" The appearance of a naked I is the innate conception of "I." That is what they say.
>
> If this ordinary mind that thinks "I" is valid, then the mind thinking "I" that is produced when someone says "You are a thief" would simply be more valid. How could it become the conception of true existence? If it is the conception of true existence, then when someone says [something equally false, such as], "The Buddha is not a refuge," then why is the mind that

> thinks, "How can he not be a refuge?" not the conception of true existence? Similarly, when someone [falsely] says, "This is not a pot," then the mind that decides, "If it is not a pot, what else is it? It is a pot" is also a conception of true existence. How is it valid? Therefore, according to their system, it seems that weak thoughts are valid, and when that very same mind becomes stronger, as if pushed by the wind, it turns into a conception of true existence. How strange!
>
> "In order to understand the view it is very important to identify the object of negation" is as well-known in the mouths of everyone as breath. If this is true, how is it possible to identify separately true establishment before understanding the view? This is because the Foremost Lama himself said: "Until one has understood emptiness, it is impossible ever to distinguish mere existence from true existence and, similarly, one cannot distinguish non-true existence from mere nonexistence" and "This is the final reason why there is no commonly appearing subject for Prāsaṅgika and Svātantrika." Thus, how can one rely on that pretense of [prior] identification of the object of negation? (289-290)

dGe 'dun chos 'phel makes two points here. He first makes note of the dGe lugs assertion that all cases of the thought "I," even among the unenlightened, are not necessarily cases of ignorance, that is, they are not necessarily cases of the innate conception of self, but are instead valid states of consciousness. The standard dGe lugs view is that ordinary sentient beings, including those who subscribe to false philosophical views, have many thoughts of "I" in which the I is not either wrongly conceived to be intrinsically existent or correctly conceived to be nominally existent. dGe 'dun chos 'phel wonders, then, why a stronger form of such a thought should somehow become invalid, should somehow become a case of ignorance, a case of the conception of intrinsic existence or, as he refers to it here, the conception of true existence (*bden 'dzin*). He then alludes to the standard technique of fabricating the false sense of self by imagining in meditation a case of being falsely accused of being a thief. If this is indeed a sense of false accusation, how can the honest and accurate thought (unlike Nixon's) "I am not a crook" be construed as a form of ignorance? If the weak thought "I am" is not a form of ignorance, why should the thought, "I am not a thief" be a form of ignorance? If it is a form of ignorance, shouldn't the dGe lugs pas claim that any veridical statement made in response to an erroneous statement is also a form of error? The difference between thinking "I am" and "I am not a thief" is only one of strength of conviction.

dGe 'dun chos 'phel's own position on the question, as he spells out earlier in the text, is that there are no valid forms of knowledge (*tshad ma*) among the unenlightened. To claim that there are, as the dGe lugs pas do, is to eviscerate Nāgārjuna's critique, to domesticate the rhetoric of enlightenment, until it does nothing more than validate the operations of ignorance. For dGe 'dun chos 'phel, all thoughts prior to the realization of emptiness, all thoughts of "I," regardless of their strength, are cases of ignorance.

His second problem with the standard instructions for identifying the object of negation is that they are offered to those who have not yet understood emptiness; otherwise, why would they need the instructions? Yet Tsong kha pa is renowned for his assertion that until one has understood emptiness, it is impossible to distinguish between mere existence or conventional existence (which is true in the sense that it exists) and intrinsic existence or true existence (which is false in the sense that it is utterly nonexistent). If this is the case, how is it possible for someone who has not understood emptiness to identify the object of negation, to pinpoint the I that does not exist in contradistinction to the I that does exist? Because the Prāsaṅgikas deny true existence and the Svātantrikas uphold true existence conventionally, it is impossible for them to engage in a debate in which the subject of the syllogism is commonly understood by both parties. What hope is there for the person undertaking his or her first meditation on emptiness? How could such a person possibly correctly identify the object of negation?

dGe 'dun chos 'phel would argue, then, that the object of negation as identified by the dGe lugs pas is little more than a scholastic epiphenomenon, a bit of sophistry ultimately designed to validate the operations of ignorance. To identify the object of negation, as defined by the dGe lugs, in the meditation on emptiness, one must have already understood emptiness, in which case the meditation would be obviated. The degree of philosophical sophistication required to identify the object of negation is necessarily absent in those for whom the instructions are apparently intended. The solution, for dGe 'dun chos 'phel, is to identify an object of negation that is more prosaic and quotidian, yet at the same time more fundamental, and hence more profound.

Moreover some say that when a valid form of awareness is produced that thinks, "A pot exists," simultaneously a conception of true existence is produced that thinks, "The pot exists as truly established," but that it is difficult to differentiate them.

Then, the so-called valid knowledge is the primary cause of attaining buddhahood and the so-called conception of true existence is the root of all faults. It is very strange that they are so similar to each other that they cannot be differentiated. If one is certain to be present whenever the other is present, then when they are refuted, they should be refuted equally. How is it possible to distinguish between the two?

The mind that thinks, "It's morning," is valid. The mind that thinks, "I am tying my belt," is valid. In the same way, if all the thoughts that think things like, "I am drinking tea," and, "I am eating tsampa," are each valid, then among all the minds that fill a day, there is not even one thing to refute. Thus, when does this object of negation, the so-called conception of true existence, occur? If the mind that is the conception of true existence, grown accustomed to from time immemorial, does not occur more than a couple of times a day, it is quite amazing. (290-291)

Notes

1. This is the list provided by Tsong kha pa in the text translated below. The Fourth Paṇ chen Lama, in his *gSung rab kun gyi snying po lam gyi gtso bo rnam gsum gyi khrid yig gzhan phan snying po*, translated by Sopa and Hopkins in *Cutting Through Appearances: The Practice and Theory of Tibetan Buddhism*, presents a version in which the last two of the four essentials differ: (3) ascertaining the absence of true sameness (*bden pa'i gcig nges pa*) and (4) ascertaining the absence of true difference (*bden pa'i tha dad nges pa*). See Sopa and Hopkins: 97. The difference seems to be that Tsong kha pa includes in the third step all of the elements required to prove the property of the position, that is, that the reason is a property of the subject. Hence, regardless of which of the many reasonings the meditator might employ, whether it be the lack of being one or many, the diamond slivers, or Candrakīrti's sevenfold reasoning, all reflections on the relation of that reason to the subject would be encompassed in the third step, with the fourth step reserved for the actual ascertainment of the thesis. In the system represented by the Paṇ chen Lama, a separate step is reserved for each element of the reason. Thus, in proving that the I is neither intrinsically the same as nor different from the aggregates, the third essential would be to determine that the I is not intrinsically the same as the aggregates and the fourth essential would be to determine that the I is not intrinsically different from the aggregates. According to this system, a meditator using the sevenfold reasoning would move through nine essentials, the first two, plus seven for each element of the reasoning. The system of the Paṇ chen

Lama, therefore, omits Tsong kha pa's final step, the ascertainment of the thesis, perhaps because such ascertainment is said to occur spontaneously after the ascertainment of the pervasion and the property of the position.

2. Although Tsong kha pa refers to the I and the aggregates being neither the same (*gcig*) nor different (*tha dad*) in steps 2 and 3 above, here in step 4 he refers to the I as being neither one (*gcig*) nor many (*du ma*).

3. A portion of this passage is cited by Ngag dbang dpal ldan in his *Grub mtha' chen mo'i mchan 'grel dka' gnad mdud grol blo gsal gces nor* (Sarnath: Bhikshu Guru Deva Lama, 1964), *dbu ma* 83b5-8. A portion of that extract is translated by Hopkins in *Meditation on Emptiness*, p. 45.

4. Bracketed material added by the translators. Translations of other instructions on how to identify the object of negation include the Fifth Dalai Lama, *The Practice of Emptiness*, trans. by Jeffrey Hopkins (Dharamsala, India: Library of Tibetan Works and Archives, 1976), pp. 10-12; Herbert V. Guenther, *Treasures on the Tibetan Middle Way* (Berkeley: Shambhala, 1973), pp. 116-118; and H.H. the Dalai Lama, *Opening the Eye of New Awareness*, rev. ed., trans. by Donald S. Lopez, Jr. (Boston: Wisdom Publications, 1999), pp. 67-72.

References

Candrakīrti

Bodhisattvayogacaryācatuḥśatakaṭīkā. P5266, vol. 98 in *The Tibetan Tripiṭaka* (see Suzuki).

dGe 'dun chos 'phel

1990 *dBu ma'i zab ngad snying por dril ba'i legs bshad klu sgrub dgongs rgyan* in *dGe'dun chos 'phel gyi gsung rtsom*, vol. 2. N.p.: Bod ljongs bod yig dpe rnying dpe skrun khang.

Hopkins, Jeffrey

1983 *Meditation on Emptiness*. Boston: Wisdom Publications.

Sopa, Geshe Lhundup and Jeffrey Hopkins

1989 *Cutting Through Appearances: Practice and Theory of Tibetan Buddhism*. Ithaca, NY: Snow Lion Publications.

Suzuki, D.T., ed.

1955-61 *The Tibetan Tripiṭaka, Peking Edition*. 168 vols. Tokyo and Kyoto: Reprinted under the supervision of the Otani University, Kyoto.

Tillemans, Tom J. F. and Donald S. Lopez, Jr.

1998 "What Can One Reasonably Say about Nonexistence? A Tibetan Work on the Problem of *āśrayāsiddha*." *Journal of Indian Philosophy*, 26: 99-129.

Tsong kha pa
1978 *dBu ma'i thal 'gyur ba'i zab lam dbu ma'i lta khrid* in *The Collected Works (gsuṅ 'bum) of the Incomparable Lord Tsoṅ-kha-pa bLo-bzaṅ-grags-pa* (*Khams gsum chos kyis* [sic] *rgyal po shar tsong kha pa chen po'i gsung 'bum*), vol. *tsha*. New Delhi: Mongolian Lama Guru Deva.

Chapter 4

Cutting the Roots of Virtue

Tsong kha pa on the Results of Anger[1]

Daniel Cozort

In the Buddhist Abhidharma literature, six root afflictive emotions are identified as the causes for episodes or entire lifetimes of suffering. Of these, anger holds a singular place. Like all other nonvirtues, it establishes "seeds" or "roots" of nonvirtue; but it is also one of a very few mental states[2] that nullify the seeds or roots of virtue that are planted by exemplary actions such as giving and patience.

Among these states, anger is uniquely destructive. The *Mañjuśrī-vikrīḍita Sūtra* warns that a single moment of anger can make a person lose a hundred *eons* of virtue. Śāntideva, the ninth-century author of the greatly influential *Bodhisattvacaryāvatāra* (*BA*), multiplies this dire warning tenfold: anger wipes out not just a hundred, he says, but a *thousand* eons of virtue.

Since most of us lose our tempers with dismaying frequency, this would seem to be terrible news. It looks as though we have little chance of ever accumulating any merit. And it must certainly make us wonder how it is possible to assert, as Mahāyāna Buddhists generally do, that all sentient beings will gain merit sufficient to attain liberation.

It appears in light of these Indian sources that apologists for the Mahāyāna tradition have a heavy burden—they must interpret statements about anger's effect on the stores of virtue as gross exaggerations spun out as a matter of "skill in means"; or, they must delimit the range of persons to whom the statements are said to apply; or, they must indicate ways in which anger's effects can be ameliorated.

I will look here at the analysis of one prominent Mahāyāna apologist, Tsong kha pa Blo bzang grags pa, who founded the Tibetan dGe lugs pa monastic order in the fourteenth century. He meticulously scrutinizes the Indian sources in two places, his *Lam rim chen mo* ("Great Exposition of the Stages of the Path," abbreviated hereafter as *LRCM*), completed in 1402, and his *dBu ma dgongs pa rab gsal* ("Illumination of the Thought, Extensive Explanation of [Candrakīrti's] *Madhyamakāvatāra*," abbreviated hereafter as *GPRS*), completed in 1418.[3] In brief, he contends that the drastic penalties mentioned before come only in the case of anger directed at *bodhisattvas* and he deftly explains that "cutting" the roots of virtue means something far less than "destroying." However, it is not clear that, in the end, Tsong kha pa has succeeded in demonstrating that anger does not, at least in some cases, prevent salvation.

Quantifying the Penalty for Anger

Let us look at Tsong kha pa's analysis. First, he attempts to quantify the penalty for anger. He must depend on just a few sources in the sūtras, for although it is clear that the Buddha regarded anger as a massively destructive force, he was seldom, according to textual evidence, more specific.

Tsong kha pa cites the *Upāli-paripṛcchā Sūtra*, the *Mañjuśrī-vikrīḍita Sūtra*, and the *Sañchaya-gāthā-prajñāpāramitā Sūtra*. The *locus classicus* appears to be the aforementioned *Mañjuśrī-vikrīḍita Sūtra*, which warns that one may lose a hundred eons of virtue in a moment of anger.

Candrakīrti, the seventh-century Mādhyamika interpreter through whom Tsong kha pa views nearly all important matters of Buddhist doctrine, probably basing his estimate on this source, also states that anger destroys a hundred eons of virtue. However, he clarifies the sūtra by indicating that hundred-eon anger is directed at a "Conqueror Child," or bodhisattva. This, of course, greatly reduces the likelihood that an ordinary person would experience such anger.

Tsong kha pa also cites Śāntideva,[4] who without specifying the recipient of anger, says (*BA*: 6.1):

> Whatever good deeds [you have done],
> Collected over a thousand eons,
> Such as giving and homage to the Ones Gone Thus
> Are destroyed in one [moment of] anger.

Aware that Candrakīrti has specified that the recipient of hundred-eon anger is a bodhisattva, Tsong kha pa surmises that the recipient of the thousand-eon anger mentioned by Śāntideva must also be a bodhisattva and, moreover, that the angry person must be a *non*-bodhisattva.[5] In that case, Tsong kha pa concludes, Candrakīrti's reference to a *lesser* penalty that also involves anger with a bodhisattva can only mean that we have one bodhisattva angry with another.

Anger is not something we normally associate with bodhisattvas, who, for Tsong kha pa, are persons always able to rouse their *bodhicitta*, the altruistic aspiration to buddhahood. However, that *bodhicitta* can arise spontaneously does not necessarily mean that it is continuously present. At least some bodhisattvas are susceptible to anger for nearly all of a period of "uncountable" eons. This is the length of the paths of "accumulation" (*saṃbhāramārga, tshogs lam*) and "preparation" (*prayogamārga, sbyor lam*), the first two of the five paths concluding in buddhahood.[6]

Anger is not precluded until one is well into the path of preparation, the second part of which is called "peak" (*mūrdhan, rtse mo*) because it is the end of the period in which one can generate anger that will sever the roots of virtue. The present Dalai Lama (Gyatso: 83) contends that a bodhisattva may become angry even after that point, but the anger is weaker than the anger to which the quotations refer and will not sever the roots of virtue.

Tsong kha pa is very specific about the consequences of being an angry bodhisattva. A mature bodhisattva who is angered by one who is lesser[7] loses a hundred eons of virtue; on the other hand, a bodhisattva angry with a *greater* one loses an eon of virtue for each instant of the anger's duration. In the latter case, Tsong kha pa has a source in the *Sañcaya-gāthā-prajñāpāramitā Sūtra*, which states:[8]

> If a bodhisattva who has not been prophesied
> Angers and disputes with another who has so been,
> He must bear the armor from the beginning for as many
> Eons as the times his mind was imbued with hatred.

Tsong kha pa interprets this to mean that a bodhisattva's anger with one who has received the prophesy of buddhahood from a buddha will impede the former's progress for many eons. Presumably the number of instants would swiftly rise above one hundred, since anger has more serious consequences for lower persons than high ones and otherwise the greater bodhisattva would pay a higher price than a lesser.

However rare or common angry bodhisattvas might be, they incur lesser "penalties" for anger than do the rest of us. A bodhisattva's anger with a non-bodhisattva would entail a penalty far less than a hundred eons. Tsong kha pa explicitly asserts that "Only a bodhisattva is an object of anger that destroys roots of virtue accumulated over a hundred or a thousand eons."[9]

We non-bodhisattvas, then, must take care. According to Tsong kha pa, it does not matter whether one knows the person with whom one is angry to be a bodhisattva. Perhaps Tsong kha pa is thinking that even if one does not realize that the person at whom one is angry is an actual bodhisattva, one certainly would have experienced that person's compassion; one therefore would have correctly identified the fundamental character of the person even if one did not realize that the person merited the title "bodhisattva."

If so, it would support the view of the contemporary dGe lugs pa scholar, Geshe Kelsang Gyatso (154), who contends that anger toward anyone who has shown one great kindness is a source of "limitless destruction of merit." To become angry even at an equal, he continues, may cost roots of virtue collected over many lifetimes. He doesn't say why, but perhaps this is because anger mixed with ingratitude contributes to pride and other *kleśas*. This modern interpretation seems consonant with the thrust of the Indian sources.

Whoever is the recipient of one's anger, clearly anger is considered an immensely negative force. We would not be surprised to learn that anger could result in rebirth in a hell for thousands of years or that it might give one who had an otherwise fortunate birth an ugly countenance. But anger is far worse. What makes anger different from most other nonvirtues is that it not only contributes to the store of causes for miserable future experiences but also affects the store of causes for fortunate experiences.

Cutting Virtue's Roots

Tsong kha pa calls the principal effect of anger, occurring in all but a few instances, "cutting" the "roots of virtue" (*kuśulamūla, dge rtsa*)[10] (Gyatso: 83). Ways to "cultivate" and "plant" roots of virtue were a major concern in early Buddhism (Buswell: 107-134). For instance, roots of virtue are a major topic in the *Abhidharma-mahā-vibhāṣā*, the document from which comes the name of the Vaibhāṣika school that, according to Tibetan doxographers, is one of the two principal Hīnayāna systems. Subsequent theoreticians of karma retained the horticultural metaphor but switched to the image of "seeds" rather than roots, and Tsong kha pa treats "roots" and "seeds" as synonymous terms. Both refer to the establishment in an individual continuum of a potential for future effects.

Again, the Indian texts seem to warn clearly and unambiguously that even a moment of anger can wipe out the virtue one has accumulated over the course of eons. What else might it mean to "destroy" (*bcom*) virtue "from the roots"? When a plant's roots are cut, it usually dies. Alternately, when its seeds are destroyed they can no longer bear fruit.

However, some plants, such as the sweet potato, do not die when their roots are cut; they lie dormant until the conditions exist for their regeneration, or they slowly produce new root systems. Tsong kha pa, it seems, considers virtue to be a sweet potato. He explains that when anger "cuts" virtue's "roots," it is not destroyed, although eons will roll on before it again becomes capable of producing the sweet fruit of a pleasant rebirth. Therefore, "destruction of the roots of virtue" is *not* equivalent to "totally cutting the roots of virtue," which for some early Buddhists meant a permanent disbarment from liberation.[11]

This is the fine-tuning in which Tsong kha pa engages as he addresses himself to certain unnamed scholars, apparently the followers of Bu ston,[12] the prolific thirteenth-century scholar of the Sa skya sect whose influential works were still reverberating when Tsong kha pa began his Buddhist studies. He affirms Bu ston's basic interpretation: despite the presence in the Indian sources of apparently unambiguous language such as "destruction" or "elimination," the "seeds" established by virtuous actions are certainly not destroyed by negative emotions such as anger; they are merely incapacitated. They cannot be destroyed by anger because only wisdom, i.e., consciousnesses at the level of the path of seeing and above, can eliminate karmic seeds. That is, until one has experienced emptiness mystically—without any dualities, without conceptuality—liberation from any sort of karma and its results is impossible. Hence, the language of the Indian texts is not literal, but must be interpreted in the following way: because the seeds of virtue cannot reach fruition, for the angry person it is *as though* the roots of virtue were destroyed.

Although it is not a question Tsong kha pa addresses explicitly, we can see that by interpreting "cutting" as something less than "destruction," Tibetan exegetes seek to avoid a serious challenge to the Mahāyāna doctrine of universal salvation (namely, that all sentient beings will eventually reach buddhahood). If anger can be so potent, and as we know too well ourselves, occur so frequently, then certainly there would be beings who had no roots of virtue at all. In that case, how could they ever have fortunate rebirths in which to make progress toward buddhahood?

Asaṅga, in his *Abhidharma-samuccaya*, asks just this question and answers that there *are* hopeless cases.[13] On the one hand, he makes a distinction between "roots" and "seeds" of virtue and nonvirtue such that it might be possible for someone to have lost "roots" but not "seeds" and therefore retain the possibility of future regeneration of the roots of virtue. However, he contends that there are some among those whose *roots* of virtue are eradicated who also have no *seeds* of virtue and therefore have no "dharma of *parinirvāṇa*." They make *samsāra* truly endless, for they themselves will never escape it.

Tsong kha pa makes no distinction like Asaṅga's between "roots" and "seeds" and does not admit the possibility that some are doomed to endless *samsāra*. He appears to think that the roots of virtue can be regenerated; they have been deadened by the poison of anger, but they can be revived by certain antidotes. As I will discuss shortly, it is not clear that his explanation succeeds.

To sum up, Tsong kha pa agrees with Bu ston and his followers that the roots of virtue continue to exist despite anger. However, he disagrees with them over whether this will entail adverse consequences. The problem, they think, with asserting that virtue might still exist despite having been "cut" is that it might then seem to follow that if certain precise conditions were to occur, virtue's seeds might yet sprout; therefore, anger would not actually have had a deleterious effect on virtue. E.g., if virtue continued to exist, could not a wayward monk whose temper too often bested him somehow still experience the effects of past virtue? Tsong kha pa's response falls under several headings below.

Seeds Can Exist Without Ripening

In the first place, Tsong kha pa wishes to establish that karmic seeds *can* exist without ripening even in the presence of conditions that ordinarily would cause them to "sprout." He uses as an example the way in which one can stop the effects of a nonvirtuous act from being issued by using the "four opponent powers." These are spelled out in Bhāvaviveka's sixth-century *Madhyamaka-hṛdaya-vṛtti-tarkajvālā* as remorse, restraint, the cultivation of specific "antidotes," and cultivating *bodhicitta*. For instance, with regard to a harsh utterance, one might regret it, pledge not to do it again, cultivate loving-kindness, and so forth. This will prevent unpleasant effects of the fruition of the act, even though it cannot actually *destroy* the seed of nonvirtue that has been established. Teachers often use the confusing term "purification" to refer to this suppression of the maturation of negative karmic seeds, which one might incorrectly assume entailed complete destruction or elimination, but which in fact means only temporary incapacitation. In just the same way, Tsong kha pa maintains, anger can prevent the pleasant effects of virtue even though it cannot destroy the seeds of virtue.

Another of Tsong kha pa's examples involves a far more advanced person who has attained the path of preparation, that level at which, according to Tsong kha pa, there has been an inferential understanding of emptiness. For such a person, the attainment of a higher path consciousness ensures that even the presence of what ordinarily would be proper ripening conditions will still not lead to the maturation of those seeds of nonvirtue that could ripen as wrong views or birth in the miserable realms of animals, hungry ghosts, and hell-beings. This level of attainment incapacitates those seeds, even though it has not yet destroyed them. Indeed, *all* "heavy" karma, the sort that results in particularly fortunate or miserable birth, suppresses the issuance of effects that are contrary to it. For instance, a hell-being never experiences pleasure, nor does a god experience pain (until, after vast stretches of time, his or her birth-impelling karma approaches exhaustion). Therefore, in Buddhist cosmology, the incapacitation of seeds of nonvirtue or virtue is a common occurrence.[14]

Tsong kha pa's final example is not as obvious as the others. In fact, it involves such a difficult point that it is included within a special list in the dGe lugs pa doxographical literature, which Tsong kha pa calls the "eight great difficult points of Nāgārjuna's *Madhyamaka-kārikās*."

Among seeds that exist without ripening are those that have *already* ripened, yet continue to exist. Commenting on a passage in the *Akṣayamati-nirdeśa Sūtra* that compares virtue to a drop of water placed in the ocean, remaining as long as the ocean endures, Tsong kha pa says (*GPRS*: 56b), "Virtuous roots are not consumed through the emergence of their effects; however, it is not the case that anger does not consume them." In *LRCM* (401) he says, "Even with regard to virtuous and nonvirtuous actions that have ceased upon issuing their own maturation, there has not been an elimination of their seeds." In brief, he says that actions can cause effects without being "used up."

How could "ripened seeds" continue to have any kind of existence? One answer is that we must recall that seeds established by virtue (or nonvirtue) cannot be destroyed by anything other than wisdom of the path of seeing or above; therefore, they are not destroyed even if their effects have already issued forth.

I think, however, that Tsong kha pa's point is considerably more subtle. He expands upon it in *GPRS*, commenting on Candrakīrti's statement in *Madhyamakāvatāra* (6.33) that:

> Because a sprout is not other [i.e., *inherently* other][15] than its seed,
> At the time of a sprout, the seed has not been destroyed.
> However, because they are not the same
> It is not said that at the time of a sprout its seed exists.

Tsong kha pa comments (*GPRS*: 127b):

> In the [non-Prāsaṅgika] systems, they think: "When a thing such as a sprout has disintegrated, everything that is part of the sprout is obliterated." Since one does not get any other thing that is different from a sprout, such as a pot, they assert that disintegratedness[16] (*zhig pa*) is utterly not a thing.

> In the [Prāsaṅgika] system, for example, one cannot designate as an illustration of Upagupta either (1) Upagupta's individual five aggregates (*skandha, phung bo*), (2) their collection, or (3) that which is a different entity from those two, and Upagupta is also unsuitable to be an illustration of those three. However, it is not contradictory that despite that, what is designated as Upagupta in dependence on his aggregates is a thing. Similarly, even though disintegratedness also cannot be an illustration of either the thing that has been destroyed or anything that is the same type as that, it is a thing because it is produced in dependence on a thing that has been destroyed.

Now we know what karmic "seeds" *really* are, according to Tsong kha pa—the "disintegratednesses" of intentional actions. When an action disintegrates, its state of *having* disintegrated—its disintegratedness—arises. This state, too, disintegrates, giving rise to the "disintegratedness of the disintegratedness" of the action, and so on, and on, until a fruition occurs. Hence, "seed" really refers to the present moment of "disintegratedness" of an original action. Asserting that "disintegratedness" is a functioning entity but denying that it is substantially existent allows Tsong kha pa to avoid either the absurdity of saying that karma persists unchanged or of proposing a substantially existent entity like the Vaibhāṣika "acquisition" (*prāpti, thob*) to account for the continuing link between a mind-stream and a karma.[17]

To continue with the quotation: Based on his understanding of Prāsaṅgika philosophy, Tsong kha pa describes all phenomena as mere imputations designated in dependence on certain bases. In his example, a man named Upagupta is not identical with the body and mind in dependence on which "Upagupta" is designated. This is Upagupta's mode of existence because he is empty of inherent existence. Nevertheless, Upagupta exists.

Similarly, says Tsong kha pa, the "disintegratedness" of a virtuous action exists upon the action's disintegration. Although there is nothing to which one can point that is the "disintegratedness" (just as there was nothing to which one could point which was Upagupta), nevertheless there is a basis—the disintegrated action—in dependence on which "disintegratedness" can be designated (just as there is a basis—a body and mind—in dependence on which "Upagupta" can be designated).

The consequence of this is that Tsong kha pa feels that it is possible to assert that even when an actions's fruition has been experienced, the action's disintegratedness, which functions as its "seed," does not cease. Of course, to look at this another way, how could "disintegratedness" ever cease to exist? After all, once something has disintegrated, it will always be true that it has disintegrated. Thus, there is no way that anger could destroy the seeds of virtuous actions.[18] (It may also be that this manner of explaining the persistence of virtue's "seeds" even when virtue has been "ripened" has to do with denying that the accumulation of merit is a "zero-sum game." That is, although virtue might ripen in fortunate rebirths, it continues to "count" toward the store of merit that comprises half—the other half being the store of wisdom—of the requisite for buddhahood.)[19]

One Can Be Virtuous Without Having Roots

The preceding discussion is one response to Bu ston's objection that if "cutting the roots of virtue" doesn't mean total destruction of them, there might still be some way that virtue will bear fruit. Continuing, Tsong kha pa explicitly argues that not only does anger not really destroy the roots of virtue, it does not preclude the performance of virtuous acts. That is, even though one cannot experience the effect of previous virtuous actions during the period in which virtuous roots have been incapacitated, one's predispositions to perform virtuous acts have not necessarily been eliminated.

We might have expected the opposite, namely, that one result of the incapacitation of virtue would be a neutralization or reversal of its "habitual" effect, the establishment of propensities for further virtuous action.[20] Apparently Tsong kha pa feels that although the seeds are incapacitated, the habits are not necessarily broken. This seems to makes sense because persons who are occasionally angry may have had much conditioning to predispose them to virtuous behavior. Certainly this would be true in the cases of the bodhisattvas who become angry with each other or with common beings. It would contradict what we observe daily to maintain that a moment of anger dramatically and permanently alters an otherwise balanced or even benevolent personality.

However, this means that one can accumulate more virtue even while sitting in the karmic penalty box. Does this mean that there are "fresh seeds" that might ripen as fortunate rebirth or pleasant experiences? If so, does this not considerably reduce the negative effect of anger? Since this would otherwise constitute a major loophole in Tsong kha pa's formulation, we can perhaps presume that these seeds, too, are incapacitated by anger. This assumption is consistent with the basic thrust of Tsong kha pa's interpretation of the meaning of "cutting the roots of virtue," since it looks *forward* toward eons in which there will be no ripening of the seeds of virtue rather than looking *backwards* at so many eons of virtue ruined.

Of course, it leads to the apparent paradox that the stores of virtue may be increased during the same period in which virtue's roots are "cut" and raises questions such as: if new roots of virtue are produced—and incapacitated—does this mean that some dormant "older" roots are activated? In other words, does anger affect a certain *quantity* of virtuous roots?

Virtue That Is Cut Only Partially

Now, let us look at Tsong kha pa's third response to Bu ston's qualms about the existence of roots of virtue. Tsong kha pa also distinguishes between degrees of anger, only the worst of which truly "cuts" the roots of virtue. Thus, he appears to think that although in general, anger prevents the seeds of virtue from ripening, there may be exceptions. He says:[21]

> The overcoming of a virtue does not mean that a virtue in one's continuum ceases to exist after one generates anger; rather, anger harms the virtue's capacity to issue forth an effect. The extent to which later fruition is harmed accords with the amount of harm done, causing a small, middling, or great extinguishment of virtue as explained above.

Tsong kha pa is referring to the *Upāli-paripṛcchā Sūtra*, which says:

> Upāli, I have not seen such a drawing of a wound or maiming as when a trainee in the pure life (*brahmacārya*) abuses [another] trainee in the pure life. Upāli, then those great roots of virtue become diminished, thoroughly reduced, and eliminated. Upāli, if you would not try to attack with your mind things such as burning logs, what can we say about a body with consciousness?

Tsong kha pa interprets "diminished," "reduced," and "eliminated" respectively as small, middling, and complete elimination. That is, he argues that although it is true that anger cuts the roots of virtue, it may do so only partially. It is not clear whether this means that in "small" or "middling" eliminations only some roots of virtue are touched or whether it means that all roots of virtue are diminished significantly, so that only partial fortunate results are possible.

In short, Tsong kha pa argues that although the Indian texts warn of draconian consequences to even a moment of anger—the loss of a thousand eons of virtue, for instance—this really means, in most cases, that there is a partial incapacitation of that virtue for a long future period. The result is that some of the seeds of virtue might actually ripen as a good body with good resources, etc., and because of this one could probably continue to make progress as a bodhisattva on the paths to buddhahood.

However, one's progress will be slow. Although a novice bodhisattva's anger at a mature bodhisattva will not de-commission her, it will impede her development. In any case, "cut" not only means nothing more than "incapacitation"; it also can mean just "mostly incapacitated." Perhaps anger incapacitates those roots of virtue that would have ripened as lifetimes with superb conditions for the study of Dharma, enabling only those roots of virtue that could ripen as lifetimes or circumstances that are relatively mediocre.

Contradictions, Apparent and Real

According to Tsong kha pa's own reckoning, the journey over the paths to buddhahood requires no less than three periods of "countless" *great* eons. In a sense, then, a moment of anger resulting in a few hundred or thousand eons in the karmic penalty box amounts to no more than a stumble on the path. On the other hand, who gets angry only once in a great while, like a thousand eons? Even with Tsong kha pa's modifications, it seems unlikely that an ordinary person would have any virtue not incapacitated by anger.

The most serious problem with any of the accounts of the effect of anger, then, is that they seem to leave open the possibility that there might be persons who would be the karmic equivalent of indentured servants, unable ever to be born into a body from which they could seek liberation. This would contradict a deeply held dogma about the possibility of universal salvation, which Tsong kha pa supports.[22] A single lifetime's episodes of anger (particularly if that life is spent largely being jealous of one or more real bodhisattvas) could easily dig a hole so deep that even innumerable eons seem too brief to permit escape. This is why vice is so vicious; it impels one into life after suffering life in which anger, among other negative emotions, is the norm rather than the exception.

The Tibetan tradition uses a famous analogy to *samsāra* which compares the chances of being born as a human who can hear the Dharma to the odds that a blind sea turtle, surfacing only once in a hundred years, will stick its head through a golden yoke floating on a vast ocean. In consideration of what we have learned about anger, we should change the setting of this scenario to outer space, where the yoke drifts through millions of cubic miles of the ether. What odds remain? In short, Tsong kha pa's efforts at moderation notwithstanding, the Indian sources seem to lead to an untenable conclusion.

Second, an apparent self-contradiction in Tsong kha pa's interpretation is that he himself maintains that regarding the roots of virtue, "cut" cannot be equated with "delay" or else there would be no great difference between anger and other negative emotions such as jealousy or gossiping, which also can delay the issuance of the effects of virtue. He actually says (*LRCM*: 401):

> The mere temporary postponement of maturation is not appropriate to be the meaning of destroying the roots of virtue; otherwise, all the nonvirtuous actions that have power would have to be set forth as destroyers of the roots of virtue.

Based on our analysis, it is difficult to see how his understanding of the destruction of roots of virtue amounts to anything *other* than delay, since anger, though much more potent than any of these other *kleśas*, seems to be different only by degree. It is true that he sees a difference in the *way* in which the other *kleśas* cause a delay; he says (*LRCM*: 401):

> The virtuous or nonvirtuous actions that have matured earlier temporarily stop the opportunity for the maturation of other actions; however, merely those [earlier maturations] cannot destroy virtue or nonvirtue and that is not set forth [in scripture as the meaning of "cut" the roots of virtue].

The fruition of the seeds of any virtuous or nonvirtuous action can result in a birth that prevents the maturation of seeds of its opposite. For instance, a seed established by nonvirtue might ripen as a birth in one of the hells. Because such a life is devoid of pleasure, seeds formerly established by virtue would lack the necessary conditions for their maturation. These seeds would not have been rendered ineffective in exactly the same way that anger renders seeds ineffective; they would not have been "cut" or "scorched" or "withered" or otherwise directly neutralized. They would be like patrons in line for a film who do not know that around the corner, near the box office, others are cutting in. But what difference does it make that anger and pride, for instance, operate differently? In practice, the result is the same. You never get to see the movie.

Other Questions

By focusing on the narrow issue of how and to what degree anger affects the stores of virtue, we have not yet asked several obvious questions. First, why is anger considered so incredibly destructive? There is no other religious tradition that approaches Buddhism in its negative assessment of the consequences of a moment's angry outburst. What is special about anger for Buddhists?

Let us look at Tsong kha pa's arguments against anger in the "patience" chapter of *LRCM* (in which he follows the lead of Śāntideva's *BA*).[23]

(1) Anger against others is irrational because others lack autonomy. They are helpless against their own conditioning, which leads them to commit acts that provoke us to anger. It is obvious that they lack autonomy because even though they themselves want happiness, they commit acts that lead to suffering.

(2) Similarly, if one thinks that others are inherently annoying, they cannot rationally be blamed, since they are merely doing what is their nature.

(3) If, on the other hand, their annoying qualities are not inherent, then those qualities are a merely adventitious product of conditioning and should not be held against them.

(4) The provocative person is only indirectly responsible for annoyance; he or she is being used by hate in the same way that a person uses a stick. One should oppose the annoyance, not the person (i.e., "love the sinner, hate the sin").

(5) Whatever makes one angry is the result of one's own past actions. Annoying persons are nothing other than the agents of one's own previous misdeeds.

(6) Only a provocative person gives one the opportunity to amass merit that can be helpful for spiritual progress. Therefore, one ought to be grateful for the provocation.

Note that his focus is on what happens to an *angry* person, not on the immediate consequences to the *recipient* of the anger. In other words, Tsong kha pa does not argue that anger ought to be avoided because it leads to violence against others or because it tends to provoke the recipient of one's anger into an equally angry state. These would be legitimate arguments, but Tsong kha pa's concern is for the mental state of the person who gets angry. He wishes to convince us that anger is simply irrational and that forbearance is beneficial, not that anger is wrong because it leads to physical or verbal acts (as he might argue if, for instance, he were addressing the faults of intoxication). It is a reminder that karma is primarily about *intention* (*cetanā, sems pa*), rather than act.

What is noteworthy about these arguments is that most of them revolve around the angry person's assumption of autonomy with respect to a provocateur—around the sort of ignorance that Buddhists identify as the "root of *samsāra*." To be angry with someone implies that one falsely imputes to that person an autonomous self, and the dynamics of anger serve to reify that misconception. Tsong kha pa also demonstrates that anger involves ignorance about oneself, for it indicates that one does not understand that harms, real or imagined, arise only in dependence upon one's own continuum.[24] Because anger reifies ignorance, it is strongly contrary not only to the development of wisdom but also to the development of compassion, which grows only where the distinction of self-and-other has been weakened.

Perhaps, then, anger is felt to be in a different class than other nonvirtues because even more than desire, etc., it solidifies that most vicious of all vices, ignorance. That is why anger joins ignorance and desire to comprise the "three poisons" functioning as the hub of the wheel of *samsāra*.

Moving to a second question, why do Buddhists say that anger affects *virtue* instead of simply saying that anger is a nonvirtuous act that carries tremendous potential for future suffering? Why place anger (and a few other nonvirtues, as described below) in a different category than any other act? Perhaps the answer is that anger does not merely set in motion a future retribution and habituate the one it grasps to further outbursts; it creates a mood, or is one, which undermines positive thoughts and actions. It would not be sufficient on the plane of ordinary experience to describe anger's effect only in terms of future negative effects. We would surely also want to add that anger diminishes positive movement. Thinking homologically, it must seem necessary in karmic theory to claim that anger produces not only roots of nonvirtue but affects the roots of virtue as well.

This is equally true of weighty virtues, such as giving. They establish roots or seeds for future pleasant lives or experiences, but they also "purify" nonvirtues (as we saw before when we considered the four powers that can temporarily nullify nonvirtues). The language of *cleaning*, rather than that of destruction, is used; for instance, we are not told that generosity "cuts the roots of nonvirtue." With virtues, what Buddhist teachers emphasize are ways in which the fruition of the virtues will enhance the attainment of liberation for oneself and others.[25]

Finally, one question that might be raised with regard to the purification of nonvirtue is what consequence this might have for virtue. We have seen that according to Tsong kha pa, anger can be nullified by the four opponent powers of remorse, restraint, etc.[26] But if anger is nullified by remorse, etc., is its nullification of virtue similarly canceled? Are the roots of virtue then freed? Or does one just establish roots of liberation? Tsong kha pa, commenting in *LRCM (402)* on Bhāvaviveka's statement that even though there is purification by the four powers, there is no destruction of seeds, concludes that "even though your accumulation of sins is washed away through purification by the four powers, this does not contradict the fact that you are slow to produce higher paths." In *GPRS* he is even more explicit; referring to the *Sarva-vaidalya-saṃgraha Sūtra*, he says:[27]

> If one abandons the doctrine as set forth in the sūtra but confesses the fault three times daily for seven years, the fruition of that deed is purified, but even at the fastest, ten eons are necessary to attain endurance [i.e., to progress to the next path]. Thus, even though confession and restraint in many ways do not restore a path that has become slower, they will purify experience of the fruition.

In other words, the purification of nonvirtues such as anger does not undo their devastating effect on virtue. "Purification" prevents the issuance of unpleasant effects, but does not rehabilitate good seeds gone bad.

Summary

This has been a complex issue, so let us summarize. Anger, identified along with ignorance and desire as a "poison" that generates *samsāra*, is singled out by Tsong kha pa as a particularly destructive emotion. It is founded on ignorance and reifies it. It establishes potentials for future occasions of suffering; it habituates its subject to react similarly in future provocative circumstances; and it also has a considerable impact on the store of previously accomplished virtue.

The *magnitude* of its effect on virtue is dependent on:

(1) the degree of anger,

(2) the status of the person toward whom it is directed,

(3) the status of the person who is angry, and

(4) whether it is "purified" by the four opponent powers.

To expand briefly on these points:

(1) Anger has "small," "middling," and "great" forms. Only anger that is of "great" intensity can "cut the roots" of virtue. While lesser instances presumably can produce painful effects, they do not also affect the ripening of virtue.

(2) Anger is most destructive when directed toward persons who display great compassion. Therefore, anger with buddhas and mature bodhisattvas is worst, anger with lesser bodhisattvas next worst, anger with persons who have shown one great kindness next worst, and so on.

(3) Conversely, the higher a person's status, the less damaging are his or her instances of anger. If a mature bodhisattva were ever angry, the anger would have only minor consequences; an ordinary person's anger with a buddha or mature bodhisattva, on the other hand, can result in the cutting of the roots of virtue for a thousand eons.

(4) Anger that is not addressed will fester and fulfill its potential for destruction. Remorse, etc., can nullify the painful effects of anger. However, it is impossible to undo anger's effect on virtue; at best the damage can be moderated.

Although the effect of anger—or, at least, intense anger—is to "cut the roots (or, destroy the seeds) of virtue," this does not actually mean that virtue is destroyed, for nothing other than a wisdom consciousness can destroy karma. Rather, the roots or seeds of virtue are incapacitated. Consequently, one may be reborn many times in the miserable realms below the level of humans, or, if born a human, will be unable to make much spiritual progress.

As I stated earlier, I do not find Tsong kha pa's attempt to explain and moderate the position of the Indian texts to be wholly convincing. On the one hand, since anger only temporarily incapacitates the roots or seeds of virtue, it is not clear how it differs from other *kleśas* such as pride. Tsong kha pa himself says "cut" must mean more than "delay" but in the final analysis it appears to mean that and nothing more.

On the other hand, even if anger means only incapacitation, its extraordinary damage spreading over many eons, based on as little as a moment's outburst, seems to make liberation a practical impossibility for most persons. Tsong kha pa's interpretation would have to be even bolder—or, anger of the root-cutting variety would have to be clearly restricted to only the most extraordinary moments of rage—to avoid this untenable conclusion.

Notes

1. The present article is a revision of an article that originally appeared in the *Journal of Buddhist Ethics*, 2 (1995): 83-104. I thank the *JBE* for permission to include it here.

2. Anger is not unique as a negative emotion that can "cut the roots" of virtue. In *GPRS* Tsong kha pa cites sūtra passages collected in Śāntideva's *Śikṣāsamuccaya* that identify other extremely counterproductive notions such as disbelief in cause and effect, boasting about spiritual attainments one does not have, etc., as root-cutters. He also mentions that the *Ākāśagarbha Sūtra* identifies root infractions of bodhisattva vows as root-cutters. See *GPRS*: 57a.5-57b.1. Of course, none of these are said to have the force of anger.

3. *LRCM* is the common name for *sKyes bu gsum gyi rnyams su blang ba'i rim pa thams cad tshang bar ston pa'i byang chub lam gyi rim pa* ("Stages of the Path to Enlightenment Thoroughly Teaching All the Stages of Practice of the Three Types of Beings"). It is Tsong kha pa's grand synthesis of Indian materials pertaining to the enlightenment path. *GPRS* is the common name for *dBu ma la 'jug pa'i rgya cher bshad pa dgongs pa rab gsal* ("Illumination of the Thought, Extensive Explanation of (Candrakīrti's) Madhyamakāvatāra"). It is Tsong kha pa's attempt, late in life, to clarify the thought of Candrakīrti, who he saw in turn as the most important of Nāgārjuna's Mādhyamika successors. Since Candrakīrti's discussion in the *MA* revolves around the ten bodhisattva grounds, *GPRS* is also concerned with many of the same issues as *LRCM* and is also characterized by copious citations from Indian texts. Tsong kha pa makes similar statements in both sources (in fact, much of the text of *GPRS* on this topic has simply been lifted from *LRCM*). The principal difference is that in the later *GPRS* he clarifies a few matters (for instance, the precise parties to whom he believes the Indian texts refer).

4. Although Tsong kha pa mentions Candrakīrti's and Śāntideva's estimates in both *GPRS* and *LRCM*, he reconciles the differences in only the later work, *GPRS*. Candrakīrti is particularly important for Tsong kha pa's understanding of Madhyamaka, but Śāntideva is particularly important for his understanding of the topic of patience.

5. Admitting that Prajñākaramati's commentary on the *BA* says otherwise, mentioning only "sentient beings," Tsong kha pa says that he finds this "difficult to believe."

6. The extensive dGe lugs pa grounds and paths (*bhūmi* and *mārga, sa lam*) literature is based on Maitreya's *Abhisamayālaṃkāra* (which in turn is based on the Prajñāpāramitā literature, where the five-path scheme can be dimly discerned) and Haribhadra's commentary; it also uses the five-path scheme of Kamalaśīla's *Bhāvanākrama* (following a much older tradition evident even in Sarvāstivādin texts—Hirakawa: 208ff.). In brief, the bodhisattva path of accumulation begins with the initial generation of *bodhicitta*, and the path of preparation with a union of calm abiding (*śamatha, zhi gnas*) and special insight (*vipaśyanā, lhag mthong*) with emptiness (*śūnyatā, stong pa nyid*) as the object.

7. The angry bodhisattva must still be a relatively low one since a bodhisattva who has progressed past the third of the ten bodhisattva *bhūmis* (a pre-Mahāyāna system adapted to Mahāyāna in, for instance, the *Daśabhūmika Sūtra*) is no longer ever subject to anger. This qualification can be found in Maitreya's *Abhisamāyalaṃkāra* and elaborated in subsequent treatments of the bodhisattva path (cf. Candrakīrti's *MA*: 3.13). The dGe lugs pa scheme would place such a person even lower, as low as the second level of the path of preparation.

8. Translation from Hopkins (1980: 212).

9. *GPRS*: 54a.5-6. Translation follows Hopkins (1980: 210).

10. It may not be the case that *all* instances of anger cut the roots of virtue. As we will see, instances of anger may be differentiated on the basis of their recipients, but are there other factors that make one instance worse than another? Tenzin Gyatso, the Fourteenth Dalai Lama, says that it is still possible for someone past the path of seeing to experience anger; however, since root-cutting anger is no longer experienced past the second part of the even earlier path of preparation, it is clear that this anger would not impel lifetimes of suffering. The implication is that a higher bodhisattva's anger is not as serious, perhaps because to some extent its root cause, ignorance, has been undermined. Does this also mean that not all instances of anger would result in severance of the roots of virtue? Would Tsong kha pa agree with the Dalai Lama's conclusion?

11. Cf. Buswell: 118-123.

12. The seventeenth-century dGe lugs pa abbot 'Jam dbyangs bzhad pa makes this identification in his *dBu ma chen mo* ("Great Exposition of the Middle Way," *BMC*: 160a), which is a commentary on Candrakīrti's *MA*.

13. Pradhan: 35/Rahula: 78. 58. Cited in Buswell: 119-120. According to Tsong kha pa's dGe lugs pa order, the mind's emptiness of inherent existence is a "natural lineage" (*rang bzhin gnas rigs*) that is the buddha-nature of each sentient

being, and hence there is no one who will fail, eventually, to attain buddhahood. (For a review of reasons why some of Tsong kha pa's followers found difficulties with these doctrines, see Lopez.) They interpret Asaṅga to mean that he sees five lineages (*gotra, rigs*) for sentient beings, respectively those who follow the path of the *śrāvakas, pratyekabuddhas,* and bodhisattvas, those who switch from one of the former to the latter, and those without a lineage for liberation.

14. The latter example is not Tsong kha pa's, but my own, which I include because it seems parallel to his. As I point out below, Tsong kha pa wants to distinguish between the temporary *suppression* of fruitions by the ripening of other, contrary, karmas, and the *incapacitation* of fruitions by anger. That is, anger is qualitatively different from most other nonvirtues. That is why I think that he himself would not use this as an example. However, there seems to be no difference between the practical effects of these nonvirtues.

15. Tsong kha pa and his followers consistently interpret the "not other than" statements in Indian Madhyamaka as meaning "not inherently other" since, of course, things such as seeds and sprouts are different from each other. On the other hand, they are individually not inherently existent (*svabhāvasiddhi, rang bzhin gyis grub pa*) and do not have a relationship of inherent otherness, i.e., they do not have a relationship that is not merely imputed by thought.

16. "Disintegratedness" is a rather ungraceful term, but it refers to a thing's state of having disintegrated, and since this state is held itself to be a functioning thing, I have nominalized it.

17. *Prāpti* and other means to account for the continuation of karma, such as the *ālayavijñāna* of Yogācāra texts, are rejected by Tsong kha pa as entities not included in the conventions of the world (which he thinks are, in contrast, upheld by sūtras of definitive meaning and in the ultimate commentarial tradition of Prāsaṅgika-Madhyamaka), not to mention the fact that as described by their proponents they could be established only by ultimate analysis. This is a major topic of the "unique tenets of Prāsaṅgika" section of 'Jam dbyangs bzhad pa's *Grub mtha' chen mo* ("Great Exposition of Tenets," *GTCM*), which I translated as part of *Unique Tenets of the Middle Way Consequence School* (Snow Lion Publications, 1998). For a recent discussion of Vaibhāṣika positions and how they are critiqued by Vasubandhu's *Abhidharmakośa-bhāṣya*, see Hayes.

18. Of course, it also raises the question of how *wisdom* could destroy seeds. This is reminiscent of a discussion by 'Jam dbyangs bzhad pa (*GTCM*: 628) on the "disintegratedness" of the obstructions to omniscience (*jñeyāvaraṇa, shes sgrib*) for buddhas. To become buddhas, of course, necessitated the destruction of those obstructions, but 'Jam dbyangs bzhad pa, wishing to avoid saying that buddhas have anything like a taint in their continuums, maintains that the disintegratedness of obstructions to omniscience does not exist. His reasoning: in order to be a functioning entity, something must be capable of producing an effect, and this disintegratedness cannot. Instead, the obstructions to omniscience are completely "extinguished into the *dharmadhātu*." I have discussed arguments for and against 'Jam dbyangs bzhad pa's position in *Unique Tenets*.

19. Although I doubt that they are that to which Tsong kha pa refers, there *are* some seeds that are capable of producing more than one effect; e.g., a single

act of killing is said to be capable of ripening into numerous lifetimes in the miserable realms. Even if some effects had ripened, those seeds would continue to exist.

20. A single action produces three effects: a "seed" (*bīja, sa bon*) for a future effect, a "predisposition" (*vāsanā, bags chags*) or tendency to repeat that type of action, and an environmental effect of contributing to the causal conditions for the world shared with other beings. Cf. Dhargyey: 87-88.

21. *GPRS*: 57a.2-3. I follow Hopkins's translation.

22. As Donald Lopez has shown (1992), Tsong kha pa seems not to have believed that all sentient beings *would* inevitably reach buddhahood, bringing an end to *samsāra;* on the other hand, he would certainly claim that it is *possible* for any individual to attain liberation and omniscience.

23. This is a summary of *LRCM*: 405-414.

24. This comes close to implying that every unpleasant occurrence is a direct result of one's own karma. Tsong kha pa would not say this, I think; however, he might argue that every unpleasant experience at least indirectly stems from one's past actions insofar as one's actions are a part of the collective karma that creates and sustains a shared environment.

25. Cf. Buswell for an analysis of the importance of giving, in particular, for the spiritual path. Giving can be seen not only as a virtuous act but one that is a conditioner of insight.

26. Kensur Yeshey Tupten, a great twentieth-century dGe lugs pa scholar, adds (Klein: 85) that even prior to the direct cognition of emptiness that begins to destroy karma on the path of seeing and above, conceptual understanding of emptiness also purifies the seeds established by anger.

27. *GPRS*: 55a.5-6. Translation follows Hopkins (1980: 212).

References

Buswell, Robert

1992 "The Path to Perdition: The Wholesome Roots and their Eradication." In Buswell and Gimello, eds. *Paths to Liberation*. Honolulu: University of Hawai'i Press.

Candrakīrti

MA *Madhyamakāvatāra*. P5261, P5262, vol. 98 in *The Tibetan Tripiṭaka* (see Suzuki). Also, edited Tibetan: Louis de la Vallée Poussin. *Madhyamakāvatāra par Candrakīrti*. Bibliotheca Buddhica IX. Osnabrück: Biblio Verlag, 1970.

Cozort, Daniel

1998 *Unique Tenets of the Middle Way Consequence School*. Ithaca, NY: Snow Lion Publications.

Dhargyey, Geshe Ngawang
1980 *Tibetan Tradition of Mental Development*, 3rd edition. Dharamsala: Library of Tibetan Works and Archives.

Gyatso, Geshe Kelsang
1980 *Meaningful to Behold*. London: Wisdom Publications.

Gyatso, Tenzin, the Fourteenth Dalai Lama
1988 *The Dalai Lama at Harvard*. Ithaca, NY: Snow Lion Publications.

Hirakawa, Akira
1990 *A History of Indian Buddhism*. Honolulu: University of Hawai'i Press.

Hayes, Richard P.
1994 "The Analysis of Karma in Vasubandhu's *Abhidharmakośa-bhāṣya*." In Katherine Young, ed., *Hermeneutical Paths to the Sacred Worlds of India*. Atlanta: Scholar's Press.

Hopkins, P. Jeffrey
1980 *Compassion in Tibetan Buddhism*. Ithaca, NY: Snow Lion Publications.
1983 *Meditation on Emptiness*. London: Wisdom Publications.

'Jam dbyangs bzhad pa Ngag dbang brtson 'grus
BMC *dBu ma chen mo / dBu ma 'jug pa'i mtha' dpyod lung rigs gter mdzod zab don kun gsal skal bzang 'jug ngogs*. In his *Collected Works*, vol. 9. New Delhi: Ngawang Gelek Demo, 1973 (Drashikyil edition).
GTCM *Grub mtha' chen mo/ Grub mtha'i rnam bshad rang gzhan grub mtha' kun dang zab don mchog tu gsal ba kun bzang zhing gi nyi ma lung rigs rgya mtsho skye dgu'i re ba kun skong*. Mundgod: Gomang, n.d. (Drashikyil edition).

Klein, Anne
1994 *Path to the Middle: The Spoken Scholarship of Kensur Yeshey Tupten*. Albany: State University of New York Press.

Lopez, Donald
1992 "Paths Terminable and Interminable." In Buswell and Gimello, eds. *Paths to Liberation*. Honolulu: University of Hawai'i Press.

Mañjuśrī-vikrīḍita Sūtra
MV *Mañjuśrī-vikrīḍita Sūtra*. P764, vol. 27 in *The Tibetan Tripiṭaka*. (see Suzuki).

Pabongka Rinpoche
1991 *Liberation in the Palm of Your Hand*. London: Wisdom Publications.

Pradhan, Pralhad, ed.
1950 *Abhidharma-Samuccaya of Asaṅga*. Santiniketon: Visva-Bharati.

Rahula, Walpola, trans.
1971 *Le Compendium de la super-doctrine (philosophie) (Abhidharma-samuccaya) d'Asaṅga*. Paris: École française d'Extrême Orient.

Śāntideva
BA *Bodhisattvacaryāvatāra*. (*Byang chub sems dpa'i spyod pa la 'jug pa*). P5272, vol. 99 in *The Tibetan Tripiṭaka* (see Suzuki).

Suzuki, D.T., ed.
1955-61 *The Tibetan Tripiṭaka, Peking Edition*. 168 vols. Tokyo and Kyoto: Reprinted under the supervision of the Otani University, Kyoto.

Tsong kha pa
LRCM *Lam rim chen mo/ sKyes bu gsum gyi rnyams su blang ba'i rim pa thams cad tshang bar ston pa'i byang chub lam gyi rim pa*. P6001, vol. 152 in *The Tibetan Tripiṭaka* (see Suzuki); also the Lhasa *Bya khyung* edition published by mTsho sngon mi rigs Printing Press, 1985.
GPRS *dBu ma la 'jug pa'i rgya cher bshad pa dgongs pa rab gsal*. P6143, vol. 154 in *The Tibetan Tripiṭaka* (see Suzuki); also, Dharamsala: Shes rig par khang edition, n.d.

Wayman, Alex
1991 *Ethics of Tibet*. Albany: State University of New York Press.

Chapter 5

Ethics as the Basis of a Tantric Tradition

Tsong kha pa and the Founding of the dGe lugs Order in Tibet[1]

Elizabeth Napper

Tsong kha pa Blo bzang grags pa (1357-1419) is considered the "founder" of the dGe lugs order of Tibetan Buddhism. It is certainly the case that the dGe lugs pas look back to him as their founder, but he himself never made a formal statement that he was founding a new order. Tsong kha pa is also widely known as a "reformer," although again, he himself never said explicitly what he was reforming, and there is some disagreement in the Western secondary literature as to exactly the extent and intent of his reforms. (See, for instance, Snellgrove and Richardson: 181; Stein: 80; van der Kuijp: 24-25.) In the absence of clear statements of intentionality, this paper proposes a careful examination of key passages from Tsong kha pa's seminal work, the *Lam rim chen mo* ("Great Exposition of the Stages of the Path")[2] in order to assess more exactly his purposes.

Tsong kha pa wrote the *Lam rim chen mo* in 1402 when he was 45 years old. It is not his first work. It is, however, the work in which he first made a systematic presentation that laid out his vision of the entire path of Buddhist practice. The text does not form a radical departure from the Tibetan religious literature that preceded it. In fact, a key concern of Tsong kha pa was to support each and every point he made with copious citation of sources in order to demonstrate how thoroughly grounded in tradition he was. However, Tsong kha pa reworked and reshaped those sources. It is often possible to locate the texts Tsong kha pa had in front of him as he was writing and then often illuminating to see what he chose to include, what to omit, and how he reordered the materials. It is such details that provide insight into what Tsong kha pa's vision was and what sort of "reform" he may have had in mind.

First, it is important to note the sources he chose to use. Tsong kha pa backs up every major point he makes with extracts from the Indian Buddhist tradition, citing figures such as Nāgārjuna, Candrakīrti, Kamalaśīla, Asaṅga, Śāntideva, and so forth. Thus, he chose to follow a particular, and rather late, strand of the Indian commentarial tradition. He does refer to sūtra sources occasionally. However, the texts of the Indian commentators are his primary referent and in fact, more often than not, when he does cite sūtra sources, they had been cited by one of the above-mentioned Indian commentators, and it is possible from textual variations to determine that Tsong kha pa was taking the passage from the commentator's citation, not from the original sūtra itself. (For example, see Napper: 735, n. 307 and 737, n. 309.)

Tsong kha pa also cites some Tibetan sources. Those come almost entirely from the bKa' gdams pa tradition that developed following the visit of the great Indian scholar Atiśa (982-1054) to Tibet. Atiśa spent the last years of his life in Tibet—according to some accounts eleven years, to others seventeen. He is credited with a major reform of Buddhism in Tibet. This will be discussed further below. For the purpose of this immediate discussion, what is significant is that Tsong kha pa cites Atiśa, but only occasionally. He also cites some of Atiśa's Tibetan followers from the early years of the bKa' gdams pa tradition. Those passages are usually short, epigrammatic exhortations to proper practice as opposed to philosophical or theoretical statements.

Tsong kha pa had studied with most of the great teachers of his time, from all different traditions. His connections to the Sa skya and rNying ma traditions are particularly well known. He cites none of them. The text he had in front of him as he was writing the *Lam rim chen mo* was a compendium of bKa' gdams pa teachings written by Gro lung pa (fl. late 11th–early 12th century) entitled the *bsTan rim chen mo* ("Great Exposition of the Stages of the

Teaching").[3] Although Tsong kha pa acknowledges this in his colophon (*LRCM*: 812), he does not cite it per se. Also, the opening chapter of the *Lam rim chen mo* is a biography and praise of Atiśa, and, from structure and wording, it is very clear that the text Tsong kha pa had in front of him as he wrote was the huge hagiography of Atiśa entitled the *Jo bo rje dpal ldan mar me mdzad ye shes kyi rnam thar rgyas pa* ("Extensive Biography of the Foremost Venerable Dipaṁkaraśrījñāna").[4] This text, generally referred to as the *rNam thar rgyas pa*, is attributed in the Tibetan tradition to Nag tsho (Nag tsho lo tstsha ba tshul khrims rgyal ba, 1011-?), a Tibetan who traveled to India, invited and accompanied Atiśa to Tibet, and stayed with him for many years as his student. In fact, it was probably compiled over a number of centuries. Although it unquestionably provides the source material for much of what Tsong kha pa wrote about Atiśa, the only passages explicitly cited are verse passages of a shorter text by Nag tsho entitled *bsTod pa brgyad cu pa* ("Eighty Verses of Praise"),[5] which is contained within the longer text.

Thus, Tsong kha pa reveals a definite preference for confining his citation of Tibetan sources to early bKa' gdams pa works, accepted across the various Tibetan traditions. Significantly, he never cites any Tibetan authors who represent any of the sects active at the time he was writing his text.[6] From this omission, it would certainly seem plausible to draw the conclusion that Tsong kha pa was choosing to distance himself from any of the orders flourishing at his time and not unreasonable to surmise that he was consciously starting something new.

After an opening homage and verse, the *Lam rim chen mo* begins with a chapter focused on Atiśa. Tsong kha pa announces that he is going to follow a tradition of composition that had its origin in the great Indian monastic university of Vikramaśila, in which one begins to compose a text by showing the greatness of the author of the teaching. He then says:

> These instructions for practice, in general, are those of the *Abhisamayālaṁkāra* composed by the venerable Maitreya.[7] In particular, the text for this [work] is [Atiśa's] *Bodhipathapradīpa* ("Lamp for the Path to Enlightenment");[8] hence, just the author of it [the *Bodhipathapradīpa*] is the author also of this [work here]. (*LRCM*: 3-4)

This passage, in which Tsong kha pa as much as says that Atiśa is the author, has been difficult for later commentators, since Tsong kha pa is the author of the *Lam rim chen mo*, not Atiśa. Essentially, the way the commentators resolve the difficulty is to point out that Atiśa's *Bodhipathapradīpa* with its quintessential instructions for practice—the differentiation into the three levels of beings with corresponding practices for each level—serves as the root text or starting point for Tsong kha pa's text.[9] And, of course, this is an important point: Atiśa's division of practitioners into three capacities has provided the essential structure of Tsong kha pa's text. Still, it is a difficult line to deal with on a literal level.

The situation becomes more interesting when one considers the actual relationship between the two texts: Atiśa's *Bodhipathapradīpa* is three folios long; Tsong kha pa's is 523. Even more significant, of the sixty-eight verses of Atiśa's text, Tsong kha pa quotes only three.[10] Hence, Tsong kha pa credited Atiśa with the authorship of the text he was about to write, and yet Atiśa's actual quoted presence in it is minuscule. Moreover, topics which are of central importance to Atiśa's text hardly appear in Tsong kha pa's and vice versa. The two texts differ enough that the *Lam rim chen mo* can in no way be considered an explication of the *Bodhipathapradīpa.*

The gain for Tsong kha pa was that he was able to begin his text by focusing on Atiśa and to use the figure of Atiśa and his life as a structure for the points he wanted make, points which then carried the weight of authority derived from the great respect with which Atiśa is regarded in the Tibetan tradition. Most of what I consider to be Tsong kha pa's primary themes are worked into his praise of Atiśa and of the *Bodhipathapradīpa*—namely, the primacy of ethics, the importance of an orderly system in which higher levels are built upon a basis of the lower, the need to study all the scriptures and then to practice from a basis of wide learning, the importance of taking and properly keeping vows, and the necessity for a system of practice in which teachings of the sūtra and tantra traditions are harmonious.

That these are important themes for Tsong kha pa is certainly well-known to anyone who has studied his work at all. However, I consider it a useful exercise to document how carefully Tsong kha pa developed them and how deliberately he chose to shape in these directions the materials he had before him. For, these themes, introduced in the opening pages of the *Lam rim chen mo* and then reiterated throughout the text, set the stage for a reordering of the priorities and structures of Buddhist life and practice in Tibet.

The Primacy of Ethics

Atiśa's great renown within the Tibetan tradition is as someone who restored the purity of the Buddhist teachings. According to traditional accounts, Buddhism was first introduced into Tibet in the seventh century, developed there over the next two centuries, and then from the ninth to tenth centuries endured a period of severe repression.[11] A revival of the tradition began in the late tenth century, but seemingly degenerate elements were to be seen in the Buddhism that remained.[12] Tibet had adopted a tantric form of Buddhism, but there was concern that not all that was being passed off as tantra was pure Buddhism.

Atiśa, a monk, renowned scholar, and tantric adept, was invited to Tibet primarily to address these issues. He arrived there in 1042, and according to the tradition Tsong kha pa accepted, taught for seventeen years, until his death. One of his greatest contributions to the Tibetan Buddhist tradition was the short text he wrote specifically for the Tibetan people, dedicated to the king who invited him, the *Bodhipathapradīpa*. It describes in brief form the path to enlightenment and introduces the concept of the different capacities of followers—those intent only on worldly happiness, those seeking their own freedom from cyclic existence, and those intent on enlightenment for the sake of all sentient beings. It is this brief work that Tsong kha pa describes in his introductory pages as the "text" of his work.

As mentioned above, Tsong kha pa was clearly looking at and relying heavily on the *rNam thar rgyas pa* as he wrote his praise of Atiśa. What is significant is how he deviated from its presentation, in terms both of order and of what he omitted. For instance, the *rNam thar rgyas pa* opens with a discussion of three qualities that an author should have: (1) a vision of one's personal deity giving permission to compose the text; (2) receipt of quintessential instructions descended in an unbroken lineage from the Buddha; and (3) mastery of the five topics of knowledge. Having these qualities was clearly considered important and Tsong kha pa did include the list and a statement that Atiśa had them (*LRCM*: 10-11). However, he put it at the end of his presentation, almost as an afterthought, a necessary back-up to show Atiśa's impeccable credentials, rather than as central to what he wanted to say. And, he reversed the order. Whereas in the *rNam thar rgyas pa*, visionary experience is first and study last, Tsong kha pa put study first and visionary experience last. Also, the *rNam thar rgyas pa* is filled with personal details of Atiśa's life, the difficulties of his travel to Tibet, his struggles once there, and so forth. All of these are omitted from Tsong kha pa's biography; what he has chosen to include instead are passages indicating Atiśa's good character, his mastery of the teachings, and how well he kept his vows.

One of Tsong kha pa's central themes, introduced in the verse homage that opens his text and then repeated in his biography of Atiśa, is the importance of studying the whole corpus of the teachings and then practicing based on that, rather than practicing based on a simplified teaching.[13] He has structured his presentation to put this across. Here and throughout this section, Tsong kha pa follows the topical outline of the *rNam thar rgyas pa*. However, he develops those topics according to his interests. Thus, the overall structure of the section dealing with Atiśa is a threefold heading: first, how Atiśa was born of good background; second, how Atiśa developed good qualities of knowledge and realization; and third, what he then did to further the Buddhist teachings. Of primary interest to Tsong kha pa was the second, how Atiśa developed good qualities of knowledge and realization, and this takes up most of the pages of the chapter.

Tsong kha pa emphasizes again and again the need for both study and practice; study alone is insufficient, but any high level realization of the teachings must be based upon a solid grounding in the meanings of those teachings. Following a long description of all that Atiśa had studied—the full corpus of general knowledge of his time, the texts of logic, philosophy, and the full range of tantric texts—Tsong kha pa concludes, "Thus, through crossing over the ocean-like tenets of our own and others' schools, he came to realize non-erroneously all the essentials of the scriptural teaching" (*LRCM*: 6). Having established this, Tsong kha pa makes the point that first Atiśa gained good qualities associated with knowledge of scripture, and then, upon that basis, good qualities of realization. The latter is the sought-for goal, with the former a necessary prerequisite.[14]

In the course of his discussion of this point, Tsong kha pa makes a linkage between the scriptural teachings being included within the three scriptural collections and the realized teachings being included within the three trainings—in ethics, meditative stabilization, and wisdom. He says:

> In general, all of the scriptural teachings of the Conqueror can be included within the three precious scriptural collections. Therefore, the realized teaching also must be included within the three precious trainings.[15] (*LRCM*: 6)

The forced linkage of these two aspects of the teachings by a rather specious causal particle is an awkward transition, not common in Tsong kha pa's work. I feel that he pushed the connection between these two more than is strictly logical because of the overriding point he very much wanted to make: namely, that knowledge of the scriptures is a prerequisite to realization, and that realization requires all three—ethics, meditative stabilization, and wisdom, the higher built upon the lower. For this then brings him to the point he really wants to make:

> Since the training in ethics is praised again and again in the scriptures and in the commentaries on their intent as the basis of all good qualities such as the trainings in concentration and wisdom, etc., initially one must possess the good qualities of realization that are within the sphere of the training in ethics. (*LRCM*: 6)

From there, Tsong kha pa goes on to establish the fact that Atiśa possessed the training in ethics. He shows that Atiśa possessed the trainings in meditative stabilization and wisdom as well, but ethics is the focus of his concern. His discussion of this point lasts for several pages; meditative stabilization and wisdom are accorded a mere paragraph each.

How does he establish that Atiśa possessed the training in ethics? By showing that he possessed the individual liberation vows, bodhisattva vows, and tantric vows. Here, Tsong kha pa is presenting Atiśa as the exemplar of another primary theme that will be developed throughout the *Lam rim chen mo*, namely that the higher levels of the teachings are built upon the lower and, far from superseding them, require them as prerequisites.

This theme will be discussed further below, but stated briefly, the assumptions of the system developed by Tsong kha pa based upon Atiśa's threefold layout of levels of practice for different levels of practitioners are as follows: The Lesser Vehicle teachings and vows provide the basis for the Mahāyāna, or Great Vehicle, teachings. The Mahāyāna teachings are of two types, sūtra Mahāyāna and tantra Mahāyāna, or Vajrayāna; these two have a common goal and motivation, but different sets of vows. Sūtra Mahāyāna is never superseded by the Vajrayāna and, in fact, its vows—the bodhisattva vows—are a necessary prerequisite for the tantric vows.

Hence, in presenting Atiśa as the exemplar of this system, Tsong kha pa establishes that Atiśa was a holder of all three levels of vows—individual liberation, bodhisattva, and tantric. Vows of individual liberation (*pratimokṣa*) are where the monks' vows are found, and Tsong kha pa emphasizes very strongly that not only was Atiśa a monk, he was someone who maintained the monastic rule impeccably:

> A yak is so attached to the hairs of its tail that when a single hair gets caught in brush, it will risk its life to guard that no hair be lost, even if it sees that it might be killed by a hunter. As is said in Nag tsho's *bsTod pa*, [Atiśa], having received the complete vows of a monk, guarded those vows as a yak guards its tail. What need to speak of major points of training that he had vowed—through guarding at the risk of his life even every *minor* point of training, he became an elder (*sthāvira, gnas brtan*) who was a great upholder of discipline. (*LRCM*: 6)

Similarly, in his upholding of the bodhisattva vows, Atiśa "never transgressed the boundaries of the formulated codes (*bcas pa*) of conqueror's children [bodhisattvas]" (*LRCM*: 7) and also upheld without transgression the tantric vows he had taken. Tsong kha pa concludes this section by repeating his point—Atiśa not only took the vows of all three levels, he kept them:

> Thus, [Atiśa] was not merely courageous with respect to promising to train in the ethics of the three vows [*śrāvaka*, bodhisattva, and tantric], but, following up on his promise, guarded [those ethics] without transgressing the boundaries of the formulated rules. And, should he transgress slightly, he would immediately purify that infraction with the respective rite for restoring [the vow]. (*LRCM*: 7)

Then Tsong kha pa mentions briefly what Atiśa did in India to further the Buddhist teachings. The main quality he singles out for praise is that Atiśa did not allow himself to be drawn into partisan presentations of the teachings, but taught from the viewpoint of the general teachings and was regarded as a teacher and an ornament of all (*LRCM*: 8-9). As is the case throughout this chapter,

Atiśa's good qualities are presented for emulation, so it seems unlikely that Tsong kha pa saw himself as engaged in a partisan mission.

Tsong kha pa then discusses what Atiśa accomplished in Tibet: ". . . in dependence upon prayers made to him that he might purify the Buddhist teachings," he composed the *Bodhipathapradīpa*, "a text that brings together the stages of practice within condensing all the essential points of sūtra and tantra." He gave instructions in sūtra and tantra all over Tibet over a period of seventeen years. He "reestablished," "reinvigorated," and "purified" the teachings (*LRCM*: 9).

Then, before giving his summary of Atiśa's contribution to the Buddhist teachings in Tibet, Tsong kha pa inserts a paragraph that seems quite out of context, almost a distraction. He says:

> In general, the glorious Śāntarakṣita and Padmasambhava introduced the practice of the [Buddhist] system of teachings to the Land of Snow [Tibet] during the early dissemination of the teaching. However, in dependence upon emptiness not being understood correctly, the Chinese abbot Hva-shang, who deprecated the factor of method and refuted all taking to mind [of anything, even virtues], caused the teaching to diminish. The great master Kamalaśila, having refuted [Hva-shang] well, settled the intent of the Conqueror; hence, his kindness was extremely great. (*LRCM*: 9)

This point is only touched on here. However, it reappears several more times later in the text[16] and becomes of central importance in the more philosophical portion of the text, where Tsong kha pa discusses the correct understanding of the teachings of emptiness. I would argue that Tsong kha pa forced it in here because he was using these introductory pages to establish his main theses, particularly the primacy of ethics, and thus it needed to be included.[17]

Following this brief digression, Tsong kha pa then concludes with a statement of Atiśa's contribution:

> In the later dissemination [of the teaching in Tibet], in dependence upon holding erroneously the meaning of the tantra sets, some who fancied that they were scholars and yogis caused great damage to the pure behavior [i.e., the maintenance of ethics] that is the root of the teachings. They were refuted well by this holy being [Atiśa], and moreover, having caused their erroneous conceptions to disappear, he reinvigorated the nonerroneous teaching. Therefore, all those of the Land of Snow were pervaded by his kindness. (*LRCM*: 9-10)

Thus, in the opening pages of the *Lam rim chen mo*, Tsong kha pa introduced what I take to be his central theme: He was concerned about a degeneration of the Buddhist tradition in Tibet, in particular about a degeneration in ethics leading to impure behavior. Ethics can be lost in one of two ways: one is through affirming the tantric tradition in such a way as to declare that it is beyond vows and supersedes those of the lower traditions. Another is through a philosophical understanding of the Buddhist teaching of emptiness in such a way that it acts to cancel out ethics, or method, or any kind of directed practice. The Samye debate and Hva shang Mahāyāna are used to exemplify this latter error, and hence the somewhat out-of-context reference to that chapter of early Tibetan history. Kamalaśīla serves as the exemplar who overcame the second sort of fault. Atiśa is the exemplar who stamped out the first. Unstated, but implicit, is that Tsong kha pa finds Tibet at yet another such juncture, and he is invoking Atiśa's name to "purify" the teachings yet again.

Sūtra and Tantra

After his presentation of Atiśa's life—the "greatness of the author of the teachings," Tsong kha pa, continuing to follow the format of using the style of composition of Vikramaśīla Monastery, goes on to discuss the greatness of the teaching itself. He says:

> Concerning the teaching, the text of these instructions for practice is the *Bodhipathapradīpa*. There are many texts composed by the Elder [Atiśa], but that which is fully complete and like a root is the *Pradīpa*. Since it teaches within having drawn together the essentials of both sūtra and tantra, its subject matter is fully complete; since it takes as chief the stages of taming the mind, it is easy to put into practice. (*LRCM*: 11)

Note that an essential quality of the text is that it draws together the essentials of sūtra and tantra. And Atiśa's text does teach both. Significantly, Tsong kha pa chose to separate sūtra and tantra, writing two "Great Expositions"—the first, the text under discussion here, the *Lam rim chen mo*, or, the "Great Exposition of the Stages of the Path," which lays out the path of practice following the sūtra system. Shortly thereafter he wrote a companion piece, the *sNgags rim chen mo* (*NRCM*), or "Great Exposition of the Stages of Mantra,"[18] in which he laid out a full presentation of the tantric path. In essence, Tsong kha pa separated sūtra and tantra by writing two separate texts and presenting in the first a system of practice in which one can put full energy into religious practice without ever engaging in tantric practices. However, he in no way questioned the need for tantra. He accepts absolutely that the tantric system is the superior one and says more than once in the *Lam rim chen mo* that eventually one should enter the tantric path.

However, he was concerned with how to integrate the two, and he praised Atiśa's success in this regard. Tsong kha pa draws out the theme of the unity of the teachings by elaborating on the point that not only are all of the teachings of the Buddha without contradiction, but one intent on attaining the highest level of the teachings, Buddhahood, must, as a means to achieving that goal, train in all the different paths set forth in those teachings. For, the whole purpose in undertaking the training of a bodhisattva is to help all beings, which includes followers of all the different lineages of the teachings, and hence one oneself must know them all, Hīnayāna and Mahāyāna alike. Tsong kha pa quotes a Perfection of Wisdom sūtra:

> Bodhisattvas should generate all paths—whatever is a path of a *śrāvaka*, whatever is a path of a *pratyekabuddha*, and whatever is a path of a Buddha—and should know all paths. They should bring all those to completion and they should do the deeds of those paths. (*LRCM*: 13)[19]

He concludes, "Thus, propounding that because one is a Mahāyāna practitioner, one should not train in the scriptural collections of the Hīnayāna is a contradictory sign" (*LRCM*: 13). "Contradictory sign" means a reason proving the opposite of what one is using it to prove—in other words, the fact that one is a Mahāyāna practitioner is a reason proving that one *should* train in the scriptural collections of the Hīnayāna. Thus, Tsong kha pa establishes that Mahāyāna practitioners should not reject the teachings of the Hīnayāna, and, in fact, since many aspects of the Mahāyāna teachings are shared with the Hīnayāna, they need to train in them.

He next addresses the qualm that some may think that whereas such may be true for sūtra Mahāyāna, it is not the case with the Vajra Vehicle, or the tantric Mahāyāna teachings. This, too, he refuses to accept, saying that the essence of the Mahāyāna, or Perfection Vehicle, "is included within the *thought* that is the generation of the spirit of enlightenment and the *deeds* of training in the six perfections" (*LRCM*: 14), and he then cites sources from tantras showing that these must also be relied on by those engaged in tantric practices. He goes on to emphasize also that the instructions for entry into the tantric teachings speak of maintaining both shared and unshared vows—i.e., bodhisattva vows and tantric vows. He concludes this section of his text by saying:

> Thus, since [the Perfection Vehicle] is like a center post for the path proceeding to Buddhahood, it is unsuitable to cast it aside. Since just this is said many times also in the Vajra Vehicle, [the causal path of the perfections] is the path common to both sūtra and tantra. If, in addition to that, one adds on the uncommon paths of Secret Mantra—initiations, pledges, vows, the two stages, and their attendant [practices], progress to Buddhahood is quicker. However, if one casts aside the paths shared [with the Perfection Vehicle], it is a great mistake. (*LRCM*: 15)

Tsong kha pa follows this with discussions making the points that what you study and what you practice are one and the same—it is not that you study the scholarly philosophical texts and then practice something completely different—and that it is a karmically serious fault to differentiate between Buddhist scriptures, saying some are the true teachings of Buddha and others are not.

Thus, in his introductory pages, Tsong kha pa has quite clearly set forth an agenda: maintaining pure ethics is of primary importance; thorough study and practice of all the scriptures is essential; the higher paths and vows are built upon a solid foundation of the lower; and sūtra and tantra are compatible and to be practiced in a complementary manner.

Vows

Tsong kha pa then begins his exposition proper. He discusses basic instructions on how to listen to the teachings, etc., and then presents his main subject matter, using the rubric taken from Atiśa's *Bodhipathapradīpa* of those practices shared with beings of low capacity, those shared with beings of medium capacity, and those of beings of great capacity.

A being of small capacity is described as someone who is involved in religious practice, but is focused mainly on attaining a good rebirth in the future. The practices set forth for a being of this capacity—i.e., the kinds of mental training that would bring one at least this level of result—are to become mindful of the fact that death is definite, but its time unknown; that there is immense suffering if one should take rebirth in one of the lower realms—as an animal, hungry ghost, or hell-being; that it is important and helpful to go for refuge to the Three Jewels—Buddha, the teachings, and the spiritual community; that one's actions have definite effects—good actions giving rise to positive effects and bad actions leading to negative effects; and that there are ways to purify negative actions done in the past. Ideally, understanding of these topics becomes the basis upon which are added the next level of practices, those of a being of medium capacity.

The types of understanding required for this level, and taught in the corresponding section of the *Lam rim chen mo*, are knowledge of the four noble truths, particularly the first two, true sufferings and true sources of suffering; knowledge of the twelve links of dependent-arising, of the sufferings of the six transmigrations—as gods, demigods, humans, animals, hungry ghosts, and hell-beings; an understanding of the afflictive emotions; and then, having seen the pervasive nature of suffering within cyclic existence, an understanding of what constitutes the path leading to liberation from that suffering. The purpose of training in these attitudes is to develop a perception of all of cyclic existence as pervaded by suffering and hence to generate a determination to become free from it by becoming liberated from cyclic existence altogether. This is the point of taking the vows of individual liberation, or *pratimokṣa* vows, the main of which are the vows of a fully ordained monk or nun. Tsong kha pa was following a tradition which sets forth a sevenfold *pratimokṣa*—fully ordained monk, fully ordained nun, nun-in-training, novice monk, novice nun, layman, and laywoman. The number of vows taken ranges from five for a lay man or woman (giving up killing, stealing, lying, sexual misconduct, and alcohol) up to 253 for a fully ordained monk and 364 for a fully ordained nun.

Tsong kha pa's clear preference is for the vows of a monk.[20] Reaching ahead in his text to bring up the question of what is the best form of vow of individual liberation for a bodhisattva, those with the highest level of motivation, he cites two texts, first the *Ugraparipṛcchā*, which says that householder bodhisattvas should aspire to full ordination (i.e., to leaving their householder state) and then the *Abhisamayālaṁkāra*, which says that a bodhisattva who observes vows is superior to a householder bodhisattva (*LRCM*: 266-267). He concludes:

> Hence, to achieve the release that is a liberation from cyclic existence, a basis of renunciation (i.e., ordination) is praised. Not only that, it is said that also for achieving omniscience by way of the Perfection Vehicle or the Vehicle of Secret Mantra, renunciation is the best support. (*LRCM*: 267)

Tsong kha pa then continues with his text. If one stops with merely the attitudes described above, and takes the vows of individual liberation, they are sufficient for assuring liberation from cyclic existence—but it will be a liberation for one's own sake alone. The preferred path is to continue on to develop the attitude of a being of great capacity, the highest level of practitioner, someone who seeks to attain the highest state, that of a Buddha, in order to be of altruistic service to all living beings. The trainings described for a being of great capacity are the development of the spirit of enlightenment (*bodhicitta*) and the training in the deeds of a bodhisattva, particularly in the six perfections—giving, ethics, patience, effort, concentration, and wisdom.

Entry into the bodhisattva path, hence into the Mahāyāna Vehicle, is marked by the taking of the bodhisattva vows. These are the vows in which one promises not to give up the bodhisattva aspiration, as well as numerous other factors.[21] Important in the tradition being followed here is a linkage between the bodhisattva vows and the vows of individual liberation. Following Asaṅga's *Bodhisattvabhūmi*, as reiterated by Atiśa and developed by Tsong kha pa, once one has taken the bodhisattva vows and entered the Mahāyāna path, one is committed to the practices of that path, the six perfections. The second of those is ethics; ethics has three subdivisions, the first of which is the ethics of vows, and these are, for most entering the bodhisattva path, the seven divisions of the vows of individual liberation. Tsong kha pa emphasizes that all who would train in the path of a bodhisattva must follow the formulations of the vows of individual liberation (*LRCM*: 394-395).

Tsong kha pa then reiterates the point he makes again and again in his text in a variety of ways, that the higher levels do not supersede the lower, but are built upon them as a basis:

> Therefore, should you, holding the thought that the vow of individual liberation is for *śrāvakas*, abandon the formulations of what should be done and what abandoned in accordance with

> that vow and say that the training of a bodhisattva is something other than that, you have not grasped the essential of the training in the ethics of a bodhisattva. For it is said many times that the ethics of vows are the basis and source of the other two types of ethics. (*LRCM*: 395-396)

Following this discussion of the ethics of a bodhisattva, Tsong kha pa then lays out the practices of the remaining perfections, and then goes on to give a more technical and philosophical explanation of the last two, concentration and wisdom, discussed now under the rubric of calm abiding (*śamatha, zhi gnas*) and special insight (*vipaśyanā, lhag mthong*).

A Philosophical View Compatible with Ethics

In the first part of the *Lam rim chen mo*, much of Tsong kha pa's discussion of ethics focuses on vows—the importance of taking them and maintaining them.[22] In the later portion, he shifts to a discussion of the philosophical understanding of emptiness, and how it must be interpreted in such a way as to make possible a viable presentation of an ethical system. The figure of Hva-shang Mahāyāna is repeatedly set forth as the negative exemplar of the wrong view that ethics, virtuous actions, or any causal actions directed towards enlightenment are all conventional and all negated in the face of correct understanding of the ultimate. However, Hva-shang is not the actual figure Tsong kha pa is refuting; he is used in the narrative as someone who was well refuted previously by Kamalaśīla, at an earlier time when the doctrine needed purifying. Now, once again, such doctrines are being asserted in Tibet (by whom is never stated; see Napper: 711, n. 241 for a list of some of those whose views Tsong kha pa questioned) and it is necessary that those wrong views be refuted again, just as they were previously.

The approach that Tsong kha pa takes is to base his argument wholly on Indian sources, primarily relying on Nāgārjuna. He frames his argument around passages in Nāgārjuna's writings that speak about the compatibility of emptiness and dependent-arising, which essentially means a compatibility of ultimate truth and conventional truth, of the final nature of reality and the phenomenal world or the world of validly established cause and effect. Maintaining this last is the essential point, for valid and reliable cause and effect means that the system of karma is maintained, one's actions do have effects, good actions give rise to good results, bad ones to negative results, and hence it is important to maintain pure ethics. Thus, Tsong kha pa delineates a very careful Mādhyamika interpretation in which any hint of reified existence is refuted, and yet the conventional world is allowed to continue to function validly and reliably—in a merely conventional way.

Tantra

Throughout his whole discussion of the stages of the path to enlightenment, Tsong kha pa makes very little reference to tantra. He praises Atiśa's *Bodhipathapradīpa* as presenting the complete essentials of sūtra and tantra. There is the brief section quoted above at the beginning of the text where he mentions that the bodhisattva vows are not superseded by tantric ones, but the tantric vows are built upon a necessary base of the "shared Mahāyāna" teachings of the bodhisattva vows and practices. At the beginning of his presentation of the three types of beings, he gives a brief overview of the entire path that includes a description of the importance of eventually entering the tantric path (*LRCM*: 92-94, especially 94).[23] Finally, at the conclusion of the text, he gives a brief summary of tantric practice:

> After training in the paths common to both sūtra and mantra, you must undoubtedly enter the secret mantra because that path is very much rarer than any other doctrine, and because it quickly brings the two collections [of merit and wisdom] to completion. (*LRCM*: 808; Lopez: 504)

After mentioning the importance of relying on a guru and receiving initiation, he then says:

> Then, at that time, you should listen to the pledges and vows to be taken, understand them, and maintain them. If you are defeated by the root infractions, they can be taken again. However, doing so greatly delays the creation of the qualities of the path in one's mind; you should strive fiercely not to be tainted by them. Strive not to be tainted by the large infractions, but even if you are tainted by a hundred of them, use the methods for restoring [the vows]. Since these are the basis of the practice of the path, without them you will become like a dilapidated house whose foundation has collapsed. The *Mañjuśrīmūlatantra* says, "The Munindra [that is, the Buddha] did not say that someone of confused ethics achieves [the attainments of] mantra." It says that none of the great, intermediate, and low attainments

> (*siddhis*) [are achieved]. And it says in the unexcelled yoga (*anuttarayoga*) tantras that those who do not protect their vows, who have inferior initiation, or who do not understand reality, do not achieve anything, even though they practice. Therefore, someone who talks about practicing the path without protecting the pledges and vows has completely strayed from the mantric way. (*LRCM*: 808; Lopez: 505)

Thus, once again Tsong kha pa emphasizes his key point: tantric teachings are the apex of the Buddhist path and are to be practiced by all who are able—but they are to be practiced within carefully maintaining ethics and vows. Tsong kha pa makes only a few more closing remarks and then concludes his text.

Conclusion

Thus, it is clear that the pervasive theme of the *Lam rim chen mo* is ethics, and within that, an unmistakable preference for the monastic life as the basis for religious practice. Tsong kha pa's theoretical basis is an inclusive and ordered system of practice in which all of the higher levels are built upon the lower, and practice is done upon a basis of thorough study. Vajrayāna practices are located solidly within the Mahāyāna tradition, sharing the same goal, but differing only in offering a quicker method. Eventually, the Vajrayāna is required, and Vajrayāna practices require full maintenance of the bodhisattva path. The bodhisattva motivation requires an attitude of wishing for a definite emergence from cyclic existence which strongly suggests taking the vows of individual liberation, and hence the ethics, concentration, and wisdom of all three vehicles must be sought and maintained. Also, all three require an understanding of emptiness in which ultimate and conventional truths are compatible, and ethics—a viable presentation of the working out of karma—are maintained.

Basically I would argue that in his opening pages of praise of Atiśa and the *Bodhipathapradīpa*, Tsong kha pa has appropriated Atiśa and made him a thinly veiled substitute for himself. Although it might appear that Tsong kha pa is merely walking briefly through a standard history, in fact he has shaped it carefully; Atiśa has been crafted to represent Tsong kha pa's ideal and his past accomplishments represent Tsong kha pa's present goals.

Although we can draw forth from Tsong kha pa's text an assessment of his purpose in writing it, we cannot know positively what he intended to accomplish in a concrete sense, such as establishing a new order, and so forth. It is interesting, however, to look at what developed among the followers of his teachings.

First, there was an unprecedented outpouring of monasticism in Tibet, with large numbers of the male population taking monk's vows. There have been various theories advanced to explain this, including the economic one of Georges Bataille (1: 93-100), but it is also the case that Tsong kha pa in his *Lam rim chen mo* crafted the theoretical support and laid out a system of practice in which it was the most desirable life choice.

Further, the three great monastic universities of central Tibet, dGa' ldan, 'Bras spung, and Se ra, were founded during Tsong kha pa's lifetime and under his direction. Within a very few years all had populations over 500 and eventually developed into the world's largest monastic universities. The curriculum studied is the great texts of the Indian philosophical tradition as a core, supplemented by extensive commentaries by Tibetan followers of Tsong kha pa. There is no attempt to study "*all* the scriptures," Tsong kha pa's exhortations notwithstanding, and it would hardly be practical given the vast range of scriptures preserved in the Tibetan Buddhist canon. However, the course of study is extensive, focused around five "great books" of the Indian Buddhist tradition, and the traditional course of study lasted twenty years or more in Tibet. It produced in Tibet, and still produces in the re-established monasteries in India, highly trained scholars with penetrating knowledge of philosophical issues and the textual tradition. Some come to be known as great practitioners as well, although the tradition is sometimes accused of emphasizing study over practice.

After the course of philosophical study is completed, advanced study of the tantric texts takes place in a separate set of monastic "tantric colleges." In the dGe lugs order, tantric study and practice takes place primarily within the context of monastic vows, and thus tantric practices are almost entirely visualized rather than actually engaged in. It is widely reported within the tradition that although Tsong kha pa might have attained enlightenment during his lifetime had he engaged in a final set of practices that require actual physical union with a consort, he chose to delay his enlightenment until the *bar do* state between lives so as not to impinge upon his monk's vows in any way. The impact upon the dGe lugs tradition is that actual physical tantric practices by monks are not condoned and cannot be used as an accepted justification for infringement of monastic vows.

Another impact of the assumption that serious religious practice is primarily done upon a basis of the monastic vows is a limited role available to the lay practitioner. And, in the absence of a lineage of full ordination for nuns and very minimal educational opportunities open to what nuns there were, a very limited role for women. Those people looking for the luminary female practitioners of the past, who can be found within the Tibetan Buddhist tradition as a whole, find very little amongst the dGe lugs pas.

Interestingly enough, the *Lam rim chen mo* is not an official part of the philosophical curriculum in the dGe lugs pa monastic universities, and in fact is sometimes seen as opposite to that curriculum. When I asked nuns at a nunnery in Lhasa if they were engaged in philosophical studies, they answered, "Oh no, we study *lam rim* (the stages of the path)." The text is most often taught at large public teachings by famous lamas, such as the Dalai Lama, his tutors, or other esteemed teachers. Such teachings are attended by a mixed audience of ordained and lay people, and for the laity it often forms the basis for their personal practice. Further, it is often the text that those who have completed the course of philosophical and tantric studies in the monastic universities choose as their focus for subsequent contemplation in meditative retreat.

Notes

1. An earlier version of this paper was presented as the Numata Visiting Professor Public Lecture in May, 1996, during my semester as Numata Visiting Professor at the University of Hawaii. Permission has kindly been granted to include this paper in the present volume. I would like to thank Gareth Sparham for reading through it and offering many helpful suggestions. My translation of the opening chapters of the *Lam rim chen mo* and a lengthy detour into research on the biography of Atiśa and Tsong kha pa's transformation of it were supported by a grant from the Tibetan Buddhist Learning Center in Washington, N.J., for which I am very grateful.

2. The full title of the text is: *sKyes bu gsum gyi rnyams su blang ba'i rim pa thams cad tshang bar ston pa'i byang chub lam gyi rim pa* (*Stages of the Path to Enlightenment Thoroughly Teaching All the Stages of Practice of the Three Types of Beings*; P6001, vol. 152 in Suzuki). The edition of the text used for all citations that follow is the mTsho sngon mi rigs dpe skrun khang (Blue Lake People's Publishing House edition), n.p., n.d., which is based on the sKu 'bum blocks.

3. An edition of this text is forthcoming from the Library of Trijang Labrang in India. It has been printed from computer data input at the Computer Center of Sera Mey Tibetan Monastic University as part of the Asian Classics Input Project. The edition is based on a rare woodblock edition held by the Library of Trijang Labrang and includes a very helpful introduction giving

valuable information about the author, Tsong kha pa's encounter with the text, and a comparison of the topical headings of Tsong kha pa's and Gro lung pa's texts. A detailed study of the relationship between this text and Tsong kha pa's is of great interest to any analysis of Tsong kha pa's "reform" of the tradition that preceded him, and will be greatly helped by the Trijang Library edition. I am most grateful to the Asian Classics Input Project for making a disk copy available to me. For other helpful information about the *bstan rim* genre in general and Gro lung pa's text in particular, see Jackson, 1996.

4. Varanasi: E. Kalsang, 1970. For more on this text, see Eimer, 1979.

5. *Khams gsum chos kyi rgyal po dpal ldan mar me mdzad ye shes la bstod pa'i rab tu byed pa tshigs bcad brgyad cu pa*. It can be found in the *Legs par bshad pa bka' gdams rin po che'i gsung gi gces btus nor bu'i bang mdzod (bKa' gdams bces btus)*, compiled by Ye shes don grub bstan pa'i rgyal mtshan (Delhi: D. Tsondu Senghe, 1985), pp. 30-39.

6. At various points in his text, Tsong kha pa refutes ideas that were current at his time. He does not cite those he is refuting by name. Mark Tatz takes this as an indication that he found such people unworthy of attribution, and also accuses him of a general antipathy to the Sa skya school (Tatz: 29 and 21). I would disagree with this and suggest as an alternative explanation that Tsong kha pa had studied widely and across all the existing traditions and because, as articulated in the *LRCM*, he took seriously strictures about respecting one's teacher, he was unwilling to criticize by name any of his teachers with whom he later came to disagree.

7. This text is considered in the Tibetan tradition to present the hidden teachings of the Perfection of Wisdom sūtras concerning the path to enlightenment.

8. *Byang chub lam sgron*, P5343, vol. 103 in Suzuki. English translation with Atiśa's autocommentary: Richard Sherbourne, S.J., *A Lamp for the Path and Commentary* (London: George Allen & Unwin, 1983).

9. The phrase in question reads: *khyad par du 'di'i gzhung ni byang chub lam gyi sgron ma yin pas de mdzad pa po nyid 'di'i yang mdzad pa po'o*. 'Jam dbyangs bzhad pa, for instance, explains it as meaning that the *Bodhipathapradīpa* is the root text for Tsong kha pa's text, and since Atiśa is the author of that, implicitly he can be considered the author of this text. 'Jam dbyangs bzhad pa sees his interpretation as supported by that fact that when Tsong kha pa discusses the greatness of the teaching to be explained, he speaks of the greatness of the *Bodhipathapradīpa* (*LRCZ*: 18).

Akya says that the meaning of Tsong kha pa's statement is as follows: Atiśa, author of the *Bodhipathapradīpa*, is also the author of the quintessential instructions of practice, having condensed into the stages of the path of the three types of persons the essentials of all the scriptures. This is the topic of discussion of Tsong kha pa's text, and Atiśa is the author of those quintessential instructions (94).

10. *LRCM*: 87-88. He also cites a few phrases from it in his section on the bodhisattva training (*LRCM*: 323-324).

11. Samten Karmay (1988) develops the case that the persecution was directed not so much against Buddhism per se but against the form it was beginning to take—centralization in large monastic institutions that drained the wealth and resources of the people and government and threatened the power of the nobility. Karmay argues that in fact it was a time of the flourishing of tantric forms. Nevertheless, it was at that point that the empire broke down, many Buddhist institutions and texts were destroyed, and Tibet entered what is traditionally considered to be a two-hundred-year period of darkness and destruction.

12. See Karmay, 1980: 154. A king of Western Tibet, Ye shes 'od, in a proclamation which Karmay tentatively dates to a few years before 985, details some of the practices being passed off as legitimate tantric Buddhist practice—"animal sacrifice," "sexual rites," "ritual of the corpse," "ritual of sacrifice," etc.

13. "Nowadays those making effort at contemplation have heard little [teaching of the great texts], while those who have heard much are not skilled in the essentials of practice" (*LRCM*: 1).

14. A basic presentation in the Tibetan tradition is that when one talks about the *teachings* (*bstan pa, dharma*) there are the scriptural teachings (*lung gi bstan pa*) and the realizational, or realized, teachings (*rtogs pa'i bstan pa*). The scriptures are how one learns the teaching; the realizational teachings are what one internalizes; internalized realizations are the teachings referred to within the refuge formula when one goes for refuge to the Buddha, dharma, or teachings, and sangha. Within this threefold refuge, it is the teachings, meaning one's realization, or internalization, of the teaching, that are the actual refuge. Hence, it is an important point to show that Atiśa has both these sorts of teachings.

15. *sPyir rgyal ba'i lung gi bstan pa thams cad sde snod rin po che gsum du 'du bas. rtogs pa'i bstan pa'ang bslab pa rin po che gsum du 'du dgos so.*

16. See for instance *LRCM*: 343ff. and 773-784. Significantly, Atiśa and Kamalaśila (and Hva-shang Mahāyāna, the proverbial "bad guy") are the only figures to appear in the *Lam rim chen mo* in any sort of historical context, i.e., with reference to their roles as historical actors, rather than merely through presentation of their philosophical views. However, they are very much straw figures, presented as exemplars of periods of purification, and used to facilitate those points that Tsong kha pa wishes to make. There is no true historical discussion. That the actual facts of the "Samye debate" would seem to differ widely from how that debate is renowned traditionally is irrelevant here; these "historical" figures are cyphers, stock characters in a mystery play.

17. This discussion might seem to have focused excessively on places where Tsong kha pa's syntax or logic seem forced, since this is the third such point

I have raised. In fact, it is because such occurrences are quite rare in Tsong kha pa's writing, which is in general remarkably clear, logical, and consistent, that I have come to see as significant those occasions where something seems forced. I find them to indicate situations where Tsong kha pa felt strongly enough about a point to make it even if he could not fully justify it grammatically or logically.

18. *sNgags rim chen mo/ rGyal ba khyab bdag rdo rje 'chang chen po'i lam gyi rim pa gsang ba kun gyi gnad rnam par phye ba*, P6210, vol. 161 in Suzuki. English translation of Chapter 1 by Hopkins, 1977, in *Tantra in Tibet* and of Chapters 2 and 3 by Hopkins, 1981, in *Yoga of Tibet*.

19. See Conze: 518 where this passage is found as V6e.3.

20. In general, Tsong kha pa's writing is quite free from overtly sexist remarks. However, throughout the section on the *pratimokṣa* vows, Tsong kha pa writes seemingly with the assumption that those who will be reading his text are monks and thus his points are framed exclusively from the viewpoint of a male readership. Given that the lineage for full ordination of nuns almost certainly did not exist in Tibet and that women were not participants in the study traditions available to monks, this exclusive focus on the vows of monks is not surprising, even if disappointing.

21. For a listing of the bodhisattva and tantric vows as well as discussion of their relationship, see Lopez. Lopez makes the very cogent point that the various types of vows do not fit together seamlessly.

22. However, it is interesting to note that in spite of the strong emphasis Tsong kha pa puts on the importance of vows, the actual details of the vows—the ceremonies for taking them and so forth—are not prominent in his text. Atiśa's text in contrast spends far more time on such aspects. The net effect is that Tsong kha pa's text remains very accessible to non-ordained as well as ordained practitioners, which may help to explain its immense popularity among the Tibetan lay populace.

23. However, he also leaves open the possibility that for some persons, entering the tantric path is not an option. He says (*LRCM*: 94), "If you cannot practice more than just the ordinary path, or do not want to do it because your inclination inherited from former lives is too weak, then just improve on these very stages of the path" (Lamrim Chenmo Translation Committee: 137).

References

Atiśa

BPP *Bodhipathapradīpa*. Tibetan translation: P5343, vol. 103 in *The Tibetan Tripiṭaka* (see Suzuki).

Bataille, Georges

1991 *The Accursed Share*. Trans. Robert Hurley. New York: Zone Books.

Conze, Edward

1990 *Large Sutra on Perfect Wisdom*. Delhi: Motilal Banarsidass.

dByangs can dga' ba'i blo gros, A kya yongs 'dzin

Akya *Byang chub lam gyi rim pa chen mo las byung ba'i brda bkrol nyer mkho bsdus pa*. In The Collected Works of A-kya Yoṅs-ḥdzin, vol. 1. New Delhi: Lama Guru Deva, 1971.

Eimer, Helmut

1977 *Berichte über das Leben des Atiśa (Dīpaṃkaraśrījñāna)*. Wiesbaden: Otto Harrassowitz.

1979 *Rnam thar rgyas pa, Materialien zu einer Biographie des Atiśa (Dīpaṃkaraśrījñāna)*. Wiesbaden: Otto Harrassowitz.

Gro lung pa Blo gros 'byung gnas

TRCM *bDe bar gshegs pa'i bstan pa rin po che la 'jug pa'i lam gyi rim pa rnam par bshad pa*. Forthcoming from the Library of Trijang Labrang, Mundgod, India.

Hopkins, Jeffrey

1977 *Tantra in Tibet*. London: George Allen & Unwin.

1981 *Yoga of Tibet*. London: George Allen & Unwin.

Jackson, David

1996 "The *bsTan rim* ("Stages of the Doctrine") and Similar Graded Expositions of the Bodhisattva's Path." In *Tibetan Literature: Studies in Genre*, pp. 229-243. Ed. by José Ignacio Cabezón and Roger R. Jackson. Ithaca, NY: Snow Lion Publications.

'Jam dbyangs bzhad pa, Ba so chos kyi rgyal mtshan, sDe drug mkhan chen ngag dbang rab brtan, and Bra sti dge bshes rin chen don grub

LRCZ *Lam rim mchan bzhi sbrags ma/ mNyam med rje btsun tsong kha pa chen pos mdzad pa'i byang chub lam rim chen mo'i dka' ba'i gnad rnams mchan bu bzhi'i sko nas legs par bshad pa theg chen lam gyi gsal sgron*. Published as: *The Lam rim chen mo of the incomparable Tsong kha pa, with the interlineal notes of Ba-so Chos-kyi-rgyal-mtshan, Sde-drug Mkhan-chen Ngag-dbang-rab-rtan, 'Jam-dbyangs-bshad-pa'i-rdo-rje, and Bra-sti Dge-bshes Rin-chen-don-grub*. New Delhi: Chophel Lekden, 1972.

Kanakura, Yensho, et al.

1953 *A Catalogue of the Tohoku University Collection of Tibetan Works on Buddhism*. Sendai: Sendai University.

Karmay, Samten

1980 "The Ordinance of lHa Bla-ma Ye-shes-'od." In *Tibetan Studies in Honour of Hugh Richardson*, pp. 150-162. Michael Aris and Aung San Suu Kyi, ed. Warminster, England: Aris and Phillips Ltd.

1988 *The Great Perfection: A Philosophical and Meditative Teaching of Tibetan Buddhism*. Leiden: E.J. Brill.

Kuijp, Leonard van der
1983 *Contributions to the Development of Tibetan Buddhist Epistemology*. Wiesbaden: Franz Steiner Verlag.

Lamrim Chenmo Translation Committee
2000 *The Great Treatise on the Stages of the Path to Enlightenment* by Tsong kha pa, vol. 1. Joshua W. C. Cutler and Guy Newland, eds. Ithaca, NY: Snow Lion Publications.

Lopez, Donald S., Jr.
1995 "A Rite for Restoring the Bodhisattva and Tantric Vows." In *Buddhism in Practice*, pp. 503-512. Donald S. Lopez, Jr., ed. Princeton, NJ: Princeton University Press.

Nag tsho lo tstsha ba tshul khrims rgyal ba
NTGP *Jo bo rje dpal ldan mar me mdzad ye shes kyi rnam thar rgyas pa*. Varanasi: E. Kalsang, 1970.
TPGC *bsTod pa brgyad cu pa/ Khams gsum chos kyi rgyal po dpal ldan mar me mdzad ye shes la bstod pa'i rab tu byed pa tshigs bcad brgyad cu pa*. In the *Legs par bshad pa bka' gdams rin po che'i gsung gi gces btus nor bu'i bang mdzod (bKa' gdams bces btus)*, pp. 30-39. Compiled by Ye shes don grub bstan pa'i rgyal mtshan. Delhi: D. Tsondu Senghe, 1985.

Napper, Elizabeth
1989 *Dependent-Arising and Emptiness*. Boston: Wisdom Publications.

sDe drub mkhan chen ngag dbang rab brtan. *See* 'Jam dbyangs bzhad pa *et al*.

Sherbourne, Richard, S. J.
1983 *A Lamp for the Path and Commentary*. London: George Allen & Unwin.

Snellgrove, David and Hugh Richardson
1968 *A Cultural History of Tibet*. New York: Frederick A. Praeger.

Stein, R. A.
1972 *Tibetan Civilization*. Stanford, CA: Stanford University Press.

Suzuki, D.T., ed.
1955-61 *The Tibetan Tripiṭaka, Peking Edition*. 168 vols. Tokyo and Kyoto: Reprinted under the supervision of the Otani University, Kyoto.

Tatz, Mark
1986 *Asanga's Chapter on Ethics with the Commentary of Tsong-Kha-Pa, The Basic Path to Awakening, the Complete Bodhisattva*. Lewiston, NY: Edwin Mellen Press.

Tsong kha pa Blo bzang grags pa

LRCM *Lam rim chen mo/ sKyes bu gsum gyi rnyams su blang ba'i rim pa thams cad tshang bar ston pa'i byang chub lam gyi rim pa*. P6001, vol. 152 in *The Tibetan Tripiṭaka* (see Suzuki). Edition used for citations: mTsho sngon mi rigs dpe skrun khang: n.p., n.d.

NRCM *sNgags rim chen mo/ rGyal ba khyab bdag rdo rje 'chang chen po'i lam gyi rim pa gsang ba kun gyi gnad rnam par phye ba*. P6210, vol. 161 in *The Tibetan Tripiṭaka* (see Suzuki).

Chapter 6

Bon rDzogs chen on Authenticity (*pramāna, tshad ma*)

Prose and Poetry on the Path

Anne Carolyn Klein

Mind-nature is primordially Buddha but
Not knowing this, one wanders in saṃsāra.
Through teaching essential precepts, your mind is known.
Like seeing your face when a mirror is shown,
To know that is to know the embodiment of Bon.

— *from* Sam gtan man ngag bde ba'i ngang
("In the Blissful Manner of Essential Precepts on Stabilization" as cited in Authenticity: *53)*[1]

This is one among many poetic statements cited in *gTan tshigs gal mdo rig pa'i tshad ma* ("Authenticity of Open Awareness, A Collection of the Essential Reasonings"; hereafter called *Authenticity)* and widely attributed to Li shu stag ring (eighth century).[2] Most succinctly, *Authenticity* emphasizes the effortless, spontaneous existence of unbounded wholeness *(thig le nyag gcig)* and its correlate, open awareness *(rig pa),* both of which go unrecognized by ordinary persons. The questions implicit in this verse and the text as a whole are religious, philosophical, and pedagogical. How is it possible to look in the mirror, that is, to be introduced to one's own face? How is such an introduction authenticated? And what place does language, particularly the type of syllogistic reasoning found in the *Authenticity*, have in this process? In short, who studies this text, and why? In examining these matters here, we consider both the pedagogical and philosophical contexts in which such study takes place.

Pedagogy

Bon rDzogs chen has two traditions by which students are introduced to their open awareness, known as Kusali and Paṇḍita.[3] The first is the system of the retreatant or hermit *(ri khrod pa'i lugs tshul)*, also known as the Kusali system[4] *(Ku sa li 'dzo*[5] *ki don nyam su len pa'i lugs tshul)*. Kusali students, after completing foundational practices[6] as described, for example, in the Oral Transmission from Zhang Zhung *(Zhang Zhung sNyan rgyud)*, begin to investigate whether their mind can be found or not; whether any identifiable color or shape can be discovered in relation to it. They use simple methods to search whether thoughts have color, shape, or location, whereas the Paṇḍita practitioners will use reasoning and logic in this investigation.

At an appropriate point in this process, Kusali students receive an introduction to their mind-nature. On the basis of this, and of a few general texts which discuss, in a relatively simple manner, the natural condition with which the student is now seeking to become familiar, they cultivate familiarity and stability with this nature. They thus experience the special calm state *(thun mong ma yin pa'i zhi gnas)* associated with rDzogs chen practice. In the course of their training, they must fully understand the practices of Setting Free *(khregs chod)* and Soaring (*thos rgal)* and be able to realize their nature *(gnas lugs)*.

In this way Kusali students realize the same nature as those in the Paṇḍita system without relying on logic to develop their understanding. They also recognize the difficulties that laxity, distraction, and lethargy *(ching ba, god pa, mug pa)* present to the meditator and ways to deflect these. What they do not have is a full conceptual understanding of the rDzogs chen view, nor of the reasoning that underlies it. Notes sLob dpon bsTan 'dzin rnam dag:

> Students in the Kusali system do not study detailed texts in their entirety. They are not concerned with cultural preservation, studying tenet systems, debating, or responding to attacks on their view. They are directed to essential portions of the text and once they receive their introduction, they are satisfied simply to practice on that basis, meditating for four one-and-a-half-hour sessions daily.

The other manner of training and introduction is a scholarly tradition known as the Paṇḍita system for "active" persons, those who take pleasure in being elaborate.[7] In Bon, this system is linked with Li shu stag ring, author of *Authenticity*, and Dran pa nam mkha', the great yogi-scholar of eighth-century Bon. Over the ensuing centuries the Paṇḍita system has waxed and waned but Bon maintains that it has continued unbrokenly since that time. Still, most meditators in fact follow the Kusali system. Those who follow the Paṇḍita system are relatively few, which is partly why many critics of rDzogs chen wrongly assert it has no logic or philosophical richness.[8]

Because Paṇḍita students study rDzogs chen in the context of the nine vehicles and Kusali students do not, Paṇḍita students are considered more advanced in terms of the rDzogs chen view and tenets in general. Students in this category accompany practice with formal debate and rigorous study of a cluster of texts associated with the *Authenticity*, which includes *Nam mkha' 'phrul mdzod* ("Magical Space Treasure") by Dran pa nam mkha', a commentary on *Ye khri mtha' sel* ("Clearing Extremes from the Primordial Mind"), which itself is one of several works foundational to the *Authenticity*. Also relevant to this style of training are early texts on the nine vehicles *(Theg rim* and *Theg 'grel)* and the *Authenticity* itself. In exile, this tradition is maintained by Tibetan monastic communities in Dolanji, India, and Kathmandu, Nepal.

Those training in the Paṇḍita system, like the Kusali students, seek to recognize their natural condition and cultivate this recognition. They are also carefully instructed that understanding their own empty nature is insufficient. For this purpose senior students in Paṇḍita training study the *Oral Transmission from Zhang Zhung*, and works including *Ye khri mtha' sel* ("Clearing Extremes from the Primordial Mind"), as well as *bGrags pa skor gsum* ("Three Cycles of Dissemination") and *Byang chub sems gab pa dgu skor* ("Nine Hidden Cycles of Enlightenment"). Another purpose of study is to prepare the student to make proper retort to those who would question the value of rDzogs chen practice. When practitioners cannot respond to such criticism, says *Ye khri mtha' sel* (812), it is as if their tongues have been cut off. Likewise, *bGrags pa skor gsum* makes it clear that without the Paṇḍita style of study and practice, it is impossible to maintain the lineage. This would undeniably have been of concern during the Bon persecution contemporaneous with King Khri srong lde btsan, the period when, according to Bon tradition, the *Authenticity* was written. The

Authenticity is of central importance in the Paṇḍita system, and barely used at all by students in the Kusali system.

Unlike the Buddhists, the Bon pos developed a system of logic and debate specifically relating to the rDzogs chen teaching (bsTan 'dzin rnam dag: 25). At g.Yas ru dben sa kha, which between 1072 and 1405 was the main seat of Bon learning in central Tibet, analysis and logic were applied to the three areas of sūtra, tantra, and "mind" or rDzogs chen *(mdo, sngags, sems gsum)*. In addition, the meditation practice of *Ah Khrid* was very important there, so much so it was referred to by the monks as *Yeru Ah Khrid*.[9]

Training in rDzogs chen debate relies especially on the *Authenticity* and *Nam mkha' 'phrul mdzod* as well as on certain parts of the above-mentioned *bGrags pa skor gsum* and *Ye khri mtha' sel* texts. In addition, at the monastery in Kathmandu, students exercise the channels and winds *(rtsa rlung)* for 100 days during winter, after which they enter the traditional forty-nine-day dark retreat. While even the most cursory description of these practices is well beyond our scope here, it is important to understand that training for the most rigorous monastic scholars—who will typically spend ten or more hours a day studying for nine to fifteen years and longer without any holiday except at New Year's—does not revolve around texts alone.

In short, meditation has long been an essential accompaniment to the scholarly style of rDzogs chen education. Students currently following this program at sLob dpon bsTan 'dzin rnam dag's monastic center in Kathmandu are required to rise at 4:00 a.m. for one hour of meditation. They do this, says their teacher, because it is not possible to identify, introduce them to, or cause them to know, that which they have not encountered in meditation. In order to be introduced to the mind-nature, you must have experienced it; otherwise, notes sLob dpon bsTan 'dzin rnam dag, "the teacher can explain things, but grasping with thought is not the system of rDzogs chen at all."

In other words, important as the texts are, they alone are unable to provide authentic knowledge of the rDzogs chen lineage. Yet, despite this apparent anti-textual bias, sLob dpon bsTan 'dzin rnam dag is adamant that those who do not do the more rigorous study are unlikely to fully comprehend, or to be able to explain, the rDzogs chen view, even though they have valid realization of it. Thus, the Paṇḍita curriculum reflects the conundrum we are here to consider—the relation of textual study and conceptual understanding to the enterprise of gaining a particular nonconceptual state.

Both Kusali and Paṇḍita students are rDzogs chen practitioners. This means that even if they do not devote their entire life to the cultivation of rDzogs chen, as do the most admired adepts of this tradition, they must at least realize the view to some degree. Whereas practitioners in the Kusali system are, according to sLob dpon bsTan 'dzin rnam dag, usually limited to focusing on only one aspect of the rDzogs chen view, those with superior training must learn to distinguish the qualities of emptiness, clarity, and spontaneous occurrence which correspond respectively to the three Buddha dimensions of emanation (*nirmāṇakāya, sprul sku*), resplendence (*sambhogakāya, klongs sku*), and reality (*dharmakāya, chos sku*).

The Bon Paṇḍita system has a long legacy in Tibet, its history intermingled with that of the *Authenticity*. Central Tibet's first Bon monastery, known as g.Yas ru dBen sa kha, was founded in 1072,[10] with logic being important virtually from its inception. We have no direct evidence of the use of the *Authenticity* in g.Yas ru dBen sa kha but, according to sLob dpon bsTan 'dzin rnam dag, they did study *Gab pa dgu skor*, one of its source texts. Thus, Bon early on developed a unique system of dialectics and debate specifically related with the rDzogs chen teaching (bsTan 'dzin rnam dag: 25).

g.Yas ru dBen sa kha was destroyed by flood in 1386 (N. T. Wangyal: 15), an event Shardza Rinpoche (142) attributes to the jealousy of Buddhist monks.[11] Notwithstanding this interpretation, the outcome of the catastrophe was that monks of dBen sa kha eventually began to attend the school for dialectics at a nearby Sa skya monastery, Brus yul skyed tshal.[12] The two remained connected for quite some time, although once g.Yung drung gling was established in 1843 as a Bon center for dialectics, the connection faded.[13] After the flood, g.Yas ru dBen sa kha was revived in 1405 as bKra shis sMan ri.[14] Founded and miraculously constructed near Shigatse by Shes rab rGyal mtshan,[15] sMan ri became the foremost Bon po monastery in Central Tibet.

g.Yung drung gling was founded at a site below sMan ri as a center for logic and debate.[16] The traditional course of study at sMan ri and g.Yung drung gling, as well as Paṇḍita training more broadly speaking, continues in exile at sMan ri Monastery in Dolanji, a small Indian town north of Simla, and includes training in the five traditional topics of logic *(pramāṇa, tshad ma),* Perfection of Wisdom *(pāramitā, phar phyin),* Madhyamaka *(madhyamaka, dbu ma),* phenomenology *(abhidharma, mdzod*) and monastic discipline *(vinaya, 'dul ba).*

To what is the student introduced? In the *Authenticity* the natural condition of mind, the ultimate mirror, is sometimes described as an unbounded wholeness *(thig le nyag gcig*), a term considered descriptive of the heart of rDzogs chen practice. *Thig le* (Skt. *bindu)* is a term with a wide and significant semantic range—it simultaneously refers to the seminal, the essential, the round, the spherical; to "drops" of semen or to other "orbs" that are essential accompaniers of certain types of meditation practice. Here *thig le* is to be understood as spherical in the sense of being complete and without sharp boundaries. At the same time it is by no means an enclosed space—on the contrary, it is open to and inclusive of everything and is therefore here translated as "unbounded." This unboundedness is moreover, to borrow from the writings of David Levin, a whole, rather than a totality.[17] This is the force of its being, *gcig,* which most literally would translate as "one" or "singular." But it is a singular kind of oneness, a wholeness which cannot be totalized; it is one because everything participates in it, there is no other. This aspect emerges, in my view, as central to the *Authenticity*'s perspective; guided by this, I am rendering *gcig* here as "wholeness."

How is wholeness known? Levin (76) observes that:

> The difference between a whole and a totality is an ontological difference which cannot be understood by a reductively calculative rationality; it can only be understood aesthetically, that is to say, in an experience grounded in our sensibility, our capacity for feeling . . . .

The marginalization of rational understanding implied here is also crucial to the *Authenticity*.

Levin's reflections are a distant echo of the *Authenticity's* own questions: What kind of authentic knowing is possible, and what sorts of ancillary authenticities contribute to this? How can the intellect be a resource for one seeking ineffable experience? A concern with aesthetics indeed seems significant to *Authenticity's* approach. The questions just noted, and many others, are addressed by our text in two different registers: logic and poetry. Let us briefly consider their connection with three crucial and crucially interrelated themes of the *Authenticity*: the place of reasoning, the nature of unbounded wholeness, and the way the narrative connecting these renders reasoning of limited value and unbounded wholeness of limitless potential.

Authentic Knowing and Open Awareness

Authenticity begins with a salutation to Samantabhadra, described as the oneness of mind and phenomena *(bon sems nyag gcig)* (*Authenticity*, 48). Indeed, the relationship between mind and all else is a central topic of this work, whose most immediate purpose, stated at the outset, is to lay to rest mistaken notions about such matters. To this end, the text puts forward numerous debates, using reasoning to establish that open awareness *(rig pa)* is uniquely authentic *(tshad ma)* in its access to unbounded wholeness. The *Authenticity's* explicit exploration of whether and how open awareness is authentic appears to be a unique feature of this text, for authenticity is not a topic generally broached in depth from a rDzogs chen perspective. Though constructed as a series of debates on topics crucial to rDzogs chen, at the same time the text is clear that conceptual thought cannot be fully valid or authentic with respect to the ultimate. Logic, though extensively employed, is irrevocably divorced from full participation in the path, for there is no way to know *rig pa* conceptually.[18] But this does not mean there is no authentic knowing in rDzogs chen.

The uneasy confluence of these concerns—using logic and getting beyond it—encourages an epistemological narrative that includes both the unspeakable and articulations of unspeakability. Partly reflective of these very different registers of human experience, the work interlaces poetic and prose descriptions of the reality known as unbounded wholeness, and its participation with open awareness.

Unlike more familiar Buddhist epistemologies, especially those of sūtra, this rDzogs chen narrative of authenticity is not embedded in a framework of subject and object. To be involved in subject and object is to be a consciousness *(shes pa)*, and the open awareness of rDzogs chen is not, in the view of many Bon as well as Buddhist texts and scholars, a consciousness. It is beyond mind *(sems las 'das pa)*. Reasoning, on the other hand, involves both consciousness and subject-object iterations. Nonetheless, reasoning has a significant role to play in the learning process, especially, as we have seen, in the context of a Paṇḍita curriculum.

For example, Buddhist epistemologies based on Dignāga and Dharmakīrti include both conceptual and nonconceptual examples of valid cognition, but in the *Authenticity* only open awareness is declared fully authentic. Words and concepts are a valid way of establishing the view, but cannot provide authentic realization of it.

Different as its own categories of authentication are from the prestigious discourse of Dignāga and Dharmakīrti, the text is in no way defensive about this; indeed, it seems quite unaware of and therefore not in any kind of explicit conversation with these elements of Indian logic nor of epistemological categories (such as inference or its subdivisions) that figure prominently in Indian-based epistemological literature. There is not a single mention of Dignāga or Dharmakīrti in the *Authenticity,* nor of any other Indian text; only the term *tshad ma* itself, the syllogistic style of reasoning, and the kinds of questions it asks tie this material to the Indian logicians. Yet we know that Tibetan Buddhism was becoming more philosophically and epistemologically oriented under the influence of rNgog Lo tsa ba (1005-1064), whose influence was already felt by the time the *Authenticity* was discovered.[19] rNgog's tradition centered around the monastery established in 1073 in gSang phu by his uncle rNgogs legs pa'i shes rab in southern Tibet (Dreyfus: 22). Assuming it was written later than is traditionally claimed, the *Authenticity* may well have been part of this general groundswell of interest in philosophical debate. In any case, the *Authenticity's* approach to logic has numerous features which radically distinguish it from classic Buddhist approaches, even while it resonates deeply with them.

Most succinctly, the *Authenticity* inquires into how unbounded wholeness is known, and what type of knower can realize it or, in more rDzogs chen terms, how to manifest the open awareness that is already united with unbounded wholeness. The text itself is framed as a kind of authenticator, a textual inquiry into that more genuine rDzogs chen authenticator, open awareness.

To this end, the *Authenticity* (52) names what it calls three "authenticators of method" *(thabs gyi tshad ma).* These three, considered methods insofar as they are causes for understanding unbounded wholeness, are scripture *(lung),* essential precepts (*man ngag*), and one's own open awareness *(rang gi rig pa).*[20] This latter, the only subjective authenticity, refers not to a conceptual awareness but, observes sLob dpon bsTan 'dzin rnam dag, to an inseparability between subject and object, for unbounded wholeness and authentic open awareness are one in essence *(ngo bo gcig).* Their union is also known as the base, clear and empty, and is also the authentic state toward which the other two authenticators, scriptural and essential precepts, are directed.

These three authenticators are intimately related. Authentic essential precepts connect the practitioner to authentic scriptures, which themselves become authenticated through authentic open awareness. These two, however, are not identified as unbounded wholeness. The methods for actually experiencing this authentic open awareness are given in the authentic scriptures *(lung tshad ma).* The *Authenticity* (49-53) describes rDzogs chen as the essence of all these teachings, the essence of the vehicles, and the fruition (*'bras bu*) which reverses delusion.

After its brief identification of the three types of authenticators, the text goes on to cite a number of tantras, no longer extant, which support its presentation, though not always directly. For example, verses cited from the *Kun rig bon gyi rje rgyud* ("Venerable Bon Awareness of Everything Tantra"), *mDo lung gsang ba* ("The Secret Scripture Collection"), *Nam mkha' rtsol 'das chen* ("Great Sky Beyond Effort Tantra"), and *sKal stong gshen rab kyi dgongs pa man ngag tu 'dus pa* ("Collection of the Essential Precepts, Thought of the Shenrabs of a Thousand Eons") do not even mention these categories. Clearly, the architecture of authenticity discourse belongs to the era of our text, not its poetic sources. Rather, the verses are implicitly interpreted to suggest a living knowingness from which scriptures, precepts, and awareness could naturally proceed. The a-logical manner in which this poetic proof proceeds is analogous to the manner in which the text as a whole unfolds.

The second text cited in this context (*Authenticity:* 52), *mDo lung gsang ba* ("The Secret Scripture Collection"), says:

> Nothing, not even one thing,
> Does not arise from me.
> Nothing, not even one thing,
> Dwells not within me.
> Everything, just everything,
> Emanates from me.
> Thus I am only one.
> Knowing me is knowing all—
> Great bliss.

In this we hear, as so often throughout the *Authenticity,* the poetic voice of Samantabhadra, the speech of reality itself, the open expression of unbounded wholeness. That open reality, fundamentally characterized by bliss, rather than by any particular cognitive content, is what open awareness recognizes and encompasses. A few lines later, the blissful nature of reality is reiterated by a quote from the *sKal stong gshen rab kyi dgongs pa man ngag tu 'dus pas* ("Collection of Essential Instructions: Thought of the Shenrabs of a Thousand Eons") (*Authenticity*: 52):

> Any mind-nature *(sems nyid)* is *bon*-nature,
> Any *bon*-nature is mind-nature.
> Dwelling inseparably
> Continuous with that very pith—
> Nonduality of things and mind
> Is called "great bliss itself."

Here we begin to get an inkling of why, in the long run, inferential cognition and the intellect will not be granted the status of an authenticator of *bon*-nature or mind-nature. It is not only that the intellect is by definition dualistic—this does not prevent it from being considered valid in a wide variety of sutric contexts which, like rDzogs chen, ultimately privilege nondualistic cognition of the ultimate—but because this reality, unlike the mere negative (*med dgag*) of classic interpretations of Madhyamaka, is itself multiple. Reasoning by its very structure points to a single focus, not a disparate array of data. Furthermore, some of the intrinsic elements of reality, such as bliss, expansiveness, and clarity, are simply not mates of the intellect but are amenable only to direct subjective experience. In short, there is a dimension to reality that cannot be circumscribed by any amalgamation of information or detail. Totalities might be so reckoned, but not wholeness. Indeed, the *Authenticity's* descriptions of unbounded wholeness celebrate its multiplicity and maintain that open awareness *(rig pa)* experiences this multitudinous yet unified expanse.

Reality, the mind-nature, is here described as an essence whose existence beckons the seeker beyond those kinds of cognitive process. The *Man ngag dam pa gsang sde dam pa* ("Excellent Collection of Essential Precepts") (*Authenticity*: 53) says:

> Clarity dwells amid noncontrivance and nondistraction
> In uncontrived mind-nature.
> No effort, no concepts: clear.
> No reflection, no analysis: naturally placed there.

"Uncontrived" is never an epithet of conceptual thought which, moreover, always involves effort. Subsequently *Authenticity* (56) states that "[The one unbounded sphere] is established by direct perception . . . it is manifest for open awareness which knows it clearly, nonconceptually, and thinglessly." When the prose text resumes, *Authenticity* (53) immediately takes up the question of one's own open awareness and its relationship to authentication:

> Regarding the authenticity of one's own open awareness *(rang gi rig pa'i tshad ma)*, [its] confidence of not contradicting the import *(don, artha)* experienced[21] via external, internal or secret essential precepts[22] in the three times[23] is known as not being separate from spontaneous meditation. In that way, authentic scripture settles the mind-nature through all the words of the tathāgathas.[24]

Essential precepts *(man ngag tshad ma)* are described as "an uninterrupted continuum of experiential essential precepts from one to another" (*Authenticity*: 53). Thus, one's own open awareness is authentic *(rang gi rig pa'i tshad ma)* as well as confident that its realization, unfolding on the basis of essential precepts, in no way contradicts the import of reality. sLob dpon bsTan 'dzin rnam dag notes that here the term *rang gi rig pa'i tshad ma* does not refer to a conceptual awareness, but rather to the inseparability of subject and object. Further authenticating power comes from its being continuously conjoined with spontaneous meditation, meaning it is effortless. Such is the manner of rDzogs chen authenticity (*Authenticity*: 53).

Next, the text (53) turns attention to the matter of authentic reflection (*rig pa'i tshad ma*):

> Regarding authentic reflection, there are two topics: (1) confidence in oneself at the time of practice, which is produced from the mind in practice, and (2) a severing of doubt (*gdar sha gcod*) by a sharp, quick, intellect in the course of debating with an opponent.

Authentic reflection, we now learn for the first time, has two subsets, nonconceptual and conceptual. Thus, the term *rig pa'i tshad ma* is not here identical with the *rang rig pa'i tshad ma* introduced above, which as we noted refers to a nonconceptual state.

Its first division, "a confidence in oneself at the time of practice that is produced from the mind in practice" (*Authenticity*: 53) refers to the nonconceptual awareness arrived at through practice and experience of rDzogs chen. This is *rang rig pa'i tshad ma*, the actual authentic rDzogs chen cognition, which we are now to understand as a subset of the more generic term "authentic reflection."

Such open awareness *(rang rig pa'i tshad ma)* is necessarily an "authentic reflection" but, notes sLob dpon bsTan 'dzin rnam dag, the reverse is not true because authentic reflection can also exist in Madhyamaka. In other words, the direct experience of emptiness discussed in Madhyamaka is also an "authentic reflection," but it is not the "self-authentic open awareness" which rDzogs chen understands as the knowing factor of emptiness itself (and thus not a knower of emptiness as in Madhyamaka). This authentic open awareness, glossed as primordial wisdom *(ye shes),* is the main subject of the *Authenticity*, and likewise of the *bGrags pa skor gsum, Ye khri mtha' sel*, and *Nam mkha' 'phrul mdzod*.

Thus, this first division in the subset of reflective awareness *(rig pa'i tshad ma)* has the same referent as the earlier term, defined above as the spontaneous confidence of not contradicting the external, internal, or secret precepts. However, the second subset here, "a severing of doubt *(gdar sha gcod)* by a sharp, quick intellect in the course of debating with an opponent," refers to a more general form of authentication, which can be either conceptual, much like an inferential consciousness, or nonconceptual. In this way, although the text's use of the term "authenticator" leaves room for the play of conceptuality, this is far from its primary meaning. The most crucial category of authentication, the actual rDzogs chen state of open awareness named in the title of the text, is unambiguously nonconceptual.

This dense but brief section is the most sustained and focused discussion the *Authenticity* provides on its own use of the term *tshad ma*. It is followed by what is perhaps the pivotal thesis of the text (54):

> The *bon* subject (*bon can*), all these, saṃsāra and nirvāṇa, is the primordial ancestor, the great vehicle, unbounded wholeness; this is the thesis, because there are many diverse perspectives.

Thus, the first project of the text is to elaborate how unbounded wholeness, in which open awareness alone authentically participates, does in fact exist, and the types of perception able to observe it. The principal point here is that although unbounded wholeness is not known to ordinary consciousnesses, it is known to yogic direct perception, and that unbounded wholeness itself cannot be described in any one way.

Multiplicity emerges as a crucial factor of unbounded wholeness and this; one important corollary of this view is that authentic open awareness is itself multivalent. We have already learned that this open awareness is not a consciousness according to the *Authenticity* and its sources; this opens the way for it being not merely an awareness, but an emptiness as well. In all these ways the rDzogs chen discussion of authenticity distinguishes itself from other well-known Buddhist discourse. Let us consider briefly how it is at variance with certain classic Mādhyamika presentations.

Comparative Perspectives

Madhyamaka, especially the Prāsaṅgika Madhyamaka made famous by Tsong kha pa and other dGe lugs philosophers, maintains that consciousnesses and other phenomena are one nature (*ngo bo gcig*) with emptiness, but does not consider these to be emptiness themselves. For Madhyamaka a table is empty of inherent existence.[25] The rDzogs chen of the *Authenticity* and related texts (and much of Buddhist rDzogs chen as well, especially that of gLong chen pa) accepts what Madhyamaka has to say about the lack of inherent existence.[26] However, in rDzogs chen the table is empty not primarily because it is unfindable, but because it arises within emptiness. This is rDzogs chen's final view. In other words, rDzogs chen points less to a phenomenon's lack of inherent existence than to its being one in nature with its source, just as a wave arising from water can only be water. This rDzogs chen emptiness is neither a mere negation nor an affirming negative *(med dgag* or *ma yin dgag);* indeed, it is neither a negative nor a positive phenomenon at all. Moreover, to realize such emptiness is not, in rDzogs chen, to realize the actual natural condition (*gnas lugs*).[27] For rDzogs chen, emptiness is beyond mind. It is not an object of knowledge, both because it is beyond mind and in the sense that there is no authentic knower of it other than itself. Thus, the main point of the *Authenticity* is to show that open awareness is authentic. To fulfill its stated purpose of clearing away doubts, the text seeks to distinguish open awareness from consciousness, including the wisdom consciousness that knows emptiness. This crucial point, to which we have already alluded, deserves further attention.

Because the knower which arises on the basis of correct reasoning is a consciousness, it is not the open awareness of rDzogs chen.

Madhyamaka holds that an inferential valid cognition of emptiness can transform into direct knowing, but for rDzogs chen, a consciousness cannot become an open awareness. Moreover, this open awareness, not being a consciousness, is neither subject nor object; it is the base, the natural condition of all things. Not being a consciousness is implicitly a correlate of its being multitudinous, like unbounded wholeness itself, and in this sense uncircum-scribable, indefinite and yet the base of everything.

The *Authenticity's* opening debates reflect on the relationship of unbounded wholeness to appearances, and to various perceptual processes such as ordinary and yogic perception. Subsequently, there is consideration given to whether either appearances or the unbounded sphere can really be described in any definitive manner; this again leads to a consideration of the relationship between mind and the unbounded sphere (*Authenticity*: 62).

In this context, the text reflects on what sort of phenomenon mind-nature and unbounded wholeness might be. Animated by a binary familiar to all students of logic, the text's unnamed interlocutor inquires: Is it permanent or is it impermanent? The opponent wishes to prove the nonexistence of the unbounded by showing that it is neither impermanent, since it is neither consciousness nor materiality, nor permanent.

The *Authenticity*, in its own archetypal kind of move, refuses to be caught in this binary. Its initial response is to inquire into the point of view from which this question is asked. This emphasis on viewpoint is a crucial and elegantly elaborated element in its manner of argument: Is it a question from the viewpoint of the essential base itself *(snying po'i gzhi)*? Or from the viewpoint of that which emerges from the base, its own dynamic display *(rtsal)* (*Authenticity*: 57)? The former is described as the unceasing nature of clarity in consciousness and open awareness, the latter as the spontaneous occurrence of its activities. In brief, the very nature of unbounded wholeness, especially its non-totalizable character, necessitates that the "reasons" establishing it are not bound by a binary structure. Indeed, nothing whatever is contradictory with unbounded wholeness. *Sems nyid me long gi mdzod phug* ("Mirror of Mind-nature Treasure") (*Authenticity*: 55) says:

> Because various diverse appearances
> Always self-rise from the unbounded whole,
> Mind-nature, great pervader of saṃsāra and nirvāṇa,
> Connects through arising with that very thing, that unbounded whole.

This diversity applies even to ontological descriptions. From the viewpoint of its own dynamic display *(rtsal)*, it is an impermanent thing *(dngos po)*. At the same time, it is also described as a non-thing *(dngos med)* and thus permanent; from the viewpoint of its own essence, it is changeless and ceaseless. The inability, and non-necessity of "resolving" any such contradiction is itself part of the dynamic nature of unbounded wholeness.

Such characterizations of unbounded wholeness represent what E. F. Schumacher (12 and 125) called a "divergent" problem, one which cannot be resolved because the more information you have about it, the more divergent description becomes. This is the type of "problem" which is not capable of solution, and thus never "dies" as an issue, whereas convergent problems, in which more information leads to a greater convergence of perspective, become lifeless; they are finished when they become contained or bounded by the parameters which emerge through research or reflection. This is clearly not the case with unbounded wholeness. We might also consider that in Buddhism and Bon generally, the "problem" of saṃsāric energies is not capable of solution, but only of active, ongoing transformation or liberation. These are persistent forces that do not resolve, or die simply through becoming fixed in understanding. As there is no "solution" available through logic, there can only be a living response to ongoing complexities that cannot possibly, by their very nature, resolve.

This crucial theme of the nature of reality and its relation to other phenomena and various types of knowing recurs in different forms throughout *Authenticity*. The way in which this conundrum is neither resolved nor unresolved but, to coin a phrase, a-resolved is key to the character of rDzogs chen logic and overall perspectives. For example: Are appearances the uncontrived body of *bon*-nature *(bon sku)*? If so, then *bon*-nature unacceptably takes on the qualities of appearances. Or, if assimilation runs in the other direction, appearances either unacceptably become attributes of the body of *bon*, or do not actually exist, or the assertion of their existence is redundant because they are merely the body of *bon*. Likewise, "if the mind is one with the object, then just as the object is material, so mind would also be material. Or, just as the object can be destroyed by the seven fires and one flood, so the mind too can be destroyed" (*Authenticity*: 65). Having sprung these seeming paradoxes on the reader, the text (*Authenticity*: 66) offers poetic a-resolution of these impossibilities prior to its own prose articulation of the matter, quoting the *Nam mkha'i ye srid gyi rgyud* ("Primordially Occurring Sky Tantra"):

> Since *bon* body is the world and its inhabitants
> Why would it not arise and cease?
> Since appearances are the mind itself
> Why would they not be conscious and aware?
> Since one's own mind is appearance
> Why would it not be a material thing?

In these and other ways, unbounded wholeness is shown to hold in harmony what other systems might call contradictions. The device of allowing a multiplicity of perspectives is crucial in setting the terms of the *Authenticity.* It is this above all which supports the principle of wholeness, a theme that pervades the entire text.

Although at various junctures in the text unbounded wholeness, like the emptiness of Madhyamaka, is described in terms of what it is not, the text never rests with this but moves on to show that inclusion of various viewpoints, rather than the elimination of all of them, is its way of understanding reality. The strategy of employing reasoning without engaging the kind of binary structure on which classic reasoning is premised becomes a major challenge faced by this text. Whereas in Madhyamaka logic the challenge is often framed as the paradox of seeking to express the inexpressible, or to stake a philosophical claim without using a thesis in the usual sense, here the deepest structural challenge is the mandate to express a wholeness from which, by definition, nothing can be excluded and to express it through words and reasonings which, by their very nature, always exclude something. The very structure of the text parallels the conundrum faced by the rDzogs chen practitioner who, using tools constructed along the binary of subject and object, must simultaneously break both those tools and the delusion they would disarm. Hence, again, the impossibility of any resolution that depends strictly on reasoning, or on consciousness.

Or, to put this another way, the challenge of both text and practice is to reconcile multiplicity with the enduring nature of reality. "The *bon*-nature, heart of the ascertained base, is utterly unchanging; yet many appearances arise from the base" (*Authenticity*: 62). Only rDzogs chen is deemed capable of this task; the lower eight vehicles are like "blind persons [who] designate various names to the body of the sturdy elephant, but the elephant itself does not become altered in any way" (*Authenticity*: 63). In certain contexts, the text is quite willing to clearly state a position;[28] however, when it comes to descriptions of reality, the vanishing of definitive description is the divergent, vitalizing conundrum that can only be liberated, never resolved. *Authenticity* (74) cites *Ye srid rnam gsum gyi mdo* ("Sūtra on the Three Aspects of the Primordial"):

> Enlightenment-mind, essence of everything,
> Mother-basis, self-risen primordial wisdom,
> Things absent, open awareness present,
> Not indefinite, spontaneously changeless and ceaseless.

No ultimate exists apart from the immediacy of unbounded everything, though this is not obvious to untrained and inauthentic perception.[29] Hope of liberation—from the bonds of reasoning as well as from other prosaic thought forms— invites both meditative inspiration and poetic intercession.

Notes

1. *Blissful Manner* is not mentioned in any catalogue known to this writer, and sLob dpon bsTan 'dzin rnam dag—whose knowledge of Bon rDzogs chen literature is encyclopedic—has never seen it. Nor has he seen most of the over one hundred poetic tantric texts cited throughout *Authenticity.*

sLob dpon bsTan 'dzin rnam dag has generously provided much oral commentary for the points discussed in this section; most of this was given during meetings in July 1998 at Sunrise Springs, New Mexico, and February, 1999 at his monastery in Kathmandu, Nepal.

I am currently completing a six-chapter introduction and annotated translation of *Authenticity* in collaboration with Geshe Tenzin Wangyal Rinpoche, "Unbounded Wholeness: Bon and the Logic of the Nonconceptual, Text and Context of 'The Authenticity of Open Awareness, a Collection of the Essential Reasonings.'"

That study, like the present article, owes much to my training with Professor Hopkins, as it comes full circle from my dissertation, published as *Knowledge and Liberation* and directed with great care by him, which examined the dGe lugs pa Sautrāntika premise that conceptual thought is not only itself valid but a vital causal condition for valid direct perception.

2. The title is given as *gTan tshigs gal mdo rig pa'i tshad ma* in the edition published by bsTan 'dzin rnam dag. Samten Karmay gives the title of this work in the *bsGrags pa skor gsum* as: *Sems nyid rdzogs chen gyis tshad ma gtan tshigs sgra don gtan la dbab pa (Catalogue,* no. 54, section 48, p. 102). Reconstructing the date of this work is a complex task, one that we begin to address in the above-mentioned manuscript.

3. The descriptions which follow are taken from discussions with sLob dpon bsTan 'dzin rnam dag at his monastery, Khri rtan nor bu rtse, in Kathmandu, Nepal, August, 1997.

4. As David Ruegg (1989: 106) observes, Sa skya mchog ldan makes an analogy between the *ku sā li pa* and the practice of stabilizing meditation or *'jog sgom* (which Ruegg terms "Fixation-bhāvāna"). He also makes an analogy between the *paṇḍita* and analytical meditation or *dpyad sgom* (which Ruegg translates as "Inspection-bhāvāna").

5. The term *'dzo* refers to a yogi. Thanks to Dan Martin on this point.

6. *sNgon 'gro*. These are often referred to as "preliminary" practices. Although this translation is literally correct, it is extremely misleading, as the practices in this category are retained throughout one's life as a basis for all other practice. They are not "preliminary" in the sense of being discarded for "higher" practices.

7. *Gang zag spros pa la dga' ba mkhas pa paṇḍita'i lugs tshul.*

8. sLob dpon bsTan 'dzin rnam dag, whose oral communication is the source of this paragraph, underscored his point by telling of conversations with two prominent lamas in the dGe lugs and bKa' brgyud traditions with whom he discussed his monastic college's nine-year curriculum. Seeing that two years were allotted to rDzogs chen, they both, in independent conversations, felt that this was too long, that there was not so much need to study in the rDzogs chen context.

9. According to comments of sMan ri Abbot Lung tog bsTan pa'i Nyima, Sunrise Springs, New Mexico, July, 1997. For a listing of the eighteen abbots of g.Yas ru dben sa kha, see Dagkar: 142, n. 8.

10. Founded in the Tsang Province of Tibet and destroyed by flood in 1386 and subsequently rebuilt. See bsTan 'dzin rnam dag: 25. For the background of this monastery and a detailed description of the present-day curriculum at Dolanji, see Cech: *passim*.

g.Yas ru dben sa kha successively produced eighteen learned scholars, the most illustrious being mKhas pa dByar mo thang ba (b. 1144) and 'A zha blo gros (1198-1263) (Cech: 6).

11. Of course there is every possibility that logic and debate came into further ascendancy because of Bon competitiveness with Buddhists.

12. This monastery is said to have been founded by Sangs rgyas 'phel (1411-1485) (Tucci, II: 642). If all these dates are correct, we are left to wonder what occurred during the approximately 50 year period between the g.Yas ru dben sa kha fire and the founding of sKyed tshal. To my knowledge, Bon narratives make no mention of this hiatus.

13. One branch of the Sa skya monastery is quite close to the present g.Yung drung gling, which latter can be seen today as one heads west on the southern route toward Shigatse from Lhasa (comments of sLob dpon bsTan 'dzin rnam dag, Sunrise Springs, New Mexico, 1998).

14. Which means "Fortunate Medicine Mountain."

15. For an account of this event, see Shardza: 142ff.

16. During the last century, nine other Bon monasteries established schools of dialectics (Cech: 7).

17. Wholeness, in his view, consists of intertwined pattern-flows, whereas a totality is a collection of discrete objects.

18. Comments of sLob dpon bsTan 'dzin rnam dag at Khri rtan nor bu rtse, Kathmandu, August, 1997.

19. If, as Bon traditions claim, the *Authenticity* was actually written in the eighth century, this would explain its lack of self-consciousness about Buddhist rationalistic hegemony. The dating of this work is an extremely complex matter that cannot occupy us here, but an attempt to come to terms with this is made in chapters I-III of *Unbounded Wholeness* (Klein: n.d.).

20. Gloss by sLob dpon bsTan 'dzin rnam dag.

21. Here a footnote from the *Authenticity* itself says: "realized."

22. Here a footnote from the *Authenticity* itself says: "of the nine [vehicles]."

23. Here a footnote from the *Authenticity* itself says: "with effortful purpose" *(ched du mi rtsol)*.

24. There is an important difference between establishing the view *(lta ba grub)* and realizing it *(lta ba rtogs)*. Thus, words and concepts are a valid way of establishing the view, but not a valid way of realizing it. In rDzogs chen, words can establish the view of what *rig pa* is, but cannot manifest experience of it.

25. These comparisons are drawn largely from discussions with sLob dpon bsTan 'dzin rnam dag.

26. See, for example, Hopkins, 1983 and 1989.

27. Distinctions between Madhyamaka and rDzogs chen are discussed in further detail in Klein, n.d.

28. For example (*Authenticity*: 64), "According to the Mind Nature of Great Completeness system, objects are not included within mind .... Objects are not destroyed or altered by mind or awareness, therefore this is not like the Ceaseless Changeless Ones [followers of Madhyamaka]."

29. For more on the theme of singleness as contrasted with sutric presentations of the two truths, see Klein and Wangyal: 780-788.

References

Anon.

BCSG *Byang chub sems gab pa dgu skor*. Delhi: Tibetan Bonpo Monastic Centre, 1967.

Anon.

DCGK *rDzogs chen bsGrags pa skor gsum*. Delhi: Tibetan Bonpo Monastic Centre, 1973

Anon.
TRNG *Theg pa'i rim pa mngon du bshad pa'i mdo rgyud kyi 'grel ba 'phrul gyi me long dgu skor.* Dolanji, India: Tibetan Bonpo Monastic Centre, 1978.

Anon.
YKTS *Ye khri mtha' sel.* Bonpo canon, 2nd reprint. Vol. 101. Also, India: Tashi Namdak, n.d.

bsTan 'dzin rnam dag
YBDT *g.Yung drung bon gyi bstan pa'i 'byung khungs nyung bsdus.* Kathmandu: Bönpo Foundation, n.d.

Cech, Krstyna
1984 *The History, Teaching, and Practice of Dialectics According to the Bön Tradition.* Solan, India: Hill Star Press for Yungdrung Bön Monastic Centre.

Dagkar, Geshi Namgyal Nyima
1994 "The System of Education in Bonpo Monasteries from the Tenth Century Onwards." In *Tibetan Studies: Proceedings of the 6th Annual Seminar of the International Association for Tibetan Studies,* ed. Per Kvaerne, vol. 1. Oslo: Institute for Comparative Research in Human Culture.

Dreyfus, Georges
1997 *Recognizing Reality.* Albany, NY: State University of New York Press.

gShen lha 'od skar
TRNS *Theg pa'i rim pa mngon du bshad pa'i mdo rgyud.* Dolanji, India: Tibetan Bonpo Monastic Centre, 1974.

Hopkins, P. Jeffrey
1983 *Meditation on Emptiness.* Boston: Wisdom Publications.
1989 "A Tibetan Delineation of Different Views of Emptiness in the Indian Middle Way School: Dzong-kha-pa's Two Interpretations of the *Locus Classicus* in Chandrakirti's *Clear Words Showing Bhāvaviveka's Assertion of Commonly Appearing Subjects and Inherent Existence*" in *Tibet Journal,* 14(1): 10-43.

Karmay, Samten G.
1977 *A Catalogue of Bonpo Publications.* Tokyo: Tōyō Bunko.

Klein, Anne
1986 *Knowledge and Liberation.* Ithaca, NY: Snow Lion Publications.
n.d. "Unbounded Wholeness: Bon and the Logic of the Non-Conceptual, Text and Context of "The Authenticity of Open Awareness, a Collection of the Essential Reasonings." Unpublished ms.

Klein, Anne and Geshe Tenzin Wangyal Rinpoche

1995 "Bon and the Logic of the Non-Conceptual: Preliminary Reflections on *The Authenticity of Innate Awareness (gTan tshigs gal mdo rig pa'i tshad ma)*." In *Asiatische Studien/ Études asiatiques*, 49(4): 769-792.

Levin, David Michael

1988 *The Opening of Vision: Nihilism and the Postmodern Situation*. New York and London: Routledge.

Li shu stag ring

TTGD *gTan tshigs gal mdo rig pa'i tshad ma*. Delhi: Tenzin Namdak, 1972.

Ruegg, David Seyfort

1989 *Buddha-nature, Mind and the Problem of Gradualism in a Comparative Perspective: On the Transmission and Reception of Buddhism in India and Tibet*. London: University of London, School of Oriental and African Studies.

Schumacher, E. F.

1977 *A Guide for the Perplexed*. New York: Harper & Row.

Shardza Rinpoche

1972 *The Treasury of Good Sayings: A Tibetan History of Bön*. Trans. and ed. Samten G. Karmay. London Oriental Series, vol. 26.

Tucci, Giuseppe

1948 *Tibetan Painted Scrolls*. 3 vols. Rome: Libreria dello Stato.

Wangyal, Nyima Tenzin

KTNB *Khri brtan nor bu rtse dang bon po'i lo rgyus*. Kathmandu: Triten Norbutse Bon Education Centre, n.d.

Wangyal, Tenzin

1993 *Wonders of the Natural Mind*. Barrytown, NY: Station Hill Press.

Chapter 7

The dGe ldan–bKa' brgyud Tradition of Mahāmudrā

How Much dGe ldan? How Much bKa' brgyud?[1]

Roger R. Jackson

Introduction

Mahāmudrā (Tibetan *phyag rgya chen po*), translated variously as "the great seal," "the great symbol" or "the great gesture," is probably best known as the name of an integral system of radical meditative practices central to the bKa' brgyud tradition of Tibetan Buddhism. Transmitted by such great masters as Tilopa, Nāropa, Maitrīpa, Mar pa, Mi la ras pa, sGam po pa, Karma pa Rang 'byung rdo rje, bKra shis rnam rgyal, and Padma dkar po, bKa' brgyud Mahāmudrā may generally be characterized as "the realization of the true nature of the mind. [It is] both an ordered series of practices and meditations, and the awakened state of enlightenment to which they lead" (Kalu: 197). The term *mahāmudrā* actually has considerably greater scope than this, however: not only is it found with a variety of usages throughout the literature of Indian Buddhist Vajrayāna, it also plays a more or less prominent role in the other traditions of Tibetan Buddhism, the dGe lugs, Sa skya, and even the rNying ma. For a term of such critical importance—it arguably has a place in Tibetan Buddhism comparable to that of *Chan/Zen* in Sino-Japanese traditions—Mahāmudrā has received surprisingly little scholarly attention. A significant number of

Mahāmudrā manuals have been translated (e.g., Evans-Wentz: 101-154; Chang: part I; Beyer: 154-161; Wang-ch'ug; Namgyal; Gyaltsen; Nyima; Rangdrol; Kongtrul; Situpa), but few include serious scholarly apparatus, and critical, historically sophisticated attempts to unravel the complexity and ambiguity of the tradition as a whole have been limited primarily to the works of Herbert Guenther (1963: 222-235, 1969, 1972), David Seyfort Ruegg (1966: 58, n. 2, 1988, 1989), Michael Broido (1984, 1985, 1987) and David Jackson (1990, 1994). These scholars have made ground-breaking contributions, but much remains to be done before we can claim to have a clear picture of the history and meaning of Mahāmudrā.

Here, I want to focus on a tradition of Mahāmudrā interpretation and practice found in a Tibetan school more often noted for gradualist scholasticism than for radical meditative practices, namely, the dGe lugs (which alternatively is known as the dGa' ldan or the dGe ldan). For all the voluminousness of dGe lugs literature, there exists in addition to the written tradition an important dGe lugs "ear-[whispered] transmission," the dGa' ldan *snyan brgyud* (or *rgyud*), named for the first and most important dGe lugs monastery. Not surprisingly, this *snyan brgyud* is traced to the tradition's founder, Tsong kha pa Blo bzang grags pa (1357-1419), who is said to have received it, via direct revelation, from Mañjuśrī, who had in turn received it from the buddha Vajradhāra. Perhaps the most important, though by no means the only, teaching in the dGa' ldan *snyan brgyud*, is of a dGe lugs tradition of Mahāmudrā. Though supposedly having its human origin in Tsong kha pa, the dGe lugs Mahāmudrā tradition apparently was not written down until the time of the First Paṇ chen Lama, Blo bzang chos kyi rgyal mtshan (hereafter: Chos rgyan, 1570-1662), who composed a brief (197-line) verse text on Mahāmudrā, the *rGyal ba'i gzhung lam* (*GBZL*; trans. Dalai Lama and Berzin: 97-102) and a prose commentary upon it (in thirty-seven folios), the *Yang gsal sgron me* (*YSGM*).[2] Chos rgyan's texts, in turn, have been commented upon at some length by later dGe lugs pas, right down to the present day. A number of brief traditional accounts of the practice have been published (First Paṇ chen; Gyatso; Rabten: part 3; Willis, 1985, 1995: 111-124), but historical-critical scholarship remains rare, limited to brief references by several historians with other interests (e.g., Karmay; D. Jackson, 1994; Seyfort Ruegg, 1989), and the more specialized study on the tradition's biographies published by Janice D. Willis (1985, 1995). Recently, the Fourteenth Dalai Lama and Alexander Berzin have published a detailed analysis of the practice (Dalai Lama and Berzin), based primarily upon two sets of discourses on the topic delivered in the late 1970s and early 1980s by the Dalai Lama; the book lacks scholarly apparatus, but reflects the Dalai Lama's broad and incisive knowledge of Tibetan Buddhist literature.

Within the scope of the whole history of Mahāmudrā, the dGe lugs tradition is, admittedly, a late and marginal development. There are, however, certain advantages to belatedness and marginality, not the least of which is an ability to look back over the developments and debates that have come before, and to attempt to arrive at some sort of summing up. Indeed, Chos rgyan and his dGe lugs successors have interesting things to say about a number of historical and practical issues in Mahāmudrā exegesis, including controversies over the existence of a Sūtra- or Pāramitā-level Mahāmudrā, the relative order of tranquillity (*śamatha*) and insight (*vipaśyanā*) in Mahāmudrā meditation, the soteriological value of various contemplations of the nature of mind, and the unity or diversity of purport among the different traditions of Mahāmudrā practice.

Here, I will focus on one issue that, while primarily a matter of intra-dGe lugs debate, has wider implications for a history of Tibetan Buddhism. The issue, quite simply put, is: Is dGe lugs Mahāmudrā actually a combined "dGe ldan–bKa' brgyud" tradition, or is it a dGe lugs tradition pure and simple? The question is in some ways a technical one, turning in part, as we shall see, on the syntactical interpretation of the titles of Chos rgyan's Mahāmudrā texts—but it is by no means trivial, for it has direct ramifications not only for our understanding of how dGe lugs pas have viewed themselves in relation to other Tibetan schools, but also for our understanding of the ways in which influences work and are explained by orthodox Tibetan traditions. In modern terms, the issues raised are those of syncretism and ecumenism. In what follows, I will examine the question of whether there is a combined dGe lugs–bKa' brgyud Mahāmudrā tradition from three viewpoints: (1) a survey of the dGa' ldan *snyan brgyud*, especially of the influences on and writings of its major transmitters; (2) the debate over the *name* of the tradition, centering on the meaning of the titles of Chos rgyan's two works on Mahāmudrā; and (3) the contents of Chos rgyan's two texts on Mahāmudrā, as compared to those of representative bKa' brgyud texts. I will return to those broader questions of syncretism and ecumenism in my conclusion. The corpus under consideration is vast, and my observations, based on a necessarily selective reading of it, are tentative. Nevertheless, I hope they may suggest some useful conclusions, both about the dGe lugs school in particular, and about inter-sectarian issues in Tibetan Buddhism in general.

The Ear-whispered Transmission of dGa' ldan

The first place we might look for evidence for or against the idea that there exists a combined dGe lugs–bKa' brgyud tradition of Mahāmudrā is in the lives and writings of the members of the lineage of masters, the *bla ma brgyud pa,* of the dGa' ldan Ear-whispered Transmission (*snyan brgyud*). Our major sources of information about the history of this tradition are a number of texts by Tshe mchog gling Yongs 'dzin Ye shes rgyal mtshan (1713-1797), most notably the *sNyan rgyud lam bzang gsal ba'i sgron me* (*NGLZ*) and the *Byang chub lam gyi rim pa'i bla ma brgyud pa'i rnam par thar pa rgyal bstan mdzes pa'i rgyan mchog phul byung nor bu'i phreng ba* (*NBPB*).[3] Here, as so often where oral transmissions are involved, there is a discrepancy between the tradition's claims and the overt historical evidence. As indicated above, the tradition maintains that the teaching has its origins in the buddha Vajradhāra, who transmitted it to the bodhisattva Mañjuśrī, who in turn revealed it to Tsong kha pa, founder of the dGe lugs. Tsong kha pa transmitted the tradition to his disciple rTogs ldan 'Jam dpal rgya mtsho (1356-1428), from whom it passed to Ba so rje Chos kyi rgyal mtshan (1402-1473), Grub mchog Chos kyi rdo rje (late fourteenth–early fifteenth century), dBen sa pa Blo bzang don yod grub pa (1505-1566), mKhas grub Sangs rgyas ye shes (1525-1591), and Chos rgyan, the First Paṇ chen Lama (1570-1662) (e.g., *NGLZ*: 214-231; Gyatso: 11; Willis, 1995: 7 *et passim*).[4] These masters received the transmission sometimes through oral teachings from their gurus, sometimes through visionary revelation, and sometimes through reading a "magical book" (*sprul pa'i glegs bam*) in which instructions were contained. Chos rgyan, who appears to be the first to *write* about the tradition, transmitted it in turn to two major disciples, Grub chen dGe 'dun rgyal mtshan and Blo bzang brtson grus rgyal mtshan, each of whom founded a stream of the teaching. Those two streams—transmitted throughout dGe lugs pa establishments in Tibet—eventually were reunited in the early twentieth-century master rJe btsun 'Phrin las rgya mtsho, better known as Pha bong kha Rin po che (1871-1941), from whom it has devolved to the present lineage-holders.

The lineage just described, the "near lineage" (*nye brgyud*) proceeding on the human plane from Tsong kha pa, is the most often cited, but it is supplemented by a "distant lineage" (*ring brgyud*) of those masters preceding Tsong kha pa. The distant lineage (*NGLZ*: 212-214) also begins with Vajradhāra, who is said to have transmitted the teaching to the bodhisattva Vajrapāṇi, who passed it on to the first human teacher, Saraha. Saraha transmitted it to Nāgārjuna, and the two of them passed it on to Śrī Śavaripa. From Śavaripa, the lineage descended in two streams, which were reunited in the great translator Mar pa. The first stream went from Śavaripa to Lūipa, Ḍārikapa, lDing kaṃ pa, Tilopa, Nāropa, and Mar pa, the second from Śavaripa to Maitrīpa to Mar pa. Mar pa transmitted Nāropa's six topics (*chos drug*) related to advanced tantric practice, as well as Maitrīpa's tradition of Mahāmudrā, to Mi la ras pa. From Mi la ras pa, it passed through a succession of Dwags po bKa' brgyud pa masters to the great 'Bri khung abbot sPyan lnga Chos kyi rgyal po, who taught it to Tsong kha pa, most likely in the form of the Fivefold teaching (*lnga ldan*), on *bodhicitta*, self-generation as the deity, *guru yoga*, Mahāmudrā, and dedication of merit (Roerich: 506; Thurman, 1982: 7, 12).[5]

Tsong kha pa also received Mahāmudrā-related transmissions from two disciples of the great Bu ston rin chen grub, namely, Khyung po lhas pa—who was expert in the Guhyasamāja and Heruka *tantras* (Roerich: 1074; Thurman, 1984: 70; but cf. Thurman, 1982: 15f.)—and the great Kālacakra adept Chos kyi dpal pa (Roerich: 794, 1075; Thurman, 1982: 14f.); and two Sa skya pas, Chos rje Don grub rin chen (Roerich: 1075ff.; Thurman, 1982: 6f.)—who was well-versed in the meditative traditions derived from Virūpa and 'Brog mi—and Red mda' ba, from whom Tsong kha pa gained much of his exposure to the traditions of Madhyamaka and the Guhyasamāja tantric corpus (Thurman, 1982: 7ff.). Since these latter topics are believed by dGe lugs pas to be crucial aspects of, respectively, Sūtra and Tantra-Mahāmudrā,[6] it is tempting to speculate that Tsong kha pa's principal human guru for the ideological framework of the dGe lugs Mahāmudrā tradition was Red mda' ba, while his principal human guru for the specific meditations that go under the name of Mahāmudrā probably was sPyan lnga Chos kyi rgyal po and/or dBu ma pa—though this conclusion must remain uncertain.

The long and short lineages we have just reviewed would seem at first to be in contradiction, the former suggesting human sources for Tsong kha pa's teaching of Mahāmudrā, the latter insisting that it derives from divine revelation. I think the contradiction can be resolved simply enough by suggesting that Tsong kha pa's human teachers provided him with the *elements* of his Mahāmudrā teaching, while Mañjuśrī provided him with the explanation that integrates the various elements. The resolution of the contradiction, however, begs certain questions that a historian is bound to ask. The most important of them is this: Granted, there is evidence that Tsong kha pa received Mahāmudrā and Mahāmudrā-related teachings at various times during his life; is there, on the other hand, any evidence that he actually taught the Mahāmudrā tradition enshrined in the dGa' ldan *snyan brgyud*? We are, obviously, face to face with a paradox, because a *snyan brgyud* is an ear-whispered transmission, not written down. Nevertheless, we might expect to find in Tsong kha pa's writings some sort of reference to Mahāmudrā *as an integral system of meditation,*[7] which would, in turn, hint at the existence of the teaching credited to him by later members of the *snyan brgyud*.

From a conscientious but by no means complete survey of Tsong kha pa's writings, it appears that he does *not* anywhere set forth Mahāmudrā as an integral system of meditation. Certainly, he discusses the Madhyamaka view that is at the heart of Sūtra-Mahāmudrā in many places (see, e.g., Thurman, 1982, 1984); and in his various tantric treatises and commentaries he mentions the place of "*mahāmudrā*" vis-à-vis other *mudrās* in the various classes of Tantra, analyzes the bliss-void gnosis (*bde stong dbyer med kyi ye shes*) that the *snyan brgyud* says is synonymous with Tantra-Mahāmudrā, and identifies the supreme achievement of the tantric path as the *mahāmudrāsiddhi* (see, e.g., Tsong-ka-pa, 1977, 1981: *passim;* Mullin: 127, 139, 158). This is not the same, however, as setting forth the integral system of Mahāmudrā meditation that later dGe lugs pas include in the *snyan brgyud*. Ye shes rgyal mtshan maintains (*NGLZ*: 218-219) that Tsong kha pa addressed issues of Mahāmudrā in several question-and-answer (*dri lan*) texts, but the quotes he furnishes make no explicit mention of Mahāmudrā, and Tsong kha pa's authorship of at least one of the texts, the *Dri ba lhag bsam rab dkar*, has been disputed, e.g., by Thu'u bkwan Chos kyi nyi ma (*GTSM*: bKa' brgyud 25a). Indeed, the quotes furnished by Ye shes rgyal mtshan make it clear that if Tsong kha pa did have a Mahāmudrā teaching, he deliberately chose not to write it down.[8] We might want to argue that the content of a dGe lugs Mahāmudrā oral tradition would not, in any case, be found in Tsong kha pa's writings, but might be hinted at in his own or others' accounts of his visionary encounters with Mañjuśrī—this, after all, is the source of the "near lineage" usually cited as the most important line of *snyan brgyud* transmission. Here, too, however, we are disappointed, for Tsong kha pa's own references to his visions (e.g., Thurman, 1982: 40-46) are indirect, and accounts by his biographers, not only by such early chroniclers as his disciple mKhas grub rje dGe legs dpal bzang po, but also by such later writers as Ye shes rgyal mtshan (Thurman, 1982: 4-34, *NGLZ*: 214-218), speak at length of Mañjuśrī's revelation of Madhyamaka, but not specifically of a Mahāmudrā tradition.[9] None of this should be taken to mean that Tsong kha pa did not teach a dGe lugs Mahāmudrā system—only that textual evidence for his having done so is belated and circumstantial.

We might turn next to the lives and writings of Tsong kha pa's first five successors in the *snyan brgyud*, rTogs ldan 'Jam dpal rgya mtsho, Ba so Chos kyi rgyal mtshan, Chos kyi rdo rje, dBen sa pa don yod grub pa and mKhas grub Sangs rgyas ye shes. I have not surveyed the complete works of these masters, but those that I have, and the titles supplied in the indexes to their *gsungs 'bums* as collected by Klong rdol bla ma (Chandra: vol. III), as well as quotations from their works embedded in later texts, give no indication that they *wrote* anything about a dGe lugs Mahāmudrā system. Chos rgyan himself composed at least two works on the lives of his lineage predecessors (e.g., *KGYT*), which quote their writings often, and make frequent references to a *snyan brgyud* descending from Tsong kha pa—but the lineage as he describes it is not exactly the same as the one analyzed by Ye shes rgyal mtshan, nor evidently a repository of Mahāmudrā teachings.[10] Ye shes rgyal mtshan quotes dBen sa pa's praise for an ear-whispered transmission that is the essence of Tsong kha pa's teachings (*NGLZ*:

225)—but the passage makes no mention of the content of the transmission. dBen sa pa's disciple (and Chos rgyan's guru) Sangs rgyas ye shes, wrote a short text on the "oral transmission" (*bka' brgyud*) of dBen sa pa, but the work is a *guru yoga* ritual, with no mention of Mahāmudrā (*CWSY* I: 91-95).[11] In short, there is good evidence that by the time of dBen sa pa (early sixteenth century), there was awareness of a *snyan brgyud*, but the writings of Chos rgyan's predecessors, while replete with discussions of *guru yoga*, show no indication of a systematic Mahāmudrā teaching. Indeed, we must remember that among the biographies of Tsong kha pa's immediate successors in the *snyan brgyud*, those most prone to seeing Mahāmudrā in the lineage (e.g., those of Ye shes rgyal mtshan) were not written before the late eighteenth century, so *their* specification that the content of the *snyan brgyud* was "instructions on Mahāmudrā" (*phyag rgya chen po'i gdams ngag*) cannot be regarded as completely reliable evidence, since they presuppose the existence of the tradition we are seeking to establish.[12]

Interestingly, only two pre-Chos rgyan dGe lugs pa writers appear to have discussed Mahāmudrā at some length: the tutor of the Second Dalai Lama, mKhas grub Nor bzang rgya mtsho (1423-1513), and the great scholar Paṇ chen bSod nams grags pa (1478-1554). Nor bzang's *Phyag chen gsal sgron* (*PCSG*)[13] is a descriptive account of the system of early bKa' brgyud Mahāmudrā. It is structured according to categories favored by bKa' brgyud pas, most notably gradualist (*rim gyis pa*) and simultaneist (*cig car pa*) practitioners, making no mention of the Sūtra-Mahāmudrā/Tantra-Mahāmudrā distinction basic to the dGe lugs *snyan brgyud* system. Nor bzang's text focuses primarily on tantric practices, and while its analysis closely resembles accounts of Tantra-Mahāmudrā in the dGe lugs *snyan brgyud*, it cannot be seen as an exposition of an independent dGe lugs Mahāmudrā system (see *PCSG*; also, *GTSM*: bKa' brgyud: 24a). bSod nams grags pa's text, the *gSang ba'i 'dus pa'i mdzub khrid phyag rgya chen po la rgyan drug tu mdzad pa'i rnam bshad*, is so far unavailable to me. Its title hints that the Mahāmudrā with which it is most concerned may be related to the teachings of the Guhyasamāja tantra-cycle and hence, like Nor bzang's text, quite different in its predominant emphasis from the *snyan brgyud* version of Mahāmudrā.[14] Still, an analysis of its contents would provide much useful information on early dGe lugs pa views of Mahāmudrā. Prior to Chos rgyan, then, there is some evidence that there was a self-conscious *snyan brgyud*, and some evidence of dGe lugs pa writers focusing on Mahāmudrā, but virtually no textual evidence that the *snyan brgyud* centered on Mahāmudrā—though certainly any tradition derived from the eclectically educated Tsong kha pa would contain the *elements* out of which a Mahāmudrā tradition might be constructed.

It is with Chos rgyan, then, that we come to the first dGe lugs pa to write about an integral system of Mahāmudrā practice. As we have seen, Chos rgyan makes a few references to a dGa' ldan *snyan brgyud*: he and his biographers make it clear that he was inspired by the life and example of dBen sa pa, the first to publicize the *snyan brgyud* (*NGLZ*: 226), and that he may even have been dBen sa pa's reincarnation (Willis 1995: 85). In his Mahāmudrā texts, he credits his teacher, Sangs rgyas ye shes, with transmitting the tradition to him (*GBZL*: 4a; trans. Dalai Lama and Berzin: 100; *YSGM*: 30b), and describes the tradition as that of Dharmavajra, father and son, i.e., Chos kyi rdo rje and dBen sa pa (*GBZL*: 1b; trans. Dalai Lama and Berzin: 97; *YSGM*: 1b). This would take the lineage (at least of the Mahāmudrā teaching) back to the late fourteenth or early fifteenth century—though not to Tsong kha pa himself. We cannot and should not discount Chos rgyan's claim that the lineage of Mahāmudrā practice precedes him by several generations, but, as we have seen, there is little textual evidence for such a claim. Whether or not Chos rgyan was the originator of the dGe lugs Mahāmudrā tradition, he was the first to expound it publicly and in detail. While some instruction on Mahāmudrā may have come from his predecessors, it is by no means unreasonable to suggest that Chos rgyan drew upon his own experience and reading as well, so it is perhaps worthwhile to seek at least some of the sources of the dGe lugs Mahāmudrā system in his own life and work.

Chos rgyan lived a long and active life (see, e.g., Tucci: I, 131f.; Kanakura: ix, 297-313; *AFPL*: Introduction; Willis, 1995: 85-96, 207-223; Shakabpa: 97-119; Cabezón), receiving his foundational education at bKra shis lhun po, but traveling later through much of Tibet, receiving teachings from a variety of lamas—and, of course, going on himself to become a scholar, diplomat, poet, and major preceptor of the Fourth and Fifth Dalai Lamas; it was the latter who designated him as the first "Paṇ chen Lama."[15] He does not seem to have had any major bKa' brgyud pa teachers, and yet:

(a) he lived in the next generation after an extraordinary efflorescence of bKa' brgyud Mahāmudrā thought, (b) he received his education in a part of Tibet (gTsang) that was under strong bKa' brgyud (especially Karma pa) influence, (c) his biographers state that he desired at various times to emulate Mi la ras pa and Śavaripa or adopt only the cotton garments prescribed by bKa' brgyud tradition (*NGLZ*: 227; Willis, 1995: 90),[16] and, most importantly, (d) there is ample evidence from his Mahāmudrā texts that he was quite familiar with bKa' brgyud literature—especially the writings of the "early" (*gong ma*) bKa' brgyud masters. The source of this familiarity is unclear. Chos rgyan clearly knew of the first dGe lugs pa to write on Mahāmudrā, mKhas grub Nor bzang rgya mtsho, but the one quotation from Nor bzang in his Mahāmudrā texts (*YSGM*: 25b-26a) is not from the *PCSG*, and there is very little overlap in citations—and virtually none of Tibetan sources—between Nor bzang's text and Chos rgyan's, making it uncertain whether he ever read the *PCSG*, and highly unlikely that he derived his understanding of bKa' brgyud from it.[17] It is conceivable that Chos rgyan extracted his bKa' brgyud citations from other, non-Mahāmudrā-related dGe lugs pa texts, but in the absence of such texts, it is perhaps most plausible to suggest that he derived them from actual bKa' brgyud texts—whether those of the early masters he most often quotes or of later systematizers who incorporate passages from the earlier masters, perhaps from reading the great bKa' brgyud pas themselves.

Was dGe lugs Mahāmudrā, then, original with Chos rgyan? He himself, and the chroniclers of the *snyan brgyud* who succeeded him, assure us that the answer is no. Such claims should not be taken lightly, and cannot be disproved, but the "paper trail" that the historian is bound to follow would seem to point to something like the following hypothesis: Chos rgyan, educated as a dGe lugs pa but deeply appreciative of bKa' brgyud traditions learned either through their preservation in dGe lugs teachings or, more likely, directly from bKa' brgyud pa texts, worked out most of the dGe lugs Mahāmudrā practice *himself*, combining various elements of his broad and sympathetic reading and learning into a unique system that knew no real precedent in the dGe lugs tradition. No doubt *a* dGa' ldan *snyan brgyud* preceded and was transmitted to Chos rgyan, and he may well have received elements of his Mahāmudrā system from the dGe lugs pa predecessors whom he so generously credits, but there is little textual evidence that the major content of the *snyan brgyud* he received was, as later chroniclers would insist, Mahāmudrā; the evidence seems to point to Chos rgyan himself as the main originator of the Mahāmudrā tradition. Even if this hypothesis is correct, of course, the fact that Chos rgyan was sympathetic to and learned in the bKa' brgyud tradition does not, *ipso facto*, guarantee that the Mahāmudrā tradition he founded is, in fact, a combined dGe lugs–bKa' brgyud system, the question with which I am centrally concerned. It is on this question that we will focus in the remainder of the paper, first by discussing possible interpretations of the name Chos rgyan gave to his tradition, then by examining the contents of his system for similarities to and differences from bKa' brgyud Mahāmudrā.

The Name of the Tradition

As hinted earlier, the titles of Chos rgyan's two texts on Mahāmudrā permit at least two competing answers to the question whether the system he founded was a combined dGe lugs–bKa' brgyud Mahāmudrā tradition. The full title of the root-verses he composed on Mahāmudrā is *dGe ldan bka' brgyud rin po che'i phyag chen rtsa ba rgyal ba'i gzhung lam*: "The Essential Path of the Victors: The Root-Text for the Mahāmudrā of the Precious *dge ldan bka' brgyud*." The auto-commentary to the root-text is entitled *dGe ldan bka' brgyud rin po che'i bka' srol phyag rgya chen po'i rtsa ba rgyas par bshad pa yang gsal sgron me*: "Lamp So Bright: An Extensive Explanation of the Root-Text of the Mahāmudrā Oral Tradition of the Precious *dge ldan bka' brgyud*." The ambiguous phrase, *dge ldan bka' brgyud*, may mean either "dGe lugs–bKa' brgyud," with *bka' brgyud* referring to the name of a school; or, alternatively, "the dGe lugs oral transmission," with *bka' brgyud* referring not to the name of a school, but simply to a lineage of orally transmitted teachings—as, e.g., Sangs rgyas ye she's reference to an dBen sa *bka' brgyud*. Quite obviously, the former reading suggests that Chos rgyan believed his tradition to be a combined dGe lugs–bKa' brgyud lineage, the latter that he considered it exclusively dGe lugs.

Two translations of the *rGyal ba'i gzhung lam* issued in the last quarter-century make it clear from their titles and their texts that their authors regard dGe lugs pa Mahāmudrā as a combined tradition. The 1975 Library of Tibetan Works and Archives translation

(First Paṇ chen) is entitled *The Great Seal of Voidness: The Root-Text for the Ge-lug/Ka-gyu Tradition of Mahamudra*, while the more recent account by the Fourteenth Dalai Lama and Alexander Berzin (1997) is entitled *The Gelug/Kagyü Tradition of Mahamudra*. In each case, not only the title of the text, but the one passage in the root-text (*GBZL*: 1b; also *YSGM*: 1b) that refers to the *dga' ldan bka'-brgyud*—*legs par 'doms mdzad dge ldan bka' brgyud pa* ("the well-instructed *dge ldan bka' brgyud pa*")—is taken to refer to a combined tradition (First Paṇ chen: 3; Dalai Lama and Berzin: 97), even though the line retains the same ambiguity as to the meaning of *dge ldan bka' brgyud* as does the text's title. We might expect that Chos rgyan's auto-commentary would shed light on the issue; unfortunately, he merely remarks that "[b]ecause it is not difficult to understand the meaning of [the foregoing], I will not write about it in detail" (*YSGM*: 2a-2b).

When we arrive at the significant commentarial literature on Chos rgyan's Mahāmudrā system, we have traversed nearly a century since the First Paṇ chen's time, and so must be wary of any claims in the literature to expose Chos rgyan's "true purport." What we find, in fact, is virtually no indication that dGe lugs pas of later centuries considered the Mahāmudrā tradition to be a combined one. The first great commentator, Ye shes rgyal mtshan (1713-1797), refers not to a *dge ldan bka' brgyud* Mahāmudrā tradition, but to a *dga' ldan phyag rgya chen po'i khrid*, i.e., a dGe lugs Mahāmudrā teaching (*NGLZ*: 201). Gu ge Blo bzang bstan 'dzin (b. 1748) also refers to it as the *dga' ldan phyag rgya chen po*, and gives an elaborate gloss on the term *bka' brgyud* to the effect that the tradition was developed by Chos rgyan "according to the *word* of Tsong kha pa" (*rje bla ma'i* bka' *bzhin du*) and was an instruction in the "ear-whispered *transmission*" (*snyan* brgyud; note the variant spelling, *brgyud*) (*CTNG*: 17). Similarly, dNgul chu Dharmabhadra (1772-1851) glosses the line from Chos rgyan's root-text thusly: "The heart or essence of [the sūtras and tantras] having all been WELL collected, it was made into the INSTRUCTION, the uncommon ORALLY-descended TRANSMISSION of Mount dGe ldan" (*NKZB*: 9).[18] Finally, Ke'u tshang Blo bzang 'jam dbyangs (eighteenth-nineteenth century) specifies that the *dge ldan bka' brgyud*, i.e., the dGe ldan pa oral transmission (*bka' brgyud*) descending from Tsong kha pa, is the general subject of Chos rgyan's text, while the particular subject is the instruction on Mahāmudrā, the uncommon oral tradition of Chos kyi rdo rje, father and son (*NGKG*: 18). It is interesting that Ke'u tshang makes a distinction between the dGa' ldan *bka' brgyud* in general and a Mahāmudrā teaching in particular: this lends support to my earlier contention that the dGe lugs *snyan brgyud* probably antedates the dGe lugs Mahāmudrā tradition with which it eventually is identified, though the more important point for our purposes here is that it demonstrates the virtual unanimity with which later commentators consider the dGe lugs Mahāmudrā tradition to be a dGa' ldan oral transmission rather than a combined dGa' ldan-bKa' brgyud practice.[19]

The commentaries we have just examined do not specifically debate whether there exists a combined dGe lugs–bKa' brgyud Mahāmudrā tradition; they announce their negative decision indirectly, through their glosses on Chos rgyan's root-text. Evidence that such a debate must have occurred, however, may be gleaned from another eighteenth-century dGe lugs work, the great history of the Tibetan schools—the *Grub mtha' shel gyi me long* (*GTSM*) of Thu'u bkwan Blo bzang chos kyi nyi ma (1737-1802; see Kapstein, 1989). In his chapter on the bKa' brgyud, Thu'u bkwan discusses a number of controversial issues regarding Mahāmudrā in general and the relation between dGe lugs and bKa' brgyud in particular. Most importantly for us, he asks the question: Do the bKa' brgyud and dGe lugs have the same purport? He cites a critique of Nor bzang rgya mtsho by a renegade student of 'Jam dbyangs bzhad pa named Blo bzang rin chen. Nor bzang had insisted in his *Phyag chen gsal sgron* that the Mahāmudrā systems of the early bKa' brgyud pas—especially the White Self-sufficient Simple (*dkar po gcig thub*) of Zhang Tshal pa—were fully Mahāyāna practices, and also in conformity with the tradition of Saraha (see *PCSG:* 10-12). Blo bzang rin chen takes Nor bzang's real point to be a demonstration that Mahāmudrā has the same purport as the teachings of Tsong kha pa, and ridicules the idea, citing familiar Sa skya pa critiques of the White Self-sufficient Simple. Thu'u bkwan is highly critical of Blo bzang rin chen, insisting that he has misrepresented Nor bzang's position (and, for that matter, the title of his text), which is *not* an attempt to argue that the dGe lugs and bKa' brgyud have the same intention. He adds, however, that there exists not the slightest disagreement between the early Mahāmudrā practices described by Nor bzang and Tsong kha pa's teaching—thereby implicitly endorsing the idea that dGe lugs and bKa' brgyud *do* have the same intention (*GTSM*: bKa' brgyud 23a-24a).

Thu'u bkwan further (*GTSM*: bKa' brgyud 24b-25a) criticizes Blo bzang rin chen for his attack on Chos rgyan's view that the various traditions of Mahāmudrā, as well as the Madhyamaka and the rNying ma Great Perfection, all have a single intention (*GBZL*: 2b; trans. Dalai Lama and Berzin: 98; *YSGM*: 12a). Blo bzang rin chen was not alone among dGe lugs pas in his rejection of this ecumenical stance: the Fifth Dalai Lama, Chos rgyan's disciple, was sympathetic to the Great Perfection, but was critical of Chos rgyan's interest in bKa' brgyud pas and their doctrines, while the Third Paṇ chen Lama, Blo bzang dpal ldan ye shes, who is a member of the dGe lugs Mahāmudrā lineage, argued that the Great Perfection was inferior to the other traditions listed (Dalai Lama 1984: 205) (whereas Blo bzang rin chen believed it superior). Thu'u bkwan further strengthens his ecumenical credentials by questioning the attribution to Tsong kha pa of a question-and-answer text, the *Dri ba lhag bsam rab dkar*, that is severely critical of the bKa' brgyud and Mahāmudrā (*GTSM*: bKa' brgyud 25a). It should be noted that while these passages from Thu'u bkwan demonstrate that there was a great deal of intra-dGe lugs discussion about the school's relationship to other traditions, and while we probably can conclude that Thu'u bkwan himself believed that the dGe lugs and bKa' brgyud have the same purport, they do not provide any evidence that Chos rgyan's Mahāmudrā system actually was a combined dGe lugs–bKa' brgyud tradition—at best, they show that at least some dGe lugs pa thinkers saw no contradiction between early bKa' brgyud Mahāmudrā traditions and the teachings of Tsong kha pa. This is a far cry, however, from maintaining that the dGa' ldan *snyan brgyud* is actually a deliberately syncretic tradition.

Still, if there is little positive evidence that Chos rgyan regarded his Mahāmudrā system as a combination of dGe lugs and bKa' brgyud, the issue cannot be considered closed. The present Dalai Lama has insisted that the tradition *should* be regarded as a dGe lugs–bKa' brgyud syncretism, because (a) while the view of reality presented in the tradition is uniquely that of Tsong kha pa, the tradition of Guhyasamāja interpretation that underlies the tantric portion of the system was received by Tsong kha pa via the bKa' brgyud (Dalai Lama and Berzin: 169-170); (b) Chos rgyan's account of Mahāmudrā, while clearly indebted to Tsong kha pa, also owes a great deal to earlier bKa' brgyud traditions of explanation (233, 234); and (c) the Fifth Dalai Lama's critique of mixing with bKa' brgyud pas is an indication that that is exactly what his guru, Chos rgyan, must have been attempting (232-233). The possibility thus is left open that Chos rgyan *did* intend to describe his system as a joint one. One other small piece of evidence—albeit circumstantial and grammatical—may be adduced at this point: the title of Chos rgyan's auto-commentary already refers to a "Mahāmudrā oral tradition" (*phyag rgya chen po bka' srol*); thus, if the *bka' brgyud* of *dge ldan bka' brgyud* meant "oral transmission," it would be redundant. Hence, it must refer to the school, the bKa' brgyud.

Probably, we never shall know exactly what Chos rgyan meant by the expression *dge ldan bka' brgyud*, but one more perspective on the relationship between dGe lugs and bKa' brgyud in his system—indeed, the most important of all—is provided by at least a brief examination of the contents of his text, and it is to an analysis of Chos rgyan's Mahāmudrā system, in comparison with those of certain bKa' brgyud pas, that we now turn.

dGe lugs and bKa' brgyud Presentations of Mahāmudrā

We cannot possibly enter here into all the details of Chos rgyan's Mahāmudrā system, let alone compare it responsibly with the vast and varied body of bKa' brgyud literature on Mahāmudrā. Nevertheless, we may be able to gain some sense of the relative mix of dGe lugs and bKa' brgyud elements in his system by briefly considering five topics and his treatment of them: (1) the sources he quotes, (2) his position on the question whether there is a sūtra-level Mahāmudrā, (3) his ordering of the stages of Mahāmudrā meditation, (4) the procedures he outlines for tranquillity meditation (*śamatha*) and (5) the procedures he outlines for insight meditation (*vipaśyanā*). Since it is Chos rgyan's own intentions that we are seeking to discern, we will largely ignore the commentarial literature, and focus our attention on Chos rgyan's own two texts on Mahāmudrā. The major bKa' brgyud sources we will use are from the generation immediately preceding Chos rgyan: bKra bshis rnam gyal's *Zla ba'i 'od zer* (Namgyal), dBang phyug rdo rje's *Phyag chen ma rig mun gsal* (Wang ch'ug), and Padma dkar po's *Lhan cig skyes sbyor 'khrid yig* (Beyer) and *Phyag chen zin bris* (Evans-Wentz).

Chos rgyan's Textual Citations

Even a cursory examination of Chos rgyan's auto-commentary reveals how conversant he was with bKa' brgyud literature, and how influenced by that literature he must have been in formulating his Mahāmudrā system. Of the slightly more than one hundred quotations or citations in the text, approximately half are from Indian sources and half from Tibetan sources. Of those from Indian sources, roughly a quarter are from texts or persons that figure prominently in the Mahāmudrā lineage preserved in Tibet by the bKa' brgyud, most notably Saraha, who is cited eleven times. More impressively, of the citations from Tibetan sources, nearly two-thirds are from the bKa' brgyud: Mi la ras pa is quoted nine times, Zhang Tshal pa four times, and 'Bri gung pa 'Jigs rten mgon po, Phag mo gru pa, Yang dgon pa and Gling ras pa twice each, just to name the most frequently cited. By comparison, among non-bKa' brgyud pas, Sa skya paṇḍita is cited seven times, Atiśa five times and—surprisingly—Tsong kha pa only four times.

As noted briefly above, the vast majority of the bKa' brgyud pas cited by Chos rgyan belong to what he and other dGe lugs pas refer to as the "early bKa' brgyud" (*gong ma bka' brgyud*), those seminal figures who first received teachings from India and established the great bKa' brgyud lineages and monasteries. In spite of the fact that bKa' brgyud pas in the generation immediately preceding Chos rgyan had produced a tremendous amount of literature on Mahāmudrā, he ignores them almost entirely, focusing his attention instead on the masters of centuries past. Why is this so? One possibility is that he was unaware of the efforts of his contemporaries. Certainly, he makes no specific acknowledgment of their work, yet he does make occasional oblique references to contemporaneous bKa' brgyud practices (e.g., *YSGM*: 20a) and, as we shall see, the structure of his text seems to have been influenced by the general style of Mahāmudrā manuals produced in the immediately preceding generation. In fact, it is likely that Chos rgyan was aware of some, if not all, of the recent bKa' brgyud literature on Mahāmudrā, but did not cite it explicitly because (a) at least part of his purpose was to establish that there is a convergence of the "stages of the path" (*lam rim*) tradition so important to the dGe lugs and the Mahāmudrā tradition so central to the bKa' brgyud, and it is in the ancient antecedents of the two modern schools—with Atiśa for the *lam rim* and the early bKa' brgyud pas for Mahāmudrā—that such a convergence is to be found (*YSGM*: 3b-4a); and (b) there were both views and practices among contemporaneous bKa' brgyud pas with which he probably disagreed, and emphasizing such disagreements would both involve him in scholastic disputes beyond the purview of a meditation manual and undercut one of his central theses—the *commonality* of such various traditions as Mahāmudrā, rDzogs chen and Madhyamaka (*YSGM*: 12a).

As noted earlier, we do not know whether Chos rgyan found his quotations from the early bKa' brgyud masters in the original texts themselves or in some more recent compendium, but the number and importance of those quotations would have to be counted as evidence for the idea he was attempting to combine dGe lugs and bKa' brgyud, much in the same way, perhaps, that sGam po pa, the fountainhead of Dwags po bKa' brgyud, had combined the *lam rim* (or "stages of the teaching" [*bstan rim*]) tradition of the bKa' gdams pas with the Mahāmudrā tradition received from Mar pa and Mi la ras pa.

Sūtra- and Tantra-Mahāmudrā

Probably the most hotly debated issue in Mahāmudrā exegesis in Tibet was whether or not there existed a sūtra-based tradition of Mahāmudrā practice in addition to the obviously tantric practices in connection with which the term generally had been used in India. The idea that there existed such a Sūtra- (or Pāramitā-) Mahāmudrā tradition seems to derive from the great systematizer of the early bKa' brgyud, sGam po pa (1079-1153), who believed that the Mahāmudrā connected with advanced tantric practice (the *saṃpannakrama*, or *upāyamārga*) was suitable only for simultaneous practitioners, *cig car pas*, while the Sūtra-Mahāmudrā was suitable for even the most dull-witted gradual practitioner (*rim gyis pa*) (Roerich: 459-460, 724-725; Broido, 1985: 12-13; D. Jackson, 1994: 14-37).[20] The tradition further developed that this Sūtra-Mahāmudrā was equivalent to Madhyamaka—whatever that meant—and that it was expressed most perfectly in the *Ratnagotravibhāga Mahāyānottaratantra śāstra* (see Roerich: 724-725; Seyfort Ruegg, 1988; Broido, 1985, 1987). It is important to note that for many bKa' brgyud pas there is no essential difference between the results of Sūtra- and Tantra-Mahāmudrā practice; it is only the methods that differ (Seyfort Ruegg, 1988: 1261; Broido, 1985: 16) The methods of Sūtra-Mahāmudrā center around a direct realization of the mind's true nature; the methods of Tantra-Mahāmudrā are based, as we might expect, on the six topics of Nāropa. This distinction of methods, it should be added, is not always maintained faithfully: not only do bKa' brgyud pas tend to frame their discussions of Mahāmudrā more along the lines of the gradualist-simultaneist division than the Sūtra-Tantra division, but there is no one-to-one correspondence between gradualism and Sūtra on the one hand and simultaneity and Tantra on the other, and—most importantly—mind-realization practices with no explicit link to the six topics of Nāropa often are regarded as tantric.

The idea that there could exist a Mahāmudrā outside the tantric context, let alone that it could issue in the same result as advanced tantric practice, was severely criticized by Sa skya paṇḍita, who insisted in his *sDom gsum rab dbye* that Mahāmudrā (a) must be considered primarily as an *achievement*, the result of a path rather than a technique on the path, and (b) must be preceded by empowerment (*abhiṣeka*). As a consequence, he regarded bKa' brgyud Mahāmudrā systems of his own time—especially the *dkar po gcig thub* of Zhang tshal ba and the *dgongs gcig* of 'Bri gung pa—to be the discredited Chinese *hva shang* quietism in disguise (*DSRB*: 315ff.; *TGRS*: 24-26; see also R. Jackson, 1982; D. Jackson 1990, 1994). Later bKa' brgyud pas expended considerable ink in the attempt to defend their doctrine from Sa skya paṇḍita's attacks, pointing out the many ways in which it differed from the *hva shang* doctrine (Namgyal: 105ff.; Broido, 1987) and providing evidence that Mahāmudrā had a much broader meaning than that assigned to it by Sa skya paṇḍita (Namgyal: 124).

It is quite evident from both the content and structure of his work that Chos rgyan essentially sides with the bKa' brgyud on the question of the legitimacy of a Sūtra-Mahāmudrā. Not only does he criticize Sa skya paṇḍita for his partiality (*YSGM*: 35a-35b), but he cites with approval both 'Bri gung pa 'Jig rten mgon po and 'Gos lo tsa ba gZhon nu dpal in their insistence that Mahāmudrā is to be found at all levels of the path, from the most elementary to the most advanced (*YSGM*: 5a-6a). Chos rgyan states quite explicitly that there are two divisions of Mahāmudrā practice, Sūtra and Tantra (*GBZL*: 2a; trans. Dalai Lama and Berzin: 98; *YSGM*: 6a), and he divides the main portion of his text into a brief analysis of Tantra-Mahāmudrā and a considerably longer discussion of Sūtra-Mahāmudrā. Thus, he is in general accord with the bKa' brgyud pas, over against the Sa skya pas, that there do exist both a Sūtra-Mahāmudrā and a Tantra-Mahāmudrā.

We will analyze the contents of Chos rgyan's version of Sūtra-Mahāmudrā shortly, but it should be noted with regard to his version of Tantra-Mahāmudrā that it differs from that of the bKa' brgyud in at least two ways: First, it is demarcated from the Sūtra-Mahāmudrā more sharply than by the bKa' brgyud pas, who, as noted above, sometimes seem to conflate the two systems and disassociate the concepts of gradual and simultaneous practice from specific relation to one or the other system. For Chos rgyan, on the other hand, (a) the gradual and simultaneous practices are closely aligned with Sūtra and Tantra levels of practice, respectively; (b) Tantra-level meditations *always* are preceded by empowerment and entail meditations within the subtle body like those prescribed in the six topics of Nāropa; and (c) it is *only* through completing the *saṃpannakrama* of an Anuttarayoga Tantra that buddhahood can be achieved; thus, the Sūtra-Mahāmudrā can be neither conflated nor confused with the tantric level, for there is a clear difference in practice and a clear difference in the result. In this latter, at least, Chos rgyan is aligned with Sa skya paṇḍita, for though he rejects the latter's narrow interpretation of the term *mahāmudrā*, he does maintain that the tantric system is separate and superior. Second, Chos rgyan and subsequent dGe lugs pas specify that tantric Mahāmudrā is practiced through *saṃpannakrama* yogas originating with such "Mother Tantra"-rooted traditions as the "inner fire" (*gtum mo*) meditation (one of the six topics of Nāropa), or the generation of the gnosis of inseparable bliss-void (*bde stong dbyer med kyi ye shes*), which are well known to bKa' brgyud pas.[21] Nevertheless, they differ subtly from bKa' brgyud pas in their understanding of these practices: dGe lugs pas interpret virtually every *saṃpannakrama* practice—even those developed in Mother Tantras—through the five-stage yoga articulated in the Guhyasamāja (a Father Tantra) literature (with Tsong kha pa's exposition being the most influential), whereas bKa' brgyud pas rely more on structures suggested by the Mother Tantras themselves. This—in addition to certain differences in the interpretation of Madhyamaka, to be noted below—will lead to variations in the interpretation of such crucial terms as *sahaja* and *yuganaddha*—and even *saṃpannakrama* itself, hence to subtle disagreements in reading such seminal texts as the *Dohās* of Saraha (Broido, 1985: 30f.). Regardless of these differences, however—and Chos rgyan alludes to neither of them—the central point of this analysis is that Chos rgyan is closely aligned with the bKa' brgyud in his view of the scope and divisions of Mahāmudrā.

The Ordering of Tranquillity and Insight

Though the terms "tranquillity" and "insight" are not always explicitly worked into accounts of Mahāmudrā meditation by the early bKa' brgyud pas, they are central elements of the accounts of those later systematizers who closely preceded Chos rgyan, such as dBang phyug rdo rje, bKra bshis rnam rgyal and Padma dkar po. All of them agree that there are two possible orderings of tranquillity and insight, and that the system in which insight comes first is the more advanced, and the system in which tranquillity has precedence is the more elementary. All of them order their texts for the elementary practitioner, hence describe tranquillity first, then insight (e.g., Namgyal: 143f.). By and large, the practices that are included under tranquillity involve bringing the mind to one-pointedness through a progressive series of ever-more finely attenuated concentrations, starting with visual objects, and moving from there to other sensory objects, the breath and—finally—the mind itself, which is gradually brought to perfect tranquillity. The practices that are included under insight are quite various, but tend to involve analyses of the nature of that mind that has been brought to tranquillity—e.g., in terms of its movement or rest, its materiality or immateriality, its oneness or multiplicity, its ultimacy or non-ultimacy—followed by a nondual realization of the mind exactly as it is, a stage that is beyond meditation in the usual sense of the word.

Chos rgyan, too, divides his account of Sūtra-Mahāmudrā into the practices of tranquillity and insight—though it should be noted in passing that he ignores other important bKa' brgyud ways of ordering Mahāmudrā, such as the triads of view, meditation and action; and ground, path and goal. He also specifies that there are two traditions for ordering tranquillity and insight, and that he will follow that in which tranquillity comes first (*GBZL*: 2b; trans. Dalai Lama and Berzin: 98; *YSGM*: 14b); unlike his bKa' brgyud predecessors, however, he does not specify which type of practitioner practices in which order, for, as we have seen, Chos rgyan takes the terms "gradual" and "simultaneous" practitioner to demarcate Sūtra- from Tantra-Mahāmudrā, not those who practice tranquillity first from those who practice insight first. Generally,

Chos rgyan's assignment of various practices as conducing to tranquillity or insight also is similar to that of his immediate predecessors in the bKa' brgyud: tranquillity *begins* with the mind as object, and proceeds through various stages of calming until one-pointed fixation upon the mind's aware, clear nature is attained; insight begins with an analysis of the nature of the meditator and of the mind, and proceeds to a nondual experience of the mind's void nature.

We will examine particular differences between Chos rgyan's and bKa' brgyud accounts of tranquillity and insight in the following two sub-sections. Here let us simply note generally that Chos rgyan seems to have more rigid standards for what may be classified as "insight" than do some bKa' brgyud pas, especially his contemporaries. First, the examination of the moving and abiding mind, which is taken by most bKa' brgyud systematizers to be part of insight (Wang-ch'uk; Beyer, 1974: 159), is included by Chos rgyan as an aspect of tranquillity (*YSGM*: 15b). Further, one of the techniques apparently taken by many of Chos rgyan's bKa' brgyud pa contemporaries to be an advanced stage of insight, namely, "settling gently, without grasping, on whatever appears," is regarded by Chos rgyan as "only the best method of accomplishing mental stabilization in a beginner," a technique that "identifies only the superficial mind" whose nature is awareness and clarity (*GBZL*: 3a-3b; trans. Dalai Lama and Berzin: 99; *YSGM*: 20a). The technique criticized here is not dissimilar to methods, listed without comment in the section on insight, that will be discussed below. These and other subtle differences in assignment indicate that Chos rgyan upholds a typically strict dGe lugs standard for what counts as insight into the ultimate: if it does not conduce directly to a realization of voidness—rather than some *conventional* nature of an object—a practice cannot count as ultimate insight, though it may aid in tranquillity, or in understanding conventionalities. This disagreement with his contemporaries notwithstanding, we see that Chos rgyan's ordering and distribution of tranquillity and insight is generally quite similar to that of the bKa' brgyud tradition of his own time.

Tranquillity

When we examine the particular sequence of practices that Chos rgyan includes in his section on tranquillity (*GBZL*: 2b-3b; trans. Dalai Lama and Berzin: 98-99; *YSGM*: 15a-19b; cf. Dalai Lama and

Berzin: 130-142, 272-290), we find that much of his material is like that found in bKa' brgyud texts. The sequence he establishes is as follows: after seating oneself and purifying via the "nine-round breathing," one should go for refuge and generate *bodhicitta*, then engage in *guru yoga* practice. At the point where, following repeated requests, one's guru is visualized as dissolving into oneself, one actually begins tranquillity meditation. One first abides in a nonconceptual, uncontrived, contentless state that nevertheless is *not* unconsciousness; then, applying mindfulness (*dran pa*) and alertness (*shes bzhin*) against wandering thoughts, one gazes intently at the aware, clear conventional nature of mind. Thoughts are to be cut off either by noting them as mere thoughts or by suppressing them. When some stability on the aware, clear nature of mind has been established, then one should relax one's effort somewhat: conceptualizations are permitted to arise, but when they do, one's continued, natural mindfulness and awareness assure that they will dissipate on their own, leaving a clear vacuity. This observation of the nature of arising thoughts is termed "the mixture of abiding and movement." The mind that has achieved equipoise (*samāpatti*) on the aware, clear nature of mind is "like clear, empty space," without the slightest trace of form, and anything that arises within it similarly is to be seen as beyond designations such as "existent" or "nonexistent," without form, and space-like.

Most of the techniques organized thus by Chos rgyan are found in bKa' brgyud Mahāmudrā literature, too, and the bKa' brgyud pas have in most cases derived them from Indian antecedents. The emphasis on suppressing thought through the application of mindfulness and alertness is rooted in the Maitreya-Asaṅga tradition common to both dGe lugs and bKa' brgyud, while the methods of alternately tightening and loosening the mind, of mixing awareness of abiding and movement, and of remaining space-like in clear awareness, all can be found in the writings of such *mahāsiddhas* as Saraha, Maitrīpa, Śavaripa, and others (Namgyal: *passim*). Not only are the elements chosen by Chos rgyan securely grounded in bKa' brgyud literature; his particular ordering of it is generally like that of bKra shis rnam rgyal (Namgyal: 146-174), and even more, quite similar to that of Padma dkar po, who also—once he begins his discussion of mind as the object of Mahāmudrā meditation—describes a procedure that moves from the suppression of thought to its allowance, to an alternation of tightening and loosening and abiding and movement, and issues in a nondual, nonconceptual, space-like state (Evans-Wentz: 128-135; Beyer: 157-159). This does not demonstrate that Chos rgyan derived his discussion of tranquillity from Padma dkar po or some other bKa' brgyud pa predecessor; it does suggest, however, that whatever the specific sources Chos rgyan may have used, both the elements and ordering of his section on tranquillity do have strong precedents in bKa' brgyud tradition—and these precedents may not be entirely coincidental.

Though there are considerably more similarities than differences between Chos rgyan's and at least some bKa' brgyud accounts of Mahāmudrā tranquillity meditation, it ought to be recollected that there are differences, too. First, as noted above, some of what is considered by certain bKa' brgyud pas to be a part of insight meditation is regarded by Chos rgyan as falling more properly under the rubric of tranquillity. Second, his specification of awareness and clarity as the two characteristics of mind on which one one-pointedly fixates does not really convey the range of characteristics that one encounters in the bKa' brgyud literature. dBang phyug rdo rje, for instance, stresses three characteristics: bliss, clarity, and nonconceptuality (Wang-ch'uk: 62), and it might not be far-fetched to suggest that Chos rgyan's neglect of the characteristic of bliss may have something to do with a sense that this is a term more properly reserved for a tantric context. Third, his insistence that the various experiences he classifies as tranquillity only relate to the conventional nature of the mind, not its ultimate reality (*dharmatā)*, is somewhat at variance with the bKa' brgyud tendency not to distinguish so strictly. Where Chos rgyan is careful to treat "mere" references to nonconceptuality or clarity as referring to the mind's conventional nature, many bKa' brgyud pa writers take them as indicating its ultimate nature (see especially Namgyal: chs. 6, 8), and hence as in some sense related to insight.

Insight

If his section on tranquillity has more similarities to than differences from equivalent bKa' brgyud accounts, Chos rgyan's section on insight (*GBZL*: 3b-5a; trans. Dalai Lama and Berzin: 99-101; *YSGM*: 20a-35b; Dalai Lama and Berzin: 143-165, 297-345) is the reverse: it only superficially resembles bKa' brgyud accounts and is, in the final analysis, the most unequivocally dGe lugs section of the text. Since it comprises nearly half of Chos rgyan's text, we can only summarize it in the most general terms here. Chos rgyan first outlines five bKa' brgyud methods for "determining the basic root of mind," i.e., (1) seeking the mind within or without, or in arising, abiding, or ceasing, (2) seeking the mind in materiality, (3) settling in uncontrived awareness in the present, (4) observing the nature of whatever object arises, and (5) allowing images to arise and pass freely into "self-liberation." Neither criticizing nor endorsing these techniques (but cf. *GBZL*: 3a-3b; trans. Dalai Lama and Berzin: 99), Chos rgyan goes on to spell out his own "essential" method for gaining insight. In an actual meditation session, this involves, first of all, analyzing whether the meditator who has achieved tranquil equipoise actually can be found in an ultimate sense. Seeking the meditator both within and apart from the various elements, one encounters the meditator nowhere; seeking ultimacy in phenomena (*dharmas*), one encounters it nowhere. Thus, one comes to abide in a space-like awareness of the void nature of both the person and *dharmas*. Next (or, alternatively) one examines more carefully whether the mind itself can be found in an ultimate sense: it is discovered to have the conventional nature of a flow of awareness and clarity, but no ultimacy, no true existence. In short, one should recognize that any existent that arises, whether an object of the mind or the mind itself, is merely conceptual, is void and—as Chos rgyan quotes his guru, Sangs rgyas ye shes, as saying—"When . . . you are equipoised one-pointedly on that, marvelous!" (*GBZL*: 4a; trans. Dalai Lama and Berzin: 100; *YSGM*: 30b). In the period between meditation sessions (*rjes thob*), one should see all appearances as deceptive (*sgyu ma*), as existing differently than they appear, but one must at the same time recognize that their ultimate voidness does not preclude their conventional functioning, any more than conventional functioning gives them true existence.

There is little in this general account that would not find acceptance by a bKa' brgyud pa: certainly bKa' brgyud pas will deny as readily as dGe lugs pas that an ultimately existent person can be found either identical to or different from that person's parts, and they also will insist that, as surely as entities may be reduced to mind, so mind, too, ultimately is void. It is when one begins to examine Chos rgyan's emphases and his particular terminology—especially in his commentary—that the idiosyncratically dGe lugs nature of his account of insight begins to emerge. In terms of his emphases, we already have seen that he mentions, but does not specifically endorse, a variety of bKa' brgyud methods of "determining the root-basis of mind," most of which center on taking the present ordinary mind as equivalent to the enlightened mind. These methods, while grounded in statements by either the *mahāsiddhas* or early bKa' brgyud masters, may, if taken out of context, lead to mistaking the conventional for the ultimate: it is for this reason that later dGe lugs pas (e.g., Thu'u bkwan) criticized the practices, and it may be for this reason that Chos rgyan does not pattern his system upon them. Indeed, the technique of "settling, without grasping, on whatever appears," whose relegation by Chos rgyan to the rubric of tranquillity we already have noted, bears a more than passing resemblance to the five techniques listed at the beginning of his section on insight. In passing over these techniques, Chos rgyan ignores an element of Mahāmudrā considered crucial by many later bKa' brgyud pas. Lhalungpa goes so far as to say that what is unique about Mahāmudrā is precisely its "extraordinary theory that an individual's 'ordinary mind' represents his original stream-consciousness, defined as being an unaltered natural state. [T]he ordinary mind is identified with a pure and valid perception regarded as natural enlightenment and usually called 'Buddha-nature'" (Namgyal: xxxviii-xxxix).

What Chos rgyan *does* emphasize in his section on insight is the sort of analysis of the person and the mind that was central to the dGe lugs version of Madhyamaka, in which a great deal of attention is paid to identifying the object of refutation (*dgag bya*), all entities are said to exist only nominally (*ming tsam*), no entity is truly existent (*bden par grub pa*), and voidness and dependent origination not only do not negate each other, but are mutually implicative. The language Chos rgyan uses, though only moderately technical, is still quite specific to the dGe lugs. His analysis of an object's "modes" of appearing, apprehension, and abiding; his discussion of "nominal" existence; his mention of a "generic image" of voidness that is a "non-affirming negation"; his refutation of particular versions of Madhyamaka that either over- or under-specify the degree of sentient beings' delusion; and his strong insistence on the perfect complementarity of emptiness and dependent origination—all these are quite particularly dGe lugs, and cannot really be understood without a familiarity with dGe lugs thought. Indeed, they differ from the standard, non-*snyan brgyud* dGe lugs treatment of voidness meditation (see, e.g., Hopkins, 1983, 1987) only in their focus on the mind as the main meditative object.

It is hardly surprising that it is in the area of insight—or correct view—that Chos rgyan's text emerges as least bKa' brgyud and most dGe lugs, for—political differences aside—it is on the level of correct view, especially on the interpretation of Madhyamaka, that Tibetan schools tend to have the most serious disagreements. They may all agree on the greatness of Nāgārjuna, and assert with equal conviction that all entities are void by nature—but what this means is a subject of almost limitless wrangling. Some of it is no doubt scholastic hair-splitting, but much of it is crucial: such questions as the role of rationality in insight, the relation between the conventional and the ultimate levels of truth, and the type of negation involved in voidness, all are questions of considerable philosophical import—and of course they are of philosophical import because they touch, finally, on the great issues of bondage and liberation. We have not the space here to examine the ways in which the dGe lugs differed from the bKa' brgyud—let alone from other schools. Suffice it to say that dGe lugs pas and bKa' brgyud pas criticized each other on all of the questions of correct view that we have just listed, and others besides (Williams; Broido, 1985; Seyfort Ruegg, 1988), and that the differences between them, while pointedly *not* emphasized by Chos rgyan, nevertheless subtly determined the shape he gave his account of insight, so that we may conclude that that account may superficially resemble bKa' brgyud accounts, but is fundamentally dGe lugs in its choices of topic and terminology.

An analysis of the structure and contents of Chos rgyan's system of Mahāmudrā, then, reveals that there are elements in it that are borrowed from the bKa' brgyud pas and elements that are idiosyncratically dGe lugs. While the "heart" of the system—insight meditation—is clearly dGe lugs, the system as a whole shows enough bKa' brgyud influence that we cannot determine on the basis of the texts themselves whether Chos rgyan explicitly set out to create a combined dGe lugs–bKa' brgyud tradition.

Conclusion

What conclusions emerge from our investigation?

First, though one always must be cautious and respectful when the claims of oral tradition are involved, the *textual* evidence we have examined seems to indicate that (a) Chos rgyan himself probably worked out the *systematization* of the dGe lugs system of Mahāmudrā meditation himself, based primarily on his own wide and sympathetic reading in both bKa' brgyud and dGe lugs texts; (b) it is not impossible that he also was the system's originator, though it is perhaps likelier that he received the basic elements of a Mahāmudrā tradition from his guru as part of a dGa' ldan *snyan brgyud*; and (c) the *snyan brgyud* did predate Chos rgyan, but it is difficult to establish textually that the tradition goes all the way back to Tsong kha pa, and more difficult still to establish that Tsong kha pa taught a system of Mahāmudrā; indeed, the generally accepted formulation of the membership and contents of the *snyan brgyud* may not precede the time of Ye shes rgyal mtshan.[22]

Second, the term by which Chos rgyan designated his Mahāmudrā system, *dge ldan bka' brgyud*, is at best ambiguous: it may refer to a joint dGe lugs–bKa' brgyud tradition, or it may refer simply to a dGe lugs "oral transmission." Chos rgyan's purport is not clear here, but the fact that most of his commentators accept the latter interpretation does not, *ipso facto*, assure that the former was not intended, for there is good evidence that, by the eighteenth century (and perhaps earlier), there was implicit or explicit debate about the meaning of the phrase.

Third, an examination of the structure and contents of Chos rgyan's two texts on Mahāmudrā shows that while there are certain crucial ways in which his understanding of Mahāmudrā differs from that of the bKa' brgyud pas, he was greatly indebted to the bKa' brgyud, which seems to have provided not only a significant number of his supporting textual citations, but also a perspective on the Sūtra-Mahāmudrā question, an ordering of meditative practices, the sequence and most of the details of his account of tranquillity meditation, and at least some of the outlines of his account of insight meditation.

Fourth—and this is a topic that I have not had sufficient space to explore here—an appreciation of Chos rgyan's unique historical role—as a scholar, meditator, and diplomat who was trained in dGe lugs monasteries in bKa' brgyud-dominated gTsang at a time when dGe lugs influence increasingly was coming to bear there—helps both to explain his familiarity with bKa' brgyud texts and traditions, and to suggest a possible "political" motive for his systematization of a dGe lugs Mahāmudrā tradition: by incorporating some of their practices, he may well have wished to make the dGe lugs seem less alien to his bKa' brgyud pa contemporaries in gTsang, or even to foster dGe lugs–bKa' brgyud cooperation.[23]

Thus, while we cannot conclude with certainty that Chos rgyan intended his system of Mahāmudrā to be dGe lugs–bKa' brgyud syncretism, there is some circumstantial evidence to this effect.

The sense that Chos rgyan may, indeed, have considered his system syncretic is further bolstered when we remember that he explicitly insisted that *all* the great Tibetan systems of meditation have "the same intention" (*dgongs pa gcig*). It would be far less difficult for a man with such a view to condone syncretism than for someone concerned with establishing the superiority of his own tradition and the inferiority of someone else's. Indeed, Chos rgyan's openness to various traditions, while far from unique in Tibetan (or even dGe lugs) history,[24] certainly is refreshing, and marks him as a figure who was not only very possibly a syncretist, but genuinely ecumenical as well. We have noted that though he does make some implicit criticisms of certain contemporaneous bKa' brgyud practices, the criticism is largely muted, and his texts are far more notable for their spirit of appreciation. This spirit is at considerable variance from that of some of his eighteenth-century commentators, who insisted that Chos rgyan's Mahāmudrā system was purely dGe lugs and who were more overtly critical of bKa' brgyud practices and views—not always, it should be added in fairness, for trivial or mean-spirited reasons: there undoubtedly really have been areas of philosophical difference worthy of scholastic exploration. In the very same century, though (see Kapstein, 1989), there were those who, like Thu'u bkwan, defended Chos rgyan's ecumenism, and dGe lugs pas have continued until the present day to differ among themselves about the exclusivity of their tradition.[25] At the very least, the spirit infused into the tradition by Chos rgyan is retained by the present Dalai Lama, who has written:

> For a long time I have had the one-pointed belief that Nying-ma, Sa-gya, Ga-gyu, and Ge-luk are all unions of sūtra and mantra as

> well as being of the [Madhyamaka] Consequence School....[A]ll four schools are getting at the same thing....Transcending sectarianism, we can find much to evoke deep realization by seeing how these schools come down to the same basic thought. (Dalai Lama, 1984: 200, 206, 224)

Notes

1. An earlier draft of this paper was presented at the Seventh Conference of the International Association of Buddhist Studies, Taipei, Taiwan, July, 1989. Funding for some of the research for the paper was generously provided by the National Endowment for the Humanities and Fairfield University. I would like to thank Profs. Luis Gómez, Lewis Lancaster, and John Newman for their helpful comments and questions on that earlier draft.

2. To be translated in my forthcoming *Lamp So Bright: Six dGe lugs pa Texts on Mahāmudrā*. This text is the basis of Dalai Lama and Berzin, part III, which includes numerous quotations from or paraphrases of it.

3. The portion of the *NGLZ* dealing with the history of the lineage will be translated in my forthcoming *Lamp So Bright: Six dGe lugs pa Texts on Mahāmudrā*, while the *NBPB* is translated in large part in Willis, 1995.

4. This lineage, the most widely recognized, is known—after its fifth recipient—as the dBen sa *snyan brgyud*. In most accountings, there is one other major dGe lugs *snyan brgyud*, the Srad, derived from Tsong kha pa's great tantric disciple, Shes rab seng ge; according to the eighteenth-century dGe lugs scholastic 'Jams dbyangs bzhad pa Ngag dbang brtson 'grus (1648-1721), Mahāmudrā teachings—especially related to the practice of *guru yoga*—also descended through the Srad *snyan brgyud*. Another, less common, division of dGe lugs *snyan brgyuds* is into a lineage of *gcod* practice and one of Mahāmudrā practice (Willis, 1995: 161). Still another scenario, sketched out in the works of the eighteenth-century dGe lugs pa masters Gung thang bzang dKon mchog bstan pa'i sgron me and A ku shes rab rgya mtsho, suggests that Tsong kha pa also transmitted Mahāmudrā teachings to his disciples at dGa' ldan Byang rtse Monastery, most notably Gung ru rGyal mtshan bzang po, from whom they may eventually have reached Chos rgyan (see Dalai Lama and Berzin: 230-232).

5. Another bKa' brgyud pa from whom Tsong kha pa may have received Mahāmudrā teachings was his friend and teacher dBu ma pa, whose guru was a 'Brug pa master who had, in turn, studied with the great Third Karma pa, Rang 'byung rdo rje (Dalai Lama and Berzin: 230).

6. Actually, the particular tantric procedures employed in dGe lugs pa Tantra Mahāmudrā are based more on the teachings of the Heruka/Cakrasaṃvara cycles, but, like virtually all dGe lugs pa tantric practices, they are structured according to the five-stage (*pañcakrama, rim lnga*) arrangement found in the commentarial literature on Guhyasamāja.

7. As opposed to Mahāmudrā as an important term in tantric texts, where it most commonly is used to denote the supreme achievement of the tantric

path, the *mahāmudrāsiddhi*. In this latter sense, to the degree that most Tibetan masters have been practitioners of Tantra, most also have been practitioners of Mahāmudrā.

8. Similarly Gung thang bzang reports that Tsong kha pa "had told another of his teachers [Red mda' ba] that he had an uncommon guideline teaching based on the mahamudra explanations of maha-madhyamaka, or great madhyamaka, but it was not yet time to propagate them widely" (Dalai Lama and Berzin: 230-231). In judging this claim—and Gung thang bzang's further contention that the written source of dGe lugs Mahāmudrā is to be found in notes taken by Tsong kha pa's disciple Gung ru rgyal mtshan bzang po—we must recall that Gung thang bzang (like Ye shes rgyal mtshan) was writing over three centuries after the events he describes, and that his own sources cannot be traced back more than a couple of generations.

9. The Dalai Lama argues (Dalai Lama and Berzin: 231-232) that there are numerous references in later dGe lugs pa texts to some "special" or "uncommon" Madhyamaka or *guru yoga* teachings transmitted by Tsong kha pa, and that these must be the dGe lugs Mahāmudrā tradition. Certainly, Madhyamaka is central to the dGa' ldan *snyan brgyud*, but most of the texts cited by the Dalai Lama belong to the eighteenth century, when dGe lugs Mahāmudrā was well publicized, and historians' motives open to question.

10. In *KGYT*, Chos rgyan examines the lives of Tsong kha pa's disciple mKhas grub rje dGe legs dpal bzang po, dBen sa pa, and Sangs rgyas ye shes. He maintains in his Mahāmudrā root-text (*GBZL*: 1b; trans. Dalai Lama and Berzin: 97; *YSGM*: 1b) that the tradition he will expound goes back to dBen sa pa's teacher, Chos kyi rdo rje (on whom see Willis, 1985: 313ff., 1995: 49-70).

11. Sangs rgyas ye shes does preface at least two songs quoted by Chos rgyan (*KGYT*: 552) with the salutation "*namo mahāmutrāya*" (*sic*), but this provides scant evidence of a systematic teaching on Mahāmudrā.

12. Indeed, it would seem that both the arrangement of the dGa' ldan *snyan brgyud* now generally accepted, as well as the claim that that lineage possessed a Mahāmudrā instruction descending from Tsong kha pa, were not fully worked out until the time of Ye shes rgyal mtshan, who might, thereby, be considered as crucial in the "formation" of the dGa' ldan *snyan brgyud* as its great early masters.

13. To be translated in my forthcoming *Lamp So Bright: Six dGe lugs pa Texts on Mahāmudrā*. Thanks to John Davenport and Tsepak Rigzin for obtaining a xeroxed copy for me from the Library of Tibetan Works and Archives.

14. He is quoted by Gung thang bzang (*DTTP*: 578) as equating Mahāmudrā with the yoga realizing the Perfection of Wisdom, but it is not clear from which text the quotation is taken. David Jackson, presumably drawing from Gung thang bzang, maintains (1994: 136) that bSod nams grags pa had written "a Great Seal manual," but does not indicate its title, or the source of his claim.

15. By another accounting, Chos rgyan's three predecessors were regarded as Paṇ chen Lamas "by courtesy," making him the fourth. Many contemporary

documents refer to the present Paṇ chen Lama, whose identification has been disputed, as the eleventh, where, more properly, he is the eighth.

16. Furthermore, he is the author of a collection of spiritual songs, *mgur*, explicitly inspired by Mi la ras pa, the *Mid la gsung mgur* (*MLSG*), which will in part be translated in my forthcoming *Lamp So Bright: Six dGe lugs pa Texts on Mahāmudrā*. He also is said to have had a visionary encounter with the great Indian forefather of Mahāmudrā, the poet-yogi Saraha (Willis, 1995: 93). The spiritual songs contained in his autobiography (*AFPL*: *passim*) have become renowned in dGe lugs circles. A selection of them will be translated in *Lamp So Bright*; segments of others are translated in Guenther, 1976: 110-127.

17. One might cite as evidence that he *was* familiar with the *PCSG* the fact that the tantric Mahāmudrā system to which Nor bzang's text devotes most of its attention is quite similar to that expounded in less detail by Chos rgyan in the *YSGM*, though this cannot be considered strong or conclusive evidence.

18. *de rnams kyi snying po'am bcud mtha' dag legs par bsdus te 'doms par mdzad pa ri bo dge ldan bka' babs kyi brgyud pa thun mong min pa ni*

19. The present Dalai Lama concedes this point (Dalai Lama and Berzin: 107) and does not speculate as to why this might have been, though he does point out (232) that the Fifth Dalai Lama resisted the idea that the tradition was a combined one, implying, perhaps, that the Great Fifth's view has affected that of later commentators. Indeed, the Fifth Dalai Lama did observe that "...it would be good if the dGe lugs pas kept themselves to themselves. What is the good of pushing in among the bKa' brgyud pa!" (Karmay: 146). This is not an explicit comment on the purport of Chos rgyan's text, but it certainly is suggestive of guru-disciple differences over policy toward bKa' brgyud pas, and perhaps, by extension, over the place of bKa' brgyud practices such as Mahāmudrā in the dGe lugs tradition.

20. As best I can tell, sGam po pa nowhere in his writings explicitly divides Mahāmudrā into Sūtra and Tantra types, but he has been accepted as doing so by virtually all later bKa' brgyud pas—who themselves accepted that Mahāmudrā had been taught in the sūtras as surely as in the tantras.

21. Indeed from at least the time of Ye shes rgyal mtshan onward, Chos rgyan's seminal dGe lugs *guru yoga* text, the *Bla ma'i mchod pa*, has been regarded as a vital ritual complement to the Mahāmudrā teachings of the dBen sa *snyan brgyud* (Dalai Lama and Berzin: 230; see also Dalai Lama, 1988). This may or may not have been Chos rgyan's intent, but the linkage between Mahāmudrā and *guru yoga* is evident in Chos rgyan's Mahāmudrā texts (where it is the context for Mahāmudrā meditation), and *guru yoga* clearly was part of the *snyan brgyud* even before Chos rgyan's time.

22. Let me reiterate, however, that there are lacunae in my textual survey; in particular, examination of Paṇ chen bSod nams grags pa's Mahāmudrā text, and closer scrutiny of the writings of other dGe lugs pa masters between Tsong kha pa and Chos rgyan, might force a reconsideration of some of these conclusions. Also, a closer study needs to be made of the possible sources of Chos rgyan's two Mahāmudrā texts.

23. This might help to explain the Fifth Dalai Lama's opposition to overtures to the bKa' brgyud—for he, as head of the dGe lugs-dominated Lhasa state, was opposed in his efforts to unify Tibet by, above all, the bKa' brgyud pas and their noble allies. An alternative interpretation, of course, is that Chos rgyan sought to co-opt, or "dGe-lugs-pa-fy," bKa' brgyud traditions as part of a concerted effort to extend dGe lugs pa hegemony over their rivals. The Fifth Dalai Lama's critique, however, suggests that if this was Chos rgyan's motive, neither he nor others was aware of it.

24. We ought to recall that the founder of the dGe lugs, Tsong kha pa, was himself both a syncretist and an ecumenist: though many of his insights were his own, or derived from visions, in developing what Geoffrey Samuel (*passim*) has called the "Gelugpa synthesis," he both borrowed from, and appreciated, the wisdom offered him by teachers from other traditions. On syncretism in Tibet, see also Kapstein, 1985.

25. This is certainly one of the issues lurking behind the intra-dGe lugs dispute over the worship of the protector deity rDo rje shugs ldan, who has been seen by both non-dGe lugs pas and by the Fourteenth Dalai Lama as a deity who may be invoked to harm the interests of other traditions.

References

Beyer, Stephan, trans.

1974 *The Buddhist Experience: Sources and Interpretations*. Belmont, CA: Dickenson.

Blo bzang chos kyi rgyal mtshan (First Paṇ chen Lama)

AFPL *The Autobiography of the First Panchen Lama Blo-bzang-chos-kyi-rgyal-mtshan*. Edited and reproduced by Ngawang Gelek Demo, with an English introduction by E. Gene Smith. Gedan Sungrap Minyam Gunphel Series, vol. 12. New Delhi, 1969.

GBZL *dGe ldan bka' brgyud rin po che'i phyag chen rtsa ba rGyal ba'i gzhung lam*. Blockprint, n.p., n.d. [Also found in Dalai Lama and Berzin: 352-355.]

KGYT *mKhas grub chen po gsum gyi yon tan mdor bsdus pa'i sgo nas rtogs brjod pa mkhas pa'i yid 'phrog grub pa'i rgyan*. In *Collected Works (gSung 'bum) of Blo bzang chos kyi rgyal mtshan, the First Paṇchen bLa ma of bKra shis lhun po*, vol. 1: 461-562. New Delhi: Mongolian Lama Gurudeva, 1973.

MLSG *Grub pa'i dbang phyug Mid la la brten pa'i bla ma'i rnal 'byor dang rnam thar du ma chud pa'i gsung mgur rnams*. In *Collected Works (gSung 'bum) of Blo bzang chos kyi rgyal mtshan, the First Paṇchen bLa ma of bKra shis lhun po*, vol. 1: 729-764. New Delhi: Mongolian Lama Gurudeva, 1973.

YSGM *dGe ldan bka' brgyud rin po che'i bka' srol phyag rgya chen po'i rtsa ba rgya par bshad pa Yang gsal sgron me*. Tibetan woodblock print: n.p., n.d.

Broido, Michael M.
1984 "Padma dKar-po on Tantra as Ground, Path and Goal." *Journal of the Tibet Society*, 4: 59-66.
1985 "Padma dKar-po on the Two *Satyas*." *The Journal of the International Association of Buddhist Studies*, 8(2): 7-60.
1987 "Sa-skya paṇḍita, the White Panacea and the Hva-shang Doctrine." *The Journal of the International Association of Buddhist Studies*, 10(2): 27-68.

Cabezón, José Ignacio
1999 "On the *Gra pa rin chen pa'i rtsod lam* of Paṇ chen bLo bzang chos rgyan." *Asiatische Studien/Études Asiatiques*, 44(4): 643-699.

Chandra, Lokesh, ed.
1963 *Materials for a History of Tibetan Literature*. 3 vols. Śatapiṭaka series. New Delhi.

Chang, Garma C. C., trans. & annot.
1963 *Teachings of Tibetan Yoga*. Secaucus, NJ: Citadel Press.

Dalai Lama, H. H. the Fourteenth
1984 "The Union of the Old and New Translation Schools." In *Kindness, Clarity and Insight*. Ithaca, NY: Snow Lion Publications.
1988 *The Union of Bliss and Emptiness: A Commentary on the Lama Choepa Guru Yoga Practice*. Ithaca, NY: Snow Lion Publications.

Dalai Lama, H. H. the Fourteenth and Alexander Berzin
1997 *The Gelug/Kagyü Tradition of Mahamudra*. [Includes Tibetan text of *GBZL*, 352-355.] Ithaca, NY: Snow Lion Publications.

dNgul chu Dharmabhadra
NKZB *Zab lam phyag rgya chen po'i rtsa ba rgyal ba'i gzhung lam gyi steng nas zab 'khrid gnad skabs kyi zin bris 'khrul pa kun sel*. In *Collected Works (gsuṅ 'bum) of dṄul chu dha rma bha dra*, reproduced from a manuscript copy traced from prints of the dNgul chu Blocks, vol. 8: 3-57. New Delhi: Tibet House, 1981.

Evans-Wentz, W. Y., ed.
1958 *Tibetan Yoga and Secret Doctrines*. New York: Oxford University Press.

First Paṇ chen Lama [Blo bzang chos kyi rgyal mtshan]
1975 *The Great Seal of Voidness: The Root Text for the Ge-lug/Ka-gyu Tradition of Mahamudra*. Trans. Geshe Ngawang Dhargyey et al. Dharamsala: Library of Tibetan Works and Archives.

Gu ge Blo bzang bstan 'dzin
CTNG *dGe ldan bka' brgyud rin po che'i bka' srol phyag rgya chen po rtsa 'grel rnams kyi 'grel bshad mchog mthun dngos grub kyi bang mdzod*. In *The Collected Works (gsuṅ 'bum) of Gu-ge yoṅs-'dzin*

Blo-bzaṅ-bstan-'dzin alias gDoṇ-drug-grub-pa'i-rdo-rje, reproduced from tracings from a set of prints from the bKra-shis-lhun-po Blocks, vol. 5: 1-454. New Delhi, 1976.

Guenther, Herbert V.

1963 *The Life and Teaching of Nāropa*. London/Oxford/New York: Oxford University Press.

1969 (trans. & annot.) *The Royal Song of Saraha: A Study in the History of Buddhist Thought*. Seattle and London: University of Washington Press.

1972 *The Tantric View of Life*. Boulder and London: Shambhala.

1976 *Treasures on the Tibetan Middle Way*. A Newly Revised Edition of *Tibetan Buddhism Without Mystification*. Berkeley: Shambhala.

Gung thang [bzang] dKon mchog bstan pa'i sgron me

DTTP *dGe ldan phyag rgya chen po'i khrid kyi zin bris zhal lung bdud rtsi'i thigs phreng*. In *The Collected Works of Guṅ-thaṅ dKon-mchog-bstan-pa'i sGron me*. Reproduced from prints from the Lha-sa blocks by Ngawang Gelek Demo, vol. 3: 563-619. New Delhi, 1972.

Gyaltsen, Khenpo Könchog, trans. & intro.

1986 *The Garland of Mahamudra Practices: A Translation of Kunga Rinchen's* Clarifying the Jewel Rosary of the Profound Fivefold Path. Co-trans. & ed. Katherine Rogers. Ithaca, NY: Snow Lion Publications.

Gyatso, Geshe Kelsang

1982 *Clear Light of Bliss: Mahamudra in Vajrayana Buddhism*. London: Wisdom Publications.

Hopkins, Jeffrey

1983 *Meditation on Emptiness*. London: Wisdom Publications.

1987 *Emptiness Yoga*. Ithaca, NY: Snow Lion Publications.

Jackson, David P.

1990 "Sa-skya Paṇḍita the 'Polemicist': Ancient Debates and Modern Interpretations." *The Journal of the International Association of Buddhist Studies*, 13(2): 17-116.

1994 *Enlightenment by a Single Means: Tibetan Controversies on the "Self-Sufficient White Remedy"* (dkar po gcig thub). Vienna: Verlag der Österreichischen Akademie der Wissenschaften.

Jackson, Roger

1982 "Sa skya paṇḍita's Account of the bSam yas Debate: History as Polemic." *The Journal of the International Association of Buddhist Studies*, 5(2): 89-99.

(n.d.) *Lamp So Bright: Six dGe lugs pa Texts on Mahāmudrā*.

Kalu Rinpoche
1986 *The Gem Ornament of Manifold Oral Instructions Which Benefits Each and Everyone Appropriately*. Ithaca, NY: Snow Lion Publications.

Kanakura, Yensho, et al.
1953 *A Catalogue of the Tohoku University Collection of Tibetan Works on Buddhism*. Sendai: Sendai University.

Kapstein, Matthew
1985 "Religious Syncretism in 13th Century Tibet: *The Limitless Ocean Cycle*." In *Soundings in Tibetan Civilization*. Ed. Barbara Nimri Aziz and Matthew Kapstein. Delhi: Manohar.
1989 "The Purificatory Gem and Its Cleansing: A Late Tibetan Polemical Discussion of Apocryphal Texts." *History of Religions*, 28(3): 217-244.

Karmay, Samten Gyaltsen
1988 *The Great Perfection: A Philosophical and Meditative Teaching of Tibetan Buddhism*. Leiden: E. J. Brill.

Ke'u tshang Blo bzang 'jam byangs
NGKG *dGe ldan snyan rgyud kyi bka' srol phyag rgya chen po'i zin bris rNam grol kun tu dge ba'i lam bzang*. In *Ke'u tshang smon lam gyi gsung 'bum*, vol. 2: 7-149. Dharamsala: Library of Tibetan Works and Archives, 1984.

Kongtrul, Jamgön (VIII) ['Jam dbyangs kong sprul Blo 'gros mtha' yas]
1992 *Cloudless Sky: The Mahamudra Path of the Tibetan Kagyü School*. Ed. & trans. into German by Tina Drasczyk and Alex Drasczyk. Trans. into English by Richard Gravel. Boston & London: Shambhala.

Mullin, Glenn H., ed. & trans.
1996 *Tsongkhapa's Six Yogas of Naropa*. Ithaca, NY: Snow Lion Publications.

Namgyal, Takpo Tashi [Dwags po bKra shis rnam rgyal]
1986 *Mahāmudrā: The Quintessence of Mind and Meditation*. Trans. & annot. Lobsang P. Lhalungpa. Boston & London: Shambhala.

Napper, Elizabeth
1991 *Dependent-Arising and Emptiness*. London: Wisdom Publications.

Nyima Rinpoche, Chokyi Nyima
1989 *The Union of Mahamudra and Dzogchen: A Commentary on The Quintessence of Spiritual Practice, the Direct Instructions of the Great Compassionate One, by Karma Chagmey Rinpoche I*. Trans. Erik Pema Kunsang. Ed. Marcia B. Schmidt. Hong Kong: Rangjung Yeshe Publications.

Nor bzang rgya mtsho, mKhas grub

PCSG *bKa' dge dgongs pa gcig bsgrub kyi phyag rgya chen po gsal ba'i sgron me*. Woodblock print, n.p., n.d. Accession no. 20379, Library of Tibetan Works and Archives, Dharamsala.

Rabten, Geshe

1983 *Echoes of Voidness*. London: Wisdom Publications.

Rangdrol, Tsele Natsok

1989 *The Lamp of Mahamudra: The Immaculate Lamp that Perfectly and Fully Illuminates the Meaning of Mahamudra, the Essence of All Phenomena*. Trans. Erik Pema Kunsang. Boston & Shaftesbury: Shambhala.

Roerich, George N., trans.

1976 *The Blue Annals*. Delhi: Motilal Banarsidass.

Sa skya paṇḍita Kun dga' rgyal mtshan

DSRB *sDom pa gsum gyi rab tu dbye ba*. In *Sa skya pa bka' 'bum*, vol. 5: 297-320. Tokyo: Tōyō Bunko, 1968.

TGRS *Thub pa'i dgongs pa rab tu gsal ba*. In *Sa skya pa bka' 'bum*, vol. 5: 1-50. Tokyo: Tōyō Bunko, 1968.

Samuel, Geoffrey

1994 *Civilized Shamans: Buddhism in Tibetan Societies*. Washington, DC: Smithsonian.

Sangs rgyas ye shes, mKhas grub

CWSY *The Collected Works (gsuṅ 'bum) of mKhas grub Sangs rgyas ye shes*. Ed. Don grub rdo rje. New Delhi, 1973. 2 vols. 1: 91-95.

Seyfort Ruegg, David

1966 *The Life of Bu-ston Rinpoche, with the Tibetan Text of the Bu ston rNam thar*. Serie Orientale Roma, 34. Rome: Istituto Italiano per il Medio ed Estremo Oriente.

1988 "A Kar ma bKa' brgyud Work on the Lineages and Traditions of the Indo-Tibetan dBu ma (Madhyamaka)," in *Orientalia Iosephi Tucci Memoriae Dicata*. Ed. G. Gnoli & L. Lanciotti. Serie Orientale Roma, 56/3. Rome: Istituto Italiano per il Medio ed Estremo Oriente.

1989 *Buddha-nature, Mind and the Problem of Gradualism in a Comparative Perspective: On the Transmission and Reception of Buddhism in India and Tibet*. London: School of Oriental and African Studies, University of London.

Shakabpa, Tsepon W. D.

1984 *Tibet: A Political History*. New York: Potala Publications.

Situpa Tenpa'i Nyinchay [Si tu pa bsTan pa'i nyin byed]

1995 *Mahāmudrā Teachings of the Supreme Siddhas: The Eighth Situpa Tenpa'i Nyinchay on the Third Gyalwa Karmapa Rangjung Dorje's*

"Aspiration Prayer of Mahāmudrā of Definitive Meaning." Trans. Lama Sherab Dorje. Ithaca, NY: Snow Lion Publications.

Thurman, Robert A. F.

1982 *Life and Teaching of Tsong kha pa*. Dharamsala: Library of Tibetan Works and Archives.

1984 *Tsong Khapa's Speech of Gold in The Essence of True Eloquence*. Princeton: Princeton University Press.

Thu'u bkwan Blo bzang chos kyi nyi ma

GTSM *Grub mtha' thams cad kyi khungs dang 'dod tshul ston pa legs bshad Shel gyi me long*. In *Collected Works of Thu'u bkwan chos kyi nyi ma*, vol. 2: 5-519. New Delhi, 1959.

Tsong-ka-pa [Blo bzang grags pa]

1977 *Tantra in Tibet: The Great Exposition of Secret Mantra*. Intro. His Holiness the Fourteenth Dalai Lama. Trans. Jeffrey Hopkins. London: George Allen & Unwin.

1981 *The Yoga of Tibet: The Great Exposition of Secret Mantra—2 and 3*. Intro. His Holiness the Fourteenth Dalai Lama. Trans. Jeffrey Hopkins. London: George Allen & Unwin.

Tucci, Giuseppe

1949 *Tibetan Painted Scrolls*. 3 vols. Rome: Libreria dello Stato.

Wang-ch'ug Dor-je, the Ninth Karmapa [dBang phyug rdo rje]

1978 *The Mahamudra Eliminating the Darkness of Ignorance*. Trans. Alexander Berzin. Dharamsala: Library of Tibetan Works and Archives.

Williams, Paul M.

1983 "A Note on Some Aspects of Mi-bskyod-rdo-rje's Critique of dGe-lugs-pa Madhyamaka." *Journal of Indian Philosophy*, 11: 125-145.

Willis, Janice D.

1985 "On the Nature of *rnam-thar*: Early dGe-lugs-pa *Siddha* Biographies." In Barbara Nimri Aziz and Matthew Kapstein, eds., *Soundings in Tibetan Civilization*. New Delhi: Manohar.

1995 *Enlightened Beings: Life Stories from the Ganden Oral Tradition*. Boston: Wisdom Publications.

Ye shes rgyal mtshan, Tshe mchog gling

NBPB *Byang chub lam gyi rim pa'i bla ma brgyud pa'i rnam par thar pa rgyal bstan mdzes pa'i rgyan mchog phul byung Nor bu'i phreng ba*. In *Collected Works of Tshe mchog gling yoṅs 'dzin ye shes rgyal mtshan*, vols. 18-19. New Delhi: Tibet House Library, 1974.

NGLZ *dGa' ldan phyag rgya chen po'i khrid yig sNyan rgyud lam bzang gsal ba'i sgron me*. In *Collected Works of Tshe mchog gling yoṅs 'dzin ye shes rgyal mtshan*, vol. 22: 201-443. New Delhi: Tibet House Library, 1974.

Chapter 8

Demons on the Mother:

Objections to the Perfect Wisdom Sūtras in Tibet

Gareth Sparham

In this paper I discuss two Perfect Wisdom (*prajñā-pāramitā*) commentaries found in the Tibetan canon. The issue of their names and who wrote them is so tangled that I propose to call them simply Gn1 and Gn2 in order to avoid any unfounded preconception about them and their authors.

In the catalogue to the Peking edition (Suzuki), Gn1 is P no. 5205, called *'Phags pa shes rab kyi pha rol tu phyin pa 'bum gyi rgya cher 'grel*. No original name is given, though if it were to have existed it would probably have been **Ārya-śata-sāhasrikā-prajñā-pāramitā-bṛhaṭ-ṭīkā* (which may be rendered in English as "Long Explanation of the *Perfect Wisdom Sūtra in One Hundred Thousand Lines*"). It is extant only in Tibetan, has no colophon, and no name of either an author or translator is given. In the same catalogue, Gn2 is P no. 5206, called *Ārya-śata-sāhasrikā-pañca-viṃśati-sāhasrikāṣṭādaśa-sāhasrikā-prajñā-pāramitā-bṛhaṭ-ṭīkā*. This is probably the original name of a work with the Tibetan title *'Phags pa shes rab kyi pha rol tu phyin pa 'bum pa dang nyi khri lnga stong pa dang khri brgyad stong pa'i rgya cher bshad pa* ("Long Explanation of the *Perfect Wisdom Sūtras in One Hundred Thousand, Twenty-five Thousand* and *Eighteen Thousand Lines*"). This text, listed as translated by the great translator Ye shes sde (fl. ca. 800), and without any mention of an author, is also extant only in Tibetan.

Who wrote these two commentaries, whether there are references to either or to both of these texts in other Indian commentaries, and the philosophical perspective from which these two commentaries interpret Her Ladyship (*bhagavatī*) the Perfect Wisdom sūtras are questions I attempt to answer here.[1] They are problems that vexed a number of fourteenth-century Tibetan writers. I shall be concerned particularly with the views of Dol po pa Shes rab rgyal mtshan (1292-1361), Bu ston Rin chen grub (1290-1364), Nya dbon Kun dga' dpal (1285-1379) and Tsong kha pa Blo bzang grags pa (1357-1419), authors whose views touch on far larger and more important issues than simply names and dates of obscure books and their authors. As Mimaki (1982, 1983) and others have shown through their investigation of early Tibetan *grub mtha'* literature, the systematic presentation of Indian thinkers in four graded schools of thought—in ascending order Vaibhāṣika, Sautrāntika, Cittamātra and Madhyamaka—and then the subcategorization of the higher schools of thought, developed in Tibet over a period of time. As I have attempted to show elsewhere (Sparham, 1993), the development of the view that the Cittamātra is simply a heuristic device and is wrong, and the parallel development of Madhyamaka subcategorizations that strongly privilege a Prāsaṅgika-Madhyamaka, are the legacy, in particular, of the later works of Tsong kha pa.[2] Here I further develop this thesis. I suggest that the development of Madhyamaka subcategorizations that conclusively devalue Cittamātra and strongly privilege Prāsaṅgika-Madhyamaka occurred in tandem with the rejection of Mahā-madhyamaka (*dbu ma chen po*). Dol po pa forcefully asserts this Mahā-madhyamaka school as fifth and superior school of thought, not a subcategory of Madhyamaka. He says that the author of the Gn2 sets forth such a Mahā-madhyamaka with great clarity and he says, repeatedly and unequivocally, that the author of Gn2 is "the Mahā-madhyamaka master Vasubandhu."

The answers to the arcane questions of who wrote Gn1 and Gn2, then, discussed at length in the long fourteenth-century scholastic commentaries on the Perfect Wisdom sūtras, allow us to plot in greater detail the development of ideas that led to a strong rejection of Mahā-madhyamaka, and as well to the development of the distinct Madhyamaka system which would, in time, become the central pillar of dGe lugs pa orthodoxy. Further investigation of this orthodoxy is timely, based as it must be on Professor Hopkins's studies of the dGe lugs pa sect.

I begin by considering a text on Perfect Wisdom attributed to a Vasubandhu and called the *paddhati* (Tib. *gzhung 'grel*, "well-trodden path"). The following facts present themselves: (1) that the word *paddhati* is used by Haribhadra in his *Ālokā* (*Āryāṣṭa-sāhasrikā-prajñā-pāramitā-vyākhyā Ābhisamayālaṃkārālokā-nāma*) in connection with Vasubandhu, though not necessarily referring to a book; (2) that Haribhadra in his *Ālokā* and *Vivṛtti* (*Abhisamayālaṃkāra-kārikā-śāstra-vivṛtti*)[3] gently criticizes Vasubandhu for his views; (3) that in the *Āmnayānusāriṇī* (*Bhagavatyāmnayānusāriṇī-nāma-vyākhyāna*) and also in works by Abhayākaragupta[4] there are extracts from a *Nyi khri gzhung 'grel* (**Pañca-viṃśati-sāhasrikā-paddhati*), a work said to be by Vasubandhu; and (4) that these extracts from *Nyi khri gzhung 'grel* are found in Gn2.

I will deal with each of these in turn.

First, in his *Ālokā* (Wogihara, 1973: 1) Haribhadra says:

> Towering on account of his pride because of a minute knowledge of views regarding the division of being and non-being, the master Vasubandhu attained a [firm] position in describing the topics in [his] *paddhati* ("well-trodden path").[5]

At this point it may be recalled that Haribhadra's work on Perfect Wisdom generated a small but not insignificant tradition in Northeast India during the Pāla dynasty (late eighth to early thirteenth century). There are a number of Indian commentaries on his work.[6] Although less well known than Śāntarakṣita and his more illustrious disciple Kamalaśīla, Haribhadra was a great influence on the Tibetan Perfect Wisdom commentarial tradition, about which I will have more to say below. His views are a complex synthesis of Yogācāra and Madhyamaka that is yet to be fully investigated. He is cited as an authority by many later Tibetan writers, and in later dGe lugs pa doxographical literature (Sopa and Hopkins: 1976) he is categorized as a *rNal 'byor spyod pa dbu ma rang rgyud pa* (**Yogācāra-svātantrika-mādhyamika*).

Second, in his *Vivṛtti* (Amano, 1975: 3) Haribhadra says:

> Vasubandhu, close companion to the aims of wandering beings, evincing his primary interest provided an interpretation based on knowables being [of the nature] of the inner [mind].[7]

There is a slight criticism of Vasubandhu (or at least of his views) evident in both these passages.

Third, the *Āmnayānusāriṇī* (I will return to the question of its author below) is closely related to Gn2 in particular. In part of a loosely extended colophon we find a passage that says that Vasubandhu is the writer one should follow, and that:

> Explanations other than that of the *Paddhati* are not to be accepted. This is because Ārya Maitreya-nātha spoke on account of the fact that the master [Vasubandhu] would explain five hundred sūtras. So how could he make a wrong explanation? Since [Vasubandhu] explains [in the opening verse of his *Paddhati*] that it is on account of [his] guru's instruction that "I want to compose clearly a *Paddhati* that is a *gNod 'joms* ('Demon Conqueror,' 'Deals with Objections')," he thus shelters in the instruction that came from Ārya Asaṅga himself.

The defense of Vasubandhu implicit in this statement is most probably in response to the criticism of Haribhadra cited above, though until the dating of the texts involved is firmly established this remains conjecture.

Fourth, at the beginning of both Gn1 and Gn2 one finds the statement "I want to compose clearly a *Paddhati* that is a *Demon Conqueror*" cited in the extract from the *Āmnayānusāriṇī*. And, though there are differences in readings between Gn2 and the extracts cited from the *Paddhati* in the *Āmnayānusāriṇī*, the *Āmnayānusāriṇī* does seems to be, in essence, a supplement to or subcommentary on Gn2 in particular. This constitutes strong evidence that the *Nyi khri gzhung 'grel* is Gn2.

The above facts greatly exercised the great Tibetan Perfect Wisdom exegetes of the fourteenth century. The immediate focus of dispute, as it emerges in their attempts to explain these facts, is whether or not Gn2 (and to a lesser extent Gn1) was written by Vasubandhu. In dealing with Tibetan opinions about this matter I discuss Dol po pa, Bu ston, Nya dbon, and Tsong kha pa. It is instructive to recall, as noted by the early twentieth-century A mdo scholar Gung thang Blo gros rgya mtsho (*TMS*: 3) that Bu ston rejects Dol po pa, that Nya dbon sees himself as the student of both Dol po pa and Bu ston, and that Tsong kha pa usually follows Nya dbon's refinements on Bu ston.

Dol po pa's Interpretation

Dol po pa is startling for his total and unequivocal rejection of Haribhadra. Even though criticism was levelled at Haribhadra long before the fourteenth century, and by his own countrymen, in particular by Abhayākaragupta (in his *Muni-matālaṃkāra* and *Marma-kaumudī*), Dol po pa goes far beyond them in his total rejection of Haribhadra. He damns him as a writer in a degenerate age.[8] Citing the *Vivṛtti*, Dol po pa says (*MDBT*: 373) that

> ... depending on his commentary, though one spends a long time working hard on the *Abhisamayālaṃkāra*, one's intense study and familiarity with this system of explanation will not give one the understanding of even a single page of the sūtra when one turns to read it. So it goes without saying that this commentary's way of explaining does not serve as an "ornament for all the Perfect Wisdom sūtras."

Dol po pa's last comment is in reference to Haribhadra's justification for his Perfect Wisdom commentaries found at the opening of his *Vivṛtti*. There Haribhadra says that he has been vouchsafed the insight that the *Abhisamayālaṃkāra* (he considers the short work to have been conveyed to Asaṅga by Maitreya-nātha) is a guide not just to the *Perfect Wisdom Sūtra in One Hundred Thousand* and *Twenty-five Thousand Lines* but to the *Perfect Wisdom Sūtra in Eight Thousand Lines* as well.[9]

Dol po pa says that he is sticking to the explanation of the Enlightened One himself and " ... ignoring the spotty (*ci rigs*), well-known traditions of interpretation of today." He says (*MDBT*: 375) that the *Maitreya-paripṛcchā* (he refers to it as *Byang chub sems dpa'i bslab pa rab tu dbye ba'i le'u*) is the Enlightened One's *Autocommentary* (*rang 'grel*) (!) on his sūtras. He says proper explanations of the Perfect Wisdom sūtras and the *Abhisamayālaṃkāra* follow the Enlightened One's *Autocommentary*. These proper explanations are those by the master Asaṅga, the Mahā-madhyamaka master Vasubandhu, the master Dignāga, as well as 'Bum ṭik mkhan po and Zhi ba 'byung gnas. He pointedly excludes from his list of authorities both Ārya-vimuktisena and Haribhadra, the champions of Tibetans following the tradition originating in rNgog Blo ldan shes rab's (1059-1109) gSang phu ne'u thog Monastery.

In this list of writers Dol po pa's reference to the Mahā-madhyamaka master Vasubandhu is to the author of Gn2. In fourteenth-century discussions of Mahā-madhyamaka in the context of Perfect Wisdom it is primarily this Vasubandhu, the putative author of Gn2, who is under consideration. The author of the *Abhidharma-kośa* or even the author of the *Triṃśikā*, etc., is not at issue, though the authority attaching to the name Vasubandhu comes from the unquestioned acceptance of his having written those scholarly treatises as well.

The "Dignāga" Dol po pa refers to is not, primarily, the author of the *Pramāṇa-samuccaya* but rather the author of the short but influential *Prajñāpāramitā-piṇḍārtha*.[10] 'Bum ṭik mkhan po ("the scholar who wrote the commentary on the *Śata-sāhasrikā*") is the author of Gn1,[11] while "the glorious king, the foremost guru living at Jagaddala, the master Śāntasaṃbhava/Śāntyākara"[12] seems to be Dol po pa's name for the author of the *Āmnayānusāriṇī*, a text which he takes to be authoritative since it is based on Gn2.

For Dol po pa, then, the *Paddhati* that is a *Demon Conqueror* referred to at the beginning of Gn2 is written by Vasubandhu. He takes Haribhadra to be referring to it by name in his *Ālokā*, and when Haribhadra criticizes Vasubandhu in his *Ālokā* and *Vivṛtti* he is referring primarily to what this Vasubandhu says in Gn2. Dol po pa totally rejects the suggestion that this Vasubandhu writes from the Cittamātra perspective. He writes from a Mahā-madhyamaka perspective as do all the great Buddhist writers, without exception, of the Golden Age (*kṛta-yuga*). Śākyamuni, particularly in his *Autocommentary* (the *Maitreya-paripṛcchā*), Nāgārjuna, and the brothers Asaṅga and Vasubandhu all say exactly the same thing. There is no need, according to Dol po pa, for a skillful hermeneutics to explain inconsistences in these Buddhist writers of the Golden Age because they all state the Mahā-madhyamaka truth clearly and without any ambiguity.

Dol po pa (*MDBT*: 378) says that one should understand the Perfect Wisdom sūtras in terms of the three natures (*parikalpita*, *paratantra* and *pariniṣpanna*) and denies that the three natures set forth the Cittamātra system. Were they to do so, then the three natures asserted by Asaṅga and Vasubandhu and, indeed, by the Enlightened One in his own *Autocommentary* would set forth the Cittamātra system. This they most assuredly do not do because then the Enlightened One would be introducing a complication and misleading readers, which he would never do.

What then is the Cittamātra and how does it differ from the Mahā-madhyamaka? Dol po pa says (*MDBT*: 386) that "... the Cittamātra notion, in the final analysis, is that the instant of consciousness free of bifurcation into subject and object is itself the ultimate." He says there is, therefore a world of difference between the Cittamātra and Mahā-madhyamaka because in the former the ultimate is mind—and therefore impermanent and so forth—while in the latter the ultimate reality (referred to as *'gyur med yongs grub chos dbying de shin nyid*) is beyond all thought and is permanent, etc.[13]

Dol po pa also deals with the question of Nāgārjuna's rejection of an ultimate in the form of mind and poses the question of whether this rejection differs from the assertions of the Mahā-mādhyamikas. He says (*MDBT*: 384) that the Compendium of Reasonings (*rigs tshogs*) is to remove the existence extreme (*yod mtha'*) and the Compendium of Praises (*bstod tshogs*) is to remove the nonexistence extreme (*med mtha'*). Since the prophecies of Nāgārjuna refer to him avoiding both extremes, "... do not be satisfied with a Madhyamaka teaching that merely refutes existence. One needs to remove both the extremes of existence and nonexistence." Equating the teaching of three natures in the works of Asaṅga with this composite teaching of Nāgārjuna that avoids both extremes, Dol po pa says (*MDBT*: 385) that it is not enough to avoid just superimposition (*samāropa*)—the cul de sac that most Tibetan Mādhyamikas of his day seem to be parked in—but must avoid deprecation (*apavāda*) as well. In this, Dol po pa delineates a mistaken Madhyamaka, different from Cittamātra and below Mahā-madhyamaka, even if he does not clearly give it the name.

Bu ston's Interpretation

As one would expect from a man known for encyclopedic knowledge and the redaction of the Tibetan canon, Bu ston has much to say about the authors of Gn1 and Gn2. He deals with the question both in his *Chos 'byung* and in his influential Perfect Wisdom commentary, *Lung gi nye ma*. This latter work is, as one would expect, based on the *Vivṛtti*. rNgog Blo ldan shes rab first introduced the *Vivṛtti* into Tibet and began the gSang phu ne'u thog tradition of using it (supplemented by the *Ālokā* and Ārya Vimuktisena's *Pañcaviṃśati-sāhasrikā-prajñāpāramitopadeśa-śāstrābhisamayālaṃkāra-vṛtti*)—rNgog revised the earlier Tibetan translations of both) to explain the Perfect Wisdom sūtras and *Abhisamayālaṃkāra*. The tradition passed down through the disciples of gNyal zhig 'Jam pa'i rdo rje (fl. ca. 1200), abbot of the upper campus of gSang phu Monastery, to Zhwa lu Monastery.

Since Bu ston spent nearly his whole life at Zhwa lu and became its most illustrious son, it is not surprising that he accepted Haribhadra's authority and used his *Vivṛtti* as the root text for his

Perfect Wisdom commentary. Specifically he says (*LNM*: 20-21) that Vasubandhu is a proponent of the Cittamātra school which his brother Asaṅga taught him in an attempt to lead him to truth. Still, Bu ston seems to accept the authority of the Vasubandhu who wrote Gn2. He praises him greatly (*LNM*: 21ff) and explains that the Cittamātra interpretation of the Perfect Wisdom is not wrong. It is based on the three natures theory. What Bu ston seems to mean is that it is a correct description of reality, but that it does not lead one the entire way along the Buddhist path to the inexpressible beyond.

Bu ston says there are four "pathbreakers" (*shing rta chen po'i srol ['byed]*), i.e. distinctive interpreters of the Perfect Wisdom sūtras. Besides Nāgārjuna, Maitreya, and Dignāga, he mentions (*LNM*: 3) "the commentary on the *Śata-sāhasrikā* by Daṃṣṭṛsena" (*daṃṣṭṛ se na'i 'bum gyi ṭīk*), clearly referring to Gn1.[14] This contrasts strongly with Dol po pa (*MDBT*: 455), who says the authors of Gn1 and Gn2, amongst others propounding the same Mahā-madhyamaka position, are the "authoritative pathbreakers" (*shing rta'i srol 'byed chen po tshad mar gyur pa*). Whether Dol po pa is refuting a tradition of four pathbreakers that precedes Bu ston, or whether Bu ston is specifically refuting Dol po pa and is the first to mention four pathbreakers is a question that cannot be answered with certainty until more Tibetan Perfect Wisdom commentaries in the gSang phu/Zhwa lu tradition come to light. But it seems likely that the issue of the number of pathbreakers in Bu ston, at least, arises in parallel with the assertion of Dol po pa that there is only one proper way to explain the Perfect Wisdom sūtras and that all other ways are wrong and there is no value in studying them.

Bu ston does not deal with the issue of the difference between Gn1 and Gn2 in his *Lung gi nye ma* because he had already dealt with the question exhaustively in his *Chos 'byung* (*bDe bar gshegs pa'i bstan pa'i gsal byed chos kyi 'byung gnas gsung rab rin po che'i mdzod;* hereafter *DSTS*). There (*DSTS*: 134-135) his tentative conclusion (based on a consideration of the old Tibetan catalogues) is that Gn2 is by Vasubandhu and Gn1 by Daṃṣṭṛsena.[15] It is this Gn1 by Daṃṣṭṛsena that Bu ston (*LNM*) says was written by a pathbreaker (probably of a Mahā-madhyamaka-type system). In regard to Gn2, Bu ston (*DSTS:* 157) explicitly says that the *gzhung 'grel*, i.e. Gn2, the *Paddhati* mentioned in the *Ālokā* as being by Vasubandhu, explains the middle turning of the wheel in accord with the Cittamātra school. Bu ston also mentions that Abhayākaragupta cites extracts from a *Nyi khri gzhung 'grel* that match statements in this text.

Bu ston is traditionally known for his knowledge of the textual tradition, not for his systematization of philosophical ideas. The amount of time he spends considering Gn1 and Gn2 demonstrates his sensitivity to the issues involved, but no obvious philosophical position emerges from the final opinion he advances on who wrote them.

Nya dbon's Interpretation

Nya dbon finished his Perfect Wisdom commentary *Nyi ma'i 'od zer (sbTan bcos mngon par rtogs pa'i rgyan 'grel ba dang bcas pa'i rgya 'grel bshad bsbyar yid kyi mun sel,* hereafter, *NMOZ*) in 1371. In the opening lines (*NMOZ*: 4) of this work he describes himself as a follower of both Dol po pa and Bu ston. Nevertheless, unlike Dol po pa, he accepts Haribhadra as authoritative and follows the gSang phu tradition in basing his commentary on the *Vivṛtti*. He explicitly says (*NMOZ*: 36) that Haribhadra in his *Ālokā* refers to a book by Vasubandhu that is called a *Paddhati*. He follows Bu ston in asserting that Vasubandhu's *Paddhati* is written from the Cittamātra point of view. But in regard to the author of Gn2 he says (*NMOZ*: 7):

> Bcom ldan [rigs pa'i ral gri] and the omniscient dharma lord (*chos rje kun mkhyen pa*) [=Dol po pa] say this ["Demon Conqueror *Paddhati* on the three Perfect Wisdom sūtras" (*Yum gsum gzhung 'grel gnod 'jom*)] [Gn2] is Vasubandhu's *Paddhati*. And it is true that finally Bu ston asserted that it is. Nevertheless the Demon Conqueror that is a commentary on the *Śata-sāhasrikā* (*'bum 'grel gnod 'joms* [Gn1]) and the Demon Conqueror *Paddhati* on the three Mother Sūtras [Gn2]) are amplified and condensed [versions of the same thing].[16] Some say that it is clear that the *Paddhati* on the three Mother Sūtras [Gn2] is by Daṃṣṭṛsena and that the *Śata-sāhasrikā* commentary [Gn1] is by the king Khri srong lde btsan.

"Mother" (*yum*) is the usual abbreviation for the Perfect Wisdom sūtras in Tibetan commentarial literature. The metaphor is first used for the sūtras in the opening verse of the *Abhisamayālaṃkāra* (*. . . buddhasya matre namaḥ*). Nya dbon's "some say" in the last sentence is probably a polite way of setting forth his own position when it disagrees with that of his gurus. Nya dbon is distinguished by his willingness to accept parts of traditions which others would insist are exclusive. Here his willingness to accept that Vasubandhu is not the author of Gn1 does not imply any rejection of it or rejection of Dol po pa's use of it as a central pillar of his interpretive system.

In passing we may describe Nya dbon as a moderate Mahā-mādhyamika. Though he bases his Perfect Wisdom commentary on Haribhadra, his intellectual debt to Dol po pa is evident. For example, he accepts (*NMOZ*: 472ff.) a Cittamātra school that is deficient insofar as it asserts the *icchāntika* ("hopeless case"). Based on this criterion Nya dbon separates out of the Cittamātra corpus a number of books which are to be privileged as Mahā-madhyamaka. In his general discussion of lineage (*gotra, rigs*) (*NMOZ*: 475) he says that the lineage described as coming down from a time without beginning in the third chapter of the *Mahāyāna-sūtrālaṃkāra* and at the beginning of the *Bodhisattva-bhūmi* are both "uncreated" (*asaṃskṛta*). This is a Mahā-madhyamaka-type assertion and differs from the position of bCom ldan rigs pa'i ral gri who says that they are the seed of transcendental wisdom on the *ālaya* ("foundation") in the case of the *Mahāyāna-sūtrālaṃkāra* and a specialness of the six sense bases in the *Bodhisattva-bhūmi* and hence mind only (*cittamātra*). Tsong kha pa will later say the same in his Perfect Wisdom commentary. Nya dbon, taking a Mahā-madhyamaka position, argues that in neither of these texts by Asaṅga is the *icchāntika* asserted. The naturally abiding lineage Asaṅga refers to is "the *dharmatā* ("true nature of dharmas") of the six sense bases, a nature from a time without beginning, the clear illumination" (*NMOZ*: 474). It is definitely not created (*saṃskṛta*).

Nya dbon's Perfect Wisdom commentary is exhaustive, and excellent for that, but a clear delineation of lower and higher schools is absent. In Nya dbon's case one suspects that he uses the *Mahāyāna-sūtrālaṃkāra's* rubrics as a general outline that includes even Vasubandhu's explanation of lineage in his *Abhidharma-kośa* because he entertains the idea that Vasubandhu is equally a Mahā-madhyamaka. On the other hand, anticipating what I will have to say about Tsong kha pa, one suspects Tsong kha pa insists that in Cittamātra the lineage is created (*saṃskṛta*)—even when the wording seems to suggest uncreated (*asaṃskṛta*)—because of his need to explain the differences between the Cittamātra and Madhyamaka schools that become, for him, clearly differentiated.

Tsong kha pa's Interpretation

Tsong kha pa finished his Perfect Wisdom commentary *Legs bshad gser phreng* (*LBGP*) in 1392. It is a subcommentary on the *Vivṛtti* based on Nya dbon, whose own commentary is mainly based on Bu ston. Tsong kha pa deals at some length with the question of the author of Gn2 and the philosophical standpoint from which Gn2 is written.

Glossing the verse from the *Vivṛtti* cited above (words cited are in inverted commas), Tsong kha pa says explicitly (*LBGP*: 25) that Haribhadra in his *Ālokā* refers to a *Paddhati* by Vasubandhu which he calls *Nyi khri gzhung 'grel* ("*Paddhati* on the *Pañca-viṃśati-sāhasrikā*"):

> ..."provided an interpretation" .... Who? ... "Vasubandhu." And where? As it says [in the *Ālokā* passage cited above]..."in his *Paddhati*" on the *Pañca-viṃśati-sāhasrikā*...based on the representation [only] (*vijñapti*-[*mātra*]) system in which it is asserted that objects that appear as "knowables are" all mere reflection "of the inner" mind and that mind is itself established as the fundamental substratum. The reason for this is that the master himself, "evincing a primary interest," was naturally drawn to the Cittamātra system.

The immediate reason that Tsong kha pa uses the name *Nyi khri gzhung 'grel* and not *Yum gsum gzhung 'grel* ("*Paddhati* on the Three Mother Sūtras"), i.e. Gn2, is because he has already, in his opening survey of Indian Perfect Wisdom commentaries, tentatively opted for the position which I have suggested above was Nya dbon's own, namely that the *Paddhati* on the three Mother Sūtras [Gn2] is by Damṣṭṛsena and the *Śata-sāhasrikā* commentary [Gn1] is by the king Khri srong lde btsan. Tsong kha pa's tenuous scriptural source for the existence of this *Nyi khri gzhung 'grel* by Vasubandhu is the *Āmnayānusāriṇī*, which uses that name and not the name *Yum gsum gzhung 'grel*. Tsong kha pa further differentiates between Gn2 and this *Nyi khri gzhung 'grel* in terms of their philosophical viewpoint. Since *Nyi khri gzhung 'grel* is the work criticized by Haribhadra in his *Ālokā*, it must be written from the Cittamātra position. Gn2, however, Tsong kha pa identifies as one of Bu ston's four pathbreaking commentaries. In arguing against four pathbreaking commentaries and for the existence of only two, Tsong kha pa says that Gn2 is not pathbreaking because it contains extracts from Nāgārjuna's *Mūla-madhyamaka-kārikās*. While he is vague about whether it is written from the same position as Nāgārjuna's *Kārikās*, Tsong kha pa says explicitly that it is not written from the Cittamātra position. Tsong kha pa is not totally happy with the standard of Gn2. Indeed, one of the reasons he gives for its not being by Vasubandhu is that it falls from the high standard of interpretation which is invariably the mark of authentic works by that illustrious writer.

Tsong kha pa exploits the lack of clarity in the relationship between Gn2 and *Nyi khri gzhung 'grel* to attempt to explain a philosophical standpoint that is not obviously of either. In a complicated passage Tsong kha pa (*LBGP*: 26-7) says (to summarize):

(1) According to the *Āmnayānusariṇī*

(1a) Gn2 takes the position of Nāgārjuna;

(1b) Cittamātra doctrines are skillful means to lead disciples to full understanding;

(1c) Haribhadra is open to criticism because Haribhadra incorrectly takes Vasubandhu, the author of Gn2, to be a Cittamātrin writing from an interpretative position, whereas the Gn2 is written from the Madhyamaka perspective;

(1d) There were mistaken Cittamātrins who took Cittamātra to be the final position of the Buddha and mistakenly changed the intention of authoritative Mādhyamikas like Nāgārjuna. Candrakīrti correctly showed the mistake in that interpretation of Nāgārjuna.

(2) The position of the *Āmnayānusariṇī* is problematic because, on Tsong kha pa's own reading of Candrakīrti, Candrakīrti rejects Dignāga's position as being the same as his own definitive one.

(3) A resolution of these problems in Tibet has been effected by saying that well-known Cittamātrin writers like Asaṅga, Vasubandhu, and Dignāga took their own Cittamātra position as the Madhyamaka and interpreted Nāgārjuna from that perspective.

(4) Later authoritative writers like Ratnākaraśānti interpret the Madhyamaka from the Cittamātra perspective in the sense of making a synthesis of two positions.[17]

Tsong kha pa does not explicitly say as much, but his unstated conclusion seems to be that there is, therefore, no need to posit a fifth Mahā-madhyamaka over and above the two schools of Cittamātra and Madhyamaka. This is something he will say explicitly some ten years later in his famous polemical tract, *Legs bshad snying po* (*LBSP*), where the rejection of a Jo nang pa Mahā-madhyamaka is central to his new formulation of a clearly hierarchical four-school system with Prāsaṅgika as the sole exponent of definitive truth at the pinnacle. The removal of a fifth, Jo nang pa Mahāmadhyamaka, was the necessary price to be paid for Tsong kha pa to give his new system coherence.

In *LBGP* Tsong kha pa is willing, like his teacher Nya dbon, to embrace inconsistencies in the received tradition. But that Tsong kha pa was able to do so in his earlier life only with difficulty is evident from his *rTen 'brel bstod pa* ("Praise of Dependent-origination"), a verse summary of *LBSP*, where he says that while sorting through the inconsistences of the Buddhist textual tradition his mind felt like "a piece of wool caught up on a thorn bush" (*CSZD*: 85). That tangle of ideas is unraveled in his *LBSP* and a decisive scheme set forth. This new scheme is a taxonomy of Buddhist beliefs within which all Cittamātra has a merely heuristic status and is simply skillful means allowing a reader to more easily approach the truth enshrined uniquely in the Madhyamaka—specifically the Madhyamaka taught in Candrakīrti's explanation of Nāgārjuna's *Kārikās*. Tsong kha pa—developing a Tibetan tradition going back to Pa tshab Nyi ma grags (b. 1055) and Jayānanda (Ruegg, 1981: 114)—calls this approach the Prāsaṅgika-Madhyamaka. In this new taxonomy there are four schools rising inexorably to the Madhyamaka, and of the two categories of Madhyamaka the highest category, Prāsaṅgika-Madhyamaka, is defined so as to exclude the complicated, syncretistic texts which attempt to reconcile the Cittamātra and Madhyamaka.

Returning for a final time in his *LBSP* (114-117; Hopkins: 231-233, 341; Thurman: 247) to the issue of Vasubandhu and the authorship of the Gn2, Tsong kha pa now categorically states that Gn2 is not by Vasubandhu because Vasubandhu was definitely a Cittamātra author and Gn2 " . . . does not admit ultimate existence capable of withstanding analysis by reasoning analytic of reality. . . . " According to Tsong kha pa's new system, all Cittamātra texts admit such, this being the main reason they are wrong and retain only a heuristic value. Tsong kha pa's final verdict on Gn2 is that it is an incorrect explanation of Madhyamaka, not in accord with Cittamātra views. He rejects it as being a definitive interpretation of the Perfect Wisdom sūtras but retains for it the general authority of an old text in the canon.

In conclusion, it may be helpful to distinguish clearly between a rejection of Dol po pa and a rejection of the Jo nang pa other-empty (*gzhan stong*) view. Dol po pa is perhaps the most famous Tibetan exponent of the Jo nang pa position, and it is well known that he was first demonized by seventeenth- and eighteenth-century dGe lugs pa chauvinists and then rehabilitated by nineteenth-century scholar-saints searching for a better future in a golden past. That, of course, is a different issue, irrelevant to an understanding of how Tibetans were thinking and writing at the end of the fourteenth century. Dol po pa is immediately distinguishable from Nya dbon and the later Jo nang pa writers Shākya mchog ldan and Tāranātha. These later Jo nang pa writers show an encyclopedic knowledge of different Tibetan Buddhist traditions, while Dol po pa justifies his more narrowly defined set of sources through recourse to a questionable theory of golden and degenerate time periods.

This perhaps explains why, in *LBGP*, Tsong kha pa consistently remains open to a discussion, at least, of a number of authors who hold Jo nang pa-type views—Dharmamitra, Ratnākaraśānti, and his own guru Nya dbon—while at the same time vehemently rejecting Dol po pa. "Learned persons," he says, "are right to cast out what he [Dol po pa] says like a gob of spit" (*LBGP*: 426).[18] Tsong kha pa's early antagonism to Dol po pa in particular—which he shared with his teacher Red mda' ba—was perhaps because of the absolutism and narrowness in Dol po pa's presentation of his views, not because of what he said.

Notes

1. Ruegg (1969: 325-327, cited by Thurman, 1984: 244) has briefly discussed the authors of the works, and again (1969: 326 n. 1, cited by Thurman, 1984: 247) says Gn2 is an authoritative Jo nang pa source. Since this paper was written two other important works that consider these questions have been published, Hopkins (1999) and Stearns (1999).

2. However, the steps in the process are yet to be fully ascertained. For instance, in Klong chen pa's *Theg mchog mdzod* (63a), in the section beginning 61b on *Mahā-yāna-siddhānta,* Klong chen pa dissolves the Madhyamaka (*dbu ma pa*) into Prāsaṅgika and Svātantrika (*thal rang gnyis)* and then says that the term *sgyu ma rigs grub* ("Reason-Established Illusionists") refers to Svātantrika (*rang rgyud pa*) (64b5).

3. The *Abhisamayālaṁkāra-nāma-prajñāpāramitopadeśa-śāstra-vivṛtti* is known in Tibetan by the abbreviation *Don gsal* (more fully *'grel pa don gsal*) and *'grel cung* (in parallel with the *Ālokā* which is called *'grel chen*). The words *don gsal* are found in the fourth of the final verses of Haribhadra's colophon in which he gives his own name and describes his commentary as such. R. Tripaṭhi (in *Abhisamayālaṅkāravivṛttiḥ Sphuṭārthā,* Sarnath: Indo-Tibetica 2, 1977) suggested the inspired, but mistaken, reconstruction **Sphuṭārthā*. The Sanskrit of the line is now available. (For bibliographical details see J. Makransky, *Buddhahood Embodied,* Albany: State University of New York Press, 1997, p. 451, and

J.W. de Jong, Review of Makransky 1997 in the *Indo-Iranian Journal*, 42 [Jan. 1999], p. 73.) It reads *kārikā-vivṛttiṁ spaṣṭām Haribhadro'karod imām*. The word *vivṛtti* may mean "commentary on [the *kārikās* of the *Abhisamayālaṁkāra*] off to the side [of the main commentary, the *Ālokā*]." Or, as the Tibetan suggests, it may be in reference to the work's clear identification of, and brief gloss on, each of the *Abhisamayālaṁkāra*'s seventy topics. Hirofusa Amano's recent Sanskrit edition of the work is unfortunately scattered in a number of Japanese publications, and the Sanskrit of the two verses from the text cited below are not found in Amano's edition (H. Amano, "Sanskrit Manuscript of *Abhisamayālaṁkāra-prajñāpāramitopadeśa-śāstra-vivṛtti*," *Bulletin of the Hijiyama Women's Junior College*, 17 [1983], p. 1).

4. I propose to deal with Abhayākaragupta and his forceful criticisms of Haribhadra elsewhere and do not deal with them in this paper.

5. *Bhāvābhāva-vibhāga-pakṣa-nipuṇa-jñānābhimānonnata ācāryo Vasubandhur artha-kathane prāptāspadaḥ paddhatau.*

6. Dharmamitra's *Prasphuṭa-padā (Abhisamayālaṃkāra-nāma-prajñāpāramitopadeśa-śāstra-ṭīkā prasphuṭa-padā)* and (Kulānta Sauvarṇadvīpa) Dharmakīrti-śrī's *Durbodhāloka (Abhisamayālaṃkāra-nāma-prajñāpāramitopadeśa-śāstra-vṛtti durbodhālokā-nāma-ṭīkā)* are both based on the *Vivṛtti*. The former writer's interests seem to be strongly influenced by Vedānta-type views, while the views of the latter, well known as a teacher of Atiśa, are traditionally characterized as Cittamātra. There are three *piṇḍārthas* ("summary") of the *Vivṛtti* as well: Prajñākaramati's *Piṇḍārtha (Abhisamayālaṃkāra-nāma-prajñāpāramitopadeśa-śāstra-vṛtti-piṇḍārtha)*, Ratnakīrti's *Kīrti-kalā (Abhisamayālaṃkāra-nāma-prajñāpāramitopadeśa-śāstra-vṛtti kīrtikalā)* and Buddhajñāna's *Pradīpāvalī* commentary *(Abhisamayālaṃkāra-bhagavatī-prajñāpāramitopadeśa-śāstra-vṛtti-prajñā-pradīpāvalī)*. Buddhajñāna also wrote a commentary *(Prajñā-pāramitā-saṃcaya-gāthā-pañjikā)* on the *Subodhinī (Bhagavad-ratna-guṇa-saṃcaya-gāthā-pañjikā-nāma)*, an explanation of the *Prajñā-pāramitā-ratna-guna-saṃcaya-gāthā* also attributed to Haribhadra. Conze (1960) contains detailed bibliographic information about all these texts.

7. *'gro don rtsa lag dbyig gi gnyen/ rang gi mos pa rtsor byed pas/ shes bya nang gi yin pa la/ yang dag rten nas rnam par bkrol.*

8. Dol po pa's understanding of the different periods of time is set forth by Matthew Kapstein (1992) in the introductory volume to the 'Dzam-Thang edition of the Collected Works of Kun-Mkhyen Dol-po-pa Shes-Rab-Rgyal-Mtshan and by Cyrus Stearns (1999).

9. *Spuṭārthā* (Amano, 1975: 3): "I bow down to perfect wisdom in order to give a breakdown of its Ornamental Verses *(*alaṃkāra-kārikā)* that will be an ornament for all." *(shes rab pha rol phyin pa la/ de'i rgyan tshig le'ur byas pa dag/ kun gyi rgyan du 'gyur bar ni/ rnam par dbye phyir gus phyag 'tshal).*

10. The name given in Tibetan sources is *Prajñā-pāramitā-saṃgraha-kārikā* but it is usually referred to as *brGyad stong bsdus don*. Frauwallner (1959) hesitantly accepts that the Dignāga who wrote the *Pramāṇa-samuccaya* also wrote it. Doubt remains, given the sudden appearance of the text in the late eighth century and the absence of references to it before that time.

11. By *'bum ṭik* Dol po pa might intend the *Vivaraṇa* on the *Ārya-śata-sāhasrikā-prajñā-pāramitā* attributed by some to Kāśmira Dharmaśrī. Its views could be Mahā-madhyamaka; cf. its rejection by Tsong kha pa (*LBGP*: 10). Jagaddala-nivāsin or some such person might then be meant as the author of the *Āmnayānusāriṇī* (cf. Peking catalogue), and a Zhi ba 'byung gnas as the author of Gn1. It is also possible that Zhi ba 'byung gnas is a garbled version of Shānti pa/Rin chen byung gnas zhi ba, i.e. Ratnākaraśānti, who wrote two well-known commentaries on Perfect Wisdom (his *Abhisamayālaṃkāra-kārikā-vṛtti-śuddhamatī* and *Ārya-aṣṭa-sāhasrikā-prajñāpāramitā-pañjikā-sāratamā*) and whose views are often cited appreciatively by followers of Mahā-madhyamaka. Tsong kha pa (*LBGP*: 26) takes Blo dpon Zhi ba 'byung gnas as the author of the *Āmnayanusārinī*.

12. *dPal ldan rgyal po ja gad da lar gnas pa'i bla mchog slob dpon Zhi ba 'byung gnas*. The person of Jagad-dala-nivasin is problematic. In the Peking Catalogue (Suzuki) the author of the *Āmnayanusāriṇi* is Jagad-dala-nivasin. Cyrus Stearns ("The Life and Legacy of the Indian *Mahāpaṇḍita* Vibhūticandra," *Journal of the International Association of Buddhist Studies*, 19(1) [1996]: 129, notes 6-8) mentions Śākyaśrībhadra and his two students Dānaśīla and Vibhūticandra fleeing from Vikramaśila to Jagaddala, a monastery located in the Varendra/ Varendri region (in the north of greater Bengal), founded by Rāma-pāla (1077?-1120?) and destroyed by invaders in about 1207. D. D. Kosambhi (Introduction to *Subhāṣitaratnadośa*, Cambridge, MA: Harvard University Press, 1957, p. xxxvii, n. 7), Y. Kajiyama (*An Introduction to Buddhist Philosophy*, Kyoto, 1957, p. 11) and S. Dutt (*Buddhist Monks and Monasteries of India*, 1962, pp. 376-380) have similar information about the monastery. Earlier, Berthod Laufer ("Bird Divination Among the Tibetans," *T'oung Pao* Series 2, 15 [1914], p. 19) says Dānaśīla "hailed from Varendrajīgatāla, that is, Jīgatīla (Jagaddala) in Varendra, in Eastern India." He dates this Dānaśīla to the ninth century on the grounds that he is made a contemporary of King Khri lde srong btsan of Tibet in the work *sGra sbyor*. Laufer says he is mentioned there with Jñāna-sena (i.e., Ye shes sde) amongst others, and speculates that there may be two Dānaśīlas.

13.Cyrus Stearns's (1999) excellent description of Dol po pa's life and distinctive views, in particular of his presentation of the *kun gzhi ye shes*, appeared after this paper was written.

14. D.K. Barua (1991: 228) mentions a Daṃṣṭṛsena who appears in the record of a gift at the Mahā-bodhi stūpa in Buddha Gayā ("Śākya-bhikṣu Daṃṣṭṛsena, resident of Tiṣyāmratirtha"). He says Tiṣyāmratirtha is a place on the island of Laṅka and that Daṃṣṭṛsena too is just a Singhalese name.

15. Bu ston says that in the Phang thang ma catalogue Gn1 is listed as written by Khri srong lde btsan but in two other catalogues it is said to be an Indian work. Yeshey Thabkay, in his recent edition of *Legs bshad snying po* (Sarnath, 1998: 116, n. 2) provides a helpful summary and also cites Dol po pa's *Ri chos nges don rgya mtsho* which agrees with Bu ston about the authorship of the two texts.

16. Ngawang Zopa's 1978 edition is very hard to read at this point. It seems to read...*ma byed sngung ngo*. I cannot make any sense of this and tentatively

emend it to *'byed sdud do*. Beneath the text, in smaller letters is written *gnod 'joms* (illegible but probably) *du gsung spos* (*sbos*?) *gnyis su lta'o*. Does this mean "Understand there are two *Demon Conquerors* on account of the increase in size of the text"?

17. This complicated passage (*LBGP*: 26.1-27.7) may be rendered into English as follows:

> In the *Āmnayānusariṇī* it explains that one cannot say that the *Paddhati* on the *Pañca-viṃśati-sāhasrikā* contradicts Nāgārjuna's system since it gives an explanation based on extracts from him as scriptural source. And it explains that it is because [of students] not being capable of comprehending the ocean of emptiness without settling on mere representation [first] that the Enlightened One took hold of the Cittamātra system, and that the Āryas [like Asaṅga] explain the consciousness philosophy likewise as well, and hence [such statements by the Enlightened One and Āryas] require interpretation (*neyartha*). Hence [the *Āmnayānusariṇī*] says:
>
> > [Haribhadra's contention that] "Vasubandhu...provided an interpretation based on knowables being of [the nature of] the inner [mind]" stands refuted.
>
> And [the *Āmnayānusariṇī* further] explains that the logicians [like the Cittamātra writer Dharmapāla] changed the texts of the Āryas [like Nāgārjuna and Asaṅga] that are definitive statements, explaining them to be representation only, and says that:
>
> > The master Candrakrīti refuted that in his *Madhyamakāvatāra*. In there, however, the ultimate Perfect Wisdom philosophy is not refuted since he himself accepts that as well. To take it otherwise and [to say that] even the Āryas [because of their teachings requiring interpretation] have different assertions, would lead to their statements lacking all cohesion. Having this in mind [Candrakīrti in his] *Madhyamakāvatāra Auto-commentary* says: "Even writers of treatises such as Dharmapāla and so forth reject the reality of emptiness."
>
> This is what Zhi ba 'byung gnas says. Nevertheless, there is an inner contradiction in his taking Dignāga's explanation to be authoritative and his quoting that extract from the *Madhyamakāvatāra Auto-commentary* as a scriptural source as well, since that extract asserts that Dignāga does not explain the profound dependent arising either.
>
> So leave aside the masters who are brothers [Asaṅga and Vasubandhu] and Dignāga, why, how could one have the capacity even to independently get a grasp of the mental calibre of those who are supposed to be just ordinary: that this one has realized that and this one's realization is not beyond that?
>
> Nevertheless, one gauges from the explanations in the works [of Asaṅga, Vasubandhu, and Dignāga] that they explain their Vijñaptimātratā interpretation to be itself the meaning of the Madhyamaka. This is a tradition well known to most Indian and Tibetan scholars and it seems to be right. For example the guru Ratnākaraśānti, within explaining that Vijñaptimātratā is itself the Madhyamaka, says the thought of Nāgārjuna

and Asaṅga is the same. [His] *Madhyamakālaṁkara* root text commentary and his *Prajñā-pāramitopadeśa*, for instance, explain that—based on establishing the illuminating and experiential dimension (*gsal myong*) of mind as being the fundamental substratum—the absence of subject-object bifurcation is the middle way. So have a look at those. Since the views in the *Demon Conqueror on the Śata, Pañca and Aṣṭādaśa* and of Zhi ba 'byung gnas seem to be pretty much in accord, I will deal with the ramifications of and the reasons for the above in brief as the occasion requires.

18. *LBGP*: 423-426 (cf. Hopkins, 1999: 225-233):

The assertion [of Dol po pa], then, that the later works of Maitreya and the scriptures of the two brothers [Asaṅga and Vasubandhu] are getting at a noncomposite, ultimately established, final outcome empty of all composites, is simply the fabricated nonsense of coarse minds. And were one to say his position agrees with the emptiness in the *gSum gyi gnod 'joms* where it [uses the language of the *Maitreya-paripṛcchā* and] says the true state eye (*dharmatā-cakṣu*) is empty of imaginary (*kalpita*) and notional (*vikalpita*) eyes, [in response we say] that if one wants to explain this approach to emptiness the way an Indian paṇḍita has, then one is going to have to harmonize with what this *gNod 'joms* says, because, together with the *'Bum gyi gnod 'joms* and the *Āmnayānusāriṇī*, which are in agreement with it, it takes the true state of dharmas as the empty basis, and explains it to be empty of imaginary and dependent phenomena. Other than this, there is not one Mādhyamika or Cittamātrin paṇḍita who has ever explained in his way. Thus, although his position and that in both *gNod 'joms* agree simply as far as mere language is concerned (where the final outcome is the empty basis, and the other two natures the dharmas of which it is empty), they are nevertheless totally in disagreement when it comes to what it means. What the *gSum gyi gnod 'joms* says is this: "This thought arises after the three [subject, object, and both] emptinesses have been set forth: Is there or is there not a form of this dharma called 'emptiness'? If there is an 'emptiness,' then emptiness exists, and a nonempty state will also come to exist, because the existence of an antidote (*pratipakṣa*) without the existence of a counterpositive (*vipakṣa*) is impossible. And if there is a nonempty state, then that will be the non-empty state all dharmas are in. After considering this, one decides: 'Emptiness' is nothing at all. Were there to be some other dharma called 'empty' then there would come to be a non-empty dharma, so there is no other dharma called 'empty of subject'." It then gives an example for this: Certain people, from seeing the city of the Gandharvas, produce an awareness of a city, and then, after exploring for it, produce an awareness empty of a city. Being 'empty of a city' [consists] in just that, there is no other dharma. Similarly, an awareness of the dharmas of form, etc. is produced. When a thorough search is made, and those objects are not found, an awareness of the empty as a nonexistence of the awareness of the dharmas is produced. 'The empty' [consists] in just that, and it cannot be that some other dharma has come about. It then says:

"Since there is no emptiness, there is no non-empty either. Since there is no non-empty there is also no emptiness." This is what should be said

> about this. One should not say that there is no emptiness [at all], because [in the sūtra it says that] all dharmas are empty. One should not say that there is emptiness, because when one searches, an 'emptiness' that is some other dharma that has come about is not there at all.

and

> If emptiness were not also empty of the characteristic mark of emptiness, then, since a non-empty dharma would have come about, that "all dharmas are empty" would be contradicted by emptiness, since it would be contradicted by this characteristic mark of emptiness. So, since there is no other dharma of emptiness called 'emptiness' that has come about, it is asserted that it is empty of the characteristic mark of emptiness.

And in the context of emptiness of the ultimate it says:

> "Even nirvāṇa is empty of nirvāṇa...." The ultimate reality—nirvāṇa—is empty of the nature of imaginary nirvāṇa. But does it not say that nirvāṇa is unmoving? Though some speculating listeners would have it that way, ultimately there is no dharma called 'nirvāṇa' at all.

Thus here and elsewhere, in many contexts, it says often that the ultimate and emptiness are empty of an own-being. And both agree in asserting that, in a fundamental state where the ultimate and emptiness are not empty of [own]-being, there is unmoving permanence.

The discussion there [in the *gNod 'joms*] of the true state of dharmas not existing in the imaginary aspect, and not not existing in the state of nonduality, is carried on within considering it to be the reality of all dharmas, out of the fear [that if it were not set forth as such], what is at an extreme might come to be established, because when that state of being free from all extremes is refuted, the heart of the matter is revealed with two refutations. It is not saying it from within asserting that, in actual reality, an unmoving permanence is established, because in the context of the emptiness of the unconditioned it says: "If even in the way of the listeners they do not ultimately exist, what need to mention that it is also the case in the way of emptiness." It thus says that the unconditioned is not established as fact (*don*).

The *Āmnayānusāriṇī* explains thus in its emptinesses section, and the *'Bum gyi gnod 'joms* also is in no way in disagreement with it. As it says: "The own-being of form not ultimately established is 'emptiness.' Do not take it like a vessel and its contents, one being empty of the other." And since there is no other great pathbreaker, besides them, either, who has ever said anything different from this, learned persons are right to cast out what he [Dol po pa] says like a gob of spit.

References

Amano, H.
1975 *A Study on the Abhisamayālaṃkāra-nāma-prajñāpāramitā-upadeśa-śāstra-vṛtti*. Tokyo: Japan Sciences Press.

Ārya Vimuktisena

PSPS *[Ārya]Pañcaviṃśati-sāhasrikā-prajñāpāramitopadeśa-śāstrābhisamayālaṃkāra-vṛtti.* Partially ed. by Corrado Pensa. Serie Orientale Roma, 37. Rome: Istituto Italiano per il Medio ed Estremo Oriente, 1967.

Bu ston Rin chen grub

DSTS *bDe bar gshegs pa'i bstan pa'i gsal byed chos kyi 'byung gnas gsung rab rin po che'i mdzod.* Partially translated by E. Obermiller in *The History of Buddhism, Being an English translation of Bu-ston's "Chos 'byung."* Heidelberg: 1932.

LNM *Shes rab kyi pha rol tu phyin pa'i man ngag gi bstan bcos mngon par rtogs pa'i rgyan ces bya ba'i 'grel pa'i rgya cher bshad pa lung gi nye ma.* Sarnath: Kagyud Relief and Protection Committee, 1979.

Barua, D.K.

1991 *Buddha Gaya Temple: Its History.* Buddha Gaya.

Conze, E.

1979 *The Prajñā-pāramitā Literature.* 'S-Gravenhage: Mouton and Co., 1960; 2nd ed. Tokyo: Reiyukai.

Dol po pa Shes rab rgyal mtshan

MDBT *Shes rab kyi phar rol tu phyin pa man ngag gi bstan bcos mngon par rtogs pa'i rgyan gyi rnam bshad mdo'i don bde blag tu rtog[s] pa.* In the *'Dzam-Thang Edition of the Collected Works of Kun-Mkhyen Dol-po-pa Shes-Rab-Rgyal-Mtshan.* Ed. by Matthew Kapstein. Vol. 4 (*mā*), part 2. Delhi: 1992.

Frauwallner, E.

1959 *"Prajñā-pāramitā-piṇḍārtha-[saṃgraha]." Wiener Zeitschrift für die Kunde Sudasiens,* 3: 140-144.

Gelugpa Student's Welfare Committee

CSZD *Chos spyod zhal 'don ner mkho phyogs bsdebs.* Varanasi: Wā ṇa mtho slob dge ldan spyi las khang, 1979.

Gn1 *'Phags pa shes rab kyi pha rol tu phyin pa 'bum gyi rgya cher 'grel*

Gn2 *Ārya-śata-sāhasrikā-pañca-viṃśati-sāhasrikāṣṭādaśa-sāhasrikā-prajñā-pāramitā-bṛhaṭ-ṭīkā*

Gung thang Blo gros rgya mtsho

TMS *bsTan bcos mngon par rtogs pa'i rgyan gyi 'grel chung don gsal ba'i mchan 'grel dun bzang shing gi nyi ma thar 'dod mun sel.* mTsho sngon mi rigs dpe skrun khang, 1991.

Haribhadra

Ālokā *Abhisamayālaṃkārālokā Prajñā-pāramitā-vyākhyā.* Ed. by Wogihara (1973).

Vivṛtti *Abhisamayālaṃkāra-nāma-prajñāpāramitā-upadeśa-śāstra-vṛtti*. Ed. by Amano (1975).

Hopkins, Jeffrey

1999 *Emptiness in the Mind-Only School of Buddhism*. Berkeley: University of California Press.

Kapstein, Matthew, ed.

1992 *'Dzam-Thang Edition of the Collected Works of Kun-Mkhyen Dol-po-pa Shes-Rab-Rgyal-Mtshan*. Delhi.

Mimaki, K.

1982 *Blo Gsal Grub Mtha'*. Kyoto: University of Kyoto.

1983 "The *Blo Gsal Grub Mtha'* and the Mādhyamika Classification in Tibetan *grub mtha'* Literature." In *Contributions on Tibetan Buddhist Religion and Philosophy*, pp. 161-167. Ed. by E. Steinkellner and H. Tauscher. Vienna: Universität Wien.

Nya dbon Kun dga' dpal

NMOZ *sBtan bcos mngon par rtogs pa'i rgyan 'grel ba dang bcas pa'i rgya 'grel bshad bsbyar yid kyi mun sel*. Delhi: Ngawang Zopa,1978.

Ruegg, D. Seyfort

1963 "The Jo Naṅ Pas: A School of Buddhist Ontologists According to the *Grub mtha' sel gyi me loṅ*." In *Journal of the American Oriental Society*, 83: 73-91.

1969 *La Théorie du Tathāgata-garbha et du gotra*. Paris: Publications de l'École française d'Extrême-Orient, 70.

1981 *The Literature of the Madhyamaka School in India*. A History of Indian Literature, vol. 7, fasc. 1. Wiesbaden: Otto Harrassowitz.

Sopa, Geshe Lhundup and Jeffrey Hopkins

1976 *Practice and Theory of Tibetan Buddhism*. London: Allen and Unwin.

Sparham, Gareth

1993 *Ocean of Eloquence*. Albany: State University of New York Press.

Stearns, Cyrus

1999. *The Buddha from Dolpo*. Albany: State University of New York Press.

Suzuki, D.T., ed.

1955-61 *The Tibetan Tripiṭaka, Peking Edition*. 168 vols. Tokyo and Kyoto: Reprinted under the supervision of the Otani University, Kyoto.

Thurman, Robert A.F.

1984 *Tsong Khapa's Speech of Gold in the Essence of True Eloquence*. Princeton: Princeton University Press.

Tsong kha pa Blo bzang grags pa

LBGP *Shes rab kyi pha rol tu phyin pa'i man ngag gi bstan bcos mngon par rtogs pa'i rgyan 'grel ba dang bcas pa'i rgya cher bshad pa'i legs bshad gser phreng zhes bya ba.* mTsho sngon mi rigs dpe skrun khang, 1986.

LBSP *Gsung rab kyi drang ba dang nges pa'i don rnam par phye ba gsal bar byed pa legs par bshad pa'i snying po.* Varanasi: dGe ldan sphyi las khang, 1973.

Wogihara, U

1973 *Abhisamayālaṃkārālokā Prajñā-pāramitā-vyākhyā. The Work of Haribhadra.* Tokyo: The Tōyō Bunko, 1932-35; reprint ed., Tokyo: Sankibo Buddhist Book Store.

Chapter 9

Gung thang and Sa bzang Ma ti Paṇ chen on the Meaning of "Foundational Consciousness" (*ālaya, kun gzhi*)[1]

Joe Bransford Wilson

Introduction

In this paper, I examine the way in which analysis of the term "foundational consciousness" (*ālayavijñāna, kun gzhi rnam par shes pa*) served as the basis for hermeneutic dialogue between two traditions of Buddhism in pre-modern Tibet and as the basis for their construction of a history of Indian Buddhist doctrinal systems. One tradition is exemplified in the politically and intellectually dominant dGe lugs pa, the other in the persecuted Jo nang pa, whose novel interpretations of Indian Buddhism nonetheless remained influential long after their apparent demise.[2]

The paper takes as its departure a section of Gung thang dKon mchog bstan pa'i sgron me's 1798 critical analysis (*YKZN*) of the topics of foundational consciousness (*ālayavijñāna, kun gzhi rnam par shes pa*) and afflicted mentality (*kliṣṭamanas, nyon mong can gyi yid*) in which he criticizes the fourteenth-century writer Sa bzang Ma ti Paṇ chen's analysis of the term "foundational consciousness." Gung thang (1762-1823) was one of the principal dGe lugs pa exegetes of his time and has given us the lengthiest of the commentaries on Tsong kha pa's (1357-1419) stand-alone work on the issue of foundational consciousness, entitled *Yid dang kun gzhi'i dka' 'grel* (*Commentary on the Difficult Points of Foundational Consciousness and Afflicted Mentality,* hereafter cited as *YKZ*). *YKZ* is a work written early in Tsong kha pa's life, in 1378.

Gung thang's *YKZN* is not, strictly speaking, a commentary on Tsong kha pa. Although most dGe lugs monastic textbooks (*yig cha*) on the subject are merely commentaries on Tsong kha pa's *YKZ*, Gung thang's text follows a different order of topics than does Tsong kha pa's and, in some cases, has a different agenda. The very issue on which Gung thang debates Sa bzang Ma ti Paṇ chen is a case in point; it is not one that is explicitly addressed in *YKZ*.

Sa bzang Ma ti Paṇ chen was one of Tsong kha pa's earliest teachers, instructing the nineteen-year-old student in Sanskrit (Kaschewsky: 24, 82, 252). Sa bzang Ma ti, in his own turn, was a disciple of Dol po pa Shes rab rgyal mtshan (1292-1361—also called Dol bu pa),[3] the great master of the Jo nang pa doctrine (Ruegg, 1963: 81 and n. 37; Stearns: 21). The assertion by Sa bzang Ma ti Paṇ chen that Gung thang finds objectionable is his doctrine of two "foundations" (*ālaya, kun gzhi*): a conventional foundational consciousness and an ultimate foundational wisdom (*CKG*: 85b-87a—cited at *YKZN*: 20b).[4] Sa bzang Ma ti Paṇ chen identifies the ultimate foundation with the buddha essence (*tathāgatagarbha*).

This two-foundations doctrine is based on the presentation of ultimate truth in Dol po pa's *Nges don rgya mtsho*—the core exposition of the Jo nang pa theory of emptiness-of-what-is-other (*gzhan stong*).[5] The two-foundations doctrine is seen, established rhetorically but not scripturally, in Dol po pa's *Kun gzhi'i rab tu dbye ba khyad par du 'phags pa* (*KZR*)and also in his *bKa' bsdu bzhi pa* (translated in Stearns: 127-173). Sa bzang Ma ti Paṇ chen's contribution is to show how such a doctrine, explicit in several sūtra passages, is also implicit in the writings of Asaṅga.

Although Gung thang's source for his critique is Sa bzang Ma ti Paṇ chen's commentary (*CKG*) on Asaṅga's *Abhidharmasamuccaya*, it should be noted that Tsong kha pa studied neither *abhidharma* nor Asaṅga's text with Sa bzang Ma ti Paṇ chen. Tsong kha pa received teaching on the *Abhidharmasamuccaya* and, most likely, on the foundational consciousness, from Red mda' ba (1349-1412) subsequent to his study with Sa bzang Ma ti Paṇ chen. At any rate, it was just after his study of *abhidharma* that Tsong kha pa composed his work on foundational consciousness (Ruegg, 1963: 85-86).

The Jo nang pa "emptiness-of-what-is-other" (*gzhan stong*) doctrine is said by its critics to be a mistaken application to sūtra system philosophy of the tantric doctrine of empty form (*stong gzugs*), form empty of materiality, set forth in the Kālacakra Tantra literature (Ruegg, 1963: 82 and n. 47).[6] This is relevant to the present discussion in that one of the distinctions between dGe lugs pa and Jo nang pa commentary is the dGe lugs insistence on keeping sūtra and tantra separate, as opposed to the more synthetic view of the Jo nang, bKa' brgyud, and rNying ma traditions in which sūtra and tantra are not seen as different hermeneutical realms.[7] Gung thang—following the dGe lugs line—speaks very negatively of such a conflation. In his critique of the Sa skya writer sTag tshang Shes rab rin chen (b. 1405), he calls such a view "a recitation of a profundity that is [merely] a confusion of fish and turnips"—mixing up things that appear to be similar when examined superficially but are actually thoroughly different, and then calling it a profound insight (*YKZN*: 10b).[8]

A Note on Terminology

The Sanskrit term *ālayavijñāna* has most often been translated by scholars of Indian and East Asian Buddhism as "storehouse consciousness." The Tibetan translation of *ālayavijñāna—kun gzhi rnam par shes pa*—on the other hand, does not suggest "storehouse," since *kun gzhi* literally means "basis of all" or, less literally, "universal foundation." Thus, Schmithausen's (1987) "fundamental consciousness" seems the best overall translation. However, the problem is that while for some Tibetan writers (for example, the dGe lugs pas), *kun gzhi* (*ālaya*) and *kun gzhi rnam par shes pa* (*ālayavijñāna*) are synonymous, for others (such as Dol po pa and Sa bzang Ma ti Paṇ chen), they are not. The trick in translating these terms in the present context is to retain (in English) the Tibetan connection between *kun gzhi* and *kun gzhi rnam par shes pa* while allowing the reader to see that the two terms may reasonably be held to have different referents. Thus, Schmithausen's "fundamental consciousness" becomes, when translating the shorter term—*kun gzhi*—"fundament." I have, therefore, opted for a clumsier term—"foundational consciousness"—since it can easily be shortened to "foundation." A more literal set of translations would be "universal foundational consciousness" and "universal foundation" but that would perhaps suggest, misleadingly, that there is only one universal foundation in which all sentient beings share.

A Note on the Literature Treating Foundational Consciousness

In the Indo-Tibetan Buddhist literature there are at least five different generic approaches to foundational consciousness—five different sorts of literary settings in which the terms *ālaya* (*kun gzhi*) and *ālayavijñāna* (*kun gzhi rnam par shes pa*) are used.

1. In the first, the term *ālayavijñāna* is used as one of a set of terms defining what was in the fourth and fifth centuries a new model for conceptualizing Buddhist karma theory, ontology, epistemology and meditative practice; this genre includes works by Asaṅga, Vasubandhu, Sthiramati, and Asvabhāva.

2. The second type of literature uses the term only indirectly, in the reporting of an opponent's position; this polemical approach to the idea is seen, for example, in Candrakīrti's *Madhyamakāvatāra*.

3. The terms *ālaya* and *ālayavijñāna* are also seen in tantric works such as Nāgārjuna's *Bodhicittavivaraṇa*.

4. The terms are also seen in the exegetical literature of India and Tibet as one of the distinctive tenets of a doctrinal system called Yogācāra or Cittamātra. Such reports must be treated separately from the first generic type (the works of Asaṅga, Vasubandhu, and their commentators), although they claim to represent it.

5. The fifth genre are those texts that focus on the term *ālayavijñāna*—for example, the *ālayavijñāna-kliṣṭamanas* literature which forms a part of the dGe lugs doctrinal curriculum (for example, *YKZ* and *YKZN*).

The first generic approach embodies the creation and systematization of the term *ālayavijñāna* seen in the works of Maitreya, Asaṅga, and Vasubandhu, and in their commentators Sthiramati and Asvabhāva. This is most readily seen in the paradigmatic innovation of texts such as Asaṅga's *Mahāyānasaṃgraha* and Vasubandhu's *Triṃśikā* and in the systematization of the new language seen in their commentaries, particularly the *Vivṛtagūḍhārthapiṇḍavyākhyā* ("Unveiling the Secret Meaning") of unknown authorship and the *Viniścayasaṃgrahaṇī*—which is part of the *Yogācārabhūmi*, a work attributed to Asaṅga.

The second generic approach is seen in the critiques of the Maitreya-Asaṅga-Vasubandhu approach by writers such as Bhāvaviveka and Candrakīrti. The third—the use of the term *ālayavijñāna* in tantric texts—has been little studied, and is only indirectly relevant to the issue being discussed here, although Dol po pa Shes rab rgyal mtshan—a secondary player in the dialogue to be examined in this paper—does invoke it.

The fourth generic approach includes both commentarial works and doxographic works. The Indo-Tibetan tenets literature (*siddhānta, grub mtha'*), commonly referred to as "doxographic," constructs an abbreviated system of assertions on a basic set of issues that it calls Yogācāra, Cittamātra, and Vijñaptimātra.[9] Various Tibetan writers use these terms in different ways. The dGe lugs usage of the term conflates the Maitreya-Asaṅga-Vasubandhu tradition and the Dignāga-Dharmakīrti tradition and stipulates that all three terms (Yogācāra, Cittamātra, and Vijñaptimātra) refer to it. For a different Tibetan usage of the terminology, see, for example, the writings of Shākya mchog ldan.[10] There seems to be some danger in using Sanskrit names for these Tibetan reconstructions. Thus, to call this doxographic construction the Mind Only system or, leaving the terminology in Tibetan, the Sems tsam system, may ultimately be preferable to translating the Tibetan into Sanskrit.

In addition to explicitly doxographic works, the term Yogācāra is also used in exegetical works that are not part of the Maitreya-Asaṅga-Vasubandhu tradition to refer to generic positions attributed to those writers and their commentators.

Texts on Universal Foundations and Foundational Consciousness

The fifth genre of literature in which the term *kun gzhi rnam par shes pa* is used is an unusual one: stand-alone presentations or analyses of the subject. The most famous has already been introduced, that written by Tsong kha pa. The many monastery textbooks used to teach Tsong kha pa's text in the dGe lugs pa tradition also belong to this genre, as does Gung thang's text on *kun gzhi* (*YKZN*). The immediate ancestors of Tsong kha pa's text would seem to be indigenous Tibetan commentaries on Asaṅga's *Abhidharmasamuccaya*. Although the *Abhidharmasamuccaya* itself presents a six consciousness system, with no mention of foundational consciousness or afflicted mentality, Tibetan commentators took their cue from the Indian commentary attributed in its Tibetan translation to Jinaputra (the *Abhidharmasamuccayabhāṣya*), who interpolates lengthy discussions of *ālayavijñāna*.[11]

Although Tsong kha pa's *abhidharma* teacher Red mda' ba is said to have written a commentary on the *Abhidharmasamuccaya*, this is no longer extant. It is possible that Tsong kha pa was also familiar with the extensive *Abhidharmasamuccaya* commentary written by Bu ston Rin chen grub (1290-1364); Bu ston devotes twenty-five folios there to *ālayavijñāna* and *kliṣṭamanas*.[12]

The Jo nang pa Dol po pa has also left us a representative of this genre (i.e., presentations devoted only to *kun gzhi*)—a text called *Kun gzhi'i rab tu dbye ba khyad par du 'phags pa* ("The Distinctive Types of Universal Foundations"—*KZR*). It consists mainly of an almost interminable list of pairs of terms, one conventional, the other ultimate. Here is how it begins:[13]

> The "universal foundation" [*ālaya*] spoken of in many scriptures *(gsung rab)* is of two types—a universal foundation which is pristine awareness *(ye shes yin pa'i kun gzhi)* and a universal foundation which is consciousness *(rnam shes yin pa'i kun gzhi)*. Alternatively, the two types [are] a universal foundation which is ultimate *(don dam)* and a universal foundation which is conventional *(kun rdzob)* [literally, "concealed"]. Alternatively, the two types [are] a universal foundation which is uncompounded *('dus ma byas)* and a universal foundation which is compounded *('dus byas)*. Alternatively, the two types [are] a universal foundation which is permanent and a universal foundation which is impermanent. Alternatively, the two types [are] a universal foundation which is natural and primordial and a universal foundation which is artificial and adventitious. Alternatively, the two types [are] a universal foundation which is ultimate virtue and a universal foundation which is undefiled and neutral *(ma sgribs lung ma bstan)*.

The list of pairs continues for some six folios, taking us through many permutations, including "a universal foundation which is the profound emptiness-of-other and a universal foundation which is the not-profound self-emptiness" (108). Along the way there are three folios of exclusively tantric terminology. At the very end of the text, in the midst of a lengthy prayer seeking freedom from various wrong views, is the petition to be free from the view that all universal foundations are "appropriating consciousnesses" (*len pa'i rnam shes*) since that is "a denigration of the foundational wisdom (*kun gzhi ye shes*), the all-pervasive great bliss" (126-129). The view that universal foundations are appropriating consciousnesses is an allusion to a reference in the *Saṃdhinirmocanasūtra* and to Asaṅga's assertion in the *Mahāyānasaṃgraha* that *ālayavijñāna* is *ādānavijñāna*, the consciousness that travels from life to life, appropriating a new body at the time of conception.[14]

Neither Tsong kha pa nor Gung thang refer to the Dol po pa text just cited. Tsong kha pa does not (in *YKZ*) cite or refer to Dol po pa at all, nor does he address the issue of the tantric use of the terms *kun gzhi* and *kun gzhi rnam par shes pa*. Gung thang, however, deals with points raised by Dol po pa at two points. First, in another context (his critique of sTag tshang lo tsa ba's invocation [in *GTKSN*] of tantric practice in explaining the *ālaya*), he invokes the normative dGe lugs pa Consequentialist (*Prāsaṇgika)[15] position which holds that references to *kun gzhi rnam par shes pa* intend emptiness. The locus classicus for this interpretation of *ālayavijñāna* is Candrakīrti's *Madhyamakāvatārabhāṣya* (6.42):[16] "One should understand that it is just emptiness which is indicated by the term *ālayavijñāna*, for [emptiness] abides as the nature of all things." Applying this to the tantric literature, Gung thang cites Tsong kha pa's commentator mKhas grub in that writer's commentary on the *Hevajra Tantra* (*brTags gnyis rnam bshad*) to the effect that in many cases *ālaya* refers to reality (*dharmatā*—for dGe lugs pas, emptiness) and afflicted mentality to the energy winds (*vāyu*, *rlung*) (*YKZN*: 6b).

In the second context in which Gung thang addresses issues raised or implied by Dol po pa, he cites (negatively) Dol po pa's *Nges don rgya mtsho* where that text associates a "pure universal foundation which is pristine-awareness [or, wisdom]" with emptiness-of-other and asserts that such an *ālaya* is "empty of all the phenomena of cyclic existence and is permanent, enduring, immutable, and eternal" (*YKZN*: 22a). Gung thang is quite clear about his agenda here, basing his criticism of Dol po pa on the dGe lugs pa assertion that "even in the [Mind Only] system, the nature of things [that is, emptiness] must be a non-affirming negative which merely eliminates"—without implying something positive (22b).

Sa bzang Ma ti Paṇ chen on the Two Foundations

The *kun gzhi* terminology used by Sa bzang Ma ti Paṇ chen in his commentary on Asaṅga's *Abhidharmasamuccaya* follows that established by Dol po pa.

It is noteworthy that despite the precedent set by Dol po pa of adducing the terminology of tantric literature to explicate the term *kun gzhi*, Sa bzang Ma ti Paṇ chen does not follow suit. However, he still manages to remain outside the boundaries of the dGe lugs analysis of foundational consciousness established by Tsong kha pa and elaborated by Gung thang.

Dol po pa had already conflated the concept of *kun gzhi* as universal foundation with the doctrine of the two truths. Sa bzang Ma ti Paṇ chen unpacks this, in the context of explaining the *vijñānaskandha* under the triple rubric of mind *(citta, sems)*, mentality (*manas, yid*), and consciousness (*vijñāna, rnam par shes pa*). The use of these three usually synonymous terms in reference to, respectively, foundational consciousness, afflicted mentality, and the other six consciousnesses, is well known as a distinctive usage of the Maitreya-Asaṅga-Vasubandhu school.[17]

Sa bzang Ma ti Paṇ chen's strategy is to relate the usage of mind (*citta, sems*) as a synonym of *ālayavijñāna* to the fairly uncontroversial assertion that the nature of the mind is clear light. Thus, the conventional foundational consciousness is mind while the ultimate foundational wisdom is the nature of mind, that nature—naturally luminous clarity—being also called sphere of reality (*dharmadhātu*) and buddha essence (*tathāgatagarbha*) (*CKG*: 86a). What is unacceptable to Gung thang about this is Sa bzang's claim that the Asaṅga who asserts an *ālayavijñāna* also asserts a *tathāgatagarbha*.

However, Sa bzang Ma ti Paṇ chen is able to establish this. He grounds his presentation of an ultimate foundation in scriptural passages.[18] One group of citations focuses on the assertion that the nature of the mind is luminous clarity and includes a sūtra passage, two verses from Maitreya's *Mahāyānasūtrālaṃkāra*, and a passage from his *Ratnagotravibhāga* (cited, of course, as *rGyud bla ma—Uttaratantra*) (*CKG*: 86a). The other group of citations is used to support the identity of the wisdom component (*ye shes kyi cha*) of the *kun gzhi* with buddha essence. Here there are two scriptural citations, both Mahāyāna sūtras, and both are explicated at length in Sa bzang's text. The first is from the *Ghanavyūhasūtra* and states (following Sa bzang's version which differs in a minor way from Gung thang's citation and from the Peking edition of the bKa' 'gyur):[19]

> The *foundation of all* the various minds[20]
> Is the buddha essence; virtuous

Is this essence that the *tathāgatas*[21] teach
Under the name "universal foundation."
Although the [buddha] essence is taught as the universal foundation,
Those of weak intellect do not understand.

All participants in the dialogue—Tsong kha pa, Sa bzang Ma ti Paṇ chen, and Gung thang—agree that a *kun gzhi* is a universal foundation because it is the foundation of cyclic existence and nirvana. This is how Asaṅga begins the *Mahāyānasaṃgraha,* and Asaṅga himself grounds this scripturally in a quotation from the *Mahāyānābhidharmasūtra,* a work that was never translated as an independent text into Tibetan:

It is the source without beginning,
The foundation of all phenomena.
Because it exists, all rebirths
And even nirvāṇa may be attained.[22]

Sa bzang Ma ti Paṇ chen capitalizes on the fact that Asaṅga also quotes this verse in another text, his commentary on Maitreya's *Ratnagotravibhāga,* but does so there in support of the assertion that there is a buddha essence (Maitreya: 72; Ruegg, 1969: 278-279). The verse stops short of actually using the term *ālaya;* it says *sarvadharmasamāśrayaḥ,* with the last member of this compound translated into Tibetan as *gnas* and not *gzhi.* Nonetheless, the consensus of commentators is that this passage serves as a substantial scriptural grounding for a foundation of some sort. Sa bzang Ma ti Paṇ chen argues that when Asaṅga cites it in defense of the position that buddha essence is the foundation of all phenomena, he is saying that there is an *ālaya* which is a buddha essence (*tathāgatagarbha*) (*CKG*: 86b).

Finally, at the very end of his presentation of two universal foundations, Sa bzang Ma ti Paṇ chen distinguishes between them, invoking the traditional Jo nang pa characterizations of conventional and ultimate (*CKG*: 87a):

> For, the universal foundation which has not transcended the nature of conventional consciousness has the characteristics of being impermanent, suffering, empty, and selfless. The universal foundation whose nature is ultimate, nondual wisdom is the final culmination, the perfection of purity, self, bliss, and permanence. Hence, the two differ greatly, like darkness and light, poison and ambrosia, or husk and kernel.

The core of Sa bzang Ma ti Paṇ chen's argument, the basic principle which informs his presentation of *kun gzhi,* is seen in that closing rhetorical flourish. It underscores what he had said in his opening statement (*CKG*: 85b-86b):

> In order to explain[23] the thought of the great systems, one requires knowledge of distinctions such as conventional and ultimate, substratum of [final] nature *(chos can)* and [final] nature *(chos nyid)*, and consciousness *(rnam shes)* and wisdom *(ye shes)*. In particular, one must know the distinction between the two truths concerning mind [that is, *ālayavijñāna*—foundational consciousness] and universal foundation [*ālaya*, that is, foundational wisdom].

Sa bzang Ma ti Paṇ chen's hermeneutics is based on the difference between conventional and ultimate. It is here that Gung thang begins his argument.

Gung thang's Critique

Gung thang, in his *YKZN*, presents Sa bzang Ma ti Paṇ chen's position at great length, quoting many of the same passages from Sa bzang's *Abhidharmasamuccaya* commentary that I have discussed above (*YKZN*: 20b ff.).

Gung thang's rejection of this claim operates at a number of levels. The deepest stems from a basic hermeneutical principle: ultimate truth must be a non-affirming negation, a phenomenon which, itself an absence of something, does not imply anything positive in place of that absent thing (*YKZN*: 22b). For Sa bzang Ma ti Paṇ chen, of course, the ultimate *kun gzhi* is something positive: nondual wisdom. The issue is a complex one. Many interpreters of Asaṅga's thought take him to be saying that in some way mind is the ultimate, the only thing that is real. dGe lugs writers reject this, but in so doing have difficulty explaining all that is said by Asaṅga and Vasubandhu.

Following Tsong kha pa, Gung thang also asserts that although the foundational consciousness is not an object to be eliminated through religious practice, nonetheless it is eliminated along the way, either when one becomes an arhat or, if a bodhisattva, when one attains the eighth stage (*bhūmi*) (*YKZN*: 14ab; Wilson: 369-379). Its continuation may then only be called a fruitional consciousness (*vipākavijñāna*)—not an *ālaya*—and, if one goes on to become a buddha, it is transformed into the mirror-like wisdom (*ādarśajñāna*). It is noteworthy that this is not brought up in the context of Gung thang's criticism of Sa bzang Ma ti Paṇ chen, although it seems to provide some common ground for the dGe lugs pa and Jo nang pa positions. Perhaps this is why it is not emphasized.

A second principle—and one that Gung thang does invoke in his critique of Sa bzang Ma ti Paṇ chen—is that the foundational consciousness as described by Asaṅga in the *Mahāyānasaṃgraha* is basically incompatible with the assertion of buddha essence as described by Asaṅga in his *Ratnagotravibhāga* commentary. The context of this argument is logical and doxographic. dGe lugs pa doxography constructs a school—the Scripturalist Mind Only (**āgamānusara-cittamātra, lung gi rjes 'brang sems tsam pa*)—based on the positions articulated by Asaṅga and Vasubandhu in works such as the *Yogācārabhūmi, Mahāyānasaṃgraha, Viṃśatikā,* and *Triṃśikā.* It is to this school that assertions on foundational consciousness and afflicted mentality belong. In so constructing this Scripturalist Mind Only doctrinal system, however, they do not include all the works of Asaṅga and Vasubandhu, notably, in the present context, excluding Asaṅga's commentary on the *Ratnagotravibhāga.* (The basic contention is that, whereas Vasubandhu is a real Mind Only thinker, Asaṅga knows better. Himself a Consequentialist [that is, a *Prāsaṅgika-Mādhyamika], he taught the Mind Only doctrines only for the sake of his duller disciples such as Vasubandhu. The doctrines presented in the *Ratnagotravibhāga* commentary represent his real thinking and are thus in many ways incompatible with his Mind Only teachings.)

This Scripturalist Mind Only system is defined—based on passages in Maitreya's *Mahāyānasūtrālaṅkāra* and in sūtras such as the *Saṃdhinirmocanasūtra* and the *Laṇkāvatārasūtra*—as teaching that it is not the case that everyone has buddha nature, but that there are those who will only become arhats and even a few who are so naturally depraved as to never attain liberation at all (Wilson: 297 ff. and *YKZ*: 10a ff.). Thus, there is no room in such a doctrinal system for an assertion of buddha essence. This is because the buddha essence taught by Asaṅga when explicating the *Ratnagotravibhāga* is present in all sentient beings.[24]

It is interesting that although Gung thang refuses to allow Sa bzang Ma ti Paṇ chen to mix Asaṅga's interpretation of the *Ratnagotravibhāga* with his statements about foundational consciousness in the *Mahāyānasaṃgraha,* Gung thang himself mixes the *Mahāyānasaṃgraha* Asaṅga with the Asaṅga held by the Tibetan tradition to be the author of the *Yogācārabhūmi*. In his critique of Sa bzang Ma ti Paṇ chen, he asserts that not only buddha essence, but, for that matter, all *gotra* (or innate enlightenment lineages) are merely seeds (*bīja*) or predispositions (*vāsanā*) in the foundational consciousness. He grounds this assertion on citations from the *Bodhisattvabhūmi* and the *Śrāvakabhūmi* (which are sections of the *Yogācārabhūmi*). Recent scholarship is reluctant to accord single authorship to the *Yogācārabhūmi* (Schmithausen: 13-14) and thus Gung thang bases his construction of Asaṅga's Mind Only in part on a text that may not have actually been written by Asaṅga.

Conclusions

Gung thang's underlying agenda is one of pointing out inherent fallacies in Asaṅga's and Vasubandhu's assertion of a foundational consciousness. dGe lugs pas hold that, in the final analysis, there is no such thing as an *ālayavijñāna* as it is defined by Asaṅga and Vasubandhu. In fact the foundational consciousness as seen in the *Triṃśikā*, especially, is barely a cognitive phenomenon. The best the dGe lugs tradition can do with it, interpolating epistemological terminology from outside Scripturalist Mind Only, is to classify it as a mind to which objects appear but which is, itself, incapable of certain knowledge of them (*snang la ma nges*) (*YKZN*: 13b, 22b). More informally, the *ālayavijñāna* is said to be stupid.

Hermeneutically, Gung thang criticizes Sa bzang Ma ti Paṇ chen for mixing the positions of the Mind-Only Asaṅga of the *Mahāyānasaṃgraha* with those of the Consequentialist, Mādhyamika Asaṅga of the *Ratnagotravibhāga* commentary. However, Gung thang himself conflates the positions of the Consequentialist Asaṅga and Candrakīrti's criterion for interpreting the term *ālayavijñāna* (seen in the *Madhyamakāvatārabhāṣya*). This interpretation reads the term *ālayavijñāna* as a reference to emptiness (the *ālaya* or universal foundation) which is to be known (*vijñāna*).

Sa bzang Ma ti Paṇ chen, on the other hand, is willing to take *ālayavijñāna* at face value. His underlying agenda is to read the Jo nang pa doctrine of two truths into references to *ālayavijñāna* and *tathāgatagarbha*. In so doing, he stays closer to the texts than does Gung thang. He is able to retain an *ālaya* which is merely a basis for carrying karmic predispositions from life to life (for him, the *kun gzhi rnam par shes pa* or foundational consciousness) while at the same time speaking of a *kun gzhi* which is cognitive and ultimately useful (foundational wisdom).

Both writers are similar in having underlying programs which, ultimately, derive from considerations other than merely presenting the thought of Asaṅga and Vasubandhu. They differ formally in that whereas Gung thang relies mainly on arguments of logical consistency, Sa bzang Ma ti Paṇ chen seems primarily concerned with explicating scriptural references.

Notes

1. Support for the research and writing of this paper was provided by a research reassignment from the University of North Carolina at Wilmington.

2. This paper was written and put in its final form prior to the publication of Cyrus Stearns's *The Buddha from Dolpo,* a study of the Jo nang master Dol po pa Shes rab rgyal mtshan. I have added a few references to this work as an aid to readers who might wish to look further into the Jo nang side of the issue.

3. David Seyfort Ruegg (1963)—following Thu'u bkvan Blo bzang cho kyi nyi ma (*GTS*: 2b)—calls him Dol bu pa.

4. See also *GTS*: 4b—translated in Ruegg, 1963: 83. See also *GTS*: 6b.

5. See Ruegg, 1963: 83 ff. Ruegg's article is in large part a translation of the chapter on the Jo nang pas from *GTS*.

6. See also *LSNC*: 10. The passage is cited in Tibetan in Ruegg, 1963.

7. See van der Kuijp: 13.

8. Gung thang's sources for this view are Tsong kha pa's commentary on the *Guhyasamāja* and mKhas grub's commentary on the *Hevajra Tantra* (quoted at *YKZN*: 6b).

9. This subject has received some attention. See for example Cabezón and Davidson.

10. See, in particular, his work on the founding (*shing rta srol 'byed*) of the Mahāyāna schools (*STSN*) and the turning of the wheel of the Dharma (*CKKN*).

11. Jinaputra, *Abhidharmasamuccayabhāṣya*: translated into Tibetan as *Chos mngon pa kun las btus pa'i bshad pa* (P5554, vol. 113 in Suzuki). The Sanskrit has been edited by Nathmal Tatia (Patna: K. P. Jayaswal Research Institute, 1976).

12. Concerning Bu ston's attitudes towards the Jo nang pa assertions, see Ruegg, 1963: 76.

13. *Kun gzhi'i rab tu dbye ba khyad par du 'phags pa* (in Collected Works—Paro, Bhutan: Lama Ngodrup and Sherab Drimay, 1984), sides 105-132. The quoted material begins at 106.2. See also Stearns: 143-144.

14. See Gung thang, *YKZN*: 15b; *Mahāyānasaṃgraha* (Lamotte edition): 1.4; and *Saṃdhinirmocanasūtra* (Lamotte edition): 5.7 (also quoted in Sthiramati's *Triṃśikābhāṣya*: 34 [Lévi ed.]).

15. I cite the Sanskrit term Prāsaṇgika merely for the convenience of those who would not otherwise recognize the term "consequentialist." Research

into the writings of the Jo nang pas, on the one hand, and Shākya mchog ldan, on the other, suggest that the normative dGe lugs pa reconstruction of Indian Mādhyamika—which they call *Thal 'gyur ba* or Consequentialist—is only one of many viable Tibetan interpretations.

16. See Wilson: 875, n. 27 for the citations of this passage in the works of Tsong kha pa. (Tsong kha pa quotes it or refers to it a number of times in his commentary on the *Madhyamakāvatārabhāṣya* and also invokes it in his treatise on Mahāyāna hermeneutics, *Drang nges legs bshad snying po*).

17. Sa bzang Ma ti Paṇ chen (*CKG*: 85b) cites the *Ghanavyūhasūtra* in this regard.

18. I use the term "scripture" in an inclusive way here. Although there is, of course, a hierarchy of canonical texts, it is not the case that only sūtras and tantras are accorded special status by Tibetan writers. Many positions on *ālaya*, for example, are scripturally grounded in writings of Asaṅga and Vasubandhu.

19. P778, vol. 39: 152.2.

20. Lhasa edition of Gung thang (20b) reads *sa rnams;* Sa bzang Ma ti Paṇ chen (*CKG*: 86b) erroneously reads *sems rnams*.

21. Lhasa edition (20b) reads *rnams;* Sa bzang Ma ti Paṇ chen (*CKG*: 86b) reads *pas*.

22. *Mahāyānasaṃgraha* 1.1 (Lamotte edition). This verse is also quoted in Sthiramati's *Triṃśikābhāṣya* (on verse 19) which is extant in Sanskrit (Lévi edition: 37): *anādikaliko dhātuḥ sarvadharmasamāśrayaḥ / tasmin sati gatiḥ sarvā nirvāṇādhigamo 'pi vā*. For its many other citations in Indian and Tibetan Buddhist literature, see Wilson: 915, n. 1.

23. Lhasa edition of Gung thang's *YKZN* (20b) reads *shes pa; CKG* (85b) reads *'chad pa*.

24. Two passages from the *Ratnagotravibhāga* are relevant here: (Maitreya: 26): *sambuddhakāyaspharaṇāt tathatāvyatibhedataḥ / gotraśca sadā sarve buddhagarbhāḥ sarīrinaḥ*—translated in Obermiller: 156. See Ruegg, 1969: 250. This passage is quoted by Gung thang elsewhere (*LSNK*: 302). The second passage is actually quoted in Gung thang's *YKZN*: 21b (Maitreya: 40): *aśuddho 'śuddhasuddho 'tha suvisuddho yathākramam / sattvadhāturiti prokto bodhisattvas tathāgataḥ*. See Obermiller: 183.

References

Asaṅga

MS — *Mahāyānasaṃgraha*. Edited by Étienne Lamotte. Louvain: Bureaux du Muséon, 1938-1939.

TCD — *Theg pa chen po bsdus ba*. Tibetan translation of *Mahāyānasaṃgraha*. P5549, vol. 112 in *The Tibetan Tripiṭaka* (see Suzuki).

Bu ston Rin chen grub

CKT *Chos mngon pa kun las btus kyi tika rnam bshad nyi ma'i 'od zer.* Known as *Kun btus ṭika* [an extensive *Abhidharmasamuccaya* commentary]. In Part 20 of *The Collected Works of Bu-ston.* New Delhi: International Academy of Indian Culture, 1971.

Cabezón, José

1990 "The Canonization of Philosophy and the Rhetoric of Siddhānta in Indo-Tibetan Buddhism." In *Buddha Nature: A Festschrift in Honor of Minoru Kiyota*, ed. Paul J. Griffiths and John P. Keenan. San Francisco: Buddhist Books International.

Davidson, R. M.

1986 "Buddhist Systems of Transformation." Ph.D. dissertation, University of California, Berkeley.

Dol po pa Shes rab rgyal mtshan

KZR *Kun gzhi'i rab tu dbye ba khyad par du 'phags pa.* In *Collected Works*, sides 105-132. Paro, Bhutan: Lama Ngodrup and Sherab Drimay, 1984.

Gung thang dKon mchog bstan pa'i sgron me

YKZN *Yid dang kun gzhi'i dka' gnas rnam par bshad pa mkhas pa'i 'jug ngog.* In *Collected Works of Guṅ-thaṅ dkon-mchog bstan-pa'i sgron-me*, vol. 2: 275-402. New Delhi: Ngawang Gelek Demo, 1972.

LSNC *bsTan bcos legs bshad snying po las sems tsam skor gyi mchan 'grel rtsom 'phro.* Blockprint; n.p., n.d.

LSNK *Drang nges rnam 'byed kyi dka' 'grel rtsom 'phro.* Sarnath: Mongolian Lama Guru Deva, 1965.

Jīnaputra

1976 *Abhidharmasamuccayabhāṣya.* Sanskrit edited by Nathmal Tatia. Patna: K. P. Jayaswal Research Institute.

CKS *Chos mngon pa kun las btus pa'i bshad pa.* Tibetan translation of *Abhidharmasamuccayabhāṣya.* In *The Tibetan Tripiṭaka* (see Suzuki).

Kaschewsky, Rudolph

1971 *Das Leben des lamaistischen Heilegen Tsongkhapa Blo-bzaṅ-grags-pa.* Wiesbaden: Otto Harrassowitz.

Maitreya

1950 The *Ratnagotravibhāga Mahāyānottaratantraśāstra.* Sanskrit edited by E. H. Johnston. Patna: Bihar Research Society.

Obermiller, E.

1931 *The Sublime Science of the Great Vehicle to Salvation. Acta Orientalia*, 9: 81-300. Leiden: E.J. Brill.

Ruegg, David Seyfort

1963 "The Jo Naṅ Pas: A School of Buddhist Ontologists According to the *Grub mtha' sel gyi me loṅ*." In *Journal of the American Oriental Society*, 83: 73-91.

1969 *La théorie du tathāgatagarbha et du gotra, études sur la Sotériologie et la Gnoséologie du Bouddhisme*. Paris: École française d'Extrême Orient.

Sa bzang Ma ti Paṇ chen

CKG *Dam pa'i chos mngon pa kun las btus pa'i 'grel pa shes bya ba rab gsal snang ba*. Gangtok: Gonpo Tseten, 1977.

Saṃdhinirmocanasūtra

1935 *Saṃdhinirmocana Sūtra: l'explication des mystères*. Edited by Lamotte. Paris: Adrien Maisonneuve.

1957 *dGongs pa nges par 'grel pa'i mdo*. P774, vol. 29 in *The Tibetan Tripiṭaka* (see Suzuki).

Schmithausen, Lambert

1987 *Ālayavijñāna: On the Origin and the Early Development of a Central Concept of Yogācāra Philosophy*. 2 vols. Studia Philologica Buddhica. Monograph Series, 4. Tokyo: International Institute for Buddhist Studies.

Shākya mchog ldan (gSer mdog Paṇ chen)

CKKN *Chos kyi 'khor lo bskor ba'i rnam gzhag ji ltar 'grub pa'i yi ge gzu bor gnas pa'i mdzangs pa dga' byed*. In *The Complete Works (gsuṅ 'bum) of Gser-mdog Paṇ-chen Śākya-mchog-ldan*. Vol. 16 (ma): 457-482. Thimphu, Bhutan: Kunzang Tobgey, 1975.

STSN *Shing rta chen po'i srol gnyis kyi rnam par dbye ba bshad nas nges don gcig tu bsgrub pa'i bstan bcos kyi rgyas 'grel*. In *Two Controversial Mādhyamika Treatises: comprising reproductions of blockprints of the "Dbu ma la 'jug pa'i rnam bśad ṅes don rnam ṅes" of Roṅ-ston Śes-bya-kun-rig and the "Lugs gñis rnam 'byed rtsa 'grel" of Gser-mdog Paṇ-chen Śakya-mchog-ldan*, pp.319-499. New Delhi: Trayang and Jamyang Samten, 1974.

sTag tshang lo tsa ba Shes rab rin chen

GTKSN *Grub mtha' kun shes nas mtha' bral grub pa zhes bya ba'i bstan bcos rnam par bshad pa legs bshad kyi rgya mtsho*. Thimphu, Bhutan: Kun bzang stobs rgyal, 1976.

Stearns, Cyrus

1999 *The Buddha from Dolpo: A Study of the Life and Thought of the Tibetan Master Dolpopa Sherab Gyaltsen*. Albany: State University of New York Press.

Sthiramati

1935 *Triṃśikābhāṣya*. In *Vijñaptimātratāsiddhi: Deux traités de Vasubandhu: Viṃśatikā et Triṃśikā*. Ed. Sylvain Lévi. Paris: Librarie Ancienne Honoré Champion.

SCS *Sum cu pa'i bshad pa*. Tibetan translation of *Triṃśikābhāṣya*. P5565, vol. 113 in *The Tibetan Tripiṭaka* (see Suzuki).

Suzuki, D.T., ed.

1955-61 *The Tibetan Tripiṭaka, Peking Edition*. 168 vols. Tokyo and Kyoto: Reprinted under the supervision of the Otani University, Kyoto.

Thu'u bkvan Blo bzang chos kyi nyi ma

GTS *Grub mtha' thams cad kyi khungs dang 'dod tshul ston pa legs bshad shel gyi me long*. Ngawang Gelek Demo, n.p.

Tsong kha pa Blo bzang grags pa

YKZ *Yid dang kun gzhi'i dka' gnas rgya cher 'grel pa legs par bshad pa'i rgya mtsho*. New Delhi: International Academy of Indian Culture, 1961.

van der Kuijp, Leonard W. J.

1983 *Contributions to the Development of Tibetan Buddhist Epistemology from the Eleventh to the Thirteenth Century*. Alt- und Neu-indische Studien 26. Wiesbaden: Franz Steiner Verlag.

Vasubandhu

1925 *Vijñaptimātratāsiddhi: Deux traités de Vasubandhu: Viṃśatikā et Triṃśikā*. Ed. Sylvain Lévi. Paris: Librarie Ancienne Honoré Champion.

Wilson, Joe

1984 "The Meaning of Mind in the Mahāyāna Buddhist Philosophy of Mind-Only (Cittamātra): a Study of a Presentation by the Tibetan Scholar Gung thang Jam-̄bay-ȳang (Gung-thang 'Jam-pa'i-dbyangs) of Asaṅga's Theory of Mind-Basis-of-All (*Ālayavijñāna*) and Related Topics in Buddhist Theories of Personal Continuity, Epistemology, and Hermeneutics." Ph.D. dissertation, University of Virginia.

Chapter 10

Authorship and Literary Production in Classical Buddhist Tibet[1]

José Ignacio Cabezón

The primary goal of this essay is twofold: (1) to examine the colophon of Tibetan texts as a literary artifact, and as a source of historical information about the composition, production and dissemination of texts, and (2) to derive from this material at least an implicit theory of authorship in Tibet. These goals (*dgos pa*), however, have ulterior motives (*nying dgos*) behind them, and it might be worth pointing these out before proceeding further.

What it means to be an author is a subject that has preoccupied Western intellectuals from Plato to Derrida.[2] This is understandable, given that in the West intellectuals are, almost by definition, authors, and given as well their penchant for self-reflection. But this preoccupation with authorship as a locus of (mostly literary critical and philosophical) investigation rarely turns outside of its own cultural boundaries in its explorations of the topic.

Are there authors elsewhere? Is what constitutes an author the same everywhere? What might be gained by bringing a different culture's views on authorship into conversation with those that are culturally proximate to us? What might such cross-cultural analysis yield by way of insight for European and American theorists in their problematization of the notion of authorship? How might such a conversation contribute to the theorization of authorship in other cultures (both by "us" and by "them")?[3]

This essay has a number of meta-goals, and one of them—one that can be gleaned from this list of questions—is theoretical and comparative: to introduce an element of alterity (in the form of a Tibetan voice) into the Western conversation concerning authorship, a voice that, by virtue of its cultural distance, prods the Western theorist of authorial subjectivity to think differently, by making the overly familiar notion of an author less so.

Western theorists of the author often slide from descriptions of what authors are to prescriptions of what authors should be. Sometimes this normative dimension is the result of aesthetic or axiological considerations: what makes a work of literature or philosophy good or beautiful or valuable is the presence—or, more recently, the absence—in the work of a certain kind of author. Hence, Bakhtin idealizes the Dostoevskian novel because of its polyphonic quality, because, that is, in it the author sacrifices his own voice so as to allow for the emergence of independent characters (Bakhtin 1981, 1984, 1990).[4] In a move that might be considered at least structurally similar, Barthes implicitly sees the shift from authors to modern scriptors not only as a historical fact, but as a desideratum.[5] Such normative claims often have broad cultural-critical implications. They not only tell us what good authors are, they also inform us as to what authors should be. Such normative implications of a theory of the author are perhaps more evident in a figure like Foucault, who, rejecting even phenomenological and structuralist options as still clinging to the privileging of the author in the "historical and transcendental tradition of the nineteenth century," presents different options as a way of "liberating" oneself from the past, thus allowing for "the possibility of genuine change" (Foucault: esp. 118, 120).

But my purpose here is not to rehearse the normative dimensions implicit in Western theories of the author. It is only to suggest that such implications do exist, and thus to argue that it is also fitting to consider the normative implications of Tibetan theorizations of the author. For I shall indeed claim, by way of conclusion, that what classical Tibetan authors were (or at least what they sometimes were) has something to teach us about how we can and should go about the task of being authors.[6]

A second meta-goal of this essay, though related to the first, has its sights set on the discipline of Buddhist Studies. In a recent essay (Cabezón, 1995), I attempt to identify some of the methodological shifts that have occurred in the discipline in recent years. Chief among these is the shift to greater interdisciplinarity, represented, on the one hand, by the desire to bring Buddhist Studies into conversation with other disciplines such as anthropology and sociology, and, on the other, by the move to apply a variety of critical perspectives (feminist, psychoanalytic, post-structuralist, Marxist, and so forth) to problems in the field. One of the things that has been missing in this movement toward greater interdisciplinarity is a sophisticated and sustained engagement with literary theory.[7] One of my hopes for the present study, then, is that it may serve as a starting point for such a dialogue. The question of authorship is a natural site for such an engagement insofar as authorship is a concern both for Buddhist Studies (and the Buddhist tradition) and for literary theory as fields of inquiry.

The third, and last, of my meta-goals is somewhat more idiosyncratic. For the last several years I have been involved with a group of colleagues in conversations whose goal it is to construct a new discipline, which we call "academic Buddhist theology." (Jackson and Makransky, 2000) To explain and defend this enterprise, and our use of the (admittedly controversial) term "theology," would take us too far afield from the focus of this essay. For our present purposes, suffice it to say that I view the exploration of the theological author, both classical and contemporary, as an essential part of this task. What makes a text theological, as opposed to, say, philosophical or fictional, has largely to do with the way that authors portray themselves in such a text, which in turn depends on a variety of other factors, not the least of which is what (in this case, the Buddhist) tradition says that theological authors are. I will say no more on this matter other than to point out that my efforts in this regard amount to the creation of what might be termed a poetics of Buddhist theological texts, one that is meant to be not only descriptive, but also normative, insofar as it is meant to guide, even if dialogically, the work of those of us who, at least in one of our guises, consider ourselves Buddhist theologians.

Not all of the meta-goals just described can of course be fulfilled in the essay you have before you, but they are nonetheless fundamental as motivating factors for the present work, and so, at the very least, worth noting.

Those familiar with the culture of contemporary native Tibetan Buddhist scholarship will probably not find it an exaggeration on my part when I say that the greatest scholars of this tradition in modern times are in large part orthographically challenged. My own experience of living among such scholars is that many (perhaps even most) of them have poor spelling and writing skills. Nor is this something that these scholars find particularly bothersome or a source of shame. Indeed, there seems to be a certain pride in knowing little by way of grammar, in having poor penmanship and in lacking spelling skills. On the one hand this stems from the fact that although writing—both in block letters (*dbu chen*) and in cursive (*dbu med*)—is taught to young monks at the beginning of the monastic curriculum, there is little need for ordinary[8] "scholarly monks" (*dpe cha ba*) ever to use it. There were in Tibet no written examinations as part of the monastic educational curriculum.[9] Scholarly monks often prided themselves on their complete devotion to the study of the texts that were the core of the curriculum. Anything that took them away from the latter—including the study of the literary sciences (orthography, grammar, poetics, etc.)—was frequently considered a distraction. Monks' inability to write proper Tibetan was thus never seen as detracting from their status as scholars. Scholarship was measured not by one's ability as a writer, but by devotion to what was considered, both intellectually and soteriologically, most important, namely the reading, memorization, and oral explanation of—as well as the tradition of scholarly debate that focused on—the classical texts of the tradition.

I have argued elsewhere (Cabezón, 1994: 83-87) that after a certain point in the history of the dGe lugs pa school of Tibetan Buddhism there arises an ethos in which the writing of new scholarly work is perceived to be not only superfluous (What necessity is there for further written clarification after that already given by the great scholars of the tradition in classical times?) but also presumptuous (How can a modern surpass those great masters of bygone ages?). This ethos, too, contributed to a relative lack of new written scholarly work, and therefore to the situation in which contemporary scholars find themselves: as chirographically handicapped.

This may be the situation today, but what of the writing of texts in more classical times, especially during the heyday of Tibetan scholasticism, roughly from the thirteenth to the sixteenth centuries? A tremendously prolific period in Tibetan scholarly history, we find during these centuries the production of a huge amount of literature of various sorts, including a plethora of the multi-volume collected works (*gsung 'bum*) of particular authors.[10] Together with expertise in explanation (*'chad pa*) and polemic (*rtsod pa*), skill in the art of composition (*rtsom pa*) has traditionally been considered one of the hallmarks of the scholar (*mkhas pa*) (Jackson, 1987; and Krang dbyi sun et al., 1993, vol. 1: 860) and it seems that, unlike what we find in modern times, in medieval Tibet this was taken seriously. Scholars were authors, but what it was to be an author in classical Tibet is a complicated matter.

I will argue that it is incumbent upon Tibetologists not precisely to *re*think—because that implies that there has already occurred a thinking—but to formulate anew, from the texts up, a notion of authorship and literary production in classical Tibet. We operate today—unconsciously, I think—under the presupposition that Tibetan scholars authored texts more or less as we do today: during free moments in the midst of busy teaching and administrative schedules, or in sabbatical-like retreat, stylus in hand and parchment on the table before them, delivering to the printers all but camera-ready copy, ready to be carved into blocks. If nothing else, I hope to show that this was not always the case, and that authorship in high-scholastic Tibet was really more varied and complex than is suggested by this rather simplistic, contemporary notion of literary composition. In particular, I hope to show that in many instances the production of literature (and my focus here will be on philosophical, or more accurately theological, literature) (1) was not the solitary enterprise of the lone scholar, but the communal work of a cluster of individuals; (2) that it involved a division of labor, with different individuals responsible for different aspects of the work (teachers, or what today we might call principal investigators, note-takers, research assistants, editors, scribes, proof-readers, and a production crew that included fund-raisers, librarians, printing supervisors, block carvers, and printers); and (3) that the initial act of literary composition was in many cases oral rather than written.

Some caveats are in order at this point. My data consists principally of the colophons of Tibetan theological texts from the fifteenth and sixteenth centuries. This of course limits my conclusions. It may be that as we examine other genres of literature, or texts from other periods, our conclusions will have to be modified. Secondly, the material examined here, in the next stage of research, will have to be supplemented with historical data, principally derived from biographical texts: data which, once again, may force us to modify our thesis. However, it is my belief that, though tentative, the thesis that I am expounding here concerning the nature of authorship and literary production holds, and that it may prove to be true beyond the historical period and genres examined in this particular study. Only further research will bear this out, however.

Why focus on colophons? The Tibetan colophon is a fascinating literary artifact, often the only source of information we possess about the composition of a particular text.[11] Although a stylistic feature of most classical texts, it has received little scholarly attention. My fascination with the colophon as a literary device will likely lead to a monograph on its stylistics at some later date (a tentative structural stylistic analysis of the colophon is provided in the appendix to this essay), but for the present purposes I am content simply to exploit this material for the information that it yields concerning authorship and literary production.

As an aside, it may be of interest to note that in Europe it is especially texts of the fifteenth and sixteenth centuries that are noted for their colophons. Interestingly, theories of medieval European authorship have been investigated based not on colophons, but on the prologues of glosses and commentaries on the Latin writers. In this regard it is A. J. Minnis's *Medieval Theories of Authorship* (1984)[12] that is the definitive work on the subject. Minnis's meta-purposes and my own overlap. Minnis believes, as do I, that the examination of authorship in radically different settings (in his case, medieval Europe) is potentially a source of insight. For Minnis that insight is both historical and theoretical: it allows us, on the one hand, to see that medieval thinkers had their own theories of authorship, and, on the other, that our modernist or postmodernist theoretical categories may not always be the best ones for understanding the medieval material. From my perspective, however, Minnis fails to realize the full implications of his work, for if medieval Western intellectuals had sophisticated notions of authorship, not only should this be brought into conversation with contemporary literary theory as a vehicle for understanding medieval texts, it should also be mined for its value to us as authors of our own texts. Thus, Minnis fails to realize the full cultural-critical implication of his otherwise outstanding scholarship.

Be that as it may, it is the Tibetan colophon, and the information that it provides, that is of interest to us here, and it is to this that we now turn. Ranging from a few lines to several folios in length, Tibetan colophons frequently give us information about places and dates of the composition and carving of the wood blocks from which the text is printed, about the scholars who requested or ordered the author to compile the work, about the principal author, donors, and the other agents responsible for the production of the work and their respective institutions, about the literary and other sources that influenced the composition, about the intellectual climate in which the text was compiled, and in the case of translations, about the translation staff.[13] Of course, not all colophons contain all of this information, but even when they do not, the Tibetan colophon is still one of the most important and interesting features of Tibetan literature. Let us now turn to some examples by way of illustrating both the style, the contents and the problematics of colophonic material.

Example 1. Author: Go bo Rab 'byams pa bSod nams seng ge (Sectarian affiliation: Sa skya) (1429-1489). Text: *lTa ba'i shan 'byed theg mchog gnad gyi zla zer.* Editions: (1) Varanasi: Sakya Students' Union, 1988 (date of preface), pp. 1-154, (2) offset edition of a written manuscript in *dpe cha* format in the collection of the Institut für Kultur und Geschichte Indiens und Tibets, Universität Hamburg (MIV 345/6, no date, catalogued 1968), most likely printed in Buxaduar, India in the early 1960s, 42 folios; (3) in the collected works of the author, *Kun mkhyen Go bo rab 'byams pa bSod nams seng ge'i bKa' 'bum,* vol. 5 (*ca*), published by Sherab Gyaltsen Lama (Kathmandu) for the Dzongsar Institute (Bir, Kangra, India), 1985, 47 folios, pp. 417-510.

> This *Distinguishing the Views: The Moonlight of Doctrinal Points of the Supreme Vehicle* is, first of all, [the result of] my studying the Madhyamaka scriptures under the omniscient Sangs rgyas 'phel [1411-1485], whose kindness is incomparable. Then, based upon the scriptures of the previous lords [of the Sa skya school],[14] whose pity [for sentient beings] is inseparable from that of Vajradhāra, I took hold of the lamp of linguistic analysis [following] the words of the great Lord Mus pa [dKon mchog rgyal mtshan, 1388-1469], whose name [so fills me with emotion] that it is difficult to pronounce.[15] [With this as background], I studied the texts of the supreme Ārya Nāgārjuna, the father, and his spiritual son [Āryadeva], and generated an ascertaining consciousness of the meaning of reality, and then, wishing to put this in written form so as to teach it to others, [I,] the Sa skya monk bSod nams seng ge, compiled [this text] following the orders of Gung ru Shes rab bzang po [1411-1475],[16] our glorious

> and holy spiritual master, who has traversed the ocean of sūtra and tantra, and who said, "First, do a brief distinguishing of the views." I began [the work] on the seventeenth day of the month of rGyal ("thirteenth" [day] also appears)[17] in the Earth Male Rat year [1468/9] (when he was forty years old) and [I completed it] on the twentieth [day] in the monastery of rTa nag gser gling. The scribe was mGon po dbang phyug. May this too become a force for the spread of the teachings of the Victor. Virtue. *Sarva maṅgalam.*
>
> The beautiful golden flowers, the Victor's teachings,
> Are the adornments of Śrī in the summer, the world.
> Skillful in melodiously proclaiming eloquent sayings
> Are the words of the Lord of Speech, the Omniscient One.
> May the mind-sun of clear-mindedness shine!
> May the lotus of intelligence blossom!
> It is I, Dhyana (*sic*), the one who established the blocks, who states this.[18]

Go ram pa's colophon begins in the usual manner, with the title of the text. He then gives a list of the figures whose writings or teachings influenced him, his experiential qualification (the generation of an ascertaining consciousness of emptiness), and the twofold motivation for compiling the text—the wish to put this understanding into written form (*yi ge bya ba*) so as to teach it to others, on the one hand, and the order of his master, on the other. There follows the identification of the date and place of compilation, the name of the scribe (who probably wrote the final, printer's copy from Go ram pa's autograph) and some auspicious words and verses. The final verses and the interstitial notes are of course the words of the individual responsible for undertaking the production of the wood blocks, and who identifies himself as Dhyana. Altogether, this is not an unusual colophon.

I have chosen to begin with this example so as not to lose sight of the fact that some classical Tibetan texts *do* in fact conform to a model of authorship that should be familiar: that of a single autonomous agent who, at least during the actual writing of the text, works in relative isolation. My thesis that some Tibetan texts are communal products involving a variety of individuals, and that the initial locus of authorship is oral, rather than written, should not be interpreted as a claim that *all* texts were authored in this way. Some, the present example among them, do seem to correspond to a model of textual authorship involving a relatively autonomous author who composes in writing, and this is an important point to keep in mind. It would be too facile—indeed, it would be outright misleading—to suggest that Tibetan authors always worked cooperatively and, as far as the composition of texts is concerned, always worked orally and dialogically. It would be overly simplistic to claim that authorship as a communal and collaborative act, when it does occur, is the direct result of Tibet's Buddhist worldview: that there is a simple and linear correspondence between the ideology of selflessness, say, and the practice of authoring texts. In this latter—and, I would claim, overly simplistic—model, the loss of autonomous agency is ascribed to a kind of kenotic process of self-emptying that is, in the authorial sphere, a practical consequence of the Buddhist no-self doctrine. That cultural practices like the authoring of texts reflect and are reflected in religious ideologies can hardly be denied, but the relationship between cultural practices and ideology are never linear, being mediated by a host of other factors. In short, it would be simplistic to suggest that the collaborative nature of the authorial practices of medieval Tibetans was the direct result of their technologies of selflessness. The time has long passed for broad generalizations of this kind, ones that succumb to a romanticism that seeks to picture everything Tibetan as radically other, and, worse, as unswervingly pure and good by virtue of their sheer otherness.

It is interesting to note Go ram pa's use of the verb "to write" (*yi ge bya ba*) in this example, especially because of its relative infrequency as a term for the authorial act in other colophons. "Writing" as the locus of authorship is more our notion than theirs, for Tibetan scholars rarely reduce authorship to writing (*'bri ba*). True, the verb *'bri ba* ("to write") is found in colophons, but this is almost exclusively an action performed by scribes, and not by authors.[19] Instead, to refer to the action of authors, the textual sources either use no verb at all (as in the next example) or (as in the conclusion of the present one), they use verbs like "do" or "make" (in its honorific, *mdzad pa*), or other verbs like "initiate," "undertake" or "compose" (*rtsom pa*);[20] "establish," "set down" or "fix in place" (*'god pa*); "begin," "compile" or "conjoin" (*sbyor ba*),[21] and this is significant. It implies that authors are perceived as free and creative agents (as opposed to, for example, being conceived as the inspired implements of a divine source, a notion not unknown to medieval Christian theorists of authorial subjectivity) who are not passive, but who must work or toil to achieve their end-result. More important, the authorial task consists of bringing other texts together. In contemporary criticism such a notion finds expression in the idea of intertextuality. As Kristeva defines the idea: "every text takes shape as a mosaic of citations, every text is the absorption and transformation of other texts" (Kristeva: 146; cited in Culler: 139).

What makes an author an author (*mdzad pa po*, literally creator or doer; or *rtsom pa po*, com-poser, one who puts-together) is not the act of writing, but the act of com-pilation or con-junction. This in turn has a number of consequences. It means that the locus of the authorial act is considered to lie elsewhere than in in-scription; that identity as an author lies more in one's ability to manipulate blocks of content-related elements rather than in any chirographic act as such.[22]

Such an analysis of authorship based on the language used to communicate the action of authors is undoubtedly useful, but more can be learned from the colophons, as our next example demonstrates.

***Example* 2**. Author: Paṇ chen Blo bzang chos kyi rgyal msthan (Sectarian affiliation: dGe lugs pa) (1567-1662). Text: *sGra pa Shes rab rin chen pa'i rtsod lan lung rigs seng ge'i nga ro*. Edition: Miscellaneous Works of the First Panchen Lama from the Zangla khar Manuscript Collection (rDzang la mkhar), published by Topden Tsering (Gemur Monastery, H.P. India), 1979, 45 folios, pp. 373-462.

> This "Lion's Roar of Scripture and Reasoning: A Response to the Arguments of sGra pa Shes rab rin chen pa" [was composed] in the temple of the great Dharma College of bKra shis lhun po by the Buddhist monk, the advocate of reasoning, Blo bzang chos kyi rgyal mtshan. [I compose it as if it were] a tax [placed on me] as a result of the insistent requests of the various scholars of the great Dharma College, the foundations of the teachings, the many holders of the *piṭaka*, who have attained the accomplishments of study and explanation; and in particular, [by the insistent requests of] the very learned one who speaks the two languages of sūtra and tantra, the great abbot of Ngam ring, Tshe brtan rgyal mtshan.
>
> The scribe was the master of ten treatises, the holder of the *piṭaka* and the three trainings, sNying stobs rgya mtsho. Afterwards, the text was completed by the scribe rJe drung Blo bzang

dbang rgyal, a Sa skya novice monk of excellent analytical [abilities], who inserted some scriptures and reasoning in the interstices and so forth.

Based on this too, may the precious teachings spread, propagate, and remain for a long time.

[Two Sanskrit mantras]

May Blo bzang bstan 'dzin's and bKra shis rab brtan's virtue [as the result of] establishing the blocks purify all their sins and obscurations, and in all of their rebirths cause them to be cared for by the glorious, holy master.

Maṅgalam.[23]

At least two things are striking about the Paṇ chen bla ma's colophon. The first is that the author identifies the place of composition of the text as the temple of the great Dharma College of bKra shis lhun po monastery.[24] Now temples (*gtsug lag khang*) are the buildings within monastic complexes that serve as meeting places for monks (where, at least today, the installation of lamas and abbots takes place, where rituals are enacted, where special debate sessions are held, and where public teachings occur). This gives us a clue as to the fact that in this instance the process of composition may have been more public than private. It is hard to imagine why a lone scholar would choose to write a text in a temple, unless, of course, he did not write but spoke the text (or more accurately, a proto-form of the text), in the form of teachings, to an audience. Secondly, two scribes are mentioned, a very learned senior monk, sNying thob rgya mtsho, and a more junior monk, rJe drung Blo bzang dbang rgyal, the latter of whom functions—like an editor and research assistant combined—to fill in arguments and add scriptural references.

From these bits of information we can surmise that the text was probably based on public lectures given by the Paṇ chen bla ma. His teachings were first set down by a senior and erudite student—which we can call perhaps the "compiling or senior scribe"—into a working document, which was then added to by a more junior, but nonetheless intelligent, student. This version of the text may have been re-written once again, to yield a clean copy that was then delivered to the printer. This latter version might have been the master from which the blocks were carved, or it might have served as the basis for the master text, which then had to be re-written by yet another (the printer's) scribe. We find the dedication (*bsngo ba*) of the men who either carved the blocks or, more likely, were responsible for their carving, in the last lines of the colophon.

That the authorship of texts often occurred as a group activity based on oral teachings, in the way I have just described, is attested to in a variety of other sources. To cite just three examples, we know, again from colophonic information, that two short Madhyamaka texts of the dGe lugs pa scholar mKhas grub dGe legs dpal bzang (1385-1438) were compiled by one of his senior students, Zhang zhung pa Phyogs las rnam rgyal Chos dbang grags pa'i dpal (1404-1469), as notes on lectures that he gave (Cabezón, 1992: 9). We know as well that the biography of the great bKa' rgyud pa translator and sage Mar pa (Mar ston Chos kyi blo gros, 1012-1096) was originally given in the form of oral teachings which were eventually compiled into a written document (Bacot: 287-288). And we know that the *rNam grol lag bcangs,* a renowned contemporary text of the "stages of the path" (*lam rim*) genre of the dGe lugs pa polymath Pha bong kha bDe chen snying po (1871-1941), was a compilation of notes taken during his 1921 *lam rim* teachings. The notes were originally taken by one of his senior students, Rwa bstod Brag gyab gDong kong rin po che. These were edited/corrected (*bka' bcos ... mdzad*) by Pha bong kha rin po che himself, but only in the first few sections. The work then sat in an unfinished state until the Ven. Khri byang rin po che (1901-1981), the junior tutor to the present Dalai Lama, who was himself present for the original teachings, took up the task of completing it. Khri byang rin po che himself states in the colophon that he did not simply edit the notes, but also added material from Pha bong kha rin po che's other teachings, as well as other material from other sources (Pha bong kha bDe chen snying po, *NGLC*: 776). Thus, the practice of literary composition as a collective activity continues to the present day.

For our last set of examples we shall turn to portions of three colophons that illustrate in greater detail the process of literary production and the agents involved therein.

Example 3. Author: Go bo Rab 'byams pa bSod nams seng ge (Sectarian affiliation: Sa skya) (1429-1489). Text: *rGyal ba thams cad kyi thugs kyi dgongs pa zab mo dbu ma'i de kho na nyid spyi'i ngag gis ston pa nges don rab gsal.* Abbreviated title: *dBu ma'i spyi don.* Edition: in *The Collected Works of Kun-mkhyen Go-rams-pa bSod-nams-seng-ge,* vol. 5 (*ca*), published in Delhi by Sherab Gyaltshen Lama for the

Dzongsar Institute (Bir, Kangra, H.P., India), 208 folios, with Arabic enumeration, 1-415 (the enumeration used here). From the same blocks as the manuscript in *Sa skya bka' 'bum*, vol. 12 (348-451, four folio sides per page). Colophon begins p. 410 (4 lines) followed by 29 numbered verses (410-414), and a postscript (414-415). Translation is from the second publisher's colophon.

> This scripture, that teaches in a clear fashion an exposition of the profound view [of emptiness], by the omniscient king of the Dharma, bSod nams seng ge, who possesses the enlightened activity of being a second teacher in regard to the Conqueror's teachings, [was published] as a basis for study and contemplation on the part of those with clear minds, and so that the pure view [of emptiness] may easily arise within our own and others' mental continua. The propitious conditions were provided by the Head Printer (*spar gnyer*), Ngag dbang 'jigs med, who possesses a mind of virtue and superior intentions. The blocks were completed in the earth monkey year of the Rab tses (1488) at the Chos mdzod sKra shis sgo mang Printing House of [the monastery of] sDe dge Lhun grub steng,[25] which was the seat of the lord of siddhas, Thang stong rgyal po. The fund-raiser was 'Jam dbyangs mkhyen rab mtha' yas, who at the same time was the proofreader, and who says: May virtue be triumphant!
>
> May there be auspiciousness in the great Go ram pa's tradition,
> Blazing in a hundred directions, and destroying the brains of elephants, his opponents,
> With the lion's roar of the errorless theory and practice
> Of the Sa skya pas, the sweet-voiced ones who are the regents of the Conqueror.
>
> *Sarva maṅgalam*
> Virtue[26]

Example 4. Author: Rong ston Shes bya kun rig (= Rong ston Sha kya rgyal mtshan, Rong ston sMra ba'i seng ge) (Sectarian affiliation: Sa skya pa) (1367-1449). Text: *dBu ma rtsa ba'i rnam bshad zab mo'i de kho na nyid snang ba*. Edition: Varanasi: Sakya Students' Union, 1988, pp. 1-337.

> [I,] a monk possessing the three vows, the man from eastern rGyal mo rong, Sha kya'i rgyal mtshan dpal bzang po, commenced [this work] in the temple of the glorious Sa skya; then, in the temple of Ngur smrig, a holy and supreme site [so pure that it seems to] survive on the essence of honey and butter, Rin

dpungs nam mkha' rgyal po,[27] victorious over all sides, the great patron of the teachings, and gYung pa dpon dge sbyong ba[28] brought together the perfect propitious conditions [for the work to continue]; finally, the compilation was completed on an auspicious day at the monastery of rTsang chos lung. May this too cause the spread and propagation of the precious teachings of the Mahāyāna in all directions and throughout all time.

[There follow 8 auspicious verses.]

Yar lungs Chu gling pa, the drop of earth,[29]
And Nam mkha' dpal ldan,[30] the advocate of scripture and reasoning,
Pray that the accomplishments of this [master], and the other masters in the lineage,
And the force of whatever other accumulations of virtue may exist,
Bring about the propagation of the Victor's teachings, the long life
Of the incomparable Lord of the Dharma, that all of his wishes come true,
That all beings constantly find happiness,
And that they quickly obtain perfect buddhahood.

Paṇḍita Nam mkha' brtan pa, rDo rje rgyal mtshan, holder of the *tripiṭaka*, and bSod nams blo gros[31] did the proofreading. The *upāsaka* from Lha mo lung wrote it down. dPon mo che dGe 'dun 'od zer, Legs bzangs brTson 'grus bzang po and bZang rin carved [the blocks]. It was finished at the great and glorious Nalendra rnam par rgyal ba'i chos sde in the first half of the month of Sa ga zla ba in the fire male dragon year[32] [1436].[33]

Example 5. Author: Rong ston Shes bya kun rig (Sectarian affiliation: Sa skya pa) (1367-1449). Text: *Shes rab kyi pha rol tu phyin pa man ngag gi bstan bcos mngon par rtogs pa'i rgyan gyi 'grel pa'i rnam bshad tshig don rab tu gsal ba.* Edition: David P. Jackson, in collaboration with Shunzo Onoda, eds., *Rong-ston on the Prajñāpāramitā Philosophy of the Abhisamayālaṃkāra: His Sub-commentary on Haribhadra's 'Sphuṭārtha'* (Kyoto: Nagata Bunshodo, 1988), 150 folios (8 lines per folio). Photo-reproduction of 15th(?) century xylograph preserved in the collection of Tibet House, New Delhi.

This "Explanatory Commentary on the *Prajñāpāramitopadeśa-śāstra Abhisamayālaṃkāra* called 'A Complete Clarification of the Meaning of the Words'" was begun by the monk, fearless in the methods of explanation, debate, composition and meditation, the man from rGyal mo rong, the great Rong ston Sha kya rgyal mtshan dpal bzang po, in the great temple of Na lendra, and compiled in the great glorious gSang phu ne'u thog, to serve as a source for limitless scholars and practitioners. It was based on my taking to the crown of my head the dust from the feet of many tutors famed for their scholarship and practice, such as the great incomparable scholar [gYag ston] Sangs rgyas dpal (1348-1414), who is renowned throughout the world. May this too cause the precious teachings to spread and to abide for a long time.

The Lord Protector of the World, the powerful Cakravartin,
Opened himself up magnanimously, a portrait of generosity.

The Du dben sha, a swirling cloud of faith,
Helped tremendously in its execution.

In addition, those who radiate purity of karma,
Stars who are the cause of propitious conditions, beautifully arranged flowers,
The nephews of scripture and reasoning, were the ones who made requests.

Exerting himself with many superior thoughts,
The prince, Grags pa by name, [made available] the wood for the blocks
So that his mother could attain emancipation.

[The blocks] were completed at Byang chub gling on the fifteenth day
Of the month of Sa ga zla ba, in the Bird Year.

May virtue as extensive as space,
As pure as the river Ganges,
And as white as the light of the autumn moon,
Cause everyone to quickly obtain unsurpassable enlightenment.

Maṅgalam bhavatu.

The corrections to the carvings of the proofread text of this Prajñāpāramitā were done by Yar lungs pa dPal 'phel. [Alternative reading: The proofreading and carving of this Prajñāpāramitā were completed, in purity, by Yar lungs pa dPal 'phel.][34]

From the above examples and similar colophonic material, and relying on our knowledge of the contemporary process of printing religious texts, we can deduce a number of interesting facts concerning the process of the literary production of this type of text in classical Tibet:

1. Texts were not always compiled in one sitting at a single place. It was often a progressive activity that moved from one monastery to another as the author moved. The movement of senior scholars

depended of course on political, but especially on economic, factors. Traveling with entourages, they were invited to different locations, where they were given financial support for limited periods of time, and this is attested in the historical and biographical sources as well. In the case of example 4 above, three different monasteries are mentioned in connection with the composition of the text, and the blocks were carved at yet a fourth. The author, we can surmise, either himself wrote portions of this commentary during his stay at each of these three locations, or else at each of the sites delivered oral commentarial teachings on the root text which were then compiled into the present text. Be that as it may, the point is that texts were sometimes written progressively at different places, and published at still other establishments.

2. In addition to monasteries—and temples within monasteries—as the sites of composition, we must mention the institution of the printing house (*par/spar khang*) as the place of publication. It was here that the process of carving the blocks, storing them[35]—and printing, storing, distributing and selling the xylographs—took place. In some instances, as in the case of sDe dge, printing houses were large and important institutions within the monastic establishments, with their own permanent staff and budgets. In other cases, they were smaller organizations, with laborers brought in either from the local community or from the ranks of the monks as the need arose. In any case, the publishing of texts was an expensive undertaking: requiring the labor of scribes, proof readers, professional block carvers, and printers, as well as raw material in the form of wood, ink, paper and a variety of tools. This meant that except for the rare instance in which the publication of a text had the subvention of a large printing house, as seems to be the case with example 3 above, it required the financial support of private donors, and this we also glean from the above colophons. Most of these issues can be subsumed under the general heading of the sociology of literary production. I will suggest, only in passing, the relevance of the work of Bourdieu in providing us with a rich theoretical base for beginning the task of dealing with such issues, something that I hope to pursue as my research in this area evolves.

3. Finally, collating the material from these and other sources, we can construct a list of the agents involved in literary production, and the stages of the process itself (see below). I should point out that the list as it is set forth here represents a variety of

possibilities, only some of which are instantiated in any given text. In other words, the following schema represents the most complex possible scenario, portions of which may not be found in any given historical instance.

1. Pre-compilation [Motivation for composition]
   - 1.1. The author (*mdzad pa po, sbyor ba po, rtsom pa po*): the author's own felt need and reasons for composing the work
   - 1.2. Students or colleagues who request the text (*bskul ba po*)
   - 1.3. The author's master (*bla ma*), who orders him to compose the text.
2. Compilation of the text.
   - 2.1. The author: the figure to whom the work is attributed, who either writes the initial draft himself, dictates it verbatim, or who expounds it in the form of general teachings that are set down by a senior student.
   - 2.2. The compiling scribe (*yi ge pa*): who takes down the words of the master verbatim, or who takes notes on his teachings and formulates them into a working document (which may then be re-examined and corrected by the author himself, or passed on to another student for further elaboration).
   - 2.3. The research assistant (*lung rigs sbyor ba po*): who, working from an original draft document (either the author's or the compiling scribe's), expands it, systematizing arguments and adding citations as proof texts, etc.
   - 2.4. Proofreaders (*zhu dag byed pa po*): who correct grammar and spelling in the text received from either the author, the compiling scribe or the research assistant.
   - 2.5. The final scribe (*yongs su rdzogs pa'i yi ge pa*): whose function is to transcribe the text in clean form after the final corrections. This individual may be identical to 4.1 (the printer's scribe) below, but need not be, since it is conceivable that even after the final scribe has completed his work, the text may be written once more to produce a final version from which the blocks are then carved.
   - 2.6. Donors (*sbyin bdag*): who sponsor the author and his entourage, and/or the public teachings, on which the text is based.
3. Printing—supervision and financing.
   - 3.1. The head printer (*spar gnyer*): director of the printing house (*par khang*) in which the blocks will be carved and housed,

and in which the text will be printed, and from which it will be distributed.

3.2. The printing supervisor (*spar kyi 'du byed po*): acts as the author's general agent in overseeing the process of publication through to its completion, from block carving to distribution (especially necessary in smaller institutions where there is no well-established printing house).

3.3. Fund raiser (*yon sbyor ba po*): finds financial support for raw materials and labor.

3.4. Printing donors (*sbyin bdag*): who donate raw materials (e.g., wood for the blocks) or funds for the raw material and/or labor.

4. Printing process

4.1. The printer's scribe (*yi ge pa*): who is responsible for the final writing of the text, from which the blocks will be carved.

4.2. The printer's editor/proofreader (*zhu dag byed pa po*): who corrects the manuscript written by the printer's scribe by checking it against the edition received from the author.

4.3. The block carvers (*spar brkos pa po*): who carve the wood blocks from which the xylograph is printed.

4.4. The proofreader of the carved blocks (*zhu dag brkos dag par byed pa po*): one possible reading of the last line in example 5 might suggest that there is an individual who corrects the blocks once they have been carved, recarving where necessary.

4.5. The printers of the blocks (*spar rgyag pa po*): cut the paper to the appropriate size, and, usually working in pairs, ink the wooden blocks with rollers and press the paper onto the blocks; they then set the pages out to dry, collate them, trim them, and color the sides of the completed text yellow or red, religiously auspicious colors, as a form of offering. The work of the printer we know from contemporary observation, since of course the *terminus ad quem* for information forthcoming from colophons is the wood-block itself.

5. Distribution (from printing houses and their outlets and through independent retailers). There are a number of individuals involved in the distribution process, that range from monks working in the printing houses of monasteries, to workers in the outlet offices of the printing houses, to lay men and women who sell xylographs in stalls on the streets of Tibet's major cities.

Conclusions

Like most of the central concepts that form the basis for the work of Western scholars in the humanities and social sciences—literature, religion, society, culture, gender—authorship is a cultural and historical construct. The work of Barthes, Foucault, and more recent literary critics and legal scholars (see Woodmansee and Jaszi) have gone a long way to exploring the historically situated nature of the author-concept in the West. What has yet to occur to any significant extent is a similar process of defamiliarization across cultures, a process that would unveil not only the historically, but also the culturally, situated character of the author-concept. The failure to do so—to realize, for example, that what it meant to be an author in high scholastic Tibet is very different from what it means to be an author in the West today—has several unwanted consequences. Let me mention just one.

Those of us who work with the Tibetan philosophical/theological literature of this period are of course quite cognizant of its extreme intertextuality. More than intertextual, however, the work of the great Tibetan scholars of this period evinces a kind of "promiscuity" that to the modern Western mind would seem to border on plagiarism. Borrowing without attribution in these sources was of course the rule rather than the exception.[36] Such practices can of course be explained by noting (a) that a good deal of scholastic literary production was commentarial in nature, thus requiring commentators to import others' work into their own, (b) that Tibetan monastic education stressed the verbatim memorization of texts, a practice which, by dislocating texts from written to oral/mental loci, blurred the boundaries of one's own and others' texts,[37] and (c) that Tibetan (and perhaps more generally Buddhist) culture was highly traditional, revering and idealizing the work of previous masters to the point where there was no felt need to restate in one's own words what had already been perfectly stated before. Such observations are, no doubt, important, but they still leave us ill at ease, failing, as they do, to completely assuage in us the feeling that the critical practices of Tibetan scholars were not only different, but arguably inferior.

This type of discomfort, however, is born, in no small part, from our presumed modernist notion of what constitutes an author,[38] a notion that, far from God-given, was the product of, among other things, Enlightenment ideologies of possessive individualism and the economic interests of publishers (see Woodmansee; Jaszi). What perhaps goes farther, then, in mitigating our feeling of unease about

Tibetan intertextual promiscuity—that is, farther than simply observing the historically constructed, and ideologically and economically motivated, character of our notion of authorship—is the contemporary scholarship concerning what authors were before they became isolated, autonomous and creative agents who enjoyed proprietary rights over their work. What emerges from this scholarship is a picture of authorship (e.g., in the Renaissance and earlier) as a collective, corporate and collaborative enterprise, where "words and texts circulated more freely," where the authorial persona is often purposely occluded,[39] and where pastiche is the rule (Woodmansee and Jaszi, Introduction). What is more to the point, the literary critics and legal experts who have unearthed this earlier author-concept argue, normatively, that even today such a notion is more representative of the way that texts are actually produced, and, pragmatically, that—whether in the realm of copyright law or in the classroom—such a notion is, especially in this day of electronic media, a more useful and viable one.

Clearly, the classical Tibetan notion of authorship has a great deal to add to this discussion. Although the similarities between the Tibetan and the premodern European conception of what authors were must be explored in greater depth, the resemblances are clearly there. Moreover, if our colleagues in literature and law are correct in their positive assessment of the earlier author-concept, then perhaps they have provided us with an even greater kindness: in the form of a means—an *upāya*—for leaving behind our unease concerning Tibetan authorial practices, and for appreciating with a new, post-critical naïveté, the genius of Tibetan authors.

Appendix:
Tentative Stylistic Structural Analysis of Colophons

[Not all of the elements are present in every text, and the order of elements may vary.]

I. Author's colophon

- 1. Prose
  - 1.1. Title (can sometimes differ from that found on title page)
  - 1.2. Intellectual factors that have influenced the author (in the first two cases, often with extensive praise)

1.2.1. Previous literature/figures in the tradition
1.2.2. The author's own teachers
1.2.3. The intellectual climate
1.3. Reason for composition
1.3.1. Requests from students/colleagues (often with praise)
1.3.2. Order of the author's master (often with praise)
1.4. Author
1.4.1. Intellectual accomplishments
1.4.2. Spiritual accomplishments
1.4.3. Titles
1.4.4. Name
1.5. Date/Period of composition
1.6. Place[s] of composition
1.6.1. District[s]
1.6.2. Monastery[ies]
1.6.3. Temple[s]
1.7. Scribe (sometimes with praise)
1.8. Research assistant
1.9. Final scribe (sometimes with praise)
1.10. Author's dedication (e.g., for the flourishing of the teachings)
2. Auspicious expressions in Sanskrit (e.g., *śubham, jayantu*)
3. Verses
3.1. In praise of the lineage
3.2. Requesting (e.g., blessings)
3.2.1. That the teachings flourish
3.2.2. That sentient beings attain emancipation
3.2.3. That generally positive conditions prevail
4. Auspicious mantras/expressions in Sanskrit (e.g., *maṅgalam bhavatu, sarva maṅgalam, om svāsti siddham*)
5. Auspicious expressions in Tibetan (e.g., *dge'o*)
II. Publisher's Colophon
1. Verses
1.1. Giving synopsis of subject matter of text
1.2. Describing intellectual climate

1.3. In praise of the lineage
1.4. In praise of the author
1.5. Of dedication, requesting
1.5.1. That the wishes of the author/lineage masters be fulfilled
1.5.2. That the teachings flourish
1.5.3. That sentient beings attain emancipation
1.5.4. Generally positive conditions (e.g., the four types of excellence = *phun tshogs sde bzhi*)
2. Prose [Some of this material can sometimes be found in verse]
2.1. Praise of the author and text
2.2. Motivation for publishing the work
2.3. Proofreader[s]
2.4. Scribe
2.5. Block carver[s]
2.6. Place of publication
2.6.1. District
2.6.2. Monastery
2.6.3. Printing House
2.7. Date of publication
2.8. Donors
2.8.1. General (individuals, groups, even entire towns)
2.8.2. Of wood for blocks
2.9. Special requests of the donor[s]
2.9.1. Related to the text (e.g., that the audience keep an open-minded attitude in regard to the text)
2.9.2. For spiritual goals
3. Auspicious expressions (e.g., *dge legs rnam par rgyal bar gyur cig*)
4. Verses
4.1. Of auspiciousness
4.2. Of dedication
4.2.1. For the emancipation of sentient beings
4.2.2. For the flourishing of the teachings
5. Auspicious mantras/expressions in Sanskrit (as above)
6. Auspicious expressions in Tibetan (as above)
7. Statement of where the blocks are housed.

Notes

1. Different versions or sections of this paper were presented—and have benefited from comments received from colleagues and students—at a variety of institutions, including the Universities of Wisconsin, Freiburg, Lausanne, Virginia, and Emory University. The "author" wishes to express his thanks to colleagues at these various institutions for their invitations and warm hospitality.

2. An important collection of primary texts on this subject is to be found in Burke.

3. Roger Jackson and I have attempted to explore related questions in regard to another topic—literature—in our introduction to Cabezón and Jackson, 1996.

4. I am not unaware of the fact that much of the discussion in the Western sources has focused on fiction, which is admittedly a quite different genre from the one that is the chief object of my investigations in this piece. That being said, I believe that there is, nonetheless, a fair amount of cross-fertilization possible when the Western and Tibetan sources on this subject are brought into conversation.

5. Barthes' most famous statement on the topic is to be found in "The Death of the Author" in Barthes, but see also "From Work to Text" in that same collection.

6. I do not wish to be misunderstood here as claiming that all comparative studies do or must have such normative implications, for some—even some very good ones—do not. Nonetheless, some such studies *do* have cultural-critical implications, and it is my hope to show that this is so in the present case.

7. This is not to say that buddhologists have been completely ignorant of the value of literary critical methods in the study of Buddhist texts. (See, for example, how Faure and Dreyfus use rhetoric in the analysis of two disparate schools of Buddhism, as discussed in Cabezón, 1995: 265, n. 82). However, in Buddhist Studies literary critical methods have yet to enjoy the popularity that they have in biblical studies, to take just one example of a cognate discipline. Even when literary theory is so used, it is usually utilized only interpretively, that is, as an explicative device that takes the Buddhist material as an object (data) on which the analysis is to be "performed," thereby ignoring or, worse, concealing the fact that Buddhism is itself a source of theory, and that it has its own views on matters literary. By contrast, the type of engagement I am advocating here calls for a more complex interaction: one that, taking, in this case, Buddhist theories of the author seriously, acknowledges the Buddhist tradition itself as a source of theory. This is not to impugn the validity or usefulness of the first form of analysis, but only to suggest that it does not exhaust all forms of literary theoretical engagement with the Buddhist tradition.

8. There is evidence to suggest that *sprul sku*s (recognized incarnate lamas), especially those who occupied a high status (*go sa*) in the ecclesiastical hierarchy, probably had more training in orthography and grammar generally.

This is probably due to the fact that their position in Tibetan society made it necessary for them to at least potentially be prepared to write.

9. This situation has changed in exile, where candidates for the *dge bshes* degree must today pass a series of written examinations in order to be granted the degree, but this is a relatively recent phenomenon that stems more from a felt need for legitimacy that comes from mimicking "Western" academic practices rather than from a sense that such written examinations are inherently useful. To a great extent the debate courtyard (*chos rwa*), where scholarly engagement takes place orally, is still the ultimate testing ground for the true scholar.

10. David Jackson (1983: 5) states that the block-printing of Tibetan-language works begins in Mongolia in the thirteenth century. Although the block printing of texts was undertaken in Tibet in the fourteenth century, it is not until the fifteenth century that this activity really begins there in an extensive way. See also Jackson, 1990: esp. 114, n. 1.

11. One of the earliest and most useful treatments of the colophon (with many important examples, edited and translated) is Bacot. See also Taube, and Jackson, 1983, 1989, 1990.

12. A portion of this seminal work is anthologized in Burke: 23-30; see also Minnis, Scott, and Wallace.

13. After writing the bulk of this paper, I came to know, through the kindness of Prof. O. v. Hinuber, of a study of colophons of Northern Thai Pali-language texts of the Lan Na tradition from the fifteenth to the nineteenth centuries: Hinduis. As with the colophons of the Tibetan xylographs, the colophons of these texts (all of them manuscripts), contain a wealth of material on the social and religious history of the culture. Hinduis's work is also valuable as a comparative literary springboard for the material presented in this essay; for example, as regards stylistics. Most important for the present work, however, Hinduis's study confirms what is one of the central theses of my essay, namely, that "the making of a manuscript was often a huge cooperative effort"(29) that required the division of labor in a collaborative enterprise that involved a number of individuals, both lay and monastic. The colophons treated in Hinduis's study are written by scribes who are copying for the most part quite ancient texts—scribes who are far removed, both temporally and culturally, from the original authors of the works being copied. Hence, the similarities with the Tibetan case—as regards stylistics and the collaborative nature of manuscript production—must be articulated carefully, given the very different natures of the Tibetan and Thai enterprises. To cite one obvious difference between the two sets of colophons, little is to be gleaned from the Thai materials about views of authorial subjectivity.

14. The five founders of the Sa skya school; see Jackson, 1983: 3.

15. This standard literary expression is a device for expressing grief for a master who has recently passed away.

16. One of the great scholars of the monastery of Ngor E vam chos ldan, where Go ram pa studied after the age of 25. See Jackson and Onoda: viii-ix,

where Jackson identifies him as the abbot of Nalendra at the time that Sha kya mchog ldan wrote his biography of Rong ston.

17. Both this and the next parenthetical expression are actually found in the Tibetan texts as interlinear notes.

18. (Edition: page = 1: 153; 2: 82; 3: 510) *lTa ba'i shan 'byed theg mchog gnad kyi zla zer zhes* (2: 83) *bya ba 'di ni/ thog mar bka' drin mnyam med kun mkhyen Sangs rgyas 'phel gyi drung du dbu ma'i gzhung lugs mnyan cing/ rJe btsun gong ma rdo rje 'chang dang mi gnyis pa'i thugs mnga' ba de dag di gsung rab kyi steng du mtshan brjod par dka' ba rJe Mus pa chen po'i gsung gis brda sprad pa'i sgron me bzung ste/ 'phags mchog Klu sgrub yab sras kyi gzhung la bltas tshe gnas lugs kyi don la nges shes skyes nas gzhan la ston pa'i yi ge bya ba* (1: *bar*) *'dod pa na/ bdag cag gi dpal ldan bla ma dam pa mdo rgyud rgya mtsho'i pha rol du song pa Gung ru Shes rab bzang po'i zhal snga nas/ thog* (1: 154) *mar lta ba'i shan 'byed mdor bsdus pa gcig gyis zhes bka' gnang ba la brten nas shakya'i dge slong bSod nams seng ges/ sa pho byi ba lo'i (dgung lo bzhi bcus tham pa'i dus/) rgyal zla'i tshes bcu bdun (bcu gsum zhes pa'ang snang ngo//) la dbu btsugs te nyi shu'i nyin rTa nag gser gling gi dgon par sbyar ba'i yi ge pa ni mGon po dbang phyug go /'dis kyang rgyal ba'i bstan pa dar rgyas su byed nus par gyur cig /dge'o/ /sarba mangga lam/*

//thub bstan gser gyi me tog bzang/ /'jig rten dbyar gyi dpal mo'i rgyan/ /legs bshad dbyangs kyis 'bod mkhas pa/ /kun mkhyen ngag gi dbang po'i gsung/ /blo gsal blo yi nyin byed shar/ /blo gros pad mo kha bye shog/ /spar du sgrub po dhya nas smras//

19. The verb *'bri ba* (past, *'bris*) has no real equivalent in the English language, since it connotes both the act of writing (as in *yi ge 'bri*), and the act of drawing (as in *ri mo 'bri*), a connotation that the verb *likh* (the Sanskrit which *'bri ba* is used to translate) also has. The other senses of the Sanskrit verb, namely, "to scratch, scrape, pick, peck, furrow, scarify, lance," and even "to unite sexually with a female" seem to be missing from the semantic range of the Tibetan verb. The Tibetan *'bri ba* is also used to translate the Sanskrit *lot* (to be mad), *upāya*, from *upa-i* (method, means, but also in the sense of stratagem, craft or artifice) *apacaya*, from *apa-ci* (diminution, decay, decline). It may of interest to note, however, that the verb *'bri ba* (past, *'bri ba*), which has the same spelling in the present tense, but a different perfect form, also means (as with Sanskrit *apa-ci*) "to diminish" or "to grow less." A good deal could be made of these various semantic connections. We might ask ourselves, for example, whether the act of writing was perceived as a diminishment of some kind. Such a hypothesis must remain speculative, however, until we find actual discussions of it in the sources themselves.

20. Krang dbyi sun et al., vol. 2: 2234, defines this as "the arranging of words and phrases, in texts, for example" (*dpe cha sogs kyi tshig sbyor sgrig pa*). It is clear from the Buddhist philosophical literature that names or words (*ming*), phrases or sentences (*tshig/ngag*), and letters, etc. (*yi ge*) cannot be reduced to their written forms. Writing (that is, the visible form of letters, words, sentences, etc.) in these sources is considered a simulacrum of the real letters and words. These latter are considered either verbal entities (that is, sound that is spoken/heard) or else entities that are neither physical nor mental (*ldan min 'du byed*). In neither case are letters, words, phrases, or texts their written form. See *Abhidharmakośa*, I: 47ab; and *AKB-tib*: 84a-85b. A more

complete treatment of writing and authorship in the Indian and Tibetan Buddhist tradition would entail a thorough examination of this, and related, literature (for example, an analysis of the claim that texts, residing in the continuum—*rgyud*—of their authors, cannot be reduced to their physical, written forms); but this is beyond the scope of the present essay.

21. Krang dbyi sun, et al., vol. 2: 2027-8, defines *sbyor ba* as "uniting (things) to make (something)" (*bsdebs nas bzo ba*), and "arranging things with respect to one another" (*phan tshun sgrigs pa*). The verb *sbyor ba* also has the sense of fastening. Both the verb *rtsom pa* and the verb *sbyor ba* have the sense of preparing, beginning something or undertaking something anew, arguably implying that there is an element of innovation or creativity involved in the act of authorship.

22. As an aside, it is worth mentioning that a similar picture of an author (*auctor*) emerges in the work of the thirteenth-century European medieval scholastic thinker Bonaventure. See Gómez: 213.

23. (p. 461) *sGra pa Shes rab rin chen pa'i rtsod lan lung rigs seng ge'i nga ro zhes bya ba 'di yang/ Chos grva chen po'i slob dpon rnam pa sogs/ bstan pa'i rtsa lag sde snod 'dzin pa 'chad nyan gyi go sar bzhugs pa mang po dang/ khyad par mdo sngags rab 'byams skad gnyis smra ba/ Ngam ring mkhan chen Tshe brtan rgyal mtshan gyis yang yang bskul ba la brten nas/ Shā kya'i dge slong rigs pa smra ba Blo bzang chos kyi rgyal mtshan gyis/ Chos grva chen po bKra shis lhun po'i gtsug lag khang du gyar khral du 'tshal ba'i yi ge pa ni/ bslab gsum sde gnod 'dzin pa'i bka'* [ed.: *dka'*] *bcu pa sNying stobs rgya mtsho dang/ slad nas mtshams rnams su lung rigs 'ga' zhig 'jugs pa sogs/ yongs su rdzogs pa'i yi ge pa ni/ rnam dpyod phun sum tshogs pa'i Shā kya'i dge tshul rJe drung Blo bzang dbang rgyal lo// //'di la brten nas kyang/ bstan pa rin po che dar zhing rgyas la yun ring du gnas par gyur cig//* [Two mantras follow.]*// Blo bzang bstan 'dzin dang bKra shis rab brtan gyis/ par du bsgrubs pa'i dge bas sdig sgrib ma lus pa 'dag cing* [ms: *tsing*]*/ dpal ldan bla ma dam pas skye ba thams cad du rjes su 'dzin par* (462) *gyur cig// //manga laṃ// //*

24. It is true that *gtsug lag khang* is the Tibetan translation for the Sanskrit *vihāra*, and that therefore it may be being used in an appositional sense to refer to the monastery (the great Dharma College) itself. I am also not unaware of the fact that it is dangerous to argue from the contemporary usage of terms to their understanding in earlier historical periods, so that it may be questionable to assume that *gtsug lag khang* refers to buildings within monastic complexes rather than to the complex in its entirety simply because this is so today. Hence, it is certainly possible to read the relevant passage in the Paṇ chen Lama's colophon "the *vihāra*, the great Dharma College" rather than as I do here, "the temple of the great Dharma college." However, the wording of another, roughly contemporary, colophon, that of mKhas grub rje's *TTC* (1972: 473), also suggests that the temple and the monastery may be different. There, mKhas grub rje states that he composed his text "in the great temple of the great Dharma College of dPal 'khor bde chen." There would be no reason, other than hyperbole, to repeat the adjective "great" twice if the reference was to the monastery as a *vihāra*.

25. Also known as the Great Monastery of sDe dge (sDe dge dgon chen), it was founded by the siddha Thang stong rgyal po in earth dragon year of the eighth *rab byung* (1448). It became the place of worship for the lineage of the

sDe dge kings, and was one of the most famous of the Sa skya pa monasteries, renowned for its library and printing facilities. See Krang dbyi sun, et al., vol. I: 1471-2.

26. */ces thub pa'i bstan pa la ston pa gnyis pa'i phrin las can kun mkhyen chos kyi rgyal po bSod rnams seng ge'i zhal snga nas mdzad pa'i gsung rab zab mo lta ba'i rnam bzhags gsal bar ston pa 'di nyid blo* (415) *gsal rnams kyis thos bsam byed pa'i gzhi dang/ /rang gzhan gyi rgyud la lta ba rnam par dag pa bde blag tu skye ba'i phyir/ /lhag bsam dge ba'i blo can spar gnyer Ngag dbang 'jigs med kyis mthun rkyen bgyis te rab tshes sa sprel lor/ grub dbang Thang stong rgyal po'i bden sa sDe dge Lhun grub steng gi spar khang Chos mdzod bKra shis sgo mang du spar du bsgrubs skabs yon sbyor ba po 'Jam dbyangs mkhyen rab mtha' yas kyis zhu dag dang chabs cig smras pa dge legs rnam par rgyal bar gyur cig /thub bstan rgyal tshab 'jam dbyangs Sa skya'i pa'i/ /lta grub 'khrul med seng ge'i nga ro yis/ /phas rgol glang po'i klad 'gems Go ram che'i/ /ring lugs phyogs brgyar 'bar ba'i bkra shis shog /sarba mangga lam/ dge'o//*

27. One of the "Powerful (noble) Disciples in Tibet"; see Jackson and Onoda: viii.

28. Also mentioned in the colophon to *dBu ma'i rigs pa'i tshogs kyi dka' ba'i gnad bstan pa rigs lam kun gsal.*

29. This is a "poetic ornament for royalty"; see Krang dbyi sun et al., vol. II: 2907.

30. See Jackson and Onoda: xi.

31. His personal attendant at the time of his death. See Jackson and Onoda: xiii.

32. The year after Rong ston pa founded Nalendra, which explains why the work was a progressive one that shifted from one monastery to another up to that time.

33. *sdom pa gsum dang ldan pa'i dge slong/ shar rGyal mo rong pa Shakya'i rgyal mtshan dpal bzang pos/ dpal ldan Sa skya'i gtsug lag khang du mgo brtsams te/ sbrang rtsi dang mar gyi snying po brten* (ms: *brang ti dar ma snying pos bsten*) *pa'i* (335) *gnas mchog dam pa Ngur smrig gi gtsug lag khang du/ bstan pa'i sbyin bdag chen po gzhan gyi phyogs las rnam par rgyal ba Rin dpungs rnam mkha' rgyal po dang/ gYung pa dpon dge sbyong bas mthun pa'i rkyen rnams legs par sbyar nas/ mthar rTsang chos lung dgon par bkra shis pa'i nyi ma la rdzogs par sbyar ba'o/ /'dis kyang theg pa chen po'i bstan pa rin po che phyogs dus kun tu dar zhing rgyas par gyur cig//*
[There follow 8 auspicious verses.]
sa yi thig le Yar lungs chu gling ba/ /lung rigs smra ba Nam mkha' dpal ldan gyis/ / 'di dang rgyud bla'i bar sogs bsgrubs pa dang/ /gzhan yang dge tshogs ji snyad mchis pa'i mthus//
thub bstan rgyas shing mtshungs med chos kyi rjes/ /sku tshe ring zhing bzhed don kun 'grub shog/ /'gro kun phan bdes rtag tu nyer 'tsho shing/ /rdzogs pa'i sangs rgyas myur du thob par shog /ches paṇḍi ta Nam mkha' brten pa dang/ sde gnod 'dzin pa rDo rje rgyal mtshan/ bSod nams blo gros rnams kyis zhus dag bgyis te/ Lha mo lung pa dge bsnyen gyis bri pas/ dPon mo che dGe 'dun 'od zer/ Legs bzangs brTson 'grus bzang po/ /bZang rin rnams kyis brkos te/ me pho 'brug gi lo sa ga zla

ba'i dkar phyogs la/ dpal Na lendra [text: *Na landa*] *rnam par rgyal ba'i chos sde chen por legs par grub pa'o// //*

34. (folio 150a) *Shes rab kyi pha rol tu phyin pa man ngag gi bstan bcos mngon par rtogs pa'i rgyan gyi 'grel pa'i rnam bshad tshig don rab tu gsal ba zhes bya ba 'di ni/ snyan pa'i grags pas sa'i steng ma lus par khyab pa/ 'gran zla med pa'i mkhas pa chen po/ Sangs rgyas dpal la sogs pa/ mkhas shing grub pa brnyas pa'i yongs 'dzin mang po 'i zhabs rdul spyi bor blangs pa la brten nas/ bde bar gshegs pa'i gsung rab dgongs 'grel dang bcas pa thams cad kyi don ji lta ba bzhin du rtogs pa/ 'chad pa dang brtsod pa dang rtsom pa dang bsgom pa'i tshul la bsnyengs pa med pa'i dge slong shar rGyal mo rong pa Rong ston chen po Shākya rgyal mtshan dpal bzang pos/ mkhas grub mtha' yas pa'i 'byung gnas su gyur pa/ Na lendra'i gtsug lag khang chen po***r mgo brtsams te*** [text: *dang tshul mtshungs pa*]*/ dpal ldan gSang phu ne'u thog gi sde chen por sbyar ba'o/ /'dis kyang bstan pa rin po che dar zhing yun ring du gnas par gyur cig// //stobs kyi 'khor los bsgyur ba'i sa skyong dbang/ /sbyin pa'i sgo 'phar yangs pa rab phye zhing/ /dad pa'i chu gter g.yo ba du dben shas/ / 'byor ba'i spobs pa rgya chen rab tu bskyed/ /gzhan yang dkar po'i las la spro rnams kyis/ /mthun rkhyen rgyu skar me tog rab bkram pa/ /rab tu skul bar byed pa lung rigs dbon/ /lhag pa'i bsam ldan du mas rab 'bad ba'i/ /par 'di'i rkang 'thung rgyal bu Grags pa'i mtshan/ /gang gi yum la thar pa bskrun pa'i ched/ /gnyis skyes lo la sa ga zla ba yi/ /dkar phyogs 'phel tshe Byang chub gling du bsgrubs/ /dge ba rnam mkha'i khams ltar yangs pa dang/ /gang gha'i chu klung lta bur dri med cing/ /ston ka'i zla 'od lta bur dkar ba yis/ /thams cad bla med byang chub myur thob shog/ /mamga lam bha va tu//* [in smaller print:] *shes phyin 'di'i/ zhu dag brkos/ Yar lungs pa/ dPal 'phel kyis/ dag par bsgrubs//*

35. Some colophons actually mention where the blocks were housed; see Bacot: 288.

36. A critically sophisticated study of this type of intertextual promiscuity that goes beyond a mere philological analysis, that is, beyond merely noting patterns of borrowing, is a desideratum in the field of Tibetan literary studies. Recent digitization of vast quantities of Tibetan material—by, e.g., the Asian Classics Input Project—make such an undertaking more feasible. This kind of intertextuality is, of course, also to be found in the Indian sources; see Deutsch: 170-172.

37. Such a blurring of boundaries has also been noted in other cases where the text is appropriated in other than written ways; see, for example, the discussion of the charges of plagiarism leveled against Helen Keller in Swan.

38. Woodmansee and Jaszi (3) describe such a notion, which they state is less than 200 years old, as follows: "... *genuine* authorship is *originary*, in the sense that it results not in a variation, an imitation, or an adaptation, and certainly not in a mere reproduction ... but in an utterly new, unique—in a word, 'original'—work which, accordingly, may be said to be the property of its creator and to merit the law's protection as such."

39. A shift away from the persona of the author to "the way in which texts 'in themselves' mean and have a significance which is not fruitfully defined according to the apparatus of authorial intent" is discussed by Clooney as a feature of Advaita literary practice; see Clooney: 32.

References

Bacot, Jacques

1954 "Titres et colophons d'ouvrages non canoniques tibétains." *Bulletin de l'École française d'Extrême Orient*, 44(2): 275-337.

Bakhtin, Mikhail M.

1981 *The Dialogic Imagination*. Ed. by Michael Holquist, trans. by Caryl Emerson and M. Holquist. Austin: University of Texas Press.

1984 *Problems of Dostoevsky's Poetics*. Ed. and trans. by Caryl Emerson, with intro. by Wayne C. Booth. Minneapolis and London: University of Minnesota Press.

1990 *Art and Answerability: Early Philosophical Essays by M. M. Bakhtin*. Ed. M. Holquist and V. Liapunov; trans. and notes by V. Liapunov; supplement translated by K. Brostrom. Austin: University of Texas Press.

Barthes, Roland

1977 *Image Music Text*. Trans. by Stephen Heath. New York: Hill and Wang.

Burke, Séan

1995 *Authorship: From Plato to Postmodernism*. Edinburgh: Edinburgh University Press.

Cabezón, José I.

1992 *A Dose of Emptiness: An Annotated Translation of the* sTong thun chen mo *of mKhas grub dGe legs dpal bzang*. Albany: State University of New York Press.

1994 *Buddhism and Language: A Study of Indo-Tibetan Scholasticism*. Albany: State University of New York Press.

1995 "Buddhist Studies as a Discipline and the Role of Theory." *Journal of the International Association of Buddhist Studies*, 18(2) (special issue "On Method"): 231-268.

Cabezón, José I. and Roger R. Jackson

1996 *Tibetan Literature: Studies in Genre, Essays in Honor of Geshe Lhundup Sopa*. Ithaca, NY: Snow Lion Publications.

Clooney, Francis X.

1993 *Theology After Vedānta: An Experiment in Comparative Theology*. Albany: State University of New York Press.

Culler, Jonathan

1975 *Structuralist Poetics: Structuralism, Linguistics and the Study of Literature*. Ithaca, NY: Cornell University Press.

Deutsch, Eliot
1989 "Knowledge and the Tradition Text in Indian Philosophy." In *Interpreting Across Boundaries: New Essays in Comparative Philosophy,* pp. 165-183. Ed. by Gerald James Larson and Eliot Deutsch. Delhi: Motilal Banarsidass.

Foucault, Michel
1977 "What Is an Author?" In *Language, Counter-Memory, Practice.* Ithaca, NY: Cornell University Press.

Gómez, Luis O.
1995 "Unspoken Paradigms: Meanderings through the Metaphors of a Field." *Journal of the International Association of Buddhist Studies,* 18(2): 183-230.

Hinduis, Harald
1990 "The Colophons of Thirty Pali Manuscripts from Northern Thailand." *Journal of the Pali Text Society,* 14: 1-173.

Jackson, David P.
1983 "Notes on Two Early Printed Editions of Sa-skya-pa Works." *The Tibet Journal,* 8(2): 3-24.
1987 *The Entrance Gate for the Wise: Sa skya Paṇḍita on Indian and Tibetan Traditions of Pramāṇa and Philosophical Discourse.* Vienna: Arbeitskreis für Tibetische und Buddhistische Studien Universität Wien.
1989 "More on the Old dGa'-ldan and Gong-dkar-ba Xylograph Editions." *Studies in Central and East Asian Religions,* 2: 1-18.
1990 "The Earliest Printing of Tsong-kha-pa's Works: The Old dGa'-ldan Editions." In L. Epstein and R. F. Sherburne, eds., *Reflections on Tibetan Culture: Essays in Memory of Turrell V. Wylie.* Lampeter, Wales: The Edwin Mellen Press.

Jackson, David P. and Shunzo Onoda
1988 *Rong-ston on the Prajñāpāramitā Philosophy of the Abhisamayālaṃkāra: His Commentary on Haribhadra's 'Sphuṭārtha'.* Kyoto: Nagata Bunshodo.

Jackson, Roger R. and John J. Makransky, eds.
2000 *Buddhist Theology: Critical Reflections by Contemporary Buddhist Scholars.* Surrey: Curzon Press.

Jaszi, Peter
1994 "On the Author Effect: Contemporary Copyright and Collective Creativity." In Woodmansee and Jaszi: 29-56.

Krang dbyi sun et al.
1993 *Bod rgya tshig mdzod chen mo.* 3 vols. Mi rigs dpe skrun khang.

Kristeva, Julia
1969 *Semiotike: Recherches pour une sémanalyse.* Paris: Seuil.

Minnis, A. J.
1984 *Medieval Theories of Authorship: Scholastic Literary Attitudes in the Later Middle Ages.* London: Scholar Press.

Minnis, A. J. and A. B. Scott, with the assistance of D. Wallace
1988 *Medieval Literary Theory and Criticism c. 1100-1375.* Oxford: Clarendon Press.

mKhas grub rje (dGe legs dpal bzang)
TTC *sTong thun chen mo.* Ed. by Lha-mkhar yoṅs-'dzin bstan-pa rgyal-mtshan. Madhyamika Text Series, vol. 1. New Delhi: 1972.

Pha bong kha bDe chen snying po
NGLC *rNam grol lag lcangs.* In *Collected Works of Pha-boṅ-kha-pa Byams-pa-bstan-'dzin-'phrin-las-rgya-mtsho,* vol. 2. Ed. by Chophel Legdan. New Delhi: 1974.

Swan, Jim
1994 "Touching Words: Helen Keller, Plagiarism, Authorship." In Woodmansee and Jaszi: 57-100.

Taube, Manfred
1966 *Tibetische Handschriften und Blockdrücke.* 4 vols. Wiesbaden: Franz Steiner Verlag.

Vasubandhu
AKB-tib. *Abhidharmakośabhāṣyam.* Tibetan translation in digital format. Asian Classics Input Project, release III. TD409OE.RAW.

Woodmansee, Martha
1994 "On The Author Effect: Recovering Collectivity." In Woodmansee and Jaszi: 15-28.

Woodmansee, Martha and Peter Jaszi, eds.
1994 *The Construction of Authorship: Textual Appropriation in Law and Literature.* Durham and London: Duke University Press.

Chapter 11

Altruism and Adversity

Perspectives from Psychoanalytic Object Relations Theory[1]

Harvey B. Aronson

The last thirty to forty years have witnessed a quantum leap in our exposure to Buddhist ideas. We of the West, whether through travel and study abroad, or through lectures and readings at home, have had the opportunity to become acquainted with a breadth and depth of Buddhist teachings unavailable at any time before. One subject that has received particular attention in talks and writings by Buddhist teachers and scholars, especially of Mahāyāna, has been that of altruism—its importance, reasons for developing it, and methods of strengthening it. In fact there are now an excellent variety of primary sources in translation on the Buddhist teachings concerning altruism, and it will not be my purpose here to summarize or rehearse what can be found in those texts.[2] Rather, I would like to consider some of the issues that arise for modern Westerners who come in contact with Buddhist instructions on altruism and attempt to practice them.

These reflections are from my observations of Westerners who have sought to enlarge their concern for others by Buddhist teachings; however, they are for the most part equally applicable to altruistic endeavors within the Judeo-Christian traditions. These observations are made mainly from the perspective of psychoanalytic object relations theory, the burgeoning field which closely explores the vicissitudes of an individual's relationships with significant others (called "objects" in the technical vocabulary of psychoanalysis based on Freud's identification of the "objects" or targets of instinctual drive).[3]

Regarding the psychological side of altruism, I discuss the following: Freud on altruism; Winnicott's contributions on True Self/False Self and their relevance to altruism; the issue of compliance; the notions of a healthy psychological self, selfishness, selfless activity, and selflessness; approaches to altruism through fullness and trial; a possible psychological explanation for the furtherance of altruism under adverse conditions; issues related to imposed adversity; and mature altruism.

Freud on Altruism

For the purposes of this paper, I suggest the following definition of altruism: The attitude of loving others as oneself and the physical, verbal, and mental activities derived from this attitude. Such an attitude is valued in Theravāda and stressed in Mahāyāna. Jesus advocated a similar norm (Matthew 7:12), and it is found also in the Hebrew Bible (Lev. 19:18). While loving others as oneself is hard enough, these religious traditions use this guide as merely the starting point, and express its fulfillment in tales of saints who value others even more than themselves.

This more selfless variant of altruism is highly favored in Mahāyāna Buddhism, which emphasizes the indebtedness of every individual to all others for kindnesses bestowed in earlier lives (Rabten: 31-53; Dhargyey: 105-138; Tsong-ka-pa, Kensur Lekden, and Hopkins: 23-79). Mahāyānists have therefore developed reflections and meditations for awakening one's sense of relatedness, and based on this, the aspiration to buddhahood: a goal which the practitioner is encouraged to adopt for the sake of others. Thereby, in the final analysis, those who follow the Mahāyāna path attempt to subordinate their own interest to the welfare of others.

As forcefully and eloquently as religious traditions praise altruism, so did Freud qualify it. There is an uncanny quality to Freud's writing on altruism when one reads it in juxtaposition to classical Mahāyāna Buddhist authors. It is almost as if the modern twentieth-century father of psychoanalysis were writing in direct response to the eighth-century Indian Buddhist author Śāntideva, who wrote:

> First of all I should make an effort
> To meditate upon the equality between self and others:
> I should protect all beings as I do myself
> Because we are all equal in (wanting) pleasure and (not wanting) pain. (Śāntideva: 8: 90)

Freud writes:

> But if he is a stranger to me and cannot attract me by any value he has in himself or any significance he may have already acquired in my emotional life, it will be hard for me to love him. I shall even be doing wrong if I do, for my love is valued as a privilege by all those belonging to me; it is an injustice to them if I put a stranger on a level with them. But if I am to love him (with that kind of universal love) simply because he, too, is a denizen of earth, like an insect or earthworm or a grass-snake, then I fear that but a small modicum of love will fall to his lot and it would be impossible for me to love him as much as by all the laws of reason I am entitled to retain for myself. What is the point of an injunction promulgated with such solemnity, if reason does not recommend it? (Freud, 1955: 82)
>
> . . . men are not gentle, friendly creatures wishing for love, who simply defend themselves if attacked, but that a powerful measure of desire for aggression has to be reckoned as part of their instinctual endowment. (85)
>
> Culture has to call up every possible reinforcement in order to erect barriers against the aggressive instincts of men and hold their manifestation in check by reaction formations in men's minds . . . hence, too, its ideal command to love one's neighbor as oneself, which is really justified by the fact that nothing is so completely at variance with original human nature as this. (87)
>
> Men clearly do not find it easy to do without satisfaction of this tendency to aggression that is in them; when deprived of satisfaction of it they are ill at ease. (90)[4]

In brief, Freud's arguments with respect to altruism in *Civilization and Its Discontents* are:

1. It is not appropriate to attempt a universal sense of close ness in the social order, where distinctions of close and distant obtain.
2. Altruism is not reasonable.

> 3. The dangers of innate instinctual aggression lead civilization to support altruism. However, this attitude is difficult if not impossible to sustain.

I do not accept Freud's view on an innate instinct to aggression in human beings, but suspect that discussions like this about the essential nature of human beings come down to metaphysical faith decisions not accessible to empirical trial (cf. Greenberg and Mitchell: 19; and Freud, 1930: 101-102).

Furthermore, I do not consider that the attempt to develop altruism is either ethically wrong or pragmatically unfeasible; rather, I consider it a valuable enterprise capable of gradual success. I base this on my observations of human kindness in general, and specifically on my contact with Mahāyāna Buddhist teachers who have embodied an attitude of universal concern in action. These advanced practitioners have demonstrated how they negotiate the delicate movement between universal concern on the one hand and ordinary social distinctions on the other. In contrast to Freud, who did not see universal concern as compatible with the particular ties of social reality, I would argue that they are. The Dalai Lama's oft-repeated humanizing words of warmth for Mao Zedong, an acknowledged enemy who brutally repressed Tibet's people and culture, conjoined with his dedication to the survival of Tibetan culture and religious freedom are a significant example of altruism which is cognizant of social reality.

Freud finds reason in opposition to altruism, but within the context of a belief in repeated rebirth, laws of karma, and the view that altruism is a beneficial state of mind, Mahāyāna Buddhists argue quite reasonably for the development of this attitude (Gyatso: 234-258; Rabten: 31-48; Tsong-ka-pa, Kensur Lekden, and Hopkins: 23-79).

Finally, in considering the "instinct to aggression," it must be stated that the psychoanalytic community no longer speaks with one voice about this particular piece of Freud's theories (Greenberg and Mitchell: 404). Some see aggression as a "personal defensive reaction against a threat to the ego" (Guntrip, 1973: 39; Kohut, 1980: 467). This view understands aggression as a socially generated response, not as an innate instinct in constant need of containment.

In sum, Freud's position in relation to altruism, though wedded to the rational, is metaphysical rather than empirical. We can argue just as validly that human beings can develop universal concern within sustaining ordinary social distinctions, and that one can present reasoned arguments in favor of altruism. Furthermore, personal observation has led me to believe that not only is altruism laudable, it is practicable. Practicable, but not easy. And here we can agree with Freud. Within the context of valuing altruism, I would like to consider several types of obstacles to this attitude from a psychoanalytic object relations perspective, or in simpler terms, from the point of view of considering relationship issues of self and other.

Healthy or True Self/False Self and Unmet Needs

When we read or hear about altruism, we often are told that we should give up selfishness or self-cherishing. As a clinician, I can't help but notice the apparent conflict that seems to obtain between the obvious importance of a healthy psychological self and guidelines to altruism which advocate selfless activity (cf. Engler: 25-26). Donald W. Winnicott, one of the most creative contributors to recent psychoanalytic object relations theory, in his writings provides a framework within which we can consider the relationship between a vital sense of self and selfless altruistic activity.

Winnicott calls the healthy sense of self the True Self and discusses both its development and qualities (Winnicott: 140-152). Winnicott sees the True Self as emerging through the mother being in tune with and responding to the infant's spontaneous gestures and needs (Winnicott: 145). He finds that it is absolutely essential to healthy development that the primary caregiver respond to the very young infant's wishes at the very moment of their arising, thereby generating in the infant a sense of near omnipotence.

Only on the basis of this healthy sense of omnipotence will the child later be able to accommodate to reality while maintaining the capacity to play (Winnicott: 146). If this earliest level of mother-child attunement does not go well, the child may attempt to secure her/his aims through developing a personality which is in compliance with environmental demands, one which Winnicott calls the False Self (Winnicott: 147). If we wish to consider the distinction between the True and False self in brief, Winnicott states that from the True Self comes the spontaneous gesture and the personal self. The spontaneous gesture is the True Self in action. Only the True Self can be creative and only the True Self can feel real. Whereas a True Self feels real, the existence of a False Self results in feeling unreal or a sense of futility (Winnicott: 148).

In the False Self there is found poor capacity for using symbols and a poverty of cultural living. Instead of cultural pursuits, one observes in such persons extreme restlessness, an inability to concentrate, and a need to collect impingements from external reality so that the living time of the individual can be filled with reactions to these impingements (Winnicott: 150).

Here we have a baseline from which to consider religious practice. Is such practice being used in the context of a healthy spontaneous personality, or as an instrument of compliance motivated by unmet developmental needs? (Of course some mixture of the two may occur.) It would be easy enough to imagine individuals who, because of some early lack of encouragement for their own self-expression in their earliest relationships, might use compliance as a means of gaining from others what should have come as a natural birthright.[5]

Case example: A young disciple from the Midwest who was not sure what to do with his life had a great interest in Buddhist practice. He found a teacher he liked in the San Francisco Bay Area and slowly began to donate a great number of presents to his teacher out of "altruism" and "devotion." Over time the teacher was unable to satisfy the student's continually escalating needs for attention. Ultimately, the teacher had to set some limits on his time with the student. As a result the student became disheartened, broke off relations with the teacher, and indicated to friends that he wanted all of his gifts back. (Here and below, case material has been altered to maintain anonymity.)

Compliance

This illustration is not given in order to disparage compliance, or concession, the subordination of our agenda to that of another person, institution, or behavioral guideline. In fact compliance is necessary for all of us. At issue is the insistence behind it and what motivates it. Far from being against compliance, Winnicott considers it necessary in health, stating that "The ability to compromise is an achievement" (Winnicott: 150). Compromise usually includes some elements of mutual concession. What is important is the psychological quality of an individual's compromises, concessions, and compliance. Clearly there are differences between the spontaneity embodied in the ballerina following the rules of classical choreography and the insecurity motivating an individual who joins an aerobics class because their best friend is doing so.[6] In the first instance, compliance to form is the structure through which the individual expresses fullness. In the second, the compliance is for the sake of satisfying psychological need.

We can speculate that a person who uses compliance out of need in response to unfortunate early deficits might use these teachings as a rationale for denying their own spontaneity, their nascent True Self. The practice then might contribute to further alienation, frustration, and ultimately revolt: short-term practice may give way to long-term disenchantment.

Case example: A young nun from New Zealand was practicing meditation in South India. She was eager to practice well and her attention to the guidelines of meditation was very sincere. She was compliant to the structure of practice. For a certain period she decided to meditate upon compassion and altruism. When some people came by her dwelling unexpectedly one day, she said with some consternation: "I wish people would leave me alone so I could meditate on compassion." Ultimately she left the order.

Here the nun was so interested in complying with the rules of practice that she was unable to experience much fellow-feeling at all towards the people who visited her even though this was the very feeling she was attempting to create through her meditations. In this case, if the psychological issues and needs fueling the compliance had received attention either through formal psychotherapy, pastoral counseling, or some unique blend of religious and/or life experience, perhaps this nun would not have found herself so constrained. As Randall Mason of the Center for Religion and Psychotherapy of Chicago says: "The love of neighbor as self implies a balanced empathic awareness of one's own needs and the needs of others . . . " (Mason: 414).

In general, discussions concerning altruism advocate abandoning selfishness and developing concern for others. In choosing to comply with such guidelines, each individual has to decide if new behavior is being adopted out of a compromise consonant with healthy/True Self, or out of a sense of personal nonexistence/False Self. One can do this by investigating deeply whether one is expecting some reward for one's altruistic attitude or behavior. When faced with a repetitive pattern of service which is accompanied by frustration or burn-out, such reflection may be more easily accomplished with clinical assistance. The Mahāyāna tradition also appears sensitive to this issue, though not using these terms, for whenever generosity is spoken of it is always emphasized that the donor should never give what he or she will regret giving (Dhargyey: 140). To do otherwise is, in Winnicott's language, to act on the basis of a False Self.

Thus both the modern psychological tradition and the classical Buddhist tradition indicate that if individuals act primarily on the basis of a False Self, they may find themselves in repeated experiences of frustration and blockage in their practice. Both traditions in their own way indicate that a False Self syndrome must be dealt with in developing selfless activity.

In some instances the combination of practice, teacher, social context, and life history may contribute to the resolution of a False Self syndrome without formal psychological intervention, a possibility requiring further consideration and investigation.

Healthy Psychological Self, Selfishness, Selfless Activity, and Selflessness

In considering the relationship between psychological language advocating a healthy self on the one hand and Buddhist language advocating selfless activity and an understanding of selflessness on the other, it becomes clear that several key terms require further discussion: (1) the healthy self, (2) selfishness, (3) selfless activity, and (4) selflessness. Jack Engler has said in the Theravāda context that an individual needs a healthy psychological self as a basis for religious development. I would prefer to avoid an arbitrary developmental model, but take his suggestion as a call for serious attention to the complex relationships between psychological and spiritual development (Engler: 51-52). One must at least have enough real psychological self to commit to an ongoing discipline of practice. Furthermore, a danger exists that individuals lacking a clear sense of self who find the Buddhist religious language particularly resonant with their psychological status will use affiliation with Buddhism to sustain their condition. Engler, a clinical psychologist who teaches Theravāda meditation, noted two groups of individuals with observable self impairment among the larger body of individuals attending his courses: (1) those who suffered some key developmental deficit early in life, and (2) those unable to deal with current life-stage tasks (Engler: 35-36). These individuals often used Buddhist idioms to legitimize essentially maladaptive and ultimately unsatisfying positions. For example, individuals facing difficulty in career choice, relationships, or decision making can seek shelter in doctrines of selflessness and then inappropriately use such doctrines to maintain an undefined self (cf. Engler: 35). Engler found that in some cases doctrine is used to rationalize behavior.

> The *anatta* (no-self) doctrine is taken to justify their premature abandonment of essential psychosocial tasks. (Engler: 35)

He also found that individuals with developmental deficits in relationship to self-integration would use Buddhist doctrine to explain and rationalize, if not actually legitimate, their lack of self-integration, their feeling of inner emptiness, of not having a cohesive self. (Engler: 36)

The individuals described are suffering from some impairment of their psychological self. While an accurate, all-encompassing definition of the self in psychological terms is an ongoing task, a useful description that has emerged is as follows:

> [T]he pattern of ambitions, skills, and goals, the tensions between them, the program of action they create, and the activities that strive toward the realization of the program are all experienced as continuous in space and time...they are the self, an independent center of initiative, an independent recipient of impression. (Goldberg: 4, citing Kohut and Wolf, 1978)

Without what I would like to call the healthy psychological self, one suffers from an array of conditions ranging from mild impairment to overwhelming incapacitation. In the former group are individuals contending with the issue of diffuse personal and occupational goals/commitments.

Case example: In the late 1960s and early 1970s many late adolescents interested in Buddhist meditation would flock to Geshe Wangyal's Buddhist center in New Jersey. There they were hoping to find a "retreat" from the over-thirty issues of work, responsibility, and family relationships. Many were surprised to find that the Buddhist lama sent them right back out into the world to find a job and a stable lifestyle before he would allow them to study Buddhist philosophy and practice, including the cultivation of altruism.

These prospective students with unclear personal direction had a mild form of self impairment. Geshe Wangyal would not allow his Buddhist center to become a refuge for individuals, to use Buddhist language, as a cover for uncompleted psychological development. While he did not verbalize his reasons, he was in effect making behavioral assessments.

In more severe forms of self-impairment, individuals lack a sense of personal cohesion, are overwhelmed by primary processes (irrational forces), have poor impulse control (often involving substance abuse), and are subject to a great deal of anxiety. These are conditions we see in schizophrenics and borderline schizophrenics. To discuss self-sacrifice, selflessness, etc., with such individuals risks exacerbating an already weak sense of self and may even play into pathological needs for self-mutilation[7] (cf. Engler: 35-38).

Clearly it is a mistake for those individuals with severe self impairment to confuse their psychological state with the ontological doctrine of selflessness in Buddhism. For, in developmental terms, self-impairment is the maladaptive contrary to the healthy psychological self, whereas Buddhist religious development assumes a certain degree of psychological health and is oriented toward finding the absence of an ontological self in the elements of our experience.[8]

On the basis of a certain degree of psychological health, an individual can take on the religious task of eradicating selfishness and cultivating altruism (cf. Mason: 416, for a Christian equivalent).[9] In this context, I understand "selfishness" as greed, pride, and narrow-minded self-interest. Buddhists have a two-pronged approach to "selfishness," both under the rubric of what we in common parlance call selflessness. The individual can work to overcome "selfishness" through cultivating selfless activity, based on a concern for others and manifested as generous deeds, actions that are not self-serving. One can also work on "selfishness" through understanding the ontological nature of the person, ultimately understanding that it lacks substantial, inherent existence: in Buddhist terms, it is selfless. Understanding the ontological status of the person in this way is said to lead to a radical alteration in attitudes such as greed and pride—ultimately leading to their extirpation (see, for example, Hopkins: 104-109 and 255-260). While in the course of this paper I have been emphasizing altruism, it must be stated that in Mahāyāna there would be a constant oscillation between cultivating an altruistic attitude and selfless activities on the one hand, and development of an understanding that in the ultimate sense the person lacks inherent, substantial, enduring existence on the other. Each in its own way contributes to the other. Ultimately the Mahāyāna practitioner maintains the healthy altruistic functioning of the psychological self while understanding that there are no inherently existent components to that self, no substantial soul to be found (cf. Engler: 39, 43-54 for Theravāda). Within this ontological understanding, the Mahāyāna practitioner would embody the most developed form of altruism.

We have said that most individuals cultivating altruism will need some psychological health as a starting point. Among those with a healthy psychological self, some will approach religious life with trust, fullness, and satisfaction (cf. the True Self of Winnicott) and continue onward to spiritual confidence and centeredness (McDargh, 1983: esp. 99-100). I would call this approach to the religious life "the approach through fullness." This group consists of psychologically healthy individuals who are either personally fortunate, or who face difficulties as challenges and with uplifted spirits garner nurture out of even adverse circumstances, moving from strength to strength.

Another approach to religious life is through disappointment and suffering, which I call "the approach through trial" (cf. McDargh, 1983: 99-100). This includes healthy individuals who face a great number of adverse environmental or physical obstacles and those who, due to some degree of self-impairment, may inadvertently find themselves sensitive to frustration and loss.

Individuals with both a healthy psychological self and few experienced hardships are, I suspect, relatively rare. The group with which I am more familiar are those who approach religion through trial. The uncomfortable truth is that individuals often see trial preceding resolution and psychological/religious growth. One of the most vexing issues is to understand how religious/psychological trials serve to foster personal growth.[10] If it is true that "religious observance and adherence to credal systems can become a vehicle for pathological tendencies and needs . . . " (Meissner: 10), why is it that some individuals' involvement with religion allows for personal and spiritual growth—forms of growth which I, in contrast to Freud, feel are possible within the context of a religious commitment?

Religious activity often involves great strain, sacrifice, and even personal suffering. How then does religious involvement take people beyond mere repetition of pathological traits? More specifically, what is it about teacher-student relationships that allow individuals with some degree of self-impairment—the vast majority of us—to work through and resolve the trials and frustrations they face in the course of their religious endeavors, e.g., in cultivating altruism? The answers to these questions will be relevant to understanding not only how the religious context serves to repair the self but also how it serves even to foster further augmentation of psychological functions. Most individuals who resolve personal difficulty in a religious context begin with a base of some intact self-structure in the form of trust in and openness towards others (cf. McDargh, 1983: 100). This may be a minimum psychological requirement for engagement in the spiritual life. For these individuals, hardships and sacrifices may be accompanied by growth if these trials involve losses or tension appropriate to them, and occur within the context of relationships with religious teachers, fellow practitioners, or belief in God/the sacred.

Marianne Tolpin is a self-psychologist who describes the process of building psychological structure in terms of "transmuting internalization" (Tolpin: 316-352). Ana-Maria Rizzuto and John McDargh also give careful consideration to the psychological functions of the representation of God/the sacred. My extrapolations from these authors, particularly Tolpin, rest on the assumptions that (1) individuals deal with loss similarly in both childhood and adulthood, and (2) the mechanisms for psychological gain in the face of loss are largely similar in both periods. Tolpin clarifies how children create psychological structure, and this process is crucial to our understanding the growth potential of trial, loss, and frustration in the religious context.

Tolpin explains the process of creating psychological structure through exploring the development of the capacity for self-soothing. This is a psychological structure many of us take for granted. When it is sometimes compromised in severe cases of neglect, trauma, or developmental arrest, severe anxiety results. Tolpin points out that a child facing temporary absence or loss of the parenting figure will often be able to substitute a soft cuddly something and attribute to it soothing functions previously provided by the mother (Tolpin: 321). In time the child will occasionally misplace the soothing object and will be forced to create the capacity for self-soothing internally. This is called "transmuting internalization," a process whereby key functions previously performed by external others are internalized and incorporated into the individual's personal psychological structure. Tolpin states:

> Repeated experiences of losing and refinding the auxiliary soother when it is needed to restore equilibrium assist the psyche in the phase-specific task of replacing maternal soothing with tension-reducing mental activity—the same process that eventually leads to the replacement of the soothing possession itself with the inner mechanisms that produce the same effect. (Tolpin: 328-332)

This process follows the basic model set out by Freud for the creation of psychic structure in the ego:

> [T]he character of the ego is a precipitate of abandoned object-cathexes and . . . it contains the history of these object choices. (Tolpin: 317, citing Freud, 1923)

In the case of self-soothing, the mother was the recipient of "object cathexis"—meaning psychic energy toward her (Brenner: 18)—but through the process described by Tolpin, the mother's function of soothing the child is precipitated in the ego structure of the child. Tolpin sees similar processes at work throughout childhood:

> When optimal (minute) loss occurs, an inherent intrapsychic process transmutes actual functions carried out by the human object into regulating psychic activity. (Tolpin: 330)

We see similar processes at work when children adopt mannerisms of loved ones. We also see it in adults when they take on the characteristics of recently departed loved ones (Brenner: 42-44). Arnold Goldberg, another psychiatrist with a self-psychology orientation, describes the same mechanism at work in adults undergoing analysis:

> Separation plays a crucial role in these analyses because the physical absence of the needed self-object [meaning the significant other person] is always traumatic. As each and every disruption or separation or empathic failure of the analyst is experienced and understood, the patient gains internal structure until, at last, he is able to contemplate the final separation from the analyst. (Goldberg: 9-10)

Analytical authors have thus pointed out similarities between the process described by Tolpin and the processes at work in adults who are mourning and those undergoing psychoanalysis. Of course, the process of structure-building will be optimal in childhood, but it seems safe to say it continues to some extent throughout life. If we consider those who approach religion through trial, I suggest that when they face losses and suffering they have the opportunity to develop new psychological structure via transmuting internalization: structure which allows them to face their respective challenges.[11] We can outline at least a few conditions for optimal results in the spiritual context: (1) the losses, trials, and frustration must occur in appropriate amounts and at appropriate intervals; and (2) these events must occur to a person (a) who is operating in a context of religious teachers or fellow practitioners, or (b) who can make use of a representation of God/the sacred (Rizzuto: 54-84 and 177-211; McDargh, 1983: 137-150). The "religious other" becomes the source from whom particular qualities are transmuted and internalized.

These basic parameters can help us define a minimal context for personal and religious growth in individuals with some self-impairment, or those who undertake a practice such as altruism and encounter either internal or external obstacles. I would add the caveat that this is by no means a simple, straightforward, clearly predictable process.The question of what else psychologically promotes structural internalization of spiritual qualities, and what else obstructs it, remains to be investigated. At a minimum, for modern Westerners, being able to discuss their feelings and thoughts about their experience with an insightful and empathic mentor, such as a psychotherapist, may be a significant component of the process (Stolorow, Brandchaft, and Atwood; Wolf, 1988).[12]

The following religious tale, which Khetsun Sangpo Rinbochay tells in teaching about compassion, illustrates the process described above and the parameters we have discussed.[13]

Dharmarakṣita was a non-Mahāyāna practitioner who aspired to become a Buddha. His compassion was very great, but his understanding of selflessness was underdeveloped. A sick person needing human flesh came, and Dharmarakṣita cut some flesh from his thigh and offered it. The man recovered and Dharmarakṣita was very pleased. When asked if he had any regrets over his sacrifice Dharmarakṣita replied no, but that he was having trouble sleeping because of the pain.

Soon thereafter Dharmarakṣita had a dream wherein a shining white being rubbed a little saliva on his thigh. Dharmarakṣita awoke cured physically and fully understanding all the profound doctrines of the Mahāyāna without having studied them. The being in his dream was Avalokiteśvara, the embodiment of compassion.

Tradition holds that through his altruism, Dharmarakṣita had purified karmic obstructions and thereby come to understand all the teachings of the Mahāyāna (Sangpo: 137). This certainly indicates the power of altruistic activity. Looking at this account from the psychological perspective developed in this paper, we can note that Dharmarakṣita underwent self-inflicted loss. In adults, loss may serve as an opportunity for transmuting internalization of new personal qualities. In Dharmarakṣita's case, following his self-inflicted loss, within the context of a relationship with a sacred being experienced in a dream, there was a change in the content of his self structure to include understanding of deep religious/philosophical truths.

Imposed Trial

How can we understand growth that—unlike Dharmarakṣita's—results from external religious challenge, that is, through trials imposed from God, the sacred, or religious teachers? Can the model of growth through loss be used to open insights into the tales of Abraham, Job, or Jesus? One hesitates to endorse what from the outside looks painful, yet the religious traditions all have instances of terrific losses and tribulations imposed from without in the name of some ultimate religious end. In the Buddhist tradition we only need think of the incredible story of Tilopa and Naropa (Guenther; Sangpo: 104-107). It seems that such stories cannot serve as models for mere humans. Surely in the name of therapy or religion we cannot advocate the imposition of suffering or deprivation on another human being. If we were to observe this in a secular clinical context we would most likely seek to work through, for example, the dependency needs of the compliant person and the search for power in the oppressor. The religious context is more complex, for what we cannot accept or sanction in secular conduct becomes here, at least in some rare instances, the avenue of considerable spiritual growth. *In retrospect*, tales of trial can be interpreted and often become the subject of the most considered religious meditations (e.g., Glatzer, Kierkegaard).

Of course, it is easy when considering religious classics to marvel at the pains the great saints have undergone in their spiritual quests. The rewards of their challenge are clear. The issue becomes much more complex when the situation is current and results are in question. We need only imagine the tragi-comical scene of Abraham discussing the divine charge to sacrifice his son with a professional clinician mandated by state law to report child abuse. Such juxtapositions help us realize that the religious and secular part ways in their understanding of what constitutes legitimate avenues of personal/spiritual growth. Lest we think such conflicts are rare or consigned just to biblical times, I would note that as a clinical social worker at Stanford Children's Hospital I regularly witnessed conflicts between religious and secular views, in life-threatening situations, around issues such as blood transfusions. I would suggest that in cases where we see religious trial imposed, we must consider the situation with utmost humility, recognizing that the individuals are in a relationship that is generating a great deal of pain but at the same time *may* ultimately be serving a larger purpose—personal or religious growth.

Case example: A lama on pilgrimage in South India with a Western disciple during the hot season continually insisted that the disciple carry more baggage and do more work. While at first the disciple readily agreed, the burden became greater and the insistence of the lama more difficult to face. At the end of a most trying week the disciple broke down and wept, saying it was unbearable. The lama responded, "Your sufferings have been very slight compared to the sufferings of all sentient beings. You should understand what they go through and dedicate yourself to relieving them of their pain." With this he experientially opened the disciple to a whole new empathic dimension.

The disciple reported that this process resulted in an increased sensitivity to others' situations. In retrospect he understood the lama's behavior in a broader perspective. Interestingly, the incident mirrors almost exactly the process described by the twentieth-century philosopher Miguel de Unamuno:

> If you look at the universe as closely and as inwardly as you are able to look—that is to say, if you look within yourself; if you not only contemplate but feel all things in your own consciousness, upon which all things have traced their painful impressions—you will arrive at the abyss of the tedium, not merely of life, but of something more: at the tedium of existence, at the bottomless pit of the vanity of vanities. And thus you will come to pity all things; you will arrive at universal love. (Unamuno: 138)

There is a traditional tale somewhat similar to the more recent account from South India: An individual with a violent temper was intent on cultivating patience. Friends, presumably from his religious context, consistently baited him, provoking him to blows. This went on until he recognized his encounters as tests and mastered his unruly reactivity (Tsong-ka-pa, Kensur Lekden, and Hopkins: 26-27).

From the perspective developed in this paper, we can say that this person had mild self-impairment—he lacked frustration tolerance, an important element of psychological structure. In the context of small frustrations with members of his own community he was able to internalize sufficient structure to master his temper.

It is clear that whether we consider healthy individuals or those with self-impairment, appropriate trials in suitable contexts can lead to personal or religious growth. However, some might still argue that we should never endorse imposed trial.

I would reply that while we must in the secular context seek to diminish the arbitrary imposition of pain by one individual onto another, in considering the religious relationship we are faced with a much more complex set of criteria. The long-term personal religious growth of the individual may be in question. The time frame for benefits to appear in the religious context may be much longer than one would accept in a secular context. When should secular individuals have intervened in the case of Abraham or Job? In either case premature termination of trial would have prevented religious growth.

But what is "premature"? There is a history of abusing power in the name of religion, and therefore withholding judgment entails great risk. Encouraging growth through imposed trial can easily be read as approval of abusive religious fanaticism, such as that which occurred in Jim Jones's People's Temple community in Guyana. Given the limitations of our ordinary capacity to understand and our fear of endorsing unproductive, harmful behavior, we are on a tightrope when we consider difficult religious relationships: respectful consideration must be delicately balanced with critical acuity. The process of experientially facing and holding such a tension when confronting difficult life situations and questions is ultimately a process of deep spiritual maturation.

It may be impossible to fully fathom the mechanisms at work in religious trial. If grace plays a role, then there are metaphysical issues which clearly transcend the expertise of the clinician (McDargh, 1983: 53). And for those who believe in grace, the interpretation of stories such as that of Dharmarakṣita will always go beyond a rationalistic, pragmatic, psychological explanation. Most Mahāyāna believers would agree with the following statement about grace made by McDargh from the Catholic perspective:

> [With grace] we are considering a reality which while it can be examined psychologically is finally not reducible to psychological processes or predictable by the analysis of genetic origins. There is that of faith which is sheer gift, supererogatory, breaking through and confounding all other categories and calculations, that is—simply graced. (McDargh, 1983: 53)

However, we can without reductionism consider the psychological aspects of growth through trial in secular terms—even when grace does occur. We can speculate that when trial leads to personal or religious growth the individual is able to internalize psychic structure or function (e.g., openness, tolerance, or altruism) that formerly had been missing or underdeveloped. This structure is internalized through experiences of loss and frustration and processes of transmuting internalization in relation to significant others. The significant other may be a religious teacher, a fellow disciple, God, the sacred, or a religious ideal (Rizzuto: 47). (The fact that there may be opportunities for psychological/religious growth in these relationships through transmuting internalization does not preclude the possibility of the intercession of the sacred through the medium of grace in these same contexts.)[14]

Thus, adversity, whether accidental or imposed, seems capable, under optimum circumstances, of leading to growth and development. The psychoanalyst Karen Horney states:

> [L]ife itself is the most effective help for our development. The hardships that life forces upon us—necessity to leave one's country, organic illness, periods of solitude and also its gifts—a good friendship, even a mere contact with a truly good and valuable human being, co-operative work in groups—all such factors can help us to reach our potential. (cited in Guntrip, 1957: 187)

Of course difficulties might outpace personal capacity. As Horney observes further:

> [T]he hardships may not only be a challenge to our activity and courage but surpass our available strength and merely crush us. (Guntrip, 1957: 187)

All religious practitioners require sufficient personal resources to face the challenges they encounter. With these resources, the individual in a religious context has opportunities for reparation of early deficits, augmentation of pre-existing skills, and development of new strengths.

Mature Altruism

We have briefly considered routes by which an individual may grow in religious life. It is clear that some individuals will begin their spiritual ventures in a state of expansiveness, while others may arrive at this through a process of personal and religious difficulty. Ultimately, the fullest manifestations of altruism will occur in those who possess a larger vision. In its most inspiring form, altruism will neither be motivated by some deep dark psychological purpose nor will it seek some ulterior personal benefit. It comes not from some inner lack but rather from fullness. Again, I think most Mahāyānists would agree with McDargh, who describes such altruism in the Christian context and states:

> Our sense of ourselves as available for communion or what I have called "loving self-donation" never proceeds from a deprivation or an inner Emptiness but rather from a taste of the satisfaction in sharing which creates a hunger and a capacity for more comprehensive and more profound sharing. Without that basic inner sustainment of which the psychoanalysts have tried to speak, the person is not wholly available for self-donation. (McDargh, 1983: 98)

The Tibetan Buddhist saint Gampopa put it simply but eloquently: "We should not make a gift if we do not rejoice at doing so . . . " (sGam.Po.Pa: 155).

Conclusion

We have considered altruism from a few select vantage points. First, Freud's somewhat ambivalent position was considered and its pseudo-empirical nature was questioned. We moved from this to consider altruism using Winnicott's categories and discussed how altruism may insinuate itself into a False Self syndrome. This led to a clarification of terms and the important point that the Mahāyāna practitioner seeks to undertake selfless/altruistic activity in the context of understanding selflessness—that is, that ontologically the self lacks any inherent existence. We noted that in the spiritual life, the relational context is able to provide opportunities for religious growth, including altruism through the mechanism of transmuting internalization. It was pointed out that transmuting internalization may occur with teachers, fellow practitioners, or in the individual's relationship with the sacred. Within the relational context, loss was seen as an opportunity for incorporation of new religious functioning and specific examples related to altruism were presented.

This led to the consideration of imposed loss as a source of religious growth. Here it became clear that we had arrived at a boundary between the psychological and religious worldview. Proponents of the former, inspired by the medical model, seek to minimize suffering and take a fairly short-term view. The religious understand that sometimes suffering facilitates religious growth and take a long-term view.

There is a further differentiation between the two in that the latter see the possibility of grace as operational in religious growth whereas the secular clinician often cannot accept the religious origins of such experience.

Altruism and religious growth were the original focii of this paper. Through these issues we were led to a consideration of adversity in the religious life. Ultimately we were led to see some clear differences between the secular and religious approaches to religious phenomena.

The call to altruism is a worthwhile challenge. Inner psychological need is not the only source of altruistic behavior. Healthy altruism is possible. Honest self-reflection and earnest engagement in the challenge provide opportunity for substantial personal religious growth and expression.

Notes

1. Dedicated to the memory of my mother Bessie Aronson (1906-1985); first presented at the Seminar on Exchange of Self and Other at the Tibetan Buddhist Learning Center, Washington, NJ, July 27, 1985.

2. See, for example, Aronson, 1980; Dhargyey: 105-138; Gómez; Gyatso; Little and Twiss: 210-250; Maxwell; Rabten: 31-53; Śāntideva; and Tsong-ka-pa, Kensur Lekden, and Jeffrey Hopkins: 23-79.

3. While much of what is said here may be of relevance to native Buddhists in Asia, there may be certain important cultural differences in the articulation

of a healthy psychological self which would require different formulation in considering the types of obstacles facing that population in practice (cf. A. Roland cited in Wolf, 1983: 124, n. 2).

4. I am indebted to Dr. Tom Roth of Stanford University Medical School for this reference.

5. Randall Mason, President, Center for Religion and Psychotherapy of Chicago, observes that in a Judeo-Christian pastoral counseling setting, many clients often confuse "self-abasement" with "self-sacrifice" (Mason: 413, n. 5).

6. The notion of structured spontaneity is one I came to appreciate through discussions with P. J. Ivanhoe, my course assistant in Comparative Religious Thought at Stanford University, 1985.

7. While it would take us too far afield to examine the question of altruistic self-sacrifice, it is important to mention that I take this to be possible in healthy individuals. Self-sacrifice by such people involves subordinating narrow-minded self-interest to a larger value held by the healthy psychological self

8. Recently, A. H. Almaas has written a thought-provoking work distinguishing self-impairment and deficient psychological emptiness from the ontological emptiness/selflessness of Buddhism, exploring also the psycho-spiritual relationship between the two (Almaas). See also Harvey, 1995 for an excellent presentation of selflessness.

9. I differ somewhat from Engler, who suggests that developmentally complete psychological structure is necessary prior to spiritual endeavor. I feel human beings are complex and it would be difficult in an *a priori* way to create a psychological foyer for spiritual practice. Engler for his part states:

> The issue in personal development as I have come to understand it is not self or no-self, but self and no-self. Both a sense of self and insight into the ultimate illusoriness of its apparent continuity and substantiality are necessary achievements. Sanity and complete psychological well-being *include both, but in a phase appropriate developmental sequence* at different stages of object relations development. What Buddhist psychology and practice appear to do instead is presuppose a more or less normal course of development and an intact or "normal" ego. For its practices, it assumes a level of personality organization where object relations development, especially a cohesive and integrated sense of self, is already complete. (Engler: 39)

Engler epitomizes this view of Theravāda when he says, "you have to be somebody before you can be nobody" (Engler: 31). I would paraphrase his Theravāda position by saying, you have to have a sound psychological self before realizing there is no ontological self. I can agree with Engler to the extent that in order to practice an individual would have to have enough psychic structure to undertake methodical behavior, to have patience and a certain amount of frustration tolerance. Barring this minimum amount of psychological structure, it is hard to see how any practice could take place. With such a minimum in place, individuals will probably proceed to pursue psychological and/or spiritual development in a manner unique to their own needs, with the possibility always present that spiritual pursuit can be, but is by no means necessarily, subverted to defensive psychological needs.

It is also worth noting that Dr. Marsha Linehan, a research clinical psychologist, using a very highly structured group relational context, has successfully used introductory mindfulness practice on a daily basis, as opposed to in a retreat, as an adjunctive therapeutic intervention with severe borderline personality disordered clients, the very type of clients it seems Engler would want to direct to therapy before insight practice (Linehan). This says much about how the amount of meditation time and the relational context within which it is practiced may be significant variables with respect to the ultimate psychological outcome of practice.

10. The following reflections were stimulated in part by questions concerning the place of trial in the religious life raised by Dr. Dick Anthony at a dinner given by the Melia Foundation, Berkeley, California, Spring 1985.

11. John McDargh, writing with respect to the Christian tradition, expresses a similar idea when he states:

> For men and women whose sense of self is deeply conflicted and bound up with a God that either requires their perfection or their destruction, some reparative psychic healing seems necessary. Perhaps Kohut's notion of "transmuting internalizations" suggestively captures the sense of the way in which the transference relationship to an idealized spiritual guide or examplar, in the context of a loving and responsive community, may work the mending. (McDargh, 1984: 359)

12. See, for example, Epstein.

13. The relevance of the respective traditional tales from Khetsun Sangpo to the material being discussed was pointed out to me by Dr. Anne Klein.

14. Aronson, n.d. gives a fuller discussion of the mechanism of transmuting internalization in a religious context. There, the issues of psychological transformation and grace are considered more fully.

References

Almaas, A. H.

1986 *The Void: Inner Spaciousness and Ego Structure*. Berkeley: Diamond Books.

Aronson, Harvey B.

1980 *Love and Sympathy in Theravāda Buddhism*. Delhi: Motilal Banarsidass.

n.d. "Guru Yoga—A Buddhist Meditative Visualization: Observations Based Upon Psychoanalytic Object Relations Theory and Self Psychology." Unpublished ms.

Brenner, Charles

1974 *Elementary Textbook of Psychoanalysis*. Garden City: Anchor Books.

Dhargyey, Geshe Ngawang

1974 *The Tibetan Tradition of Mental Development*. Dharamsala: Library of Tibetan Works and Archives.

Engler, Jack

1984 "Therapeutic Aims in Psychotherapy and Meditation: Developmental Stages in the Representation of Self." *Journal of Transpersonal Psychology*, 16(1): 25-61.

Epstein, Mark

1995 *Thoughts without a Thinker*. New York: Basic Books.

Freud, Sigmund

1923 *The Ego and the Id. Standard Edition of the Complete Psychological Works*, vol. 19. London: The Hogarth Press.

1927 *The Future of an Illusion. Standard Edition of the Complete Psychological Works*, vol. 21. London: The Hogarth Press.

1955 *Civilization and Its Discontents*. London: The Hogarth Press.

Glatzer, Nahum N.

1969 *The Dimensions of Job*. New York: Schocken.

Goldberg, Arnold

1980 "Introductory Remarks." In *Advances in Self Psychology*. Ed. Arnold Goldberg. New York: International Universities Press.

Gómez, Luis

1978 "Karunabhavana: Notes on the Meaning of Buddhist Compassion." In *The Tibet Journal*, 3(2): 33-59.

Greenberg, Jay R. and Stephen A. Mitchell

1983 *Object Relations in Psychoanalytic Theory*. Cambridge, MA: Harvard University Press.

Guenther, H.V.

1971 *Life and Teaching of Naropa*. New York: Oxford University Press.

Guntrip, H.

1957 *Psychotherapy and Religion*. New York: Harper and Brothers.

1973 *Psychoanalytic Theory, Therapy and the Self*. New York: Basic Books.

Gyatso, Geshe Kelsang

1980 *Meaningful to Behold*. Cumbria, England: Wisdom Publications.

Harvey, Peter

1995 *The Selfless Mind: Personality, Consciousness, and Nirvana in Early Buddhism*. Surrey, England: Curzon Press.

Hopkins, Jeffrey
1983 *Meditation on Emptiness*. London: Wisdom Publications, 1983.

Kierkegaard, S.
1983 *Fear and Trembling: Repetition*. Ed. and trans. H. Hong and E. Hong. Princeton: Princeton University Press.

Kohut, Heinz
1971 *The Analysis of the Self*. New York: International Universities Press.
1980 "Reflections on Advances in Self Psychology." In *Advances in Self Psychology*. Ed. by Arnold Goldberg. New York: International Universities Press.

Kohut, Heinz and Ernest S. Wolf
1978 "The Disorders of the Self and their Treatment: An Outline." In *International Journal of Psychoanalysis*, 59: 413-425.

Linehan, Marsha M.
1993 *Cognitive-Behavioral Treatment of Borderline Personality Disorder*. New York: The Guilford Press.

Little, David and Sumner B. Twiss
1978 *Comparative Religious Ethics: A New Method*. San Francisco: Harper and Row.

Mason, Randall C.
1980 "The Psychology of the Self: Religion and Psychotherapy." In *Advances in Self Psychology*. Ed. Arnold Goldberg. New York: International Universities Press.

Maxwell, Natalie
1975 "Great Compassion: The Chief Cause of Bodhisattvas." Ph.D. dissertation, University of Wisconsin.

McDargh, John
1983 *Psychoanalytic Object Relations Theory and the Study of Religion*. Lanham, MD: University Press of America.
1984 "The Life of the Self in Christian Spirituality and Contemporary Psychoanalysis." *Horizons*, 11(2): 344-360.

Meissner, W.W.
1984 *Psychoanalysis and Religious Experience*. New Haven: Yale University Press.

Rabten, Geshe
1974 *The Preliminary Practices*. Dharamsala: Library of Tibetan Works and Archives.

Rizzuto, Ana-Maria
1979 *The Birth of the Living God*. Chicago: University of Chicago Press.

Sangpo Rinbochay, Khetsun

1982 *Tantric Practice in Nying-ma*. Translated and edited by Jeffrey Hopkins; co-edited by Anne Klein. Ithaca, NY: Gabriel/ Snow Lion.

sGam.Po.Pa

1981 *The Jewel Ornament of Liberation*. Trans. by Herbert V. Guenther. Boulder: Prajna Press.

Shantideva

1979 *A Guide to the Bodhisattva's Way of Life*. Trans. by Stephen Batchelor. Dharamsala, India: Library of Tibetan Works and Archives.

Stolorow, Robert D., Bernard Brandchaft, and George E. Atwood

1987 *Psychoanalytic Treatment: An Intersubjective Approach*. Hillsdale, NJ: The Analytic Press.

Tolpin, Marian

1971 "On the Beginnings of a Cohesive Self: An Application of the Concept of Transmuting Internalization to the Study of the Transitional Object and Signal Anxiety." In *Psychoanalytic Study of the Child*, 26: 316-352.

Tsong-ka-pa, Kensur Lekden, and Jeffrey Hopkins

1980 *Compassion in Tibetan Buddhism*. Valois, NY: Gabriel/Snow Lion.

Unamuno, Miguel de

1921 *The Tragic Sense of Life*. Trans. J. E. Crawford Flitch. London: Macmillan and Co.

Winnicott, D. W.

1965 "Ego Distortion in Terms of True and False Self (1960)." In *The Maturational Processes and the Facilitating Environment*. New York: International Universities Press.

Wolf, Ernest

1980 "On the Developmental Line of Self-Object Relations." In *Advances in Self Psychology*. Ed. Arnold Goldberg. New York: International Universities Press.

1988 *Treating the Self*. New York: Guilford Press.

Chapter 12

Drawing the Steel Bow[1]

A Bibliographic Appreciation of the Literary Legacy of Paul Jeffrey Hopkins and His Program at the University of Virginia[2]

Paul G. Hackett

Walk into any used bookstore and you will find books on Buddhism nestled between odd volumes of the *Śrīmad Bhāgavatam* and exposés on the Loch Ness Monster. In such a place, in a small bookstore in Tucson, Arizona, I found my first book on Tibetan Buddhism, a slightly worn copy of *Kindness, Clarity and Insight* by His Holiness the Dalai Lama. Though at the time many of the terms and concepts were foreign to me, the learned and yet practical disposition of the book spoke to me on many levels. Because of this, I sought out more books by the Dalai Lama as well as those by the man His Holiness had chosen to speak through, Jeffrey Hopkins. Over the years since that time, I have often reflected on my good fortune in finding that book, which laid the foundation for my eventual graduate study with Hopkins—for such fortuitous circumstances did not always exist.

In the early 1970s, access to the intellectual content of Tibetan Buddhism was available only to a privileged few.[3] One of those few was Jeffrey Hopkins, who, in 1973 at the age of thirty-three, had just completed his doctoral dissertation, an extensive response to T. R. V. Murti's contention that meditation in Prāsaṅgika-Madhyamaka lacked an object. *Meditation on Emptiness* presented a detailed exposition of the Madhyamaka position in the context of Buddhist tenets and practice. In the years since its publication (Wisdom, 1983), *Meditation on Emptiness* has been translated into at least sixteen languages, including a rumored bootleg Russian translation circulated during the Soviet era. In that time, too, both the level of access to and the demographics of American interest in Tibet and Tibetan Buddhism have broadened, and so has the scholarship of Jeffrey Hopkins.

I have heard Hopkins say to students, on a number of occasions, that it is best to gain a well-founded, solid understanding of one individual thing from at least one perspective, before attempting to launch into the unknown and speculative territory which surrounds it. His lectures and texts reflect this attitude as well. For this reason, a novice student opening one of Hopkins's books for the first time may find the level of detail to be nearly overwhelming. Hopkins has never sacrificed attention to the particular for the sake of presentation, and over time one comes to appreciate and even savor his style. I can still recall my first attempt at reading *Meditation on Emptiness*. Admittedly, I found it difficult, and as questions arose in my mind I turned to my fellow students for help, only to be referred back again to *Meditation on Emptiness*, where indeed the answers to my questions could be found. Over time, I learned that all that was really required was effort on my part. So it is with all of Hopkins's works.

A Complete Course in Tibetan Buddhism

One of the hallmarks of the Buddhist religion is the apparently superfluous nature of its cultural trappings — both spatially and temporally. Even so simple an aspect as the image of the Buddha — whether carved in schist and draped in Grecian robes, mustached and emblazoned on Silk Road cave walls, or flickering on celluloid in the likeness of Keanu Reeves — remains unrestrained by any one culture for the simple reason that it stands not as the be-all-and-end-all of the religion, but rather as the central icon of the profound teachings which go by his name and in which so many have found value. Because these teachings are grounded in the shared experiences of all men and women, the social mores and lineage figures that may rigidly define other religions are much more fluid across the Buddhist world. Nonetheless, fixed reference points do exist, though in the form of practices and provocative ideas.

Within the Tibetan tradition, different schema and curricula designed to explicate the teachings of Śākyamuni Buddha have thrived over the centuries. Since the eighteenth century, however, many Tibetan lineages have adopted a standardized curriculum that spans sectarian boundaries. Whether evinced as the thirteen treatises of mKhan po gZhan dga' (a.k.a. gZhan phan chos kyi snang ba) or the textbooks of 'Jam dbyangs bzhad pa, a number of key points deemed essential to a solid understanding of Buddhist thought remain in common.

One such instructional scheme is the program of studies for the *dge shes* degree offered at the larger monastic universities of 'Bras spungs, Se ra, and dGa' ldan. A simplified version of this was devised in the 1970s as a thirteen-year regimen covering the basic categories of Buddhist thought and knowledge:[4]

I. Epistemology
  1. Small, Middling and Greater Paths of Reasoning
  2. Knowledges and Awarenesses
  3. Signs and Reasonings

II. The Perfection of Wisdom
  1. Grounds and Paths
  2. The Seventy Topics

III. General Tenets

IV. Mind-Only
  1. Tenets
  2. The Definitive and the Interpretable

V. Middle Way

VI. Stages of the Path
  1. Calm Abiding
  2. Special Insight

VII. Tantric Grounds and Paths

VIII. Secret Mantra—The Lower Tantras
  1. Action Tantra
  2. Performance Tantra
  3. Yoga Tantra

IX. Highest Yoga Tantra
  1. Generation Stage
  2. Completion Stage
  3. Kālacakra

This simplified plan for a comprehensive Buddhist education reflects a range of subjects central to Buddhist thought. In structuring the Tibetan Buddhist Studies program at the University of Virginia, Hopkins looked to such a preestablished curriculum as a model, as a solid foundation upon which exploratory and comparative research could take place. Indeed, part of the genius of Hopkins's approach lay in his recognition of the dynamism of the Tibetan monastic textbook literature where, by comparing presentations of core subjects at the sub-commentary level, disputes between authors could be mined to reveal the detail sought in the more primary texts.

This approach was in radical contrast to previous "orientalist" approaches at many universities, where individual texts were examined out of context and *in vacuo*. The approach of viewing texts as objects suitable for scientific dissection proved to be of limited success. Although Hopkins was criticized for contextualizing his research within the traditional Tibetan environment, his methods proved to be quite fruitful. Evidence of this can be seen in the breadth and depth of Hopkins's literary legacy—his works, and those produced by students under his direct supervision in the Tibetan Studies program at the University of Virginia. Taken as a whole, these works can be seen as the first nearly comprehensive set of English language textbooks and study materials geared towards a coherent and informed presentation of higher Buddhist studies.

Amonxg these works, no discussion of the literary legacy of Jeffrey Hopkins could begin without making reference to the foundations established in *Meditation on Emptiness*. Taken alone, this first major work by Hopkins stands as a fit introduction to more than half of the topics listed above. Although primarily presented as an exposition on the object of meditation in Prāsaṅgika-Madhyamaka, the contextual materials presenting both the textual and philosophical history, comparative tenets, and overall Buddhist path structure themselves serve as substantial presentations of these topics.

In several respects, many of the works by Hopkins and his students are refinements and amplifications of topics that received their initial treatment in Hopkins's dissertation. The role and application of epistemological categories, for example, is presented by Hopkins as it is employed in the Prāsaṅgika-Madhyamaka system. Likewise, the Buddhist path structure—grounds and paths, the generation of calm abiding (*śamatha, zhi gnas*) and special insight (*vipaśyanā, lhag mthong*)—and systems of tenets are all covered by Hopkins as they relate to and inform the practice of meditating on emptiness.

To the foundation provided by *Meditation on Emptiness*, Hopkins's later works added more detail and broader perspectives. Nonetheless, just as *Meditation on Emptiness* was a starting point for Hopkins, so too it remains a starting point for serious students interested in gaining a thorough knowledge of Tibetan Buddhist theory and practice.

Buddhist Epistemology

Beginning in the late eleventh century, the students of Atiśa, the gSang phu abbots, began to give a great deal of attention to the mastery of epistemology. Sa skya Paṇḍita Kun dga' rgyal mtshan reinforced this pedagogical trend, emphasizing in particular Dharmakīrti's *Pramāṇavārttika*. This emphasis was perpetuated by later scholars such as Tsong kha pa,[5] and has continued to this day. The topic of Valid Cognition (*pramāṇa, tshad ma*)—generically referred to as Buddhist epistemology—covers three separate issues: ontological categories,[6] the states of consciousness which correctly or incorrectly perceive them, and specifics regarding the forms of logical statements concerning them. These issues are dealt with in the literary genre known as *bsdus grwa* ("collected topics"). Texts in this genre typically consist, correspondingly, of three parts: *rigs lam* ("the path of reasoning"),[7] *blo rig* ("knowledge and awareness"), and *rtags rigs* ("signs and reasonings").

Jeffrey Hopkins studied Buddhist epistemology in depth with the former abbot of the Tantric College of Lower Lhasa (rGyud smad), Kensur Ngawang Lekden.[8] From 1974 to 1975 Hopkins taught the introductory *rigs lam* texts in the Tibetan language class. In March of 1976, Laṭi Rinbochay arrived at the University of Virginia and taught on these and other subjects though May of 1977, followed by Denma Lochö Rinbochay in 1978, and Geshe Gedün Lodrö from January to August of 1979. With Hopkins serving as interpreter and facilitator, several of his graduate students were able to study these topics with traditional scholars. Based on this work, Daniel Perdue presented the material contained in Phur bu lcog's *Rigs lam chung ngu* ("Introductory Path of Reasoning") for his dissertation (1983).[9]

Other topics found in the *rigs lam* texts were also studied in other contexts. The presentation of "specifically and generally characterized phenomena" (*rang mtshan dang spyi mtshan*), which a student initially encounters in the second chapter of the introductory *rigs lam* books, was studied in expanded form through bsTan dar lha ram pa's *Rang mtshan spyi mtshan gyi rnam gzhag*. Similarly, classes at Virginia studied the topic of "negative and positive phenomena" (*dgag sgrub*) as encountered in the greater *rigs lam* text for the sGo mang College of 'Bras spungs, Ngag dbang bkra' shis's *Sras bsdus grwa* ("A Spiritual Son's Collected Topics"). Anne Klein, working with Denma Lochö Rinbochay, Kensur Jambel Shenpen and others from 1978 to 1981, included portions of these texts in her doctoral dissertation (1981).

The first group of Hopkins's students[10] also received explanatory commentary from Laṭi Rinbochay and Geshe Gedün Lodrö on the "knowledge and awareness" (*blo rig*) aspects of epistemology. With Hopkins as her advisor, Elizabeth Napper translated, analyzed, and presented a text on this subject for her master's thesis (1979).

The last of these topics, the underlying framework for the logical representation of the epistemological system, discusses the concept of validity in the reasoning process itself. Hopkins and his students studied the "signs and reasonings" (*rtags rigs*) aspects of epistemology during the early years of the Tibetan Studies program. Beginning with the work of those first classes with Hopkins, Katherine Rogers composed the only complete English language presentation of this material, which served as the subject of both her master's thesis (1980) and Ph.D. dissertation (1992).

To date, the last major contribution to the understanding of Buddhist epistemology to come out of the University of Virginia Tibetan Studies program was made by Georges Dreyfus (a.k.a. dGe bshes Sangs rgyas bsam grub) for his dissertation (1991) under the direction of Hopkins.

Perfection of Wisdom

The sixth of the Great Vehicle Buddhist "perfections" (*pāramitā; phar phyin*) is known as the perfection of wisdom. Much has been written concerning the perfection of wisdom as the crux of disagreements over the centuries since the literature bearing its name first began to be propagated. The subject matter contained in the Perfection of Wisdom sūtras has been presented in two different strands of thought. The first, following Nāgārjuna, concentrates on what is called the "manifest teaching" of the sūtras, the doctrine of emptiness (*śūnyatā, stong pa nyid*) and is generically referred to as Madhyamaka or "Middle Way." The second, following Maitreya, concentrates on what is called the "hidden teaching," the path structure and clear realizations of the three vehicles, and is studied primarily through the lens of Maitreya's *Abhisamayālaṃkāra* together with Haribhadra's *Spuṭhārtha*.

Maitreya's *Abhisamayālaṃkāra* presents the clear realizations in terms of eight subjects and seventy topics. During the course of this presentation, the paths (*mārga, lam*) leading to liberation and the bodhisattva grounds (*bhūmi, sa*) which mark one's progression along the paths are also explicated in the context of the three Buddhist vehicles. The two genres of literature which have arisen pedagogically out of this tradition are known, respectively, as the Seventy Topics (*don bdun cu pa*) and Grounds and Paths (*sa lam*). 'Jam dbyangs bzhad pa's presentation of the former was translated by Hopkins with oral commentary by Denma Lochö Rinbochay in 1978 but currently remains unpublished;[11] Hopkins's translation of dKon mchog 'jigs med dbang po's (1728-1791) presentation of the latter, together with the oral commentary of Denma Lochö Rinbochay is also unpublished though forthcoming.

Doxographically, these explanations accord with the Svātantrika-Madhyamaka ("Middle Way Autonomy") school in that they assert a different object of negation (*pratiṣedha, dgag bya*) for each of the three vehicles, *śrāvaka*, *pratyekabuddha*, and bodhisattva. A contrasting perspective, Blo bzang rta mgrin's presentation of the grounds and paths from the standpoint of one common object of negation—that of the Prāsaṅgika-Madhyamaka ("Middle Way Consequence") school—was translated by Jules Levinson as part of his dissertation (1994) under Hopkins.

Other topics included in the field of the Perfection of Wisdom, subsumed by the rubric of "supplementary topics" (*zur bkol*), include "Concentrations and Formless Absorptions" (*bsam gzugs*), "Dependent-arising" (*rten 'brel*), "Twenty Sangha" (*dge 'dun nyi shu pa*), and the "Definitive and the Interpretable" (*drang nges*). The first of these, the "Concentrations and Formless Absorptions," was taught by Laṭi Rinbochay, Geshe Gedün Lodrö, and Denma Lochö Rinbochay with reference to Paṇ chen bSod nams grags pa's *Phar phyin spyi don*. This work served as the core of Leah Zahler's master's thesis (1981), and later her Ph.D. dissertation (1994). The last of these, the "Definitive and the Interpretable," Hopkins has incorporated into his presentation of Mind-Only philosophy (1999a).

General Tenets

Tenets (*siddhānta, grub mtha'*) as a genre of literature refers to the systematic delineation of the established conclusions of philosophical schools, both Buddhist and non-Buddhist. In general, there are three reasons for studying tenets:

- to delineate coherent and consistent systems from the disparate Buddhist teachings,
- to serve as a framework in which to present the system of Prāsaṅgika-Madhyamaka in contrast to other ("lower") tenets systems, and
- ultimately, to understand the correct view of selflessness.

This first point has been discussed by Hopkins in his article "The Tibetan Genre of Doxography" (1996a), while the last point—bringing the subject out of the realm of the scholastic and into the practical—is evoked by dKon mchog 'jigs med dbang po at the opening of his presentation of tenets.

> [Those] who seek liberation from the depths of their hearts must work at the means of understanding the correct view of selflessness. For, no matter how much you have internalized love, compassion, and the altruistic aspiration to enlightenment, if you are without the profound view of selflessness, you are unable to remove the root of suffering. (Sopa and Hopkins, 1976b: 147)

Thus, for dKon mchog 'jigs med dbang po, Buddhist scholasticism exists only in the service of soteriology.

Historically, some of the first textual references to tenets as a subject are found in Bhāvaviveka's *Tarkajvālā* and Śāntarakṣita's *Tattvasaṃgraha*. Numerous treatises on this subject were written in Tibetan over the centuries, from the early rNying ma translator Rog Shes rab 'od to contemporary authors such as dGe bshes Ye shes dbang phyug of Se ra sMad. In terms of contemporary pedagogy, however, the treatises which have defined the genre date from the high scholastic epoch of such figures as 'Jam dbyangs bzhad pa and lCang skya Rol pa'i rdo rje in the seventeenth and eighteenth centuries. Following in close succession to these two figures was dKon mchog 'jigs med dbang po. Hopkins, together with Geshe Lhundup Sopa, translated the latter's abbreviated presentation of tenets in 1968 in preparation for what was later to become his dissertation. Though Hopkins taught this text to his fellow graduate students in Wisconsin, the translation was not published until 1976 in *Practice and Theory of Tibetan Buddhism*.

With dKon mchog 'jigs med dbang po and *Meditation on Emptiness* as guides, Hopkins and his students began an exploration of the field of tenets, looking particularly to the work of lCang skya which Hopkins had previously studied. Anne Klein, working with Hopkins and several Tibetan scholars,[12] translated the Sautrāntika sections of lCang skya's tenets along with other presentations of the two truths in that tenet system for her dissertation. Jules Levinson worked on the general introduction to tenets and non-Buddhist tenets, while Craig Preston worked on the general introduction to Buddhist tenets and Vaibhāṣika section of lCang skya's presentation of tenets. Both of these works currently remain unpublished.

Ngag dbang dpal ldan's *Grub mtha' bzhi'i lugs kyi kun rdzob dang don dam pa'i don rnam par bshad pa* ("The Explanation of the Conventional and the Ultimate in the Four Tenet Systems") was also used to shed light on certain points. Working with Hopkins and Kensur Yeshey Tupden in Virginia and other Tibetan scholars abroad,[13] John Buescher completed his dissertation on the first chapter of this text, focusing on the two truths in the Vaibhāṣika system as compared with Theravāda.

Cittamātra

Hopkins's work on the Mind-Only system began with a series of lectures by Laṭi Rinbochay in the Spring of 1977. This was followed by a lecture course which Hopkins gave in the Fall of 1980. In 1982, however, during Hopkins's two-month stay at dGa' ldan Shar rtse Monastic University, His Holiness the Dalai Lama lectured on Tsong kha pa's *Legs shes snying po.*[14] Thus began what Hopkins has described as his earnest study of the Mind-Only system and the topic of "the definitive and the interpretable." When this study neared publication seventeen years later, Hopkins had read and synthesized over twenty separate commentaries on Tsong kha pa's root text, received countless hours of oral commentary from His Holiness and other teachers, taught graduate level seminars in the material several times, and produced three books (1999a and forthcoming) addressing the various issues contained in Tsong kha pa's *Legs shes snying po*.

During this time, Hopkins also worked closely with several of his graduate students on Mind-Only issues. In 1977, coincident with Laṭi Rinbochay's lectures, Joe Wilson began a study of the Mind-Only system, with particular attention to the concepts of the "afflicted mentality" (*kliṣṭamanas, nyon mongs can gyi yid*) and the "mind-basis-of-all" (*ālayavijñāna, kun gzhi rnam par shes pa*) through reference to Gung thang dKon mchog bsTan pa'i sgron me's commentary to Tsong kha pa's text of the same name. In the process, Hopkins and Wilson investigated not only the Mind-Only chapter of lCang skya's *Grub mtha'*, but other canonical and post-canonical sources for studying the Mind-Only system, including the *Saṃdhinirmocana-sūtra*, Vasubandhu's *Triṃśikā*, Asaṅga's *Mahāyāna-saṃgraha*, and sTag tshang Shes rab rin chen's *Grub mtha'*.

Shortly after Wilson completed his dissertation in 1984, John Powers arrived in Charlottesville following his master's work at McMaster University. Pursuing his interest in Mind-Only, he and Hopkins began a detailed study of the primary scriptural basis for the Mind-Only tenet system, the *Saṃdhinirmocana-sūtra*. Powers consulted with 'Bras spung Blo gsal gling Geshe Ye shes thab mkhas in Sarnath and other Tibetan scholars in Charlottesville—including Geshe dPal ldan grags pa, Geshe Jampel Thardo, and Kensur Yeshe Tupden, resulting in his dissertation (1991).

In the late 1980s, Greg Hillis arrived at the University of Virginia with the idea of exploring tantra through the tenets of Mind-Only. Working with Hopkins, he studied and translated the first half of Vinitadeva's *Prakaraṇaviṃśakāṭikā* ("Explanation of [Vasubandhu's] Commentary on the 'Twenty Stanzas'") for his master's thesis

(1993). During this same period, William Magee completed his master's thesis (1987) with Hopkins which investigated *tathāgatagarbha* theory, a subject which arises in conjunction with both Mind-Only and Middle Way tenets.

Besides investigating the philosophical aspects of the Mind-Only tenet system, Hopkins has explored the relationship between Mind-Only and the Yogic Practice school (*yogācāra, rnal 'byor spyod pa*). Although this distinction appears to have lost any real meaning by the time of Tsong kha pa, some scholars have argued that a definite difference did exist during the genesis of many key Indian texts by authors such as Asaṅga and Vasubandhu. Hopkins presented an analysis of this issue and some Tibetan perspectives on it in "A Tibetan Contribution on the Question of Mind-Only in the Early Yogic Practice School."

Middle Way Philosophy

Hopkins's dissertation, *Meditation on Emptiness,* remains today the *locus classicus* of English language presentations of Madhyamaka philosophy. Hopkins began his study of Middle Way tenets through the lens of 'Jam dbyangs bzhad pa's monumental text *Grub mtha'i rnam bshad* under the direction of Geshe Wangyal in 1963.[15] It was not until the Fall of 1968, however, with the arrival of the sGo mang scholar Kensur Ngawang Lekden in Freewood Acres, New Jersey, that Hopkins was able to begin his in-depth study of the text. Over the next three years both in New Jersey and in Wisconsin, Hopkins and Kensur Lekden read not only all of 'Jam dbyangs bzhad pa's *Tenets* but also Ngag dbang dpal ldan's annotations to the same, as well as almost all of 'Jam dbyangs bzhad pa's *dBu ma chen mo.*

After the deaths of both his advisor Richard Robinson and Kensur Lekden, Hopkins continued his studies in Germany with Geshe Gedün Lodrö for three months before traveling on to India. Once in India, Hopkins studied with His Holiness the Fourteenth Dalai Lama, attending both public and private lectures on such texts as Tsong kha pa's *Lam rim 'bring,* the six texts of Nāgārjuna known collectively as the "Collections of Reasonings," the Seventh Dalai Lama's brief *dBu ma'i lta khrid dran pa bzhi (Song of the Four Mindfulnesses),* and His Holiness's own compositions, *The Buddhism of Tibet* and *The Key to the Middle Way* (1975a). Hopkins subsequently finished his dissertation in 1973[16] and published translations of these last three texts along with Nāgārjuna's *Ratnāvalī* in 1975.

Meditation on Emptiness, however, did not see publication until 1983. Between its completion and its publication, Hopkins published a number of smaller works related to his study of Middle Way philosophy: *The Practice of Emptiness* (1974a), a translation of the Perfection of Wisdom chapter of the Fifth Dalai Lama, Ngag dbang blo bzang rgya mtsho's "Stages of the Path" (*lam rim*) text *'Jam dbyangs zhal lung,*[17] and *Analysis of Going and Coming* (1976a), a translation of the second chapter of Candrakīrti's *Prasannapadā* along with the corresponding section from Tsong kha pa's *Rigs pa'i rgya mtsho* in *Ocean of Reasoning* (1977a). In addition, Hopkins edited a series of fifteen lectures by Kensur Lekden in *Meditations of a Tibetan Tantric Abbot: Kensur Lekden* (1977b). These lectures were republished as part of *Compassion in Tibetan Buddhism* (1980), a volume which also included Hopkins's translation of the first five chapters of Candrakīrti's *Madhyamakāvatāra.*

Hopkins's work on Candrakīrti's *Madhyamakāvatāra* continued with Anne Klein, who, like Hopkins, had been initially introduced to the text by Kensur Lekden in Wisconsin. Having studied the text on and off for twenty years, Klein synthesized Hopkins's translation of portions of the sixth chapter (together with Tsong kha pa's commentary) with the oral commentary of Kensur Yeshey Tupden, producing a testament to this great luminary of Tibet. It was published as *Path to the Middle: The Oral Scholarship of Kensur Yeshey Tupden* (1994).

Hopkins also worked extensively on another major work by Candrakīrti, the *Prasannapadā*. Besides his translation of the second chapter (1976a), numerous other sections have been translated. In one such publication, Hopkins discusses the differences between Candrakīrti's and Bhāvaviveka's interpretations of Nāgārjuna. Addressing this issue in general, and the meaning of "inherent existence" (*svabhāvasiddha, rang bzhin kyis grub pa*) in particular, Hopkins summarized the debate and Tsong kha pa's analysis of it in a brief article entitled "A Tibetan Delineation of Different Views of Emptiness in the Indian Middle Way School" (1989a).

Emptiness Yoga (1987a) was, in a sense, a complementary work to *Meditation on Emptiness*. Drawn from the Prāsaṅgika-Madhyamaka section of lCang skya's *Grub mtha'* and Hopkins's own lectures, here Hopkins adopted lCang skya's style of a "free-flowing discussion" of the issues surrounding this tenet system—in contrast to 'Jam dbyangs bzhad pa's *Grub mtha'* and *Meditation on Emptiness*, where a more complex and structured style holds sway. Perhaps because of this open, more "personal" style, *Emptiness Yoga* has proven to be a favorite text among both Hopkins's students and general readers alike.

Hopkins has continued to revisit the subject of Madhyamaka over the years. In 1997, twenty-five years after he first received commentary on Nāgārjuna's *Ratnāvalī* by His Holiness the Dalai Lama, Hopkins turned his attention once again to that text. Deciding to retranslate the text in order to broaden its accessibility, Hopkins listened to his tapes of His Holiness' lectures anew, producing a new translation with an expanded introduction, copious notes and a detailed presentation of rGyal tshab's outline of the text. The result was *Buddhist Advice for Living & Liberation: Nāgārjuna's "Precious Garland"* (1998a).

Hopkins also encouraged his students to pursue detailed investigations of these so-called higher tenet systems. One of Hopkins's first degree candidates, John Buescher, presented his master's thesis under Hopkins's guidance in 1975. An exploration of the two truths and the Madhyamaka reasonings known as "ultimate analysis," Buescher's thesis included a translation of the sixth chapter of Candrakīrti's *Prasannapadā*. Likewise, Donald Lopez, who entered the doctoral program in 1974, studied and eventually translated for his dissertation (1982) the Svātantrika-Madhyamaka chapter of lCang skya's *Tenets*.

Like Lopez, Guy Newland also spent his undergraduate years at the University of Virginia prior to entering the doctoral program in Tibetan studies. During his course of study, Newland produced both a master's thesis and doctoral dissertation on subjects related to Madhyamaka. For his master's thesis (1983), Newland worked with Hopkins and mKhan zur 'Jam dpal gzhan phan on rJe btsun Chos gyi rgyal mtshan's commentary to Candrakīrti's *Madhyamakāvatāra*, exploring the extensive meaning drawn from Candrakīrti's expression of worship and amplifying through detailed analysis several of the themes discussed in *Compassion in Tibetan Buddhism*. Following his exploration of Candrakīrti's *Supplement*, Newland translated for his dissertation (1988) sections of the sixth chapter together with Candrakīrti's own commentary, the corresponding sections of the Madhyamaka commentaries of 'Jam dbyangs bzhad pa and rJe btsun Chos gyi rgyal mtshan, and the "Two Truths" section of the Consequence school chapter of lCang skya's *Grub mtha'*. Daniel Cozort, too, for his dissertation translated portions of lCang skya's *Tenets* and 'Jam dbyangs bzhad pa's *Grub mtha'* dealing with the "unique tenets" of the Middle Way Consequence School. Working with Hopkins, mKhan zur 'Jam dpal gzhan phan, and Kensur Yeshey Tupden, Cozort completed his dissertation in 1989.

Stages of the Path

Serving as the praxis to Madhyamaka's gnosis, the "Stages of the Path" (*lam rim*) literature applies Buddhist philosophical tenets to the spiritual development of the individual practitioner. Central to *lam rim* presentations are the instructions on generating the mental states of calm abiding—the fixing of the mind on an object of observation, and special insight—the state of mind in which one is able to analyze the object of observation.

During the spring and summer of 1979, Geshe Gedün Lodrö taught three classes a week on the generation of calm abiding and special insight. Hopkins served as translator for these lectures, which were transcribed by Anne Klein and reviewed by Geshe Lodrö just prior to his death later that year. The transcripts were edited again by both Hopkins and Leah Zahler and published initially as *Walking Through Walls* (1992c), and again, with substantial revision, as *Calm Abiding and Special Insight* in 1998.

A wide range of topics beyond calm abiding and special insight are covered in the Stages of the Path literature. In 1963, His Holiness the Dalai Lama composed a succinct yet thorough overview of Buddhist doctrine and religious practice intended for both Tibetan and non-Tibetan readers, *Opening the Eye of New Awareness*. Although a paraphrased rendering of the text into English was published in the early 1970s, the definitive translation was prepared by Hopkins and Lopez with the assistance of Kensur Yeshey Tupden (1985a).

In 1984, His Holiness the Dalai Lama gave a series of lectures in London in which he discussed the stages of the path and the twelve links of dependent-arising. Hopkins, who served as interpreter during the teachings, retranslated these lectures for publication in book form as *The Meaning of Life from a Buddhist Perspective* (1992d).

This approach to instruction through simplifying and summarizing key points for direct application to a practitioner's life has a long history in Buddhist literature. Indeed, many Indian treatises found in the bsTan 'gyur promote themselves as nothing more than condensations of the core teachings of the Buddhist sūtras; in Tibet, this style of composition continued. Tsong kha pa, for instance, composed a fourteen-verse summary of the path to enlightenment commonly known as *Lam gyi gtso bo rnam pa gsum*. Subsequent generations of dGe lugs scholars have singled this work out as a concise and pointed presentation of the Buddhist path. Hopkins, working with Geshe Sopa in the early 1970s, translated Tsong kha pa's text along with one of its many commentaries, the meditation manual by the Fourth[18] Paṇ chen Lama Blo bzang dpal ldan bsTan pa'i nyi ma. This translation was published by Hopkins and Sopa in *Practice and Theory of Tibetan Buddhism* (1976b).

Elizabeth Napper, like Joe Wilson and Anne Klein, began the academic study of Tibetan Buddhism at the University of Wisconsin. Following her master's work, Napper worked closely with Hopkins on the "Special Insight" (*lhag mthong*) chapter of Tsong kha pa's *Lam rim chen mo* and the corresponding section of *Lam rim mchan bzhi sbrags ma*, working as well with mKhan zur 'Jam dpal gzhan phan, Kensur Yeshey Tupden and other geshes abroad. Her dissertation (1985) contained a translation of the section of Tsong kha pa's text concerned with "refutation of an object of negation which is too broad" (*dgag bya ngos 'dzin khyab che ba dgag pa*).

William Magee's dissertation (1998) took up the discussion of Tsong kha pa's "refutation of an object of negation which is too narrow" (*dgag bya ngos 'dzin khyab chungs ba dgag pa*). When taken in combination with Napper's dissertation, the result is a complete presentation of the avoidance of extreme views in understanding the actual object of negation to be used in meditative practice.

Tantric Grounds and Paths

As is repeatedly pointed out in tantric teachings, the path to enlightenment presented in a tantric context is different from that of a sūtra-based presentation. With mKhan zur 'Jam dpal gzhan phan, Hopkins and his students[19] read Ngag dbang dpal ldan's tantric presentation of "Grounds and Paths" entitled *gSang chen rgyud sde bzhi'i sa lam gyi rnam bzhag*. A finished translation with commentary by mKhan zur 'Jam dpal gzhan phan is being prepared for publication at this time; however, excerpts and a summary of the Action Tantra section were published in *The Yoga of Tibet* (1981; reprinted as *Deity Yoga*). This material also served as the basis for Daniel Cozort's master's thesis (1983), which summarized the Highest Yoga Tantra section of Ngag dbang dpal ldan's text.

In 1984, having published more than ten books centered around textual translations, Hopkins brought out *The Tantric Distinction*, a less formal, narrative presentation of Buddhist theory and practice (1984c). Based on two sets of lectures from 1974 and 1978 edited by Anne Klein, Hopkins sets forth in the context of common human experience the roles of wisdom and compassion in both sūtra and tantra. He then explains the distinguishing feature of tantra, the practice of deity yoga, using everyday analogies and accessible language.

Hopkins's exploration of tantra, however, has not been confined to traditional Tibetan perspectives. In an article contextualizing Buddhist notions of spiritual development and soteriology, Hopkins explored a variety of issues surrounding the Buddhist idea of "path" (*mārga, lam*) in the context of both sūtra and tantra. Hopkins's article "A Tibetan Perspective on the Nature of Spiritual Experience" (1992b) presents several of the ideas found in the Stages of the Path literature, such as the types of religious practice and beings, as well as items peculiar to tantra, such as the mind of clear light, but draws as well on the work of Western thinkers such as Rudolph Otto and Carl Jung. In other contexts as well, Hopkins has referred to Jung's ideas, answering his qualms concerning tantric practice. The notion of ego inflation and Jung's ideas about psychological well-being are explored by Hopkins in "The Ultimate Deity in Action Tantra and Jung's Warning against Identifying with the Deity" (1985c) as well as in other as yet unpublished works on tantra and its distinguishing feature, deity yoga.

The topic of deity yoga and the general distinctions between the Buddhist "vehicles" (*yāna*) also served as the subject of Donald Lopez's master's thesis (1977). Working with Hopkins and Laṭi Rinbochay, Lopez presented a translation of the first section of the *bsTan pa spyi dang rgyud sde bzhi'i rnam par gzhag pa'i zin bris* by the First Paṇ chen Lama, Blo bzang chos kyi rgyal mtshan.

Secret Mantra: The Lower Tantras

In 1972, during a private audience, His Holiness the Dalai Lama suggested to Hopkins that he translate Tsong kha pa's *sNgag rim chen mo,* or "Great Exposition of Secret Mantra." In the moment, Hopkins recalls, he laughed at the magnitude of what was being suggested. After reflection, however, he decided to take on the project on the basis of His Holiness's confidence in his abilities, and began receiving oral commentary from His Holiness on the text during his second visit to Dharamsala in 1974. The first chapter of Tsong kha pa's text, along with His Holiness' commentary, was published by Hopkins in *Tantra in Tibet* (1977c). Included in the book was a supplementary exposition by Hopkins drawn from the oral teachings of Kensur Lekden. As with many of Hopkins's books written during this time, invaluable assistance was provided by Laṭi Rinbochay and Geshe Gedün Lodrö, for whom Hopkins translated his work back into Tibetan for verification, thus allowing for the clarification and refinement of the meaning of the points presented. This pattern of research—textual translation, oral commentary, translation back into Tibetan, and final revision—was applied many times over the years and used by Hopkins for the sequel to *Tantra in Tibet.*

Deity Yoga (originally published as *The Yoga of Tibet,* 1981) presented chapters two and three of Tsong kha pa's text dealing with the first two of the three "lower" tantra sets: Action Tantra (*kriyā tantra, bya rgyud*) and Performance Tantra (*caryā tantra, spyod rgyud*). Together with the edited commentary of His Holiness also from the 1974 visit, Hopkins produced the second volume in this series, synthesizing and presenting the overall structural context of the practices associated with these two tantra sets.

Highest Yoga Tantra

In the wake of the Chinese invasion of Tibet and the acts of genocide perpetrated on the Tibetan people during the "Cultural Revolution" (1966-1976), it became clear to a number of high-ranking lamas that many of the instructional lineages preserved in Tibet for centuries were in danger of extinction. For this reason it was decided to "declassify," as it were, the traditionally restricted teachings on tantra in general and Highest Yoga Tantra in particular. This decision was made despite the dangers associated with the tantric teachings through their openness to misinterpretation of statements about alcohol, violence, and sexual desire—the primary reason for their restricted status. Hopkins addressed the issue of misconstruing sexual imagery in his contribution to the *Buddhist-Christian Studies* journal, "Tantric Buddhism, Degeneration or Enhancement" (1990a). Framed as a response to the misinterpretation of tantric materials as a degenerate corruption of Buddhism, Hopkins presents the basic role and function of tantra within traditional Buddhist practice as elucidated by Tsong kha pa and later dGe lugs scholar-yogis. In a lighter vein, Hopkins also relates an encounter he had with Geshe Wangyal concerning another tantric issue—alcohol consumption. In a recent brief contribution to *Tricycle* magazine (1998c), Hopkins describes drinking in his youth and Geshe Wangyal's unique and insightful attitude toward this subject.

In Highest Yoga Tantra, another topic traditionally discussed concerns yogic techniques for the manipulation of the subtle body constituents in a manner similar to natural processes which occur at the time of death. Thus, the process of dying, the states of mind which occur during it, and their simulation during meditative practice form a subset of topics within the general category of Highest Yoga Tantra. In consultation with Laṭi Rinbochay, Hopkins translated a short explanatory text on these processes written by the Thirteenth Dalai Lama's tutor, A kya Yongs 'dzin dByangs can dga' ba'i blo gros. The text, *gZhi'i sku gsum gyi rnam gzhag*, gives a presentation of these issues from within the context of the Guhyasamāja cycle of Highest Yoga Tantra, drawing on the tantric works of Nāgārjuna as well as sutric sources. The final translation was published as *Death, Intermediate State and Rebirth in Tibetan Buddhism* (1979).

In general, Highest Yoga Tantra practice can be divided into two stages, known as "generation stage" (*utpatti-krama, bskyed rim*) and "completion stage" (*niṣpanna-krama, rdzogs rim*). Hopkins has done much work on both of these, and while the vast majority of his material remains unpublished, it has served as a rich resource for his graduate students. Alan Cole presented his master's thesis (1988) under Hopkins's direction on aspects of Highest Yoga Tantra. The thesis entailed a discussion of both traditional and non-traditional scholarship on Highest Yoga Tantra together with a translation of the First Paṇ-chen Lama Blo bzang Chos kyi rgyal mtshan's Vajrabhairava meditation manual, *dPal rdo rje 'jigs byed dpa' bo gcig pa'i rdzogs rim gyi rnam gzhag 'jam dpal dgyes pa'i mchod sprin.*

As a final subject in both Highest Yoga Tantra and the scheme of a Buddhist education, the system of tantric practice known as the "Wheel of Time" or Kālacakra is sufficiently different from other cosmological and tantric systems that it is usually addressed separately. The Kālacakra system of Tibetan tantric practice was one of the main Highest Yoga Tantras promulgated over the centuries for general practice. Like other Highest Yoga Tantras, the primary aim of the Kālacakra practice is "to manifest and utilize the mind of clear light, a subtle, powerful, innermost level of consciousness, to make it conscious and then use it to realize truth."[20] Explanatory texts for this system, however, tend to stand apart from other tantric presentations. For example, there are separate presentations of the "Grounds and Paths" which apply only to the Kālacakra system. Indeed, in some redactions of the Tibetan canon the Kālacakra root tantras themselves are broken out of the general "Tantra" division of the bKa' 'gyur and set apart in their own section.

Numerous lineage holders of the Kālacakra system have given the empowerment cycle both in the United States and abroad. Following the 1981 initiation ceremony given by His Holiness the Dalai Lama in Wisconsin, Hopkins took the explanations given to him by His Holiness both during the ceremony and in private meetings prior to each lecture, and edited them together into a singular coherent presentation of the ceremony. *The Kalachakra Tantra: Rite of Initiation* (1985b) was first published for the Kālacakra initiation in Switzerland. It has seen two more editions since that time.

Additional Works

Though many of Hopkins's works reflect the dGe lugs perspective of his numerous teachers and textual sources, Hopkins has explored issues outside this area as well. During his 1972 visit to India and later during the visits of Khetsun Sangpo Rinbochay to Virginia, Hopkins and his students received teachings on rNying ma presentations of tenets, sūtra, and tantra, including works by Klong chen pa Dri med 'od zer and Mi pham rgya mtsho. Comprising these teachings, *Tantric Practice in Nying-ma* (1982a) summarizes dPal sprul 'jigs med chos kyi dbang po's *Kun bzang bla ma'i zhal lung,* as well as the general subject of the Great Perfection (*rdzogs chen*).

Hopkins has also contributed as a scholar of Tibet in fields other than religion. For instance, he has made contributions to the study of Tibetan medicine, which has become increasingly popular within "alternative medicine" circles. In 1981, Hopkins worked with researchers from the Harvard Medical School as part of a scientific team exploring the physiological side-effects of meditation. With the consent of His Holiness the Dalai Lama, researchers collected empirical data on the physiological changes experienced by advanced practitioners of "heat" yoga (*gtum mo*). The results of this study were later published in the journal *Nature* (1982b).

As a larger contribution to the understanding of Tibetan medicine by English speakers, Hopkins translated and edited a series of lectures by Dr. Yeshi Donden. Published as *Health Through Balance* (1986a), this series of lectures presents a broad overview of the Tibetan approach to medicine from the general topics of physiology and diagnosis to treatment and a discussion of the religious dimensions of medicine.

Besides serving as interpreter for Dr. Donden and other Tibetan scholars,[21] Hopkins has served as interpreter to His Holiness the Dalai Lama during many of his trips around the world. *Kindness, Clarity, and Insight* (1984d) and *The Dalai Lama at Harvard* (1989b) both consist of talks by His Holiness which Hopkins originally translated and then edited for publication.

Hopkins has participated in interreligious dialogue as a scholar, translator, and practitioner on several occasions. In these contexts, Hopkins has presented Buddhist perspectives on ultimate reality, the notion of liberation, and has made an effort at explaining the easily misconstrued image of Tibetan tantric Buddhism for a non-specialist audience.

On three separate occasions Hopkins has testified as a witness before both Senate and House committees on the political and social conditions existing in present-day Tibet. Hopkins's commitment to promoting social action and awareness has continued most recently with his arrangement and coordination of the landmark Nobel Peace Laureates Conference held at the University of Virginia in November of 1998.[22]

The issue of sexuality and the role it plays in the interaction between American culture and Tibetan Buddhism was one which Hopkins began to explore in the early 1990s. He began translation of a work by the so-called "renegade monk" dGe 'dun Chos 'phel, *'Dod pa'i bstan chos*, in New Jersey in 1967 at the suggestion of Mrs. Dorje Yudon Yuthok, but it remained unfinished until 1991. Seeing publication in 1992 as *Tibetan Arts of Love*, this work was to become one of Hopkins's best-selling books (1992e). Simultaneously

Hopkins continued the trend he began in *The Tantric Distinction* of moving to a more "personalized" style rather than writing "as a voice for the tradition." Both of these directions of content and methodology are reflected in an article from this time—"The Compatibility of Reason and Orgasm in Tibetan Buddhism: Reflections on Sexual Violence and Homophobia" (1993b) and in the follow-up book to *Tibetan Arts of Love*, entitled *Sex, Orgasm, and the Mind of Clear Light* (1998b). This latter book, a gay male variation on dGe 'dun Chos 'phel's original text, reflected what Hopkins felt was a need "to live up to [his] responsibilities to [his] own community," commending the work—as dGe 'dun Chos 'phel had done with his own—"for those of my own nature" (Hopkins, 1998b: xii). Hopkins concludes this book with four chapters of "ruminations" reflecting on issues of sex, religion, psychology, and tantra. Despite the presumed complete lack of background knowledge about Buddhism on the part of the intended audience, or perhaps because of it, these "ruminations" contain a very clear and straightforward presentation of Buddhist tantra, echoing sentiments which Hopkins stressed earlier in *The Tantric Distinction*: the warning against confusing subsidiary practices—the generation of sexual desire (used with altruistic motivation)—with the core of the path—compassion and wisdom.

Hopkins has continued to instruct and to read with students, to research issues in Buddhist religion and philosophy, and to produce language reference works. In reviewing Hopkins's literary output—without accounting for the works of his students to which he contributed, let alone the vast number of unedited manuscripts, lectures, and translated teachings in his possession—one is struck by the accomplishment. His dedication to the clear and detailed exposition of the entire range of Buddhist religious philosophy is reminiscent of the great polymaths of earlier generations. The bibliography which follows is, in this sense, a tribute to Hopkins and all those who have had the honor and privilege of being his students. One of Hopkins's students eloquently stated what all of us have realized at one time or another:

> It is often the case that after studying with one person for an extended period of time we sadly reach the end of his or her learning. This has not been my experience with Professor Hopkins.[23]

As Hopkins enters his seventh decade and his publications continue to emerge, this sentiment rings demonstrably true.

Chronological List of the Published Works of Paul Jeffrey Hopkins

1973 *Meditation on Emptiness*. Ph.D. dissertation, University of Wisconsin. Revised for London: Wisdom Publications, 1983; second edition, Boston: Wisdom Publications, 1996.

1974a *Practice of Emptiness*. By the Fifth Dalai Lama; trans. by Jeffrey Hopkins in accordance with instruction from Geshe Rapden. Dharamsala: Library of Tibetan Works and Archives.

1974b "An Anatomy of Body and Disease." With Dr. Yeshi Dhonden. *Tibetan Review* (September 1974): 18-20.

1975a *The Buddhism of Tibet and the Key to the Middle Way*. By Tenzin Gyatso, the Fourteenth Dalai Lama. Trans. by Jeffrey Hopkins and Lati Rinbochay. London: George Allen & Unwin; New York: Harper & Row. Reprinted (together with 1975b) as *The Buddhism of Tibet* by Snow Lion Publications, 1987.

1975b *Precious Garland and the Song of the Four Mindfulnesses*. By Nāgārjuna and Kaysang Gyatso, the Seventh Dalai Lama. Trans. and ed. by Jeffrey Hopkins and Lati Rinbochay, with Anne Klein. London: George Allen & Unwin; New York: Harper & Row. Reprinted (together with 1975a) as *The Buddhism of Tibet* by Snow Lion Publications, 1987.

1975c "Three Natures of Every Phenomenon." *Tibetan Review* (April 1975): 18-19.

1976a *Analysis of Going and Coming: the Second Chapter of Candrakirti's* Clear Words. Trans. by Jeffrey Hopkins in accordance with instruction from Kensur Nawang Lengden. Dharamsala: Library of Tibetan Works and Archives.

1976b *Practice and Theory of Tibetan Buddhism*. With Geshe Lhundup Sopa. London: Hutchinson; NY: Grove. Revised and expanded as *Cutting Through Appearances: The Practice and Theory of Tibetan Buddhism*. Ithaca, NY: Snow Lion Publications, 1990.

1977a *Chapter Two of* Ocean of Reasoning *by Tsong-ka-pa*. Trans. by Jeffrey Hopkins in accordance with instruction from Kensur Nawang Lengden. Dharamsala: Library of Tibetan Works and Archives.

1977b *Meditations of a Tibetan Tantric Abbot: Kensur Lekden*. Dharamsala: Library of Tibetan Works and Archives. Reprinted Ithaca, NY: Snow Lion Publications, 2001.

1977c *Tantra in Tibet*. With the Dalai Lama and Tsong-ka-pa. London: George Allen & Unwin. Reprinted Ithaca, NY: Snow Lion Publications, 1987.

1978a "Goiter in Tibetan Medicine." With Gerard N. Burrow, Yeshi Dhonden, and Lobsang Dolma. *Yale Journal of Biology and Medicine*, 51: 441-447. Reprinted *gSo-rig Tibetan Medicine*, 5: 39-46.

1978b "In Praise of Compassion." *Tibet Journal*, 3(3): 21-28.

1979 *Death, Intermediate State, and Rebirth in Tibetan Buddhism*. With Laṭi Rinbochay. London: Rider/Hutchinson. Reprinted Ithaca, NY: Gabriel/Snow Lion, 1980 and Ithaca, NY: Snow Lion Publications, 1985.

1980 *Compassion in Tibetan Buddhism*.By Tsong-ka-pa, with Kensur Lekden. Ed. and trans. by Jeffrey Hopkins, with Lati Rinbodchay and Barbara Frye. London: Rider/Hutchinson; Ithaca, NY: Snow Lion Publications.

1981 *Yoga of Tibet*. By H. H. the Dalai Lama, Tsong-ka-pa and Jeffrey Hopkins. Trans. and ed. by Jeffrey Hopkins. London: George Allen & Unwin. Reprinted as *Deity Yoga*, Ithaca, NY: Snow Lion Publications, 1987.

1982a *Tantric Practice in Nying-ma*. With Khetsun Sangpo Rinbochay. London: Rider/Hutchinson; Ithaca, NY: Snow Lion Publications, 1983.

1982b "Body Temperature Changes during the Practice of gTum-mo Yoga." With Herbert Benson, John W. Lehmann, M. S. Malhotra, Ralph F. Goldman, and Mark D. Epstein. *Nature*, 295: 234-236. [Letters & Replies (by Benson) to this article appeared in *Nature*, 298: 402.]

1983 *Meditative States in Tibetan Buddhism*. By Laṭi Rinbochay and Lochö Rinbochay. Trans. by Leah Zahler and Jeffrey Hopkins. Boston: Wisdom; revised edition, Boston: Wisdom Publications, 1997.

1984a "Reason as the Prime Principle in Tsong kha pa's Delineation of Deity Yoga as the Demarcation Between Sūtra and Tantra." *Journal of the International Association of Buddhist Studies*, 7(2): 95-115.

1984b "A Session of Meditating on Emptiness." *The Middle Way: Journal of the Buddhist Society*, 59(1): 3-9.

1984c *The Tantric Distinction*. London: Wisdom; revised edition, Boston: Wisdom Publications, 1999.

1984d *Kindness, Clarity, and Insight*. By the Fourteenth Dalai Lama, Tenzin Gyatso. Trans. and ed. by Jeffrey Hopkins, co-ed. Elizabeth Napper. Ithaca, NY: Snow Lion Publications.

1984e "Tribute to Lama Yeshe." *Wisdom Magazine*. Available at: http://www.cuenet.com/~fpmt/Teachers/Yeshe/tribut03.html

1985a *Opening the Eye of New Awareness*. By the Dalai Lama. Trans. and introduced by Donald Lopez, with Jeffrey Hopkins. London: Wisdom; revised edition, Boston: Wisdom Publications, 1999.

1985b *The Kalachakra Tantra: Rite of Initiation for the Stage of Generation*. By the Dalai Lama. Trans., ed., and introduced by Jeffrey Hopkins. London: Wisdom; revised editions, Boston: Wisdom Publications, 1989, 1999.

1985c "The Ultimate Deity in Action Tantra and Jung's Warning against Identifying with the Deity." *Buddhist-Christian Studies*, 5: 158-172.

1985d "Reply to Alex Wayman's Review of *The Yoga of Tibet*." *The Journal of the Tibet Society*, 5: 73-95.

1986a *Health Through Balance: An Introduction to Tibetan Medicine*. By Dr. Yeshi Donden. Trans. and ed. by Jeffrey Hopkins, with Lobsang Rabgay and Alan Wallace. Ithaca, NY: Snow Lion Publications, 1986.

1986b "Altruism in Great Vehicle Buddhism." *Thoughtlines* (Spring 1986): 34-38.

1986c "Jeffrey Hopkins Replies [to Bruce Burrill's review of *The Tantric Distinction*]." *Journal of the International Association of Buddhist Studies*, 9(2): 184-187.

1987a *Emptiness Yoga*. Ed. by Joe B. Wilson. Ithaca, NY: Snow Lion; second edition, 1996.

1987b "Liberation from Systemic Distortion and to Altruistic Endeavor in Tibetan Buddhism: Response to David Tracey's 'The Christian Understanding of Salvation-Liberation,'" given at the Second Buddhist-Christian Theological Encounter, Vancouver (March 1985). Published in "Responses to David Tracey." *Buddhist-Christian Studies*, 7: 139-148.

1987c "Dge-lugs-pa" in *The Encyclopedia of Religion*. Ed. Mircea Eliade. New York: Macmillan.

1988 "Ultimate Reality in Tibetan Buddhism." *Buddhist-Christian Studies*, 8: 111-129.

1989a "A Tibetan Delineation of Different Views of Emptiness in the Indian Middle Way School." *Tibet Journal*, 14(1): 10-43.

1989b *The Dalai Lama at Harvard*. By His Holiness the Dalai Lama, Tenzin Gyatso. Trans. and ed. by Jeffrey Hopkins. Ithaca, NY: Snow Lion Publications.

1989c "J. W. de Jong's Review of Jeffrey Hopkins's *Meditation on Emptiness*: An Exchange." *Journal of the International Association of Buddhist Studies*, 12(2): 123-129.

1990a "Tantric Buddhism, Degeneration or Enhancement: The Viewpoint of a Tibetan Tradition." *Buddhist-Christian Studies*, 10: 5-12.

1990b "Book Review: *A History of Modern Tibet, 1913-1951: The Demise of the Lamaist State* by Melvyn C. Goldstein." *Journal of Asian Studies*, 49(4): 901-902.

1990c "Three Case Reports of the Metabolic and Electroencephalographic Changes During Advanced Buddhist Meditation Techniques." With Herbert Benson, M. S. Malhotra, Ralph F. Goldman, and Gregg D. Jacobs. *Behavioral Medicine*, 16(2).

1992a "A Tibetan Contribution on the Question of Mind-Only in the Early Yogic Practice School." *Journal of Indian Philosophy*, 20: 275-343.

1992b "A Tibetan Perspective on the Nature of Spiritual Experience." In *Paths to Liberation*, pp. 182-217. Ed. by Robert Buswell and Robert Gimello. Honolulu: University of Hawai'i Press.

1992c *Walking Through Walls*. By Geshe Gedün Lodrö. Trans. and ed. by Jeffrey Hopkins; co-ed. Anne C. Klein and Leah Zahler. Ithaca, NY: Snow Lion Publications. Revised as *Calm Abiding and Special Insight*, Ithaca, NY: Snow Lion Publications, 1998.

1992d *The Meaning of Life from a Buddhist Perspective*. By His Holiness the Fourteenth Dalai Lama, Tenzin Gyatso. Trans. by Jeffrey Hopkins. Boston: Wisdom Publications. Reprinted as *The Meaning of Life: Buddhist Perspectives on Cause and Effect*. Boston: Wisdom Publications, 2001.

1992e *Tibetan Arts of Love*. By Gedün Chöpel. Intro. and trans. by Jeffrey Hopkins, with Dorje Yudon Yuthok. Ithaca, NY: Snow Lion Publications.

1993a *Fluent Tibetan: A Proficiency Oriented Learning System*. By William Magee and Elizabeth Napper. Jeffrey Hopkins, General Editor. Ithaca, NY: Snow Lion Publications.

1993b "The Compatibility of Reason and Orgasm in Tibetan Buddhism: Reflections on Sexual Violence and Homophobia." In *Gay Affirmative Ethics*, pp. 5-25. Ed. Michael L. Stemmeler and J. Michael Clark. Gay Men's Issues in Religious Studies, Series 4. Las Colinas, TX: Monument. Reprinted in *Que(e)rying Religion*, pp. 372-383. Ed. Gary Comstock and Susan E. Henking. New York: Continuum, 1997, and in *Queer Dharma: Voices of Gay Buddhists*, pp. 335-347. Ed. Winston Leyland. San Fransisco: Gay Sunshine Press, 1998.

1994 *Path to the Middle: The Oral Scholarship of Kensur Yeshey Tupden*. By Kensur Yeshey Tupden. Trans., ed., annotated, and intro. by Anne Carolyn Klein, with textual trans. by Jeffrey Hopkins and Anne Klein, and annotation by Jeffrey Hopkins. Albany: State University of New York Press.

1996a "The Tibetan Genre of Doxography: Structuring a Worldview." In *Tibetan Literature: Studies in Genre*, pp. 170-186. Ed. José Ignacio Cabezón and Roger R. Jackson. Ithaca, NY: Snow Lion Publications.

1996b Prologue to *Tibetan Portrait: the Power of Compassion* by Phil Borges. New York: Rizzoli.

1998a *Buddhist Advice for Living & Liberation: Nāgārjuna's "Precious Garland."* Analyzed, trans. and ed. by Jeffrey Hopkins. Ithaca, NY: Snow Lion Publications.

1998b *Sex, Orgasm, and the Mind of Clear Light: The 64 Arts of Gay Male Love*. Berkeley: North Atlantic Books.

1998c "On the Incongruities of Getting Enlightened and Getting Drunk." *Tricycle: The Buddhist Review* 8(1): 83.

1998d "A Tibetan Contribution to the Doctrine of Mind-Only." Paper presented at the 1998 AAR Seminar on Yogacāra Buddhism. Available at http: //www.uncwil.edu/iabs/yogacara/External_Objects/TibetanContribution.html

1998e "Nirvana, Buddhahood, and the Spiritual Life." In *The Gethsemani Encounter: A Dialogue on Spiritual Life by Buddhist and Christian Monastics*, pp. 19-27. Ed. James Wiseman and Donald Mitchell. New York: Continuum.

1998f "Death, Sleep, and Orgasm: Gateways to the Mind of Clear Light." *Journal of Chinese Philosophy*, 25(2): 245-261.

1999a *Emptiness in the Mind-Only School of Buddhism*. Berkeley: University of California Press.

1999b "Equality: The First Step in Cultivating Compassion." *Tricycle: The Buddhist Review*, 8(4): 26-29.

2000 *The Art of Peace: Nobel Peace Laureates Discuss Human Rights, Conflict and Reconciliation*. By José Ramos-Horta et al. Edited by Jeffrey Hopkins. Ithaca, NY: Snow Lion Publications.

Congressional Testimonies

U.S. Senate Committee on Foreign Relations, *U.S. and Chinese Policies Toward Occupied Tibet: Hearings Before the Committee on Foreign Relations*, 102nd Congr., 2nd sess., 28 July 1992, pp. 39-42 (transcript), pp. 42-46 (prepared statement).

U.S. House Committee on Foreign Affairs, *Religious Persecution: Hearing Before the Subcommittee on International Security, International Organizations and Human Rights*, 103rd Congr., 2nd sess., 9 March 1994, pp. 41-44 (transcript), pp. 151-60 (prepared statement), pp. 161-67 (c.v.).

U.S. Senate Committee on Foreign Relations, *U.S. Policy Towards China: Hearing Before the Subcommittee on East Asian and Pacific Affairs*, 103rd Congr., 2nd sess., 4 May 1994, pp. 63-66 (transcript), pp. 66-68 (prepared statement).

Interviews and other selected works on or about Jeffrey Hopkins

Murray Illson

"Ex-Ivy Leaguers aim to be monks: Three Studying at Buddhist Monastery in Jersey." *New York Times*, 15 December 1963: 71 col.1.

Dawa Norbu

"Interview: Jeffrey Hopkins—Emptiness is Dynamic and Rich." *Tibetan Review*, Oct/Nov. 1973: 23-26.

"An Interview with Professor Jeffrey Hopkins." *Dreloma*, 7 (1981): 35-36.

Marc Vassallo

"Speaking Words of Wisdom—Jeffrey Hopkins, Translator to the Dalai Lama." *Albemarle*, 27 (April-May 1992): 20-25.

Robina Courtin

"Jeffrey Hopkins Reconstructs His Mind." *Mandala*, May-June 1995: 30-33.

Mark Epstein

"In the Realm of Relationship: Mark Epstein interviews Jeffrey Hopkins." *Tricycle: The Buddhist Review*, 5(4) (Summer 1996): 53-58.

Anon.

"The Nobel Peace Laureates Conference: Bringing Together Great Hearts and Minds." *Albemarle*, 68 (February-March 1999): 32-37.

A Selected List of University of Virginia Theses and Dissertations Directed by Jeffrey Hopkins

Buescher, John Benedict

1975 Master's thesis: "Madhyamika Reasoning."

1982 Ph.D. dissertation: "The Buddhist Doctrine of Two Truths in the Vaibhāṣika and Theravāda Schools."

Cole, Alan Robert

1988 Master's thesis: "Tantric Buddhism: A Translation and Analysis of a Ge-luk Text on Highest Yoga Tantra."

Cozort, Daniel Geoffrey

1983 Master's thesis: "The Completion Stage of the Highest Yoga Tantra." Published as *Highest Yoga Tantra*. Ithaca, NY: Snow Lion Publications, 1986.

1989 Ph.D. dissertation: "Unique Tenets of the Buddhist Middle Way Consequence School." Published as *Unique Tenets of the Middle Way Consequence School*. Ithaca, NY: Snow Lion Publications, 1998.

Dreyfus, Georges Bernard Jacques

1987 Master's thesis: "Some Considerations on Definition in Buddhism: An Essay on the Use of Definitions in the Indo-Tibetan Epistemological Tradition."

1991 Ph.D. dissertation: "Ontology, Philosophy of Language, and Epistemology in Buddhist Tradition." Published as *Recognizing Reality: Dharmakīrti's Philosophy and Its Tibetan Interpretations*. Albany: State University of New York Press, 1997.

Hillis, Gregory Alexander

1993 Master's thesis: "An Introduction and Translation of Vinitadeva's Commentary on Vasubandhu's *Twenty Stanzas*, with Appended Glossary."

Klein, Anne Carolyn

1981 Ph.D. dissertation: "Mind and Liberation: The Sautrāntika Tenet System in Tibet: Perception, Naming, Positive and Negative Phenomena, Impermanence and the Two Truths in the Context of Buddhist Religious Insight as Presented in Ge-luk Literary and Oral Traditions." Analysis published as *Knowledge and Liberation: Tibetan Buddhist Epistemology in Support of Transformative Religious Experience*. Ithaca, NY: Snow Lion Publications, 1986; revised ed., 1998. Translations published as *Knowing, Naming and Negation: A Sourcebook on Tibetan Sautrāntika*. Ithaca, NY: Snow Lion Publications, 1991.

Levinson, Julius Brooks

1983 Master's thesis: "The Process of Liberation and Enlightenment in the Buddhism of Tibet."

1994 Ph.D. dissertation: "The Metaphors of Liberation."

Lopez, Donald Sewell

1977 Master's thesis: "The Difference Between the Buddhist Vehicles: Hīnayāna, Mahāyāna, and Vajrayāna."

1982 Ph.D. dissertation: "The Svātantrika-Mādhyamika School of Mahāyāna Buddhism." Published as *A Study of Svātantrika*. Ithaca, NY: Snow Lion Publications, 1987.

Magee, William Albert

1987 Master's thesis: "*Tathāgatagarbha* in Tibet: Including a Translation and Analysis of Parts of Ngak-wang-bel-den's *Annotations* for Jam-yang-shay-ba's *Great Exposition of Tenets*."

1998 Ph.D. dissertation: "Tradition and Innovation in the Consequence School: Nature (*rang bzhin, svabhāva/prakṛti*) in Indian and Tibetan Buddhism." Published as *The Nature of Things: Emptiness and Essence in the Geluk World*. Ithaca, NY: Snow Lion Publications, 1999.

Napper, Elizabeth Stirling

1979 Master's thesis: "A Contemporary Tibetan Explanation of Consciousness: Oral Commentary on Ge-shay Jam-bel-sam-pel's *Presentation of Awareness and Knowledge, Composite of All the Important Points, Opener of the Eye of New Intelligence*." Published as *Mind in Tibetan Buddhism*. Valois, NY: Gabriel/Snow Lion, 1980; repr. Ithaca, NY: Snow Lion Publications, 1986.

1985 Ph.D. dissertation: "Dependent-Arising and Emptiness: A Tibetan Buddhist Interpretation of Mādhyamika Philosophy Emphasizing the Compatibility of Emptiness and Conventional Phenomena." Published as *Dependent-Arising and Emptiness: A Tibetan Buddhist Interpretation of Mādhyamika Philosophy Emphasizing the Compatibility of Emptiness and Conventional Phenomena*. Boston and London: Wisdom Publications, 1989.

Newland, Guy Martin

1983 Master's thesis: "Compassion in Mādhyamika Buddhism." Published as *Compassion: A Tibetan Analysis*. London: Wisdom Publications, 1984.

1988 Ph.D. dissertation: "The Two Truths: A Study of the Mādhyamika Philosophy as Presented in the Monastic Textbooks of the Gelukba Order of Tibetan Buddhism." Analysis published as *The Two Truths*. Ithaca, NY: Snow Lion Publications, 1992.

Perdue, Daniel Elmo

1976 Master's thesis: "Tibetan Monastic Debate." Published as *Debate in Tibetan Buddhist Education*. Dharamsala: Library of Tibetan Works and Archives, 1980.

1983 Ph.D. dissertation: "Practice and Theory of Philosophical Debate in Tibetan Buddhist Education." Published as *Debate in Tibetan Buddhism*. Ithaca, NY: Snow Lion Publications, 1992.

Powers, Chester John

1991 Ph.D. dissertation: "The Concept of the Ultimate (*don dam pa; paramārtha*) in the *Saṃdhinirmocana-sūtra*: Analysis, Translation, and Notes." Translation published as *Wisdom of Buddha: the Samdhinirmocana Sutra*. Berkeley: Dharma Publishing, 1995. Analysis published as *Hermeneutics and Tradition in the Saṃdhinirmocana-sūtra*. Leiden: E. J. Brill, 1993.

Rogers, Katherine Manchester

1980 Master's thesis: "Tibetan Logic: A Translation with annotations of Pur-bu-jok Jam-ba-gya-tso's *The Topic of Signs and Reasonings* from the "Great Path of Reasoning" in *The Magic Key to the Path of Reasoning, Explanation of the Collected Topics Revealing the Meaning of the Texts on Valid Cognition*."

1992 Ph.D. dissertation: "Tibetan Logic: The Role of Reasoning in the Ge-luk-ba System of Tibetan Buddhist Education."

Wilson, Joe Bransford

1984 Ph.D. dissertation: "The Meaning of Mind in the Buddhist Philosophy of Mind-Only (Cittamātra): A Study of a Tibetan Presentation of Mind-Basis-of-All (*ālayavijñāna*)."

Zahler, Leah Judith

1981 Master's thesis: "Meditative States in Tibetan Buddhism: The Concentrations and Formless Absorptions." Published as *Meditative States in Tibetan Buddhism*. By Lati Rinbochay, Lochö Rinbochay, Jeffrey Hopkins, and Leah Zahler. Boston: Wisdom Publications, 1983. Revised and reprinted, Boston: Wisdom Publications, 1997.

1994 Ph.D. dissertation: "Concentrations and Formless Absorptions." Forthcoming from Snow Lion Publications under the title *Tibetan Interpretations of Meditative States*.

Visiting Tibetan Scholars in the University of Virginia's Tibetan Studies Program

1974 (Spring): Khetsun Sangbo Rinbochay (mKhas btsun bzang po rin po che)

1976 (Mar.)–1977 (May): Laṭi Rinbochay (Bla ṭi rin po che, b. 1923)

1978: Denma Lochö Rinbochay (lDan ma blo chos rin po che, b. 1927)

1979 (Jan.–Aug.): Geshe Gedün Lodrö (dGe 'dun blo gros, 1924-1979)

1979: H.H. Tenzin Gyatso, the Fourteenth Dalai Lama (bsTan 'dzin rgya mtsho, b. 1935) [H.H. the Dalai Lama gave several private lectures to Hopkins and students at Virginia. *Kindness, Clarity and Insight* (Hopkins, 1984d) contains edited transcripts of some of these talks]

1980 (June)–1981 (June): Kensur Jambel Shenpen ('Jam dpal gzhan phan, b. 1919), a.k.a. Losang Wangdu (Blo bzang dbang sdud)

1982: Kensur Yeshey Tupden (Ye shes thub ldan, 1916-1988)

1985: Khetsun Sangbo Rinbochay (mKhas btsun bzang po rin po che)

1987 (Spring): Geshe Belden Drakba (dPal ldan grags pa)

1989 (Spring): Geshe Gönchok Tsering (mGon mchog tshe ring)

1990 (Summer): Geshe Jampel Thardo ('Jam dpal thar 'dod, b. 1925)

1991 (Spring): Khetsun Sangbo Rinbochay (mKhas btsun bzang po rin po che)

1991 (Summer): Geshe Thupden Jinpa (Thub bstan sbyin pa)

1992 (Spring): Khenpo Palden Sherab (dPal ldan shes rab, b. 1941)

Notes

1. The metaphor of the steel bow and arrow (*lcags mda' lcags gzhu*) has been applied to Tsong kha pa's *Legs bshad snying po* ("Essence of Eloquence")—the subject of one of Hopkins's latest books. To summarize one explanation, the meaning of the metaphor is that "just as it is hard to pull a steel bow and arrow to its full extent but if one can, the arrow will course over a great area, so even the words—not to consider the meaning—of this text are difficult to understand but, when understood, yield great insight" (Hopkins, 1999a: 16).

2. I gratefully acknowledge the scholarship of Anne Klein, whose attention to the historical details of her work with and around Hopkins greatly facilitated the writing of this article. Thanks also to Bill Magee, Daniel Perdue, and Craig Preston for helpful comments on earlier drafts of this paper.

3. In 1998 in the United States alone, of the 2,791 commercially published books on "religion," more than fifty titles related to Tibetan Buddhism. Just twenty-five years earlier, in 1973, a total of 1,374 books on "religion" were published in the United States, and of these, sixty were on the subject of Buddhism in general and of these, only six related to its Tibetan form. General category statistics drawn from *Bowker Annual Library and Book Trade Almanac*, 43rd Edition (1998) and *Bowker Annual of Library & Book Trade Information*, 19th Edition (1974); sub-category statistics based on data drawn from OCLC/WorldCat and the Library of Congress.

4. Scheme drawn from Tenzin Dorjee, "Namgyal Dratsang: A 413-Year-Old Monastery," *Tibet Journal*, 14(3): 33-46.

5. Tsong kha pa blo bzang grags pa, 1357-1419. Although it should be noted that Tsong kha pa himself never wrote an extensive commentary on Dharmakīrti's presentation of epistemology, both of his main students, rGyal tshab dar ma rin chen (1364-1432) and mKhas grub dge legs dpal bzang po (1385-1438) did, and these texts serve as the basis of later study within the dGe lugs tradition.

6. Though whether or not an ontological commitment is implied by them has been debated among some scholars. This issue is discussed at length by

Georges Dreyfus in *Recognizing Reality: Dharmakīrti's Philosophy and Its Tibetan Interpretations* (Albany: State University of New York Press, 1997).

7. For a breakdown of these texts by subject, see Daniel Perdue, *Debate in Tibetan Buddhism* (Ithaca, NY: Snow Lion Publications, 1992), pp. xvi-xvii.

8. Ngag dbang legs ldan, 1900-1971. Doctorate of Religious Philosophy (*dge bshes*, "geshe") from 'Bras spungs sGo mang Monastic University and Abbot emeritus (*mkhan zur*) of the Lower Tantric College (rGyud smad) of Lhasa.

9. Full citations for this work and others may be found in the reference list at the end of this article.

10. This first class of students who would eventually complete their Ph.D.s under Hopkins included: (from the class of 1972) John Buescher, Anne Klein, Donald Lopez, Elizabeth Napper, Daniel Perdue, and Joe Wilson; (from the class of 1974) Katherine Rogers.

11. In addition, Hopkins compiled a synthetic presentation of the Seventy Topics drawing on not only the work of 'Jam dbyangs bzhad pa, but also from Paṇ chen bSod nams grags pa, 1478-1554, Se ra Byes rJe btsun Chos kyi rgyal mtshan, 1469-1546, and others. Made available to Hopkins's students as "The Topics of Enlightenment," this too, however, remains unpublished.

12. Working with Laṭi Rinbochay (Bla ṭi rin po che, b. 1923) and Denma Lochö Rinbochay (lDan ma blo chos rin po che, b.1927) on lCang skya, and with Geshe Gedün Lodrö (dGe 'dun blo gros, 1924-1979) on 'Jam dbyangs bzhad pa.

13. Notably Geshe dPal ldan grags pa who was then at Tibet House in New Delhi, and Geshe bsTan pa rgyal mtshan at the Tōyō Bunko in Tokyo.

14. In particular, the Introduction and Mind-Only sections; Hopkins's account of this period is presented in *Emptiness in the Mind-Only School of Buddhism* (Hopkins, 1999a), pp. viii-ix.

15. Hopkins's presence along with other Americans at the monastery in New Jersey was viewed as a curiosity by the media at the time: see Murray Illson, "Ex-Ivy Leaguers Aim to Be Monks: Three Studying at Buddhist Monastery in Jersey," *New York Times*, 15 December 1963, p. 71.

16. Hopkins's thoughts during this time are reflected in an interview with Dawa Norbu: "Interview: Jeffrey Hopkins, 'Emptiness is Dynamic and Rich,'" *Tibetan Review*, Oct/Nov. 1973: 23-26.

17. Published as *The Practice of Emptiness* (1974a), this work also served as the basis for the later article by Hopkins, "A Session of Meditating on Emptiness" (1984b).

18. There are two different enumerations of the lineage of the Paṇ chen Lama used in bibliographic and other sources. The system used by the Library of Congress begins with the incarnation Blo bzang chos kyi rgyal mtshan (1567/70-1662), who received the title from the Fifth Dalai Lama. The other system of enumeration, used primarily in contemporary Chinese documents, takes Blo bzang chos kyi rgyal mtshan to be the fourth member in a previously existing incarnation lineage that begins with Tsong kha pa's student mKhas grub dge legs dpal bzang po (1385-1438). In the latter system, Blo bzang dpal ldan bsTan pa'i nyi ma would be the Seventh Paṇ chen Lama.

19. This class of students included: Elizabeth Napper; (from the class of 1976) Guy Newland and Leah Zahler; (from the class of 1978) Daniel Cozort, Jules Levinson, and Craig Preston.

20. "Speaking Words of Wisdom—Jeffrey Hopkins, Translator to the Dalai Lama," interview by Marc Vassallo. *Albemarle*, 27 (April-May 1992): 24.

21. Hopkins discusses some of the difficulties associated with such translation work in a brief interview, "An Interview with Professor Jeffrey Hopkins," *Dreloma*, 7 (1981): 35-36.

22. Chronicled in a number of newspaper articles at the time and in *Albemarle* magazine; transcripts of the conference were also published in *The Art of Peace*. See: "The Nobel Peace Laureates Conference: Bringing Together Great Hearts and Minds," *Albemarle*, 68 (February-March 1999): 32-37; Jeffrey Hopkins (ed.), *The Art of Peace: Nobel Peace Laureates Discuss Human Rights, Conflict and Reconciliation*. Ithaca, NY: Snow Lion Publications, 2000.

23. Donald S. Lopez, Jr., *A Study of Svātantrika* (Ithaca, NY: Snow Lion Publications, 1987), p. 10.

References to Tibetan Texts

Citations to "P" refer to the catalog of the Peking edition of the Tibetan canon published in Suzuki, D.T., ed., The Tibetan Tripiṭaka: Peking Edition *(Tokyo-Kyoto: Tibetan Tripiṭaka Research Institute, 1955-61); citations to "Toh." refer to the catalog of the Derge (sDe ge) edition of the Tibetan canon published in Ui, Hakuju,* A Complete Catalogue of the Tibetan Buddhist Canons (Bkaḥ-ḥgyur and Bstan-ḥgyur) *(Sendai, Japan: Tôhoku Imperial University, 1934).*

A kya yongs 'dzin dbyang can dga' ba'i blo gros

ZKSN *gZi'i sku gsum gyi rnam gzag rab gsal sgron me.* In *The Collected Works of A-kya Yongs-'dzin*, vol. 1. New Delhi: Lama Guru Deva, 1971.

Bhavaviveka

MHTJ *Madhyamaka-hṛdaya-vṛtti-tarka-jvāla.* Tibetan translation: P5256, vol. 96; Toh. 3856.

Blo bzang bstan pa'i nyi ma, the Fourth Paṇ chen Lama

LTSK *Gsung rab kun gyi snying po lam gyi gtso bo rnam gsum gyi khrid yig gzhan phan snying po.* N.p., n.d.

Blo bzang chos kyi rgyal mtshan, the First Paṇ chen Lama

DRNZ *dPal rdo rje 'jigs byed dpa' bo gcig pa'i rdzogs rim gyi rnam gzhag 'jam dpal dgyes pa'i mchod sprin.* Delhi: 1972.

GDZN *bsTan pa spyi dang rgyud sde bzhi'i rnam par gzhag pa'i zin bris.* In *Collected Works*, vol. 4. New Delhi: Gurudeva, 1973.

Blo bzang rta mgrin

PPSL *Phar phyin theg pa'i lugs kyi sa dang lam gyi rnam par bzhag pa mdo tsam du brjod pa zab don rgya mtsho'i snying po*. In *Collected Works of Rje-btsun Blo-bzang-rta-mgrin*, vol. 4. New Delhi: Gurudeva, 1975-76.

bsKal bzang rgya mtsho, the Seventh Dalai Lama

BMTK *dBu ma'i lta khrid dran pa bzhi ldan gyi mgur dbyangs dngos grub char 'bebs*. N.p, n.d.

bsTan dar lha ram pa

RTPT *Rang mtshan spyi mtshan gyi rnam gzhag*. In *Collected gSung 'bum of bsTan-dar Lha-ram of A-lag-sha*, vol. 1. New Delhi: Guru Deva, 1971.

Candrakīrti

MVPP *Mūla-madhyamka-vṛtti-prasanna-padā*. Tibetan translation: P5260, vol. 98; Toh. 3860.

MAB *Madhyamakāvatāra-bhāṣya*. Tibetan translation: P5263, vol. 98; Toh. 3862.

Dharmakīrti

PVK *Pramāṇavārttikakārikā*. Tibetan translation: P5709, vol. 130; Toh. 4210.

dGe 'dun chos 'phel

DTC *'Dod pa'i bstan bcos*. Delhi: T.G. Dhongthog Rinpoche, 1967.

dPal sprul 'jigs med chos kyi dbang po

LMZL *Kun bzang bla ma'i zhal lung/ rDzogs pa chen po klong chen snying thig gi sngon 'gro'i khrid yig kun bzang bla ma'i zhal lung*. Bhutan: n.p., 1969.

Gung thang dKon mchog bstan pa'i sgron me

YKZN *Yid dang kun gzhi'i dka' gnas rnam par bshad pa mkhas pa'i 'jug ngog*. In *Collected Works of Guṅ-thaṅ dkon-mchog bstan-pa'i sgron-me*, vol. 2: 275-402. New Delhi: Ngawang Gelek Demo, 1972.

gZhan phan chos kyi snang ba, gZhan dga'

TTGP *The Thirteen Treatises of mKhan-po Gźan phan chos-kyi snaṅ-ba*. Thimbhu, Bhutan: n.p., 1976.

Haribhadra

SPHU *Sputhārtha*. Full Title: *Abhisamayālaṃkāra-nāma-prajñāpāramit-opadeśa-śāstra-vṛtti*. Tibetan translation: P5191, vol. 90; Toh. 3791.

'Jam dbyangs bzhad pa'i rdo rje ngag dbang brtson 'grus

GTNS *Grub mtha'i rnam bshad/ Grub mtha'i rnam bshad rang gzhan grub mtha' kun dang zab don mchog tu gsal ba kun bzang zhing gi nyi ma lung rigs rgya mtsho skye dgu'i re ba kun skong*. In *Collected Works*. New Delhi: Ngawang Gelek Demo, 1972-74.

BMNS *dBu ma rnam bshad/ dBu ma la 'jug pa'i mtha' dpyod lung rigs gter mdzod zab don kun gsal skal bzang 'jug ngog*. Buxadur: 1967.

lCang skya Rol pa'i rdo rje

GTNZ *Grub mtha' rnam gzhag/ Grub pa'i mtha'i rnam par bzhag pa gsal bar bshad pa thub bstan lhun po'i mdzes rgyan*. Varanasi: Pleasure of Elegant Sayings, 1970.

Maitreya

AAPP *Abhisamayālaṃkāra-nāma-prajñāpāramitopadeśa-śāstra*. Tibetan translation: P5184, vol. 88; Toh. 3786.

Nāgārjuna

PMMK *Prajñā-nāma-mūla-madhyamaka-kārikā*. Tibetan translation: P5224, vol. 95; Toh. 3824.

RPRN *Rāja-parikathā-ratnāvalī*. Tibetan translation: P5658, vol. 129; Toh. 4158.

Ngag dbang bkra bshis

SNDG *Sras bsdus grwa/Tshad ma'i dgongs don rtsa 'grel mkhas pa'i mgul rgyan*. Mundgod, Karnataka, India: Drebung Gomang Buddhist Cultural Association, 1984.

Ngag dbang blo bzang rgya mtsho, the Fifth Dalai Lama

JBZL *Byang chub lam gyi rim pa'i khrid yig 'jam pa'i dbyangs kyi zhal lung*. Thimphu: Kun bzang stobs rgyal, 1976.

Ngag dbang dpal ldan

GTCG *Grub mtha' chen mo mchan 'grel*. Sarnath: Pleasure of Elegant Sayings, 1964.

GTZL *Grub mtha' bzhi'i lugs kyi kun rdzob dang don dam pa'i don rman par bshad pa*. New Delhi: Guru Deva, 1972.

SGSL *gSang chen rgyud sde bzhi'i sa lam gyi rnam bzhag gzhung gsal byed*. In *The Collected Works of chos-rje Ṅag-dbaṅ-dpal-ldan of Urga*, vol. 2. Delhi: Mongolian Lama Guru Deva, 1983.

Paṇ chen bSod nams grags pa

PPPD *Phar phyin spyi don*. In *Collected Works*, vol. 3 *(ga)*. Mundgod: Drebung Loseling Library Society, 1982.

Phur bu lcog byams pa rgya mtsho

DGNZ *Tshad ma'i gzhung don 'byed pa'i bsdus grwa'i rnam bzhag rigs lam 'phrul gyi lde mig*. Buxa, India: 1965.

rGyal tshab dar ma rin chen

URCP *dBu ma rin chen 'phreng ba'i snying po'i don gsal bar byed pa*. In *The Collected Works gsung 'bum of Rgyal-tshab Rje Darma Rin-chen*. New Delhi: Ngawang Gelek Demo, 1980-81.

rJe btsun Chos kyi rgyal mtshan

BMPD *bsTan bcos dbu ma la 'jug pa'i rnam bshad dgongs pa rab gsal gyi dka' gnas gsal bar byed pa'i spyi don legs bshad skal bzang mgul rgyan.* New Delhi: lHa mkhar yongs 'dzin bstan pa rgyal mtshan, 1973.

Saṃdhinirmocana-sūtra

SNC *Saṃdhinirmocana Sūtra: l'explication des mystères.* Edited by Lamotte. Paris: Adrien Maisonneuve, 1935. Tibetan translation: P774, vol. 29; Toh. 109.

sTag tshang shes rab rin chen

GTKS *Grub mtha' kun shes nas mtha' bral grub pa.* Thimphu: Kun bzang stobs rgyal, 1976.

Śāntarakṣita

TSK *Tattvasaṃgrahakārikā.* Tibetan translation: P5764, vol. 138; Toh. 4266.

Tsong kha pa Blo bzang grags pa

DGRS *dBu ma la 'jug pa'i rgya cher bshad pa dgongs pa rab gsal.* P6143, vol. 154; Toh. 5326. In *The Collected Works of Rje Tsoṅ-kha-pa Blo-bzaṅ-grags-pa.* Delhi: Ngawang Gelek, 1975. Also: Sarnath: Pleasure of Elegant Sayings, 1973.

KZNS *Kun bzhi rnam bshad/ Yid dang kun bzhi'i dka' ba'i gnas rgya cher 'grel pa legs par bshad pa'i rgya mtsho.* P6149, vol. 154; Toh. 5414. In *The Collected Works of Rje Tsoṅ-kha-pa Blo-bzaṅ-grags-pa.* Delhi: Ngawang Gelek, 1975.

LRB *Lam rim 'bring/ sKyes bu gsum gyi nyams su blang ba'i byang chub lam gyi rim pa.* P6002, vols. 152-153; Toh. 5393. In *The Collected Works of Rje Tsoṅ-kha-pa Blo-bzaṅ-grags-pa.* Delhi: Ngawang Gelek, 1975.

LRCM *Lam rim chen mo/ sKyes bu gsum gyi nyams su blang ba'i rim pa thams cad tshang bar ston pa'i byang chub lam gyi rim pa.* P6001, vol. 152; Toh. 5392. In *The Collected Works of Rje Tsoṅ-kha-pa Blo-bzaṅ-grags-pa.* Delhi: Ngawang Gelek, 1975.

LRCZ *Lam rim mchan bzhi sbrags ma/ mNyam med rje btsun tsong kha pa chen pos mdzad pa'i byang chub lam rim chen mo'i dka' ba'i gnad rnams mchan bu bzhi'i sko nas legs par bshad pa theg chen lam gyi gsal sgron.* In *The Lam rim chen mo of the incomparable Tsong-kha-pa; with the interlineal notes of Ba-so Chos-kyi-rgyal-mtshan, Sde-drug Mkhan-chen Ngag-dbang-rab-brtan, 'Jam-dbyangs-bzhad-pa'i-rdo-rje, and Bra-sti Dge-bshes Rin-chen-don-grub.* 2 vols. New Delhi: Chos-'phel-legs-ldan, 1972.

LSNP *Legs bshad snying po/ Drang ba dang nges pa'i don rnam par phye ba'i bstan bcos legs bshad snying po.* In *The Collected Works of Rje Tsoṅ-kha-pa Blo-bzaṅ-grags-pa.* P6142; Toh. 5396. Delhi: Ngawang Gelek, 1975.

LTNS *Lam gyi gtso bo rnam pa gsum/ Tsha kho ba dbon po ngag dbang grags pa la gdams pa.* P6087, vol. 153; Toh. 5275 (85). In *The Collected Works of Rje Tsoṅ-kha-pa Blo-bzaṅ-grags-pa.* Delhi: Ngawang Gelek, 1975.

NRCM *sNgags rim chen mo/ rGyal ba khyab bdag rdo rje 'chang chen po'i lam gyi rim pa gsang ba kun gyi gnad rnam par phye ba.* P6210, vol. 161; Toh. 5281. In *The Collected Works of Rje Tsoṅ-kha-pa Blo-bzaṅ-grags-pa.* Delhi: Ngawang Gelek, 1975.

TSTC *dBu ma rtsa ba'i tshig le'ur byas pa shes rab ces bya ba'i rnam bshad rigs pa'i rgya mtsho/ rsta shes ṭik chen.* P6153, vol. 156; Toh. 5401. In *The Collected Works of Rje Tsoṅ-kha-pa Blo-bzaṅ-grags-pa.* Delhi: Ngawang Gelek, 1975. Also Sarnath: Pleasure of Elegant Sayings, n.d.

Vasubandhu

VK *Viṃśatikā-kārikā.* Tibetan translation: P5557, vol. 113; Toh. 4056.

Vinitadeva

PVT *Prakaraṇa-viṃśakā-ṭikā.* Tibetan translation: P5566, vol. 113; Toh. 4065.

Contributors

Harvey B. Aronson is Co-director of Dawn Mountain (Tibetan temple, community center, and research institute) in Houston, Texas, where he is also a psychotherapist in private practice. He is the author of *Love and Sympathy in Theravada Buddhism* (South Asia Books).

John Buescher is Director of the Tibetan Broadcast Service for Voice of America.

José Ignacio Cabezón is Professor of Philosophy of Religion at Iliff School of Theology. His publications include *Scholasticsm* (SUNY) and *Buddhism and Language* (SUNY).

Daniel Cozort is Associate Professor of Religion at Dickinson College. His books included *Highest Yoga Tantra* (Snow Lion) and *Unique Tenets of the Middle Way Consequence School* (Snow Lion).

Paul G. Hackett is an independent scholar based in Charlottesville, Virginia.

Roger R. Jackson is Professor of Religion at Carleton College. His publications include *Buddhist Theology* (Curzon) and *The Wheel of Time: The Kalachakra in Context* (Snow Lion).

Anne Carolyn Klein is Professor of Religious Studies at Rice University. Her work includes *Meeting the Great Bliss Queen* (Beacon) and *Path to the Middle* (SUNY).

Donald S. Lopez, Jr. is Carl W. Belser Professor of Buddhist and Tibetan Studies in the Department of Asian Languages and Cultures at the University of Michigan. His publications include *Elaborations on Emptiness* (Princeton) and *Prisoners of Shangri-la* (University of Chicago).

Elizabeth Napper is Co-director of the Tibetan Nuns Project in Dharamsala, India. Her published work includes *Mind in Tibetan Buddhism* (Snow Lion) and *Dependent Arising and Emptiness* (Wisdom).

Guy Newland is Professor of Religion at Central Michigan University. His publications include *The Two Truths* (Snow Lion) and *Appearance and Reality* (Snow Lion).

Gareth Sparham is Visiting Assistant Professor of Tibetan Language at the University of Michigan. His publications include *The Fulfillment of All Hopes* (Wisdom) and *Memoirs of a Tibetan Lama* (Snow Lion).

Joe Bransford Wilson is Associate Professor of Religion at the University of North Carolina, Wilmington. His publications include *Translating Buddhism from Tibetan* (Snow Lion).